TEJANO PATRIOT

TEJANO PATRIOT

*The Revolutionary Life of
José Francisco Ruiz, 1783–1840*

BY ART MARTÍNEZ DE VARA

Texas State Historical Association
Austin

The publication of this book was supported by generous donations from the Texas Historical Foundation, Dr. Carlos Hamilton, and Mr. Sam Clegg. Cover portrait courtesy of the Alamo Mission Foundation.

Library of Congress Cataloging-in-Publication Data

Names: Martínez de Vara, Art, author.
Title: Tejano patriot : the revolutionary life of José Francisco Ruiz,
   1783–1840 / by Art Martínez de Vara.
Description: Austin : Texas State Historical Association, [2020] | Includes
   bibliographical references and index. | Summary: "Art Martínez de
   Vara's Tejano Patriot: The Revolutionary Life of José Francisco Ruiz,
   1783-1840 is the first full-length biography of this important figure in
   Texas history. Best known as one of two Texas-born signers of the Texas
   Declaration of Independence, Ruiz's significance extends far beyond that
   single event. Born in San Antonio de Béxar to an upwardly mobile
   family, during the war for Mexican Independence Ruiz underwent a
   dramatic transformation from a conservative royalist to one of the
   staunchest liberals of his era. Steeped in the Spanish American liberal
   tradition, his revolutionary activity included participating in three
   uprisings, suppressing two others, and enduring extreme personal
   sacrifice for the liberal republican cause. He was widely respected as
   an intermediary between Tejanos and American Indians, especially the
   Comanches. As a diplomat, he negotiated nearly a dozen peace treaties
   for Spain, Mexico, and the Republic of Texas, and he traveled to the
   imperial court of Mexico as an agent of the Comanches to secure peace on
   the northern frontier. When Anglo settlers came by the thousands to
   Texas after 1820, he continued to be a cultural intermediary, forging a
   friendship with Stephen F. Austin, but he always put the interests of
   Béxar and his fellow Tejanos first. Ruiz had a notable career as a
   military leader, diplomat, revolutionary, educator, attorney, arms
   dealer, author, ethnographer, politician, Indian agent, Texas Ranger,
   city attorney, and Texas Senator. He was a central figure in the saga
   that shaped Texas from a remote borderland on New Spain's northern
   frontier to an independent republic"-- Provided by publisher.
Identifiers: LCCN 2020006828 | ISBN 9781625110589 (paperback) | ISBN
   9781625110596 (ebook)
Subjects: LCSH: Ruíz, José Francisco, 1783-1840. | Texas. Declaration of
   Independence--Signers--Biography. | Indian agents--Texas--Biography. |
   Texas--History--Revolution, 1835-1836--Biography. | Texas--Politics and
   government--To 1846. | LCGFT: Biographies.
Classification: LCC F389.R85 M37 2020 | DDC 974.4/04092 [B]--dc23
LC record available at https://lccn.loc.gov/2020006828

To Marina, "*pho*"
To Rebecca, "El Moo"
And to Iñaki, "ecce homo"

Contents

Maps

Illustrations follow page 93

Foreword

Biography continues to be a popular genre of non-fiction. Its appeal rests in making general social, economic, and political currents more immediately accessible through the experience of the individual. Not surprisingly, both major and minor Anglo Americans in the drama of nineteenth-century Texas have received biographical attention as a way of better explaining the times in which they lived. Tejanos* have not fared so well, however.

Although the integration of Tejanos into the mainstream of Texas history is not new, it is only recently that in-depth biographical studies have been conducted on a relatively few individuals. Along with David Mc-Donald's *José Antonio Navarro: In Search of the American Dream in Nineteenth-Century Texas* (2010), Ana Carolina Castillo Crimm produced a family biography, *De León: A Tejano Family History* (2003), and I published *A Revolution Remembered: The Memoirs and Selected Correspondence of Juan N. Seguín* (1991, 2002) and edited a book of biographical essays, *Tejano Leadership in Mexican and Revolutionary Texas* (2010).

Farther back, Rubén Rendón Lozano, a San Antonio banker, took advantage of the centennial of Texas independence from Mexico to produce *Viva Tejas: The Story of the Mexican-born Patriots of the Republic of Texas*, which was published by the Southern Literary Institute. The very short work included brief biographical sketches of a considerable number of Tejanos, among them Ruiz. Unfortunately, his entry confuses José Francisco and his son Francisco Antonio, one of numerous problems that Martínez de Vara addresses in this biography. Those shortcomings should not be held against Rendón Lozano; they are an indication of how hard it was to find Tejanos in Texas historiography. Yet his little book serves as

---

* The term Tejano is here used in reference to Texans of Mexican heritage, whether or not they were born in Texas.

a reminder that twentieth-century Tejanos were unwilling to forget about their ancestors' hard-fought right to be called Texans.

In this book, José Francisco Ruiz finally joins his nephew José Antonio Navarro in getting the full biographical treatment long overdue him. Yes, there was Walter G. Stuck's short *José Francisco Ruiz: Texas Patriot*, written in the 1940s, but although that work tried to illustrate the importance of its subject to the story of the emergence of Texas as a republic, it was incomplete and error prone.

That Ruiz is worthy of a full biography is made clear in the pages that follow. Art Martínez de Vara has given us a new window on a period of Texas history that has lacked for Tejano protagonists. In this regards, Martínez de Vara is part of a movement to uncover the story of Tejano history makers who have long been seen only on the margins of the state's colorful, triumphalist, and largely Anglo-centric nineteenth-century history.

Like David McDonald's *José Antonio Navarro: In Search of the American Dream in Nineteenth-Century Texas*, the present work explores themes of family, service, and loyalty not just across sovereignties but across the cultural gulf that separated an ascendant Anglo American world and a retreating Hispano-Mexican one. Just as McDonald and other authors have sought to understand the problem of shifting loyalties through the lens of devotion to Texas, Martínez de Vara traces the story of a man who defined his homeland first and foremost as the Texas he knew. The interests of his *patria chica* (little homeland) outweighed any loyalties to more remote sovereigns, whether in Madrid or Mexico City.

As the following pages make clear, despite the repeated assertion over the years that Ruiz favored annexation by the United States, his words and actions in the last years of his life do not allow for such a claim. His admonition to his son-in-law in late 1836 would seem to indicate a preference for an independent Texas: "by no means should you take arms against the Texans. Give the same advice to your friends for only God could possibly return the territory of Texas to the Mexican Government. Texas has the arms and money for her defense and shall remain forever free."

Art Martínez de Vara's use of the terms "revolutionary" and "patriot" are amply supported by the story he tells of José Francisco Ruiz as family man, public official, and political firebrand. But we should understand both words in the broader context of a life lived across multiple sovereignties. His revolutionary activities did not just take place in 1835–1836 with regard to Texas independence from Mexico, but in 1812–1821 with regard to Texas and Mexican independence from Spain. Likewise, his patriotic beliefs focused on Texas first and all other loyalties second.

There certainly can be other perspectives on Ruiz. For Spanish royalists he was a traitor, as he was for Mexican centralists and even for Mexican federalists who might have seen in his decision to sign the declaration of independence a betrayal of Mexico as an ideal. To an increasing number of Anglo Texans, he was the representative of an increasingly suspect group whose loyalty and status were more and more being called into question. For Chicano activists he, along with other Tejanos who took part in the Texas Revolution, was a sell-out. And, to a growing middle-class of Tejano descendants he is a hero and inspiration that should make Tejanos proud to be called Texans. With this biography you have the opportunity to make up your own mind about Ruiz from the most complete record of his life yet assembled, as Martínez de Vara makes his case for a Tejano revolutionary and patriot.

Jesús F. de la Teja,
Regents' Professor Emeritus,
Texas State University
September 2019
Austin, Texas

Acknowledgments

May the sun and earth grant unto [you] the light, the abundance,
and the serenity of happy days.

> —José Francisco Ruiz, " [José] Francisco Ruiz in
> the Mexican Army," in Malcolm D. McLean (ed.), *Papers
> Concerning Robertson's Colony in Texas* (19 vols.; Arlington:
> University of Texas at Arlington, 1974–1993), *IV*, 35.

I am indebted to a great number of people who have helped me over
the eight years of researching and writing this book. I begin with my
mother, Sally Ann Martínez, who inspired me to write this study with
the stories of José Francisco Ruiz she told me as a child. The tales she recounted were not found in the history books I was given at school. I recall
vividly the day she took me to the library at Rice University in Houston, Texas, and showed me the rich accounts of Tejanos in Frederick C.
Chabot's *With the Makers of San Antonio*. Far too often the lives, trials, and
aspirations of our Tejano forefathers have survived only in oral history and
family remembrances. But the keepers of these stories have passed down
to our time a legacy that inspires us to reclaim, revisit, and revive the rich
history of Spanish and Mexican Texas.

Sister Francis Marie Bordages of Seton Junior High School was my
Texas history teacher when I was in the seventh grade. Under her guidance, I won the TAPPS State Academic Championship in Texas history
and launched a lifelong interest that I have yet to shake. Dr. Jesús F. de
la Teja of Texas State University, author of several pioneering works in
Tejano biography, inspired me to attempt to write a full-length study of
Ruiz. I remain especially indebted to him for his persistent willingness to
help translate archaic Spanish abbreviations and his magical ability to read
blurry, darkened nineteenth-century handwriting on microfilm. The staff

of the Texana Collection at the San Antonio Public Library assisted me in locating sources, answered countless questions, and on many occasions allowed me to stay on the microfilm machine until the minute they closed. I thank I wish to thank Dr. Caroline Castillo-Crimm for sharing her wisdom and helping me complete the thesis version of this manuscript. Dr. Rosanne Barker, Dr. Jeffery Littlejohn and Dr. Brian Domitrovic served as my thesis advisors at Sam Houston State University. Dr. Janice Roberts of the Sabine Parish Clerk of Court office and the office staff of the Sabine Parish Tax Assessor were tremendously helpful in helping me locate the Santa Barbara Río Hondo Ranch. Stephanie Ann Brady is simply the best sister, editor, and manuscript critic there ever was. Kay Hindes, San Antonio City Archaeologist, edited the book for accuracy and made several critical corrections. Dr. David Carlson, Bexar County Spanish Archivist, edited early drafts of this book and expanded my available sources. Ryan Schumacher served as the managing editor of this manuscript. Dr. Richard McCaslin was the developmental editor. David Timmons did the layout and design. Jay Knarr was the indexer. Others who contributed to this manuscript include Dr. Alston Thoms, Chris Marrou, David McDonald, Evie Patton, Maria "Vee" Gomez, Martha Celina Saldaña Vásquez and Rudy de la Cruz. I thank my wife, Marina, for accompanying me to what seems like nearly every library and museum in Texas and a few in Louisiana and Mexico City. She is the love of my life and a gifted translator of Spanish and its legal terminology.

Introduction

¡Díos y Libertad!¹

—José Francisco Ruiz

In 2012 the Star of the Republic Museum at Washington-on-the-Brazos had a grand exhibit on the signers of the Texas Declaration of Independence. A short sketch of the personal achievements of each signer was proudly displayed next to their likenesses. The entry for José Francisco Ruiz, one of two native-born Texans who signed the declaration, simply stated that "since he did not speak English, he did not take an active part in the convention."[2] This brief statement summarized the conclusions of several generations of Texas historians who have generally overlooked Ruiz. But Ruiz actually played important roles in pre-Revolutionary Texas. He became a cultural broker who lived on a physical, cultural, and political frontier. He bridged the Spanish, Mexican, indigenous, and Anglo American spheres, and he took center stage in many of the prominent political and military events in Texas during the early nineteenth century, including the convention at Washington-on-the-Brazos in 1836.

Before and after Texas's independence, Ruiz had a notable career as a public servant, military leader, diplomat, revolutionary, educator, attorney, arms dealer, author, ethnographer, and politician. His revolutionary activity included participating in three rebellions, suppressing two others, and enduring extreme personal sacrifice for the republican cause. As a diplomat, he negotiated nearly a dozen peace treaties for Spain, Mexico, and the Republic of Texas, and he traveled to the imperial court of Mexico as an agent of the Comanches to secure peace on the northern frontier. He was fluent in the Comanche and Cherokee languages and communicated with other Indians without an interpreter. His *Report on the Indian*

Tribes of Texas, 1828 has been lauded by historians as the most authentic
and insightful contemporary account of Texas Indian culture. One anthropologist, Thomas W. Kavanagh, wrote that Ruiz's "descriptions have an
authority unsurpassed by any other historical writer." Historian Brian De-
Lay has noted, "[Ruiz] probably knew more about the native peoples of
the southeastern plains than any of his contemporaries."[3] He was elected
to serve in the *ayuntamiento* (town council) of Béxar, three revolutionary
juntas, and the senate of the Republic of Texas. His military career included leading the battered Tejano[4] forces from the battlefield at Medina;
facilitating a proxy war against the Spanish from the Neutral Ground in
Louisiana; founding an outpost, Tenoxtitlán, in Central Texas; and serving
as a Texas Ranger in his later years. He was an adviser and confidant to
Stephen F. Austin, Jean Louis Berlandier, Comanche leader Paruakevitsi,
José Antonio Navarro, Sam Houston, and other notable figures of Texas.

The great respect that many of Ruiz's contemporaries had for him is
evident in their early publications. The earliest known account of him appeared in 1844, four years after his death, in the popular Mexico City journal *El Museo Mexicano*. The article by naturalist Jean Louis Berlandier,
entitled "Caza del Oso y Cíbolo, en el Nor-oeste de Tejas," chronicled a
hunting expedition led by Ruiz that involved more than sixty Comanche
warriors. This same article was reprinted in Mexico City as part of a longer work in 1850 under the title *Diario de Viage de la Comisión de Límites.*[5]
Ruiz also appeared in accounts of the life of his nephew José Antonio
Navarro, including the latter's memoirs that were published serially in the
San Antonio Ledger during the 1850s.[6] Jacob de Cordova briefly included
Ruiz in his 1858 book, *Texas: Her Resources and Her Public Men.*[7] Ruiz's son,
Francisco Antonio Ruiz, mentioned his father in his narrative of the fall of
the Alamo, which was published in the 1860 edition of the *Texas Almanac.*[8]
This widely read account became a source for many other authors, at least
one of whom attributed the actions of Francisco to his father. An "Old
Texan," who was most likely Narciso Leal, published a biography of Na-
varro in 1876 that included much about Ruiz from Navarro's memoirs.[9] In
1878, *The Magazine of American History* published an article on the Texas
Revolution by Reuben M. Potter that discussed the roles played by Ruiz,
Navarro, and Lorenzo de Zavala.[10]

Despite his historical importance, Ruiz remains an enigmatic figure.
How could such a major figure in Texas history be overlooked? The scant
attention paid to Ruiz was explained by historian Raúl A. Ramos in *Be-*

yond the Alamo: "The relative abundance and availability of Anglo American sources has resulted in a history of Tejanos largely shaped by Anglo assumptions and observations structured within the larger periodization of American history."[11] Simply put, Tejano figures such as Ruiz do not fit into the Anglo-focused narrative of Texas and so are typically obscured, if not completely omitted. While recent historians—including Ramos, Jesús F. de la Teja, Arnoldo De León, and others—have begun to challenge this narrative, it persists in the popular understanding of Texas history. This work attempts to fill the void left by more than a century and a half of omission. This oversight is regrettable, but it allows for a contemporary examination of Ruiz's life and legacy without the considerable interpretive baggage attached to other early Texas figures.

The reasons for Ruiz's absence from Texas historiography need more explication. If he was mentioned at all in early Texas histories, Ruiz appeared on the historical stage as a fully developed Mexican federalist, signing the Texas Declaration of Independence, and then exiting into obscurity.[12] His obscurity is surprising in light of the voluminous records and letters related to him that remain in various archives and his participation in many events of nineteenth-century Texas. His life, however, did not fit within the Anglo-dominated narrative of Texas, which supported a simplified view of national identity in which Tejanos could identify with either Texas or Mexico, but not both. From this perspective, no obvious or natural motive arose for Ruiz to sign the Texas Declaration of Independence. He was thus given the same motivation as the Anglo colonists; as Sam Houston Dixon wrote, Ruiz "espoused the cause of the Texas colonists against Mexican tyranny."[13] A study of Ruiz requires the reader to see beyond the Anglo Texan experience and into the Tejano experience, which goes farther back in time and involves a complex history of frontier survival and previous political struggles.

There is a compelling reason that nearly all early historiography concerning Ruiz focused on his role in Texas's independence. The United States during the nineteenth and much of the twentieth century was a *Herrenvolk* democracy[14] that maintained a distinction between white and nonwhite or mixed-race peoples. The displacement and oppression of Tejanos by Anglos was justified by portraying the former as mixed-race people who had the stereotypically negative attributes of their indigenous ancestors such as indolence, untrustworthiness, and defective morality. In contrast, a few Tejano elites such as Ruiz, Navarro, and Juan N. Seguín were "Europeanized" to explain their virtue in siding with the "white" (and therefore superior) colonists. To reconcile the apparent contradiction of a "Mexican" siding with Anglo neighbors, early twentieth-century historians attempted to de-Mexicanize Ruiz by creating a European origin myth to justify his participation. Ruiz, as a "Spaniard," had European origins, education, and virtues that separated him from indolent, untrustworthy, or tyrannical Mexicans. Ruiz's nephew Navarro, the only other Tejano who signed the declaration, underwent a similar transformation, partly through his own authorship. Navarro's Corsican blood cleansed him of Mexican identity and cast him as a European on a par with his Anglo counterparts. However, Ruiz was far from European in his birth, education, or culture. He was born and educated in Spanish Texas, and his political beliefs were heavily influenced by his life on the northern borderlands of New Spain (the colonial name for Mexico). Distance from the administrative center of New Spain gave him and other Tejanos the intellectual space to espouse a radical position within the Mexican political dialectic. Ironically, while Ruiz did not share many of the political or racial views of Anglos, he was also ideologically distant from his countrymen in the center of Mexico. Either way, since he did not fit the Anglo narrative, Ruiz had to be redefined, and accounts of him focused sharply on his role in Texas independence.[15]

While racial attitudes have changed since the nineteenth century, racist thinking has affected Texas historiography, where Tejanos have often been given brief, frequently superficial attention, and in broader narratives and biographical sources with contemporary interpretive methods frequently lacking. Sam Houston Dixon published what may have been the first biographical sketch of Ruiz in his 1924 book, *The Men Who Made Texas Free*. This work confusingly blended the lives of José Francisco Ruiz, his father, Juan Manuel, and his son, Francisco Antonio. Dixon's work was influential in molding popular views on Texas independence into a nationalist story that pitted courageous Americans against indolent Mexicans in a brave struggle against centralization and murderous tyranny.[16] There being no room for complexity within this simple narrative, Dixon presented Tejanos who supported independence as having adopted the cause of the Anglo colonists. Thus, Dixon's conflation of Ruiz's motivations with those of most Anglo Texans. Other nineteenth- and twentieth-century historians also adopted a reverential attitude towards Anglo Texan culture and political aims. Only occasionally was the voice of a Tejano heard, and when it was included it was usually written by an Anglo, told from within the Anglo narrative, and directed at an Anglo audience.

Tejano apprehensions concerning slavery, annexation by the United States, the influx of Protestant Christianity, their loss of political control to an Anglo majority, and their desire for statehood within Mexico rather than independent nationhood were rarely noted by Anglo historians. Dixon overlooked the Tejano perspective altogether and told his readers only that the Tejanos at San Antonio hesitated to join with Anglo colonists in demanding independence, but "when the Washington convention was called . . . they no longer hesitated to join their forces with the American settlers to work out a governmental policy that would result in freedom from Mexican tyranny."[17] This portrayal of the Tejanos apparently influenced even early Tejano authors such as Ruben Rendón Lozano, who wrote a biographical sketch of Ruiz in his landmark 1936 work, *Viva Texas: The Story of the Mexican Born Patriots of the Texas Revolution.* Lozano also placed Ruiz within the context of Anglo political designs, writing, "[Ruiz] was exceptionally zealous, as he always favored annexation of Texas by the United States." Lozano's last sentence attempted to bolster Ruiz's importance by recalling that James Bowie was his great nephew by marriage.[18]

The simplified Anglo hagiography of Ruiz influenced a generation of historians. Frederick C. Chabot included a sketch and genealogy of Ruiz in his 1937 self-published book, *With the Makers of San Antonio.* Chabot cited Dixon's volume as well as Ruiz family members whom he had interviewed. Walter G. Struck's 1943 work, *José Francisco Ruiz: Texas Patriot* was the first fairly well-researched study of his life. That short book, which was published by the Witte Museum in commemoration of the relocation of the Ruiz home to the grounds of the museum, was the first to address the lengthy career of Ruiz prior to Texas independence, though it did so in less than six pages. Struck also only briefly touched upon Ruiz's career as an Indian negotiator, an important aspect of his life that had been overlooked by earlier biographers. Some factual errors entered Struck's work from Dixon and Chabot, such as Ruiz's father being from "Querétaro, Spain," and the claim of a Spanish education for the younger Ruiz.[19]

Starting about twenty years after the publication of Dixon's book, works began to appear on different aspects of Ruiz's life that provide some other perspectives on him. Louis W. Kemp in 1944 produced *The Signers of the Texas Declaration of Independence,* which added important details from primary sources regarding Ruiz's service during the Texas Revolution. Carlos E. Castañeda's multivolume *Our Catholic Heritage in Texas, 1519–1936* does not focus upon Ruiz specifically, but he does appear in a brief introduction in volume 6 that outlines his service as the commander at Tenoxtitlán. Malcolm D. McLean, in several volumes of his *Papers Concerning Robertson's Colony in Texas*, translated many of Ruiz's writings into English.[20] A fine historical essay appears in an archaeological study by Al J. McGraw and V. Kay Hindes entitled *Chipped Stone and Adobe: A Cultural Resources Assessment of the Proposed Applewhite Reservoir, Bexar County, Texas*. Hindes also wrote a useful introduction for *The Herrera Gate: An Archival, Architectural and Conservation Study*. David R. McDonald's *José Antonio Navarro: In Search of the American Dream in Nineteenth-Century Texas* is a fine study of Navarro that provides good insights on Ruiz.[21] Ruiz's work with Indians is discussed in Pekka Hämäläinen's *The Comanche Empire* as well as in Gary Clayton Anderson's *The Conquest of Texas* and Thomas W. Kavanagh's *The Comanches*. Raúl Ramos's *Beyond the Alamo* investigates Ruiz's role as a cultural broker between the Indians, Mexicans, and Anglo Americans. Jack Jackson's *Indian Agent: Peter Ellis Bean in Mexican Texas* describes Ruiz's rivalry with Bean and the tension during the Fredonian Revolt.[22] Patsy M. Spaw's first volume of *The Texas Senate* provides a detailed account of the Senate session that Ruiz attended during the brief life of the Republic of Texas.[23]

This study of Ruiz blends the best from the aforementioned secondary sources with primary research to provide a thorough account of the man within the context of his place and times. In so doing, it requires the reader to abandon the presentist perspective of Texas history. Modern Americans typically perceive the United States as a receiver of immigrants and Mexico as an exporter, with the former struggling to regulate the flow of people from the latter. In Ruiz's time, the reverse was true. He was an early advocate for American, European, and Native American immigration into Texas, and he also carried out military orders that halted illegal immigration from the United States. "Manifest Destiny" and westward expansion are mainstays of American history. In this study, American motivations for immigration to Texas are different. Stephen F. Austin and other colonizers were expected to secure the Mexican frontier against Indian incursions and thwart American expansionism. These Americans became Mexican citizens who conversed officially in Spanish, pledged to practice the Catholic faith, and took oaths of allegiance to Mexico. Austin, as leader of this group, was a late supporter of independence. Narratives of American history generally portray expansion as east to west, but Texas was a cultural and political borderland with immigrants from all points of the compass. This flow included not just people whose origins lay in European nations and their post-colonial republics, but also indigenous polities whose military, cultural, and political authority were acknowledged. Most narratives of Texas and American history have given primary attention to the Anglo perspective; this one gives primary attention to the Tejano one that molded Ruiz.

Tejanos held different views on race than their Anglo counterparts, and so a study of Ruiz must also present his perspective. He was born in Béxar (San Antonio), a frontier town mostly populated by mixed-race people of European, Indian, and African heritage. Adherence to the Spanish *sistema de castas* (caste system) was minimal in Béxar due to isolation, scarcity of available spouses, and the constant threat of Indian hostilities, which drew the community together. Ruiz and his immediate family were classified as *criollos españoles* (Spaniards born in the New World) and benefited socially from their racial classification. The fluidity of classifications in Béxar can be seen in the family of Ruiz's son-in-law, Blas María Herrera, whose grandfather was classified as a *lobo* (mixed African and indigenous ancestry) upon his arrival in Béxar, but whose sons were elevated to *mestizos* (mixed indigenous and Spanish ancestry) and then *españoles* as they rose in social status and wealth. Ruiz also lived eight years among the Comanches, whose group identity was primarily cultural and not racial. More important distinctions for Tejanos were labels, such as *indios bárbaros* and *gente de razón*, into which they classified the numerous indigenous groups around them. Over time many indigenous peoples became Hispanicized and blended into Tejano society through settlement, marriage, and military service, thereby becoming *gente de razón*.[24] The later acceptance of Anglo American and European groups into Texas fit into the established Tejano heritage of mixing with what they perceived as "people of reason," for the common benefit of resisting the persistent threat of "barbarous" people.[25]

Tejano social structures must also be considered. In addition to family ties by blood and marriage, Tejanos placed near equal importance on *compadrazgo*, a term that describes an institutional relationship between the parents and godparents of a child. In this relationship, the parents of a child and the godparents of the same child refer to each other as *com-*

padres, literally meaning "co-parents." This relationship is formalized in the Catholic baptism ceremony, during which the godparents promise to accept shared responsibility for raising the child according to the dictates of the Church, and to assist in education, marriage, and personal development. Compadrazgo played a central role in Tejano society. Understanding the social history of Béxar, and the Ruiz family, requires a knowledge of compadrazgo relationships. When these are considered, previously hidden patterns, affiliations, and affinities are revealed.[26]

Lastly, the politics of Tejano society differed from their Anglo counterparts. Ruiz was heavily influenced by Iberian traditions of provincial autonomy. Defenders of this tradition in early Mexico came to be known as Federalists, and it put them into conflict with another powerful group, the Centralists, who believed that a strong central government in Mexico City should rule the country with very limited room for regional discretion. Federalists championed a liberal constitution, a weak central government with strong regional autonomy, and statehood for Texas. Many Tejanos, including Ruiz, fought in the early battles of the Texas Revolution for the restoration of the federalist Mexican Constitution of 1824, not for independence or annexation by the United States. After the convention at Washington-on-the-Brazos declared independence in March 1836, Tejano support for the Anglo cause wilted. Ruiz, Navarro, Seguín, and other leaders of Béxar became exceptions.[27] This study will explore why the political elites of Béxar supported independence while Tejanos elsewhere rejected it. Ruiz's act of signing the Texas Declaration of Independence was a profound political statement by him and the Bexareños who elected him.

A multi-racial Tejano cultural and political milieu thus defined Ruiz's life. He became a cultural broker who passed freely between Anglo American, indigenous, and Hispanic societies. His lengthy career was characterized by this multiculturalism. In particular, this study will reveal the close and mutually advantageous relationships that Ruiz developed with Navarro, Austin, and Comanche leader Paruakevitsi, which were vital in his successful career as an Indian agent, military leader, politician, and merchant. Ruiz became one of the most ardent Texas revolutionaries, but his zeal for liberty developed slowly and was tempered with pragmatism and a statesmanlike sense of political timing. His public career was filled with critical decisions in which he often chose the path of stability and safety for the people of Texas over unwise rashness. In his private actions, in contrast, he was prone to taking personal risks, especially in politics, which brought him great calamity, admiration, and ultimately success. For his wisdom in political affairs, he gained and kept the trust of many Texans of all varieties. Ruiz was thus an exceptional Texas leader, yet he has been among the least studied participants of the Texas Revolution. His life exemplified the trials of Tejanos, whose culture was the product of the Texas frontier and whose survival required an artful balance of political, military, and cultural ideals. A study of his life provides the opportunity to not only know him better, but to explore the intellectual origins and practical application of the Tejano liberal tradition as expressed in his writings, actions, and remembrances, all of which reveal the cultural, intellectual, and physical influence of the borderland in which he lived.

CHAPTER I

Origins

It is necessary to seek recruits outside the province because here there is no population whatsoever; and some time is needed to court them.

— Governor Fernando Pérez de Almazán, 1724[1]

José Francisco Ruiz was born on January 28, 1783, in San Fernando de Béxar, where his father, Juan Manuel Ruiz, had settled about twenty-five years earlier.[2] Like his father, José Francisco was a product of his home town. His worldview was shaped not only by his father and mother, the former Manuela de la Peña y Valdés, but also by his extended family and the characteristics of "Béxar," as it was commonly known, as a borderland settlement on the northern periphery of New Spain. Béxar was a multiethnic community, and José Francisco's ability to gain and hold status in the indigenous and Spanish spheres became the key to much of his success in life. Therefore, to begin to understand him, one must consider both his family background and the development of the town where he was raised. Béxar served as the capital of the Provincia de Tejas y las Nuevas Filipinas, often shortened to "Tejas" or "Texas."[3] Unlike other provincial capitals such as Santa Fe and New Orleans, Béxar received few immigrants, struggled to support its population, and was threatened by ever-present Lipan Apaches and Comanches. Spanish authorities tried various strategies to meet these challenges, but Béxar remained a borderland community, and the Ruiz family adapted well to that environment.

The Ruiz family traces its lineage in Mexico back to the seventeenth century in the town of San Luis de la Paz in the province of Querétaro, which today lies in the state of Guanajuato. San Luis de la Paz was founded on August 25, 1552, upon the Spanish Camino de la Plata ("Silver Road"), which linked the mines near Zacatecas with Mexico City.

The community served as an administrative center for Querétaro and an important Spanish military and political base during the late sixteenth-century war of extermination against the Chichimecas, who threatened Spain's rich mining operations in the region.[4] Otomí, Tlaxcaltecan, and Huisache allies were imported to repopulate the area, and San Luis de la Paz became a center for trade, culture, and education. This pattern of indigenous extermination, repopulation by allied indigenous groups, and the establishment of presidios and missions was repeated along a chain of settlement that stretched north to Saltillo and eventually Texas.[5] By the early eighteenth century, the community was the provisioning post for silver mines operated by Jesuits in the nearby Sierra Gorda Mountains. The Jesuits also established a college in San Luis de la Paz, which became one of the most renowned in all of New Spain.[6] The region had a small number of Spanish merchants, government officials, and soldiers along with its majority population of Chichimecas and Otomís. To encourage settlement, indigenous colonists were given rights equal to those of the *españoles* (Spanish), which drew the Otomís from southern Querétaro. San Luis de la Paz was connected to both the northern frontier and colonial capital via the Silver Road, which carried travelers north as far as Saltillo as well as south to Mexico City.[7]

The Ruiz family established itself in San Luis de la Paz by the late seventeenth century and became involved in the fields of trade and education. The earliest Ruiz family records were created when José Francisco Ruiz's paternal great-grandparents, Manuel Ruiz and Augustina Servín de Mora, had their son, Joseph, baptized in February 1695 in the local church of Santiago de Querétaro.[8] Thirteen years later, in June 1708, another son, Augustín, was baptized in the same church—he became the grandfather of José Francisco Ruiz of Béxar.[9] A merchant, he sold trade goods and mining supplies that he acquired in the provisional capital of Santiago de Querétaro.[10] Among his children was Juan Manuel Ruiz, born about 1730.[11] Since Juan Manuel later became a teacher, he may have received a formal education from the Jesuit college in San Luis de la Paz.

The Ruiz family's northward migration from Querétaro to Texas is contemporaneous with a highly organized effort to colonize the region between the Pánuco River and Texas led by José de Escandón. In December of 1748, the Escandón expedition left Querétaro with 2,500 colonists and 755 soldiers. Over the next seven years, Escandón founded 23 civil settlements along the Rio Grande in Nuevo Santander (present-day State of Tamauli-

pas) drawing colonists from Querétaro, the surrounding Sierra Gordo and
the northern provinces of Coahuila, Nuevo Leon, and Chihuahua. Juan
Manuel Ruiz and his family migrated even further than most, to the village
of San Fernando de Béxar on the northern frontier of New Spain.[12]

Founded in 1731 and commonly known as Béxar under Spanish and
Mexican rule, it was not officially renamed San Antonio until 1837, after
Texas had become an independent republic. To secure the borderlands, the
Spanish implemented a three-pronged strategy of religious missions, military presidios, and, ultimately, civil settlements, including San Fernando
de Béxar, in 1731.[13] For decades, the administration of the village of San
Fernando de Béxar remained distinct from the presidio of San Antonio de
Béxar, although the former was taxed to provision and develop the military
outpost.[14] The political complexity of the town increased further when
the community became the provincial capital in 1772; governors tended to
dominate local politics, although this did not prevent the occasional turf
battle between the town councilmen and a governor. To further complicate
local politics, clustered to the south was a string of five mission settlements
operated by Franciscans. Beginning in 1792 with Mission Valero, the missions were secularized, transforming into self-governing communities,
each with its own governing body.[15]

Juan Manuel brought with him other family members, including his
mother, Ana María de Cumplido, and sister, María Gertrudis Ruiz.[16] The
family lived in a stone house on the south side of the Plaza de Armas, in
the Barrio del Sur. This was in the neighborhood established to house
the early presidio soldiers, and in the late 1750s it remained distinct from
the adjacent *villa* of San Fernando de Béxar.[17] Nineteen families from the
Canary Islands (*Isleños*) formed the nucleus of the villa and would dominate local affairs for much of the eighteenth century. The physical layout
of Béxar had been adapted to the local terrain, thus it did not have the
customary streets laid out at right angles. It had two unimposing plazas
in the center, the Plaza de Armas (Military Plaza) to the west of San
Fernando church (later cathedral) and the Plaza Principal (Main Plaza)
to the east. Surrounding these were several single-story, flat-roofed stone
residences (such as the Ruiz's), the San Antonio de Valero mission, the
military barracks, and a government building. On the periphery of town
stood four neighborhoods, or *barrios*, where poorer residents lived in *ja-
cales*—thatch-roofed houses made of upright wooden poles chinked with
adobe and sometimes plastered.[18]

Carol Zuber-Mallison / ZMGraphics.com

Ruiz family origins in eighteenth-century Bajío region of Mexico. Santiago de Querétaro can be seen in the Bajío region north of Mexico City, and San Antonio de Béxar is
located in the far north.

Land allocation and access to water became sources of contention in
the early history of Béxar, the latter being a limited resource. By 1740, all
of the irrigable land in Béxar had been appropriated with the exception
of *propios*, or tracts reserved by the municipality, which surrounded the
urban center. They were typically set aside for public use or rented for
public income. Seeking to alleviate this land stress, residents successfully
petitioned the governor to allow more rentals of propios. Water, of course,
was the key to the effective production of land. Captain Toribio Urrutia
wrote to the viceroy in December 1740, complaining about the actions of
the Isleño-controlled town council: "Anyone who is not an Islander owns

no land, water, nor anything assigned to them to be able to subsist as citizens of the town." Debates over access to water and land, essential to the development of parts of the community, continued for years, generating a culture of litigation and a need for legal professionals, a career which José Francisco Ruiz pursued early in life.[19]

Juan Manuel found agricultural opportunities somewhat restricted in the rigid structure of early Béxar, where farming was limited to those who had vested irrigation rights. Subsistence agriculture and cattle and horse ranching were the main endeavors of the early families. Few of them engaged in trades such as blacksmithing, tailoring, or carpentry. This void afforded some of the new immigrants opportunities to establish themselves economically and build personal wealth, and they came to dominate the skilled trades in Bexar. Ruiz was one of nine tailors during the last third of the eighteenth century in Béxar, a time when almost no ready-to-wear clothing was available.[20] His stone house on the south side of the Plaza de Armas, which he bought from José Antonio Rodríguez, served as his place of business as well as his home. This was a prime location near the presidio and its garrison of mounted troops, the city's greatest economic asset.

Having settled in Béxar, Juan Manuel quickly established himself as a political and business leader.[21] The earliest surviving record of him in the Béxar Archives is a testimony he gave in 1760; in it he swore to facts that occurred while he was serving as a *regidor* (councilman) on the *cabildo* (town council), or *ayuntamiento*, as it became known in the late eighteenth century.[22] He was re-elected to serve in the ayuntamiento for 1761.[23]

Juan Manuel's rapid entry into an elected office reflected the opportunity afforded to artisan immigrants in Béxar at that time. Most immigrants to Béxar in the late eighteenth century immigrated from the provinces of Nuevo León, Coahuila, and Nuevo Santander to serve as soldiers in the presidio, but a small minority, typically artisans and merchants, came from elsewhere in New Spain, Europe, and America. Other immigrant families who prospered in Béxar and by marriage became linked to the Ruiz family were the Navarros (Kingdom of Corsica, 1777), Veramendis (Kingdom of Navarre, 1770), Gil Y'Barbos (Los Adaes, Louisiana, 1773), and Seguíns (Aguascalientes, New Spain, 1750).[24]

To supplement his income, Juan Manuel, along with Cristóbal de los Santos Coy, became a private schoolmaster in Béxar and probably tutored his pupils at his residence.[25] He also in 1782 purchased at auction a royal concession to operate the games of *chusa* (a form of roulette) and *bolas* (bocce), which were played under tents during the popular dance celebrations called fandangos.[26] The people of Béxar had long enjoyed these public dances, which often transgressed the social boundaries of acceptable public mores and morality of the time. In 1784, as related by historian Jesús F. de la Teja, "the town council at something of a wits' end complained to the governor because much of the crowd attending or congregating outside fandangos was composed of 'unbridled youths and marked women.' They asked that fandangos should be restricted to certain hours and confined to the inside of houses, 'making the homeowners responsible for the offenses to God committed through the bad things that were sung, the fights, and disorders that occur.'"[27] Despite these attempts at regulation, fandangos remained popular in Béxar. When American immigrants arrived later, their Protestant views on public morality and social comportment clashed with the activities of the fandango. George W. Smyth of Tennessee wrote in 1830 that "the priest and all participated, so contrary to all my preconceived notions of propriety."[28] But clearly not all American immigrants shared Smyth's loftier moral rectitude, since many Texan militia defenders of the Alamo, for example, were enjoying a fandango when news came of the Mexican army's arrival in February 1836.[29]

Additionally, Juan Manuel began a ranching operation of his own on the Medina River, southwest of Béxar, in present-day Von Ormy.[30] This ranch was one of a string of such estates established by various families along the banks of the Medina and San Antonio Rivers and Cibolo Creek from Béxar to La Bahía. The Ruiz family papers in the Bexar Archives indicate that Ruiz received his Medina River grant in 1774. The Ruiz ranch lay north of the Medina River across from the 1808 grant of Juan Ignacio Pérez. It also was adjacent to the ranch of Ruiz's son-in-law, Ángel Navarro, as well as upstream from that of his brother-in-law, Ignacio de la Peña.[31]

Ruiz's ranching operations were small in comparison to neighboring ranchers and involved rounding up unbranded stock and selling them to the presidio and in local markets as dried salted beef, tallow for candles, and leather. The *comandante general* of the province, Teodoro de Croix, decreed in 1778 that all wild cattle and horses belonged to the Spanish crown and that those taking or branding them had to be licensed and pay taxes. His list of men who had unlawfully branded cattle on the Medina River included Juan Manuel, who marked "two calves and two *añejas*."[32] The relatively few cattle noted in the 1778 report is due to an extended war between residents of Béxar and confederations of Comanches and Taguayas, during which ranches on the Medina River were largely abandoned and their stock dispersed.[33] Four years later, in 1782, Ruiz filed a petition to extend the deadline to pay his fine.[34] This debt may have prompted him to establish his gaming business that same year. Conflict with the Comanches ended in 1785, but by then Ruiz's ranch was no longer the primary focus of his economic activity. The Ruiz family would not have a permanent presence on the Medina River again until 1828, when José Francisco Ruiz's son-in-law, Blas María Herrera, permanently re-established the ranch.[35]

Tallow and hides from Béxar were exported and sold in markets such as the fair in Saltillo, the largest annual trade event for Tejanos; Nuevo Santander (modern day Tamaulipas); Nuevo León; and Nueva Extremadura (Coahuila).[36] Maintaining close social networks and personal relationships in Saltillo, which is located in what is now the Mexican state of Coahuila, was very advantageous for members of the merchant class of Béxar, and both the Ruiz and Navarro families did so. For Juan Manuel, the Saltillo fair also afforded a good opportunity to buy supplies for his tailoring business. Spanish officials collected a sales tax at the fair known as *la alcábala*, which varied between 2 and 8 percent.[37] This and similar taxes greatly inflated the cost of goods, which merchants sought to avoid by engaging in illicit trade. José Francisco Ruiz later learned this tactic from his father, and records clearly reveal that the Ruiz, Navarro, and Veramendi families of Béxar engaged in illicit trade—regarded as "smuggling" by crown officials—consistently over multiple generations.[38]

Despite his various efforts, Juan Manuel never became a wealthy man in Béxar. A 1779 ad valorem tax on the residents of Béxar assessed him a tax of only four reales, compared to the highest assessment of six pesos for Fernando de Veramendi and Marciano Zambrano and two pesos for Ruiz's son-in-law, Ángel Navarro.[39] (At that time a peso was equal to eight reales.) This meant that Ángel's property was assessed to be worth four times that of his father-in-law. All reports of Juan Manuel Ruiz's ranching activity indicated that it was a modest enterprise. His 1782 request to extend the payment deadline on his taxes and his 1783 concession to operate games of chance reveal that in this period he needed to supplement his income. No records indicate that he managed to advance his economic status much further. The Veramendi and Zambrano families had eight times as much wealth as the Ruiz family. The marriage of Juan Martín de Veramendi and Josefa Navarro in 1810 solidified the Ruiz-Navarro-Veramendi family into an influential commercial, political and military alliance in the decades before Texas independence. Clearly the Ruiz family entered this union with the least financial resources of the three.

Juan Manuel died on July 30, 1797, leaving his widow, Manuela de la Peña y Valdés, as the primary parental influence in José Francisco Ruiz's life during his teen years. Due to the limited role women played in public life at that time, there is little direct information outside of family records on the early life of Manuela. She was born on June 24, 1748, to Martín de la Peña and Ana Petra Valdés in Saltillo.[40] The De la Peña family had long served as military and political elites of Saltillo, having been there since shortly after its founding in 1591.

Manuela's distant ancestors, Alonso Martín and María de la Peña, arrived in Saltillo among its first settlers and established themselves among the city's political and business elites, with succeeding generations building upon their influence.[41] José Martín de la Peña, the son of Lieutenant General Martín de la Peña and Manuela's grandfather, was a captain in the Spanish army.[42] He retired in Texas about the time that Juan Manuel Ruiz arrived in Béxar, and ran unsuccessfully for *alcalde de segundo voto* in 1768.[43] His son, Ignacio de la Peña, established a successful ranch on the San Antonio River named San Ildefonso de Chayopín,[44] which was one of the largest ranches on the Béxar to La Bahía road and was among those that supported the Continental Army during the American Revolution by sending cattle to New Orleans.[45] Ignacio married Francisca de Urrutia, the daughter of a prominent Béxar family, in 1759.[46] He served as *alcalde de segundo voto* in 1775 and employed his nephew-by-marriage, Juan Manuel Ruiz, as *testigo de asistencia* in various legal proceedings that year.[47] Through Manuela, then, Juan Manuel did gain at least some connection to Béxar's elite.

The historical record does not indicate when or where Manuela met Juan Manuel, and the marriage records of San Fernando Church for this time are incomplete, so no marriage certification has been located for them. What is clear was that Manuela and Juan Manuel were married by 1766, when the first of their thirteen children was born. As was not uncommon in that era, Manuela lost eight children in infancy, but those who survived did well and strengthened the Ruiz's ties with other prominent families.[48] Manuela's eldest surviving daughter, María Josefa, born in 1766, married Ángel Navarro, a merchant from Corsica eighteen years her senior, in 1782.[49] The couple purchased a house across the street from the

Ruiz home. Since María Josefa was seventeen years older than José Francisco and Ángel was thirty-five years older than him, they seem to have become his surrogate parents after Juan Manuel died.

Following the death of her husband, Manuela resided with her eldest son, José Antonio Pablo Longino Ruiz, until he married in 1804. She then lived with her daughter María Josefa, whose husband Ángel served as a mentor and benefactor for José Francisco until his death in 1808.[50] María Josefa's sons—José Ángel, José Antonio, and José Luciano—all developed close relationships with José Francisco Ruiz, since they were nearby and not far apart in age. But the influence of Manuela and María Josefa should not be overlooked. The Ruiz women were the matriarchs of the extended Ruiz-Navarro clan for nearly thirty years and maintained the family through the difficult period after the Battle of Medina, when its fortunes were shattered.[51] José Francisco Ruiz always maintained a close relationship with both women. When his mother died of cholera at Béxar in 1834, her will affectionately directed that "for the services and nursing which my children María Josefa and José Francisco have so willingly given me they shall each receive a third of the [my] estate."[52] Other older siblings played important roles in José Francisco's upbringing as well; he was born fifth among the five who survived to adulthood.

José Francisco's sister María Antonia was born on October 24, 1771, and was widowed three times.[53] Her first husband was Marcos Gil Y'Barbo, the son of Antonio Gil Y'Barbo, the erstwhile lieutenant governor of the province of Texas. Marcos died on December 28, 1792.[54] She then married Francisco Antonio Calvillo, who died in 1799. Her third husband was Francisco Xavier Rodríguez, a family friend and son of the original builder of the Ruiz home.[55] He joined the ill-fated republican army during the Gutiérrez-Magee Expedition and followed José Francisco into exile in the Neutral Ground between Texas and Louisiana, where he died in 1814.[56]

José Francisco's brother José Antonio Pablo Longino was born on March 13, 1775, and became a professional soldier in the Béxar Company.[57] After the death of his father he supported his mother and younger siblings. In 1804, he married María Fernanda Seguín, daughter of Ermeregildo Seguín and Juana Flores, and began his own family in Béxar.

María Rosalía Ruiz was born on May 12, 1777, and married Pedro de la Zerda in 1800.[58] They settled next door to the Ruiz home on Plaza de Armas. When José Francisco moved into the house in 1802 and used it as a schoolhouse, Francisco de la Zerda, Pedro's father, lived with him.[59]

José Antonio Francisco Victoriano was born on August 31, 1780, and also served in the Béxar Company before his death in 1812 at Béxar.[60] His ranch in the Neutral Ground was where José Francisco resided during his exile. José Francisco secured an American title to this property for his mother after the Adams–Onís Treaty of 1819 gave control of the Neutral Ground to the United States.[61] His mother left it to José Francisco and his siblings in her will, and he tried to sell it in 1836, following the Battle of San Jacinto.[62]

Having a family network proved fortunate for José Francisco, who was fourteen years old when his father died. His widowed mother Manuela de la Peña was left to care for him, his younger brother, who did not survive to adulthood and who was also named José Francisco, and his sister María Rosalía.[63] Soon after his father's death, José Francisco's eldest brother, José Antonio Pablo Longino, a presidio soldier, moved back in with the family.[64] In his will, Juan Manuel directed his oldest son to care for his affairs if Manuela was unable. He left half of his property to his wife "because we acquired it together during our marriage" and the remainder "equally divided among my said children that they may possess it and enjoy with the blessing of God and my own."[65] No mention was made of the Ruiz ranch on the Medina River in the will, possibly reflecting the fact that it had been abandoned.[66]

Family in this era was comprised not only of biological relatives but also relatives sealed by a religious bond of friendship and trust. Compadrazgo, an institutional relationship between parents and godparents during which godparents promise to accept shared responsibility for raising the child, was often used to strengthen extended family ties. In this relationship, the parents and godparents of the same child refer to each other as *compadres*, or literally "co-parents." This relationship is formalized in the Catholic baptism ceremony, during which godparents promise to accept shared responsibility for raising the child, according to the dictates of the Church, and for helping the child to live a fruitful life, including education, marriage, and personal development. The child would subsequently call the godparents *"padrino"* and *"madrina."* Godparents also participated in the sacraments of marriage and confirmation.

José Francisco Ruiz's padrinos for his 1783 baptism at San Fernando Church were José Hernández and Luisa Guerrero, the uncle and aunt of his future wife, María Josefa Hernández.[67] The padrinos at his wedding in 1804 were Lieutenant Colonel Juan Ignacio Pérez and his wife, Clemencia

Hernández, María Josefa's eldest sister. On June 20, 1809, José Francisco and María Josefa welcomed the birth of a second daughter, María Antonia. Her padrinos were José Ignacio Pérez and his sister Gertrudis. Ruiz solidified his extended family relationships by entering several compadre relationships. He and María Josefa first served as padrinos at the baptism of María de Jésus Rodríguez on December 20, 1808.[68] Upon returning to Béxar from his exile in the Neutral Ground, he was a padrino to the marriage of his nephew, José Luciano Navarro, to Teodora Carbajal (April 11, 1823) and for the baptisms of Juan Ancelmo Losoya (July 19, 1822), Juan Martín de Veramendi (April 19, 1823), and José Guadalupe Morales (December 19, 1824).

Compadrazgo also created family-like ties in the absence of traditional family structures. While in exile, José Francisco served as a padrino several times for fellow exiles in Natchitoches, which signified his role as a leader. It was also used to formalize relationships between people of different classes and racial backgrounds. These socially mixed compadre/padrino relationships sometimes had different meanings from traditional relationships between persons of similar classes. In Béxar, racial designations took on a more social meaning, such that persons of known mixed racial heritage, known as castas, were sometimes classified as español upon achieving suitable social status. (A notable example of racial/socio-economic rise from casta to español in Béxar was the Herrera family, who will be discussed later in this work.) The Ruiz family, though not among the wealthiest families in Béxar, was certainly considered among the ruling elites and was uniformly referenced as españoles.

José Francisco grew up in a household that included indigenous members and castas. These persons held various positions from servants to full members of the family, and for a select few, these relationships were socially cemented through the institution of compadrazgo. On August 30, 1763, Juan Manuel Ruiz became padrino of a mixed race (coyote) child, José Viterbo Caemusquis, the son of Javier Caemusquis and Clara de Sandoval.[69] This was the case of Ruiz serving as padrino for the child of a couple who worked for him, or in some other subservient relationship. Servants who resided in a household were known as criados and Ruiz, who was a tailor, had much use for them. He became a padrino again on November 3, 1763, for an Apache child named José Manuel.[70]

Young captives were a common source of labor in early Béxar. In 1761, the Spanish signed a peace treaty with the Lipan Apaches in the aftermath of the San Sabá massacre. Under the treaty the Spanish built Mission San Lorenzo and Mission Candelaria on the Nueces River, and in return the Lipans promised to accept Christianity and live in peace with the nearby Spanish settlements. By September 1762, the ayuntamiento of Béxar protested to Governor Ángel de Martos y Navarrete that in spite of the so-called "peace," Apache raids were continuing in Béxar.[71] Smallpox struck the missions in 1763, and they closed shortly thereafter. It is impossible to know whether José Manuel was the victim of either Spanish-on-Indian violence, or Indian-on-Indian violence, or perhaps orphaned by the smallpox epidemic and brought to Béxar. But he and other captive Apache children were baptized in the fall of 1763 at San Fernando Church.[72] These children typically became domestic servants in the households of their padrinos and became part of their extended family. Juan Manuel Ruiz thus not only took an Apache child into his household as a domestic servant, but sponsored his Christianization through the institution of compadrazgo. Thus, compadrazgo served as an institution for the adoption and integration of Indian and mestizo children into the Spanish way of life, including religion. José Francisco grew up in a multi-racial household with indigenous culture, language, and lifeways present. This would prove beneficial to him in the years to come.

For migrants like the Ruiz family, compadre relationships enhanced their integration into Béxar by transforming friendships into familial relationships. José Francisco benefited from family relationships and established many of his own with other prominent families in town. Among the family names for those who served as compadres to him and his siblings were Arocha, Bustillos, Cortinas, Curbier, Durán, Farías, Gortari, Lucero, Salinas, Seguín, Travieso, Urrutia, and Zambrano.[73]

The Ruiz family briefly left Béxar following the death of its patriarch Juan Manuel Ruiz. Neither José Francisco, his mother, nor his brothers were listed in the census records for Béxar during the period of 1797 to 1802. This may indicate that the family left with José Francisco's older brother, José Antonio Pablo Longino Ruiz, on a military assignment. Exactly where the Ruiz family went is not known, but José Antonio served later in East Texas, at Nacogdoches, and in Louisiana. José Francisco's sister, María Rosalía, who was twenty years old at the time, stayed in Béxar and married Pedro de la Zerda in February 1800 at San Fernando Church.[74]

Among the important features of Béxar that influenced and molded young José Francisco was the house in which he was born and lived until he was a teenager, and to which he later returned.[75] Because the Ruiz home stood in the center of the community on the Plaza de Armas, José Francisco grew up surrounded by people and places that would long be the center of his world. Across Calle de los Flores from his house, was the home of his brother-in-law and sister, Ángel and María Josefa Navarro, who married in 1782, a year before José Francisco was born.[76] The three Navarro brothers, though technically his nephews, were close to José Francisco, and he formed a particularly strong bond with José Antonio Navarro, who was twelve years his junior. After the death of Ángel Navarro in 1808, José Francisco served as a father figure and mentor to José Antonio for the rest of his life. In later years, Navarro wrote fondly of his uncle, often referring to him as "my venerable uncle," and acknowledged his formative influence. José Francisco's future wife, María Josefa Hernández, was among the many children who lived on the Plaza de Armas.[77] The two certainly knew each other since the Ruiz and Hernández families were related by compadrazgo. José Francisco's padrino was José Hernández, the uncle of María Josefa.[78]

The Ruiz home was never very large, nor was it particularly valuable, but it has proven to be a durable reminder of its owner. The house was described in the estate of José Francisco as "a stone house situated on the southside of the Plaza de Armas made fifteen varas from the front, and two and five eighth varas without buildings on Nueva Street, valued at six hundred pesos." It remained in his family for many generations and served in several private and public capacities including residence, tailor shop, school, grocery, and general store. In 1942 it was moved to the grounds of the Witte Museum on Broadway Street near the San Antonio Zoo and Brackenridge Park, where it became an educational facility and later served as a museum store. In 1973, the Texas Historical Commission placed historical marker number 4386 at the site where the house formerly stood on Dolorosa Street, on the south side of the Military Plaza (the former Plaza de Armas).[79]

Born into a Béxar family that was several generations removed from life in Spain, and raised on the northern frontier of New Spain, José Francisco Ruiz was far more of a borderland settler than a European. In his community, he lived within a flexible multiethnic environment that fostered ideas that were very different from those common in Spain, his ancestral homeland, or even in distant Mexico City. Fortunately for him, he had strong support from his parents and siblings, and compadrazgo created an extended family network on which he would depend throughout his life. His father was not wealthy, but young José Francisco always had a home and never seemed to want for necessities.

CHAPTER II

Early Years

José Francisco Ruiz . . . is selected for [schoolmaster], provided
his minority does not render him incompetent to fill it.
—Minutes of the Ayuntamiento of San Fernando, 1803[1]

With the death of his father, José Francisco not only lost his provider, but also his best mentor and teacher. Juan Manuel had been one of the early private schoolmasters in Béxar and had educated his sons in the Ruiz home.[2] Though illiterate herself, Ruiz's widowed mother, Manuela, did not allow her son's education to be neglected.[3] Some historians have stated that José Francisco was educated in Spain, but there is no evidence for this claim.[4] It would have been cost prohibitive for even the wealthiest family of Béxar to send a son to Spain for four years. In 1796, the Ruiz family was in good shape economically compared to most Béxar residents, but they were not wealthy and simply did not possess the financial resources to send José Francisco to Spain. Events in Spain also seem to have precluded José Francisco from traveling there. Spain was involved in the Napoleonic Wars at this time. The British established a naval blockade of all Spanish ports during 1797 to impede Spain's primary source of revenue, colonial shipping.[5] The blockade continued until 1802, when a temporary end of hostilities was negotiated. José Francisco's alleged formal education in Spain spanned these same years, 1798–1803. In all of his writings, he never once mentioned traveling to Spain, which certainly would have been a monumental event in his life. It seems much more likely that Ruiz was schooled at home or in Saltillo, which had two schools at the time: one run by the Franciscans that opened in 1774 and a public school opened in 1776 when the governor of Nueva Vizcaya, Felipe de Barri, ordered the establishment of public schools in all ayuntamientos.[6] Manuela de la Peña and her eldest daughter, María Josefa, faced with a similar decision twelve years later concerning José Antonio Navarro, sent him to a school in Saltillo.[7]

José Francisco Ruiz returned to Béxar in 1802 and settled in the "dilapidated" house he inherited from his father. He was appointed as the first public schoolmaster of Béxar in 1803, at just twenty years of age, and repaired the home to serve as a school.[8] Public education in early Béxar had been non-existent apart from the efforts of Franciscan friars. There were three private school masters who tutored in Béxar before 1789. These were Cristóbal de los Santos Coy, José Francisco de la Mata, and Juan Manuel Ruiz, the father of José Francisco Ruiz.[9] Scant mention was made of their teaching activities in existing records, and it is not known for how long each taught. Public education in the Spanish empire came in response to the exclusion of the Jesuits in 1767, which crippled the educational system of Spain and its colonies.[10] In response, the crown ordered the establishment of public schools to replace those formerly operated by Jesuits. On May 1, 1789, De la Mata appeared before the ayuntamiento and requested official authorization and public funds for his school.[11] His effort was short lived because three years later he was jailed for "unworthy criticism of the Governor of the Province." No further references to his school have been found in the Bexar Archives.[12] When Juan Manuel Ruiz died in 1797, there was no public school for his children.

In January 1802, the new governor of Texas, Juan Bautista Elguézabal, issued a long list of reforms, including an order to all alcaldes to ensure that parents placed their children in school. He stated that this "was of the greatest importance to the religious and political life of the community."[13] The governor suggested that each community create at least a one-room school and parents pay a tax of two *reales* for each child attending.[14]

The decree was implemented one year later. The ayuntamiento of Béxar met to discuss the formation of a public school and selection of a schoolmaster. José Francisco was selected as the schoolmaster with the added comment, "provided his minority does not render him incompetent to fill it." It was further noted that "his residence for the present is to constitute the schoolhouse."[15] This was the same house in which his father taught. Ruiz's youth and inexperience were probably excused by the ayuntamiento because most if not all of the officials knew him well, including his brother-in-law, Ángel Navarro, the alcalde, and his uncle José Ignacio de la Peña, a regidor (a voting member of the town council).[16] It was also possible that Ruiz's father had tutored members of the ayuntamiento or their children. It must be noted that Ángel Navarro's son, José Antonio Navarro, then eight years old, was among Ruiz's students.[17] José Francisco would serve as mentor and father figure for his nephew for the remainder of his life, especially after Ángel Navarro died in 1808. This was the start of public education in Béxar, and with it came official limitations on what was taught. In 1804, for example, a decree banning philosopher Jean-Jacques Rousseau's *The Social Contract* was proclaimed in Béxar.[18]

José Francisco served as the schoolmaster for only one year.[19] He resigned just prior to marrying María Josefa Hernández. The position of schoolmaster was not a well-paid job and held little prospect of supporting a new family. Governor Elguézabal recommended replacing Ruiz with the presidio paymaster, who agreed on condition that a schoolhouse was provided. A plan to construct a schoolhouse made of *cojines* (woven branches) was devised. The governor relayed his plan to the comandante general, Nemesio Salcedo, along with a note that he knew of an unnamed "mozo" (young man), a clear reference to the young Ruiz, who could "read and do arithmetic adequately" and "who was agreeable to serve as school master," but declined because of the low salary.[20] Ruiz was succeeded as public schoolmaster of Béxar by Francisco Barrera, who later petitioned the ayuntamiento for permission to change professions to that of notario público because teaching had left him destitute and unable to care for his family.[21]

José Francisco married María Josefa on March 8, 1804, at Mission Concepción near Béxar.[22] The Ruiz and Hernández families were related by compadrazgo, and pursuant to Catholic practice of the time, the priest investigated the families of the bride and groom to determine whether or not they were impeded from marrying by being too closely related by blood or affinity. They were not.[23] He was twenty-one years old, while she was about seventeen. No baptismal record has been found for María Josefa, but from her age in census records, it can be determined that she was born about 1787, probably on her family's El Rincón ranch at the confluence of the San Antonio River and Cíbolo Creek.[24]

The Hernández family descended from Francisco Hernández, a member of the Alarcón expedition that established the San Antonio de Béxar presidio in 1718. María's grandfather, Andrés Hernández, was granted land between the San Antonio River and Cíbolo Creek from the point where the two flowed together to a distance of six leagues up the Cíbolo. He called his ranch San Bartolo, but it was commonly called El Rincón (The

Josépha Nuñes Arocha | Manuel Nuñes | Padre Francisco Maines | Nepomenceno Arocha | Maria de Jesusa Treviño | Brijida Treviño | Angel Navarro

Calle de Presidio

Ignacio Perez

Rastro (Slaughterhouse) formerly the Compania de Bexar Cuartel (Barracks Building) | José Francisco Sosa

José Alejandro Treviño

Juan Antonio Urrutia

Calle de Armagura

PLAZA DE ARMAS (circa 1820)

Calle de Flores

Parish Church of San Fernando

Josefa Cadena

Antonia Bueno

Apolinar Masmela

Antonio Arocha

Luisa Benites —

Maria Ignacia del Rio

Matias Carillo —

José Cassiano

Calle Dolorosa

José Andres Hernandez | José Maria Moral | Placido Hernandez | José Francisco Antonio Ruiz | Francisco Travieso | José Maria Salinas

Carol Zuber-Mallison / ZMGraphics.com

Landowners of the Plaza de Armas, c. 1820. Data courtesy of Clint McKinzie and Jake Ivey.

Fork).[25] The Hernández ranch headquarters was near the site of Fuerte de Santa Cruz del Cíbolo.[26]

The story of María Josefa's family at Béxar was not as peaceful as that of the Ruiz clan. Andrés suffered for years from a debilitating illness, so his wife, Juana de Ollos (Hoyos), and sons operated the ranch. In the late 1770s María Josefa's father, Plácido Hernández, and his family engaged in a lengthy boundary dispute with Mission Espíritu Santo over the rounding up of free-range cattle on lands claimed by both. Andrés died in 1779 and in his will, Plácido and his brother Miguel, did not receive any of their father's cattle. Instead, all were given to their brothers José Andrés and José Joaquín because "they had worked more than the others." The Hernández ranch had to be temporarily abandoned after a Comanche raid in 1783 and was eventually divided among the heirs. Plácido named his ranch San Bartolo de Cerrito. In 1791, he moved his family, including young María, to Béxar. He purchased a lot on the Plaza de Armas across from the Ruiz home (see map on page 27). That same year, the ayuntamiento compiled a list of improved ranches, which included San Bartolo de Cerrito. The report noted that no one lived there at that time. Placido served on the ayuntamiento in 1794. That year Governor Manuel Muñoz reported that ten ranches in the vicinity of Béxar had been repopulated, including Placido's place. Nevertheless, the family, including María Josefa, relocated to Béxar, settling in a house on the Plaza de Armas near the Ruiz home.[27]

María was six months pregnant at the time of her marriage to José Francisco. What, if any, influence this situation had on José Francisco's resignation as schoolmaster is unknown, but it does not seem to have had any lasting negative social effect. The couple was not married at San Fernando Church but at nearby Mission Concepción. The compadres at the Ruiz wedding were Lieutenant Colonel Juan Ignacio Pérez and his wife, Clemencia Hernández, María's eldest sister. Ruiz thus married into a family that provided him additional connections with Béxar elites. His new brothers-in-law, Pérez, José María Zambrano, José Damien Arocha, Manuel Peres Casanova, and Leonardo San Miguel, all played important roles in Béxar. Over the next decades these brothers-in-law would participate, along with Ruiz, in the political and military turmoil of various revolutions.

Following their wedding, the couple settled in the Ruiz home on Plaza de Armas, where they were surrounded by family. They lived with Francisco de la Zerda, an elderly widower, and the father of Ruiz's brother-in-law, Pedro de la Zerda. Pedro lived next door with Ruiz's sister, María Rosalía, who had a new baby in April 1804 named María Ancelma de la Zerda. Ruiz's mother, Manuela, was listed in the 1803 and 1804 censuses of the presidio company of San Antonio de Béxar as residing with her oldest son, José Antonio Pablo Longino Ruiz, her youngest son, also named José Francisco Ruiz, and a granddaughter, María Y'Barbo, who was apparently the daughter of María Antonia Ruiz and Marcos Gil Y'Barbo.[28] In 1804, José Antonio married María Fernanda Seguín, so by the end of the same year Manuela settled with her daughter María Josefa and her husband, Ángel Navarro, whose home stood across the street from the newlyweds. Future relatives lived close as well: Benito Herrera lived two doors down and his one-year-old son, Blas María Herrera, later became Ruiz's son-in-law.[29]

On June 15, 1804, Ruiz's wife, María Josefa, gave birth to a daughter named María Lugarda de Jesús, who died at seven days of age on the day after her baptism.[30] On June 20, 1809, she had a second daughter, María Antonia.[31] Her padrinos were José Ignacio Pérez and his sister Gertrudis, children of her oldest sister, Clemencia, and Juan Ignacio Pérez. The relationship between José Francisco and José Ignacio was quite complex and deserves explanation. In addition to being compadres, they operated adjoining ranches on the Medina River that had been founded by their fathers. Only four years after the baptism of María Antonia, during the Battle of Medina, Ruiz and Pérez served on opposing sides. Pérez, however, tended to the Ruiz property while José Francisco was in exile, and later accounts note that Ruiz resided at José Ignacio's ranch after the latter retired from the army.[32] Later Ruiz and Pérez again found themselves on opposite sides of the Texas War for Independence. Pérez granted Ruiz power of attorney to tend to his property while he went into exile after Mexico's defeat in 1836. They managed to maintain the affinity and obligations of compadres, while publicly being political and military enemies.

Following his marriage, José Francisco pursued law and public service. On December 20, 1804, he was elected to serve as a regidor on the ayuntamiento of Béxar for 1805.[33] Ruiz's term on the ayuntamiento was vital to the development of his views on government.

Because of its status as a villa under the Laws of the Indies, Béxar annually elected two *alcaldes ordinarios* and six regidores.[34] The *alcalde ordinario de primer voto* had superior rank over the *alcalde ordinario de segundo voto*. Candidates for alcalde ordinario had to be members of the ayuntamiento. José Francisco served as the sixth regidor, the most junior member of the Béxar ayuntamiento, in 1805 under Juan Ignacio Pérez, his brother-in-law, as alcalde ordinario de primero voto. Among the issues addressed by the ayuntamiento that year were the secularization of the Mission San Antonio de Valero (Alamo), management of a secular school, preparation of a census, establishment of weekly mail service with Coahuila, administration of the hospital, regulation of cotton processing, preparations for the use of the smallpox vaccine, and defense against numerous Indian attacks.

Of primary concern for the ayuntamiento were tensions related to the transfer of the Louisiana Territory to the United States in 1803, in part because the Texas border remained in dispute. As tensions rose, Bexareños made preparations for possible military action by the United States. In or-

der to strengthen the Spanish position, a treaty was signed with the Caddo
Indians and a new trading post and settlement were established at Bayou
Pierre.[35] José Francisco's brother, José Antonio Francisco Victoriano Ruiz,
was among the soldiers from Béxar who were sent to the new eastern
post.[36] He was stationed at both Bayou Pierre and La Nana and patrolled
the banks of the Arroyo Hondo.[37] He established a homestead on Bayou
Santa Bárbara on the road named Santa Bárbara Río Hondo north of
present day Many, Louisiana.[38]

Tensions were complicated by the frequent arrival of American military
deserters, fugitive slaves seeking asylum, and the activities of American
smugglers. Governor Juan Bautista Elguézabal prohibited American immigration into Texas, required passports for all foreigners, and prohibited
trade with Louisiana.[39] The militia companies of Nuevo Santander and
Coahuila were relocated to Béxar, which Elguézabal further reinforced by
requiring all residents to be armed and ready for militia service. The influx
of new soldiers placed a strain on available resources, and the burden of
building new barracks and an infirmary fell on the ayuntamiento.[40]

In order to pay part of the growing military costs, José Francisco and
his fellow regidores used the most reliable funding source available to
them: royal cattle. Large herds of wild cattle and horses collectively known
as *mesteños* roamed south of Béxar. Ranchers rounded up these animals for
sale to the presidio and in local markets and for export. By law, the king
owned the animals, so ranchers paid a tax for each one. Part of the tax,
which ranchers avoided paying whenever possible, was allocated to the
ayuntamiento and known as the mesteño fund. Ruiz's own father had been
caught not paying the mesteño tax, but in 1805, as regidor, he supported
reform designed to increase compliance with the tax and reduce the trade
in contraband cattle.[41]

Provisioning the presidio became of greater importance due to the
military buildup. The presidio was the largest consumer of beef in Béxar,
and its quartermasters had long complained about the quality and availability of beef. Following the military buildup, the demand for beef was far
greater than any individual could supply and no bidders were forthcoming.
José Francisco played a central role in resolving the issue. Under the old
system, the ayuntamiento awarded a single, year-long concession to provide beef. Under new rules, competition and availability were increased by
shortening the length of the contract into a manageable term. In a decree
on November 23, 1805, Elguézabal ordered that any Béxar resident could

slaughter beef for sale to the presidio or the public. Anyone who wished to participate would be given a fifteen-day concession, during which no other person could slaughter beef for commercial sale.[42] In order to participate, the concession holder had to ensure a consistent level of quality and in return was granted a short-term exclusive right to sell. During 1805, Ruiz inspected the operations of four new *carniceros* (butchers), Juan Ignacio Pérez, Juan Manuel Zambrano, Francisco Arocha, and José Miguel Flores. All four passed his inspections.[43] This unassuming and humble duty of inspecting the presidio's beef supply provided Ruiz with some practical experience that likely contributed to his appointment as a military quartermaster a few years later.

Ruiz's ayuntamiento service also provided the opportunity to begin a career in the legal profession. Along with his duties as the commissioner of butchers, Ruiz was appointed assistant to the *síndico procurador* (city attorney). This was the beginning of five years of legal education, which led in turn to him being elected *procurador* in 1810.

Due to the lack of universities or other formal institutions for legal training on the northern frontier of New Spain, a system of informal education had developed. Estate inventories reveal the presence of legal texts and jurisprudence manuals in Béxar, specifically within the Navarro and Veramendi families to which Ruiz had access.[44] Despite the lack of access to formal education, the legal system at Béxar operated like others in the Spanish empire, following the same legal procedures, standards of evidence, and formalities. A typical alcalde received his training by being previously elected or appointed to a series of lower level offices, during which he was able to observe legal proceedings.[45] One constant problem plaguing Béxar was the lack of a *notario* (notary) and *escríbano* (secretary). Spanish law required the presence of both to record and maintain transcripts of the legal proceedings, but on the frontier compliance with this requirement was an infrequent occurrence.[46] The use of sworn witnesses known as *testigos de asistencia* helped compensate for the lack of such officials.[47]

José Francisco was given opportunities to serve as testigo de asistencia by Navarro in 1806, which allowed him to observe and study legal proceedings. One of the criminal proceedings that year was a charge of theft against Bernardo Contreras, who was ultimately sentenced to permanent exile from Texas.[48] Ruiz continued to serve under succeeding alcaldes, including Luis Galán in 1807, Victor Blanco in 1808, and Juan Ignacio Pérez in 1809. These duties included a range of criminal and civil matters. An

1807 case filed by Don Manuel Francisco Peres, a soldier of the Laredo Company, against Don Antonio Baca, for non-payment of rent was heard by alcalde Galán with Ruiz and Francisco Barrera assisting due to the lack of a notary public.[49] The death of María Josefa Carrió, who died suddenly and without confession, required Ruiz to "examine the body and to make the proper investigation" along with assisting alcalde de segundo voto Victor Blanco. Blanco and Ruiz took depositions from José Fernando Carrió, Doña Guadalupe Carrió, and Doña María Ygnacia Carrió.[50] That same year, 1808, Ruiz witnessed the bill of sale of an African slave from Antonio Baca to Manuel Salinas.[51] By participating in these and many other matters Ruiz gained the legal skillset and procedural experience to hold the office of procurador.

In December 1809, Ruiz was elected to be procurador, a voting member of the council elected by the the regidores, on the ayuntamiento of Béxar.[52] The structure and jurisdiction of the 1810 ayuntamiento were significantly reduced compared to Ruiz's service just five years prior. The military buildup in Texas that resulted from tensions with the United States led to a restructuring of civil authority concentrated in the governor. Initially consisting of two alcaldes (judges), one procurador (attorney) and six regidores (aldermen), the number of regidores was reduced by four and its jurisdiction was reduced to ordinances dealing with "sanitation, hospitals, charity, schools, and policing the villa."[53] As procurador, José Francisco was the general counsel for the ayuntamiento and advised its members on legal matters, represented the town in business affairs, acted as principal negotiator, represented his area before the *audiencia* (regional court of appeals) and assisted the alcaldes in prosecuting those arrested or accused of crimes.

As with other aspects of life on the frontier, court procedure required modification to the realities of Béxar. In large cities, court was held daily, except on Sundays; in Béxar it was held only as needed.[54] Additionally, Spanish law required that court proceedings be held in the *palacio municipal,* but Béxar lacked this public building. Proceedings often occurred at the presidio or elsewhere. The governor served as a court of appeals, and could review the decisions of the municipal court; if one wished to appeal even further, the case was sent to the audencia in Guadalajara.[55]

Among the cases procurador Ruiz worked on in 1810 were the convictions of José Rodríguez, alias "Jocito," for horse theft, and Máximo Mejía for assault, contempt, and concubinage.[56] An investigation into José Andrés Patiño resulted in charges of resisting arrest.[57] A *sumaria* (a summary of charges following an investigation) against Gil Guillermo de la Barr (William Barr) for treason was also signed by Ruiz.[58] Barr, a partner in the trading firm of Barr and Davenport based in Nacogdoches, was accused of violating a trade embargo that prohibited trade with Louisiana.[59] By far the most common criminal charge was smuggling. Ruiz filed different cases against José Megúe (probably Joseph Magee), Julían Lartigue, Juan de la Forcade, Francisco Álvarez, and associates. The court auctioned the smuggled contraband, including that taken from Álvarez.[60]

Civil cases clogged the Béxar courts in 1810, most of which involved nonpayment of debts. These civil cases were usually filed by the litigants without the aid of an attorney. The inhabitants of Béxar were notably litigious and frequently sued over issues involving personal character and gossip. In 1810, Vicente Travieso sued Francisco Travieso for defamation. Mariano Rodríguez filed a vindictive, politically charged petition to review the legitimacy of the birth of Francisco Javier Bustillos.[61] Frustrated by badly written, trifling legal proceedings, Governor Manuel María de Salcedo angrily denounced in 1810, "the injuries and inconveniences" that resulted from them. Believing the cause to be attorneys working in "ignorance" or "bad faith," he declared only a handful of attorneys were competent to present cases to the court: "Don Juan Lira, Don Francisco Barrera, Don Francisco Ruiz, and Don José Bustillos."[62] As a result of this decree, José Francisco became one of only four authorized private civil attorneys in Béxar.

Frivolous litigation was far from the greatest challenge facing Béxar that year. The 1810 session of the ayuntamiento had to address the consequences of the war in Spain that began when Napoleon invaded in 1808. The capture of King Ferdinand VII resulted in the organization of juntas, or governing councils, to rule in the name of the monarch throughout the Spanish Empire, on both sides of the Atlantic.[63] These governing juntas were organized for the purpose of providing legitimate government in the absence of legal national authority or in response to national authority perceived as illegitimate. There was almost uniform rejection among the Spanish of Napoleon's installation of his brother Joseph Bonaparte as their king. Instead, the remaining "free" cities of Spain created governing juntas, which eventually consolidated into a *Junta Suprema Central*.[64] In September 1808, the Junta Suprema Central called for a meeting of representatives from throughout the empire to form a legislative body and write a constitution. Ruiz, serving as procurador, argued that Béxar did not possess the financial resources to send a delegate to the Cortes (national assembly) that was set to convene at Cadíz, Spain, in September 1810. He also declared that there was no native-born Bexareño who was educated enough to serve, including himself.[65] No deputy was sent to represent Texas. The events in Spain rippled throughout the empire, however, and 1810 would be a particular turbulent year in New Spain, the viceroyalty of which Béxar was a part.

Without question the most significant political development in New Spain during 1810 was Father Miguel Hidalgo's revolt. Like a bolt of lightning, Hidalgo's "Grito de Dolores" flashed across New Spain, illuminating the inequities of the colonial system and encouraging the discontented to take up arms against the "bad government" of peninsular-born Spaniards, who were pejoratively called *gachupínes*. The life of José Francisco changed course at that stormy moment and revolution came thundering toward Béxar.

CHAPTER III

Royalist

At the request of the interested party [José Francisco Ruiz], we
are failing to record for him the actions and campaigns in which
he took part against the First Patriots during the time of the
Spanish Government.

—Notation in the Military Service Record of
José Francisco Ruiz, 1831[1]

The Hidalgo revolt grew out of one of the many plots that emerged
out of the crisis of authority in the Spanish empire that came as
a result of Napoleon's installation of his brother on the throne. In
the summer of 1810, in the town of Querétaro, located in the region north
of Mexico City known as the Bajío, the local literary club became the
source of one of the many plots since 1808 that sought to wrest power in
New Spain away from Iberian-born *peninsulares* and place it in the hands
of Mexican-born *criollos*. Among the group leaders were two priests, José
María Morelos and Miguel Hidalgo. The group professed their loyalty to
King Ferdinand VII and called for confiscation of *peninsular* property in
the Bajío region and to use the proceeds of pillage—or expropriation, if
you prefer—to fund an insurgency intended to liberate the rest of the colony. Some plotters intended to abolish slavery and end the *sistema de castas*,
which would eliminate the preferential rights held by peninsulares. These
revolutionary proposals would inspire much more widespread appeal for
this particular plot than others, which tended to be restricted to expand-
ing rights only for criollo elites. The uprising was set for December 8 and
the conspirators began contacting allies in other cities. Before that date,
however, the secret plot became known to the Spanish officials in Mexico
City, who ordered the arrest of the conspirators. News of the arrest orders
reached Hidalgo, who lived in Dolores; his reaction was not to flee, but to

start the rebellion immediately. On Sunday, September 16, 1810, he rang the church bells to call the people to the church and delivered a speech that has come to be known as the Grito de Dolores, which famously ended: "Viva nuestra Madre Santísima de Guadalupe. Viva Fernando VII. Viva la América. Y muera el mal gobierno." (Long live our holy mother the Virgin of Guadalupe. Long live Ferdinand VII. Long live America! Death to bad government).[2]

News of Hidalgo's revolt at Dolores swept rapidly northward, finding many eager supporters and worrying government officials. On October 24, 1810, Comandante General Nemesio de Salcedo issued an address to the people of the Internal Provinces, which included Texas and others on the northern frontier, warning them not to be misled by Hidalgo's revolutionary rhetoric. He characterized the priest as an agent of Napoleon, whose true intention was not to bring happiness to the people, but to gain control of the Spanish colonies, destroy the Catholic religion, and enslave the people. He ended the letter with a declaration that anyone giving aid to French agents and sympathizers would be accused of high treason and executed within twenty-four hours of being found guilty. Anyone found spreading propaganda would be hanged as a traitor.[3]

Hidalgo realized that his poorly provisioned peasant army would need supplies and reinforcements if he had any hope of defeating the Spanish. He planned a northern campaign to reach the United States, whose anti-colonial sympathies he hoped would be a source of financial, military and political support. Rebel General Mariano Jiménez undertook the first northern operations. He captured San Luis Potosí in November 1810 and called on the revolutionaries of the northeast to rush to Coahuila, the next likely target of the rebellion. Among those who answered the call were two brothers, Antonio and Bernardo Gutiérrez de Lara. These two, the former a priest, the latter a blacksmith, would bring the revolution to Texas.

Governor Manuel Antonio Cordero y Bustamante of Coahuila underestimated the sentiment of his troops.[4] When he ordered a march from Saltillo to attack Jiménez, he was surprised when his forces peacefully joined the revolution and he became a prisoner of war. In Nuevo León, seeing the fate of his neighbor, the governor in Monterrey also joined the revolution. Jiménez made Saltillo his headquarters and set about strategizing to bring the revolution to Nuevo Santander and then Texas. If they had Texas, the reasoning went, the revolutionaries would have a lifeline to the United States. The Gutiérrez de Lara brothers offered their loyalties to Jiménez, who sent them to incite revolt in the five cities on the Río Grande: Laredo, Mier, Camargo, Reynosa, and Revilla. The appeal was well received and during February 1811, the governor of Nuevo Santander wrote to the Viceroy of New Spain that "revolution and terror rage in the settlements along the Río Grande."[5]

In Texas, worries of invasion extended north as well as south. Fearful rumors that American filibusters were preparing to invade from Louisiana spread rapidly.[6] North Americans seemed willing and eager to assist the revolt against Napoleon. In one surviving letter in the Bexar Archives, John F. Smith of Natchitoches wrote to Father José María Huerta of Nacogdoches with an offer to raise 1,000 men for the revolution. Smith advised Huerta, "You should abandon your King at once, for he is unworthy to rule you, having submerged his sovereignty beneath the tyranny of Napoleon."[7] In Bexar, two promoters of the revolution were caught working among the presidio troops. Lieutenants Francisco Ignacio Escamilla and Antonio Sáenz were charged with treason and imprisoned in the Alamo.

In the early days of 1811, Governor Manuel María de Salcedo of Texas, nephew of Comandante General Nemesio de Salcedo, had the unique position of being the only remaining loyalist governor in northeastern New Spain. But the revolution was at his doorstep on the Río Grande and sympathetic Americans in Louisiana were planning incursions and filibuster expeditions. Both movements threatened to take Texas for the revolutionaries.

Governor Salcedo appealed to the people of Texas to remain loyal to the king. Both sides accused the other of being agents of Napoleon. The ayuntamiento, on which José Francisco Ruiz still sat, professed its loyalty to the king and governor. Unlike Coahuila, Nuevo León, and Nuevo Santander, Texas had remained relatively quiet since the start of the uprising in distant central Mexico. The province was uneasy with rumors of rebellion and insurrection. News of the rebel army's northward advance trickled into town. Travel restrictions were put in place and settlers were forbidden from traveling to Béxar.[8]

Even public festivals were placed under tighter controls. Governor Salcedo issued an edict on the celebration of the feasts of Our Lady of Guadalupe and the Immaculate Conception citing the fear that "revolutionary leaders may have some partisans here," while wishing "to afford this settlement [Béxar] the annual diversion of the feasts they customarily celebrate." Strict rules were laid out to ensure "amusement for everyone with peace and the prevention of evil intentions of disturbances of the public peace." José Francisco Ruiz was ordered to work with the feast-day committee to select the location of the bazaar booths and bullfighting ring to ensure "order" and "ample room for the traffic and recreation of the public." As a member of the ayuntamiento, he was further tasked with patrol duty "to watch and preserve good order and public tranquility . . . and arrest anyone found drunk or anyone disturbing the peace." A report by a townswoman of an unknown officer prowling the back streets added to the atmosphere of suspicion and fear.[9]

The new year began with the same strains and stresses that had characterized the last months of 1810. Ominous signs of unrest were in the air. Governor Salcedo quietly sent his wife and daughter to East Texas for greater security. When their absence was noticed, public speculation and anxiety intensified.[10] On January 2, 1811, Salcedo ordered the troops at Béxar to gather in the Plaza de Armas for an expedition to the Río Grande to assist in quashing the rebellion there. Rumors quickly spread that the governor was going to abandon Texas and leave it exposed to hostile Indians. Discontent and unease spread through the military ranks, while near panic set in among the civilian population.[11] In an attempt to counter the rumors, the governor issued a proclamation on January 6 denouncing them. He cautioned against believing rebel propaganda and urged residents to remain steadfast in backing their Spanish system of values. Ruiz remained a loyal supporter of Salcedo. In October 1810, a few months prior, he had stubbornly insisted on Salcedo's election as the Texas delegate to the Spanish Cortes in Cádiz despite its extra-legality.[12] On January 13, the governor called on the loyal citizens of Béxar to join the militia to protect the province from rebels.[13] That day Ruiz made a fateful decision to begin a military career. José Francisco had almost no prior military service, except for a brief mandatory enlistment in 1807 that amounted to little more than receiving a flintlock musket in dubious condition.

On January 14, 1811, the day after Salcedo's second call, José Francisco joined the Béxar militia at the rank of *tercer capitán,* or third captain. Trouble began the next day.[14] On January 15, Lieutenant Antonio Sáenz escaped from his prison cell in the Alamo, gathered a group of fellow conspirators to plan the overthrow of Governor Salcedo and Comandante General Simón de Herrera, and declared Texas for the revolution. The plot soon collapsed and Sáenz and his conspirators were returned to the Alamo, this time under heavy guard. Two days later a junta was called with representatives of the three estates—ayuntamiento, the Catholic Church, and military garrison. They discussed Sáenz's plot and formally denounced it and all other revolutionary activity. They reiterated their loyalty to the king and Church. The assembly also gave a vote of approval for Governor Salcedo and Comandante General Herrera as their political and military leaders.[15] The members of the junta approved a plan to abandon the march to the Río Grande and instead bolster local defenses. Calm was restored, but many Bexareños still distrusted Salcedo's motives.[16]

A retired militia officer from Nuevo Santander who resided in Béxar, Juan Bautista de las Casas, was among those who distrusted Salcedo. He took action on January 21, 1811, when the governor announced to the troops that they would march to Cíbolo Creek or the Guadalupe River for field exercises. Later that night, infantry officer Vicente Flores visited Alcalde Francisco Travieso and told him that the soldiers did not want to leave Béxar and were ready to follow Casas in a revolt. Travieso also feared the impending removal of the military from the community, which would make defense his direct responsibility. The alcalde met with Casas at his home to discuss the next day's events. In the morning, Travieso, Flores, and Casas planned to walk to military headquarters and ask the soldiers to denounce their officers, accept Casas as their leader, and arrest Salcedo and Herrera. Accordingly, this group, accompanied by a handful of soldiers, approached military headquarters at dawn. The sentinel on duty stopped them but upon recognizing Casas allowed him to enter the quarters of the officer on duty, who refused to surrender, so the conspirators took him prisoner. Casas then addressed the assembled troops, who received him enthusiastically. He marched to the Plaza de Armas, where he seized Salcedo and Herrera. Salcedo asked to join the revolt as a common soldier, but Casas refused. He did grant them permission to remain under house arrest in the Governor's Palace (then the home of Juan Ignacio Pérez).[17]

Casas followed Hidalgo's model in not calling for outright independence and insisting on loyalty to the absent King Ferdinand VII and the Catholic Church. Casas quickly wrote to Hidalgo about his success. Rebel General Mariano Jiménez in Saltillo received the letter and duly appointed Casas to be the military governor of Texas. Casas soon proved he was not fit to assert his new power judiciously. His decisions to arrest popular priests, confiscate the property of Europeans regardless of their loyalty, and detain the avowed revolutionary Lieutenant Sáenz, as well as his distrustful and jealous nature, made him many enemies and led to his downfall. Historian Carlos Castañeda asserts that Casas was largely ignorant of the reasons and events of the Hidalgo revolt, and he concluded that his motivations clearly manifested a "personal desire for power."[18]

José Francisco, as a captain of militia, did not support the Casas revolt, nor was he among those singled out by Casas for arrest.[19] He also was not among the leadership who formed the ruling junta under the brief Casas interregnum. Ruiz just remained quietly in service, following the events closely with the other members of his extended family. Ruiz's conservative response is notable in its marked contrast to his later boldness in political and revolutionary affairs. It can possibly be explained due to his youth and inexperience in such matters, or the result of a concerted effort by royalists to remain in positions of influence until a better opportunity for response arose. Meanwhile, Casas became concerned with the large number of prisoners in Béxar and requested that they be transported elsewhere for trial. Permission was given to take all of them in chains to Presidio San Juan Bautista del Río Grande for trial. Salcedo, Herrera, and others were escorted there and then held under house arrest on the hacienda of Ignacio Elizondo, the commander of the presidio.[20]

Both local royalists and would-be revolutionaries had grown unhappy with the despotic Casas. In particular, a small group of royalists in Béxar bound by compadrazgo, including Ruiz, Juan Ignacio Pérez, José Dario Zambrano, Erasmo Seguín, Juan Martín de Veramendi, and José María Zambrano, had witnessed enough of Casas's abuses to finally take decisive action. During the last week of February 1811, they called a meeting at the home of José Dario Zambrano and plotted the overthrow of Casas. They selected as their leader Juan Manuel Zambrano. They also decided to enlist the help of other leading families and army officers before proceeding.[21]

Juan Manuel Zambrano took the bold step of covertly entering the revolutionary camp to seek support. Earlier General Jiménez had sent two emissaries to the United States to seek assistance on behalf of the revolution. These emissaries, Ignacio Aldama, a ranking revolutionary, and Father Juan Sálazar, the chaplain for Jiménez's improvised army, reached Béxar in late February. Zambrano first approached Sálazar, pretending to be a supporter of the Hidalgo revolution. He complained about Casas and sought support for his removal. Sálazar declined to assist but frankly and openly spoke of the inevitable failure of the revolution after a series of military defeats.[22] This emboldened the counter-revolutionaries, and they took action.

On March 1, Juan Manuel Zambrano, Ruiz, and other conspirators marched in the footsteps earlier trod by Casas to the army barracks. They disarmed the sentries and overpowered the officers in command. The simple *soldados* or privates now joined the counter-revolutionaries. News spread rapidly in Béxar and armed residents committed to the past administration hurried to the barracks to reinforce the counter-revolutionaries' counter-coup. Zambrano and others publicly addressed the crowd, denouncing the tyranny of Casas. By midnight, the sentiment of the townspeople was won over, and they set about electing a new counter-revolutionary governing junta. Juan Manuel Zambrano was elected its president.[23] The junta then led soldiers and civilians to the building where Casas resided. There the troops stood in formation while residents gathered in silence. Awakened but only partially dressed, Casas emerged before the assembly. Zambrano read a prepared statement by the junta, and Casas surrendered. Immediately the junta called for the election of a new ayuntamiento and the reorganization of all military forces.[24]

The members of the junta prepared an officious proclamation defending their actions:

North America has just given us examples of monstrous treason and disorder ... Juan Bautista Las Casas, ambitious to enter into favor with the execrable Hidalgo, raised the standard of rebellion in the capital of Béxar ... Casas and his followers were the only ones who got the fleeting fruit of his perfidy, in the military ranks and in the despotic management of the public fortune, while anarchy and injustice reigned in all branches of the administration ... Thus it was that the plotters confiding frankly in those who were deserving of confidence of such importance, took with others action to let it be known that their designs were only against the despotism of Casas, and against the disorders of the government; hence they were able to draw many away from the partisans of the insurrection.[25]

The proclamation ended with a list of Bexareños distinguished for rendering service "to Religion, the Country, and the King." Among those listed was José Francisco Ruiz.[26]

The junta next sent two emissaries to make contact with the royalist forces to the south. Luis Galán, former alcalde and mentor of Ruiz, and José Martín Muñoz met some resistance in Laredo but continued to

San Fernando de Austria (present-day Zaragoza, Coahuila), where they found José Menchaca of Béxar in command. On March 13, 1811, Menchaca took them to the hacienda of Elizondo, the presidio commander who had Salcedo and Herrera under house arrest. Upon hearing the news of the counter-revolution in Béxar, Elizondo returned to the royalist cause and promptly freed his prisoners. Both immediately planned an ambush of Hidalgo, who was fleeing north through Chihuahua toward Texas.

Around the same time, the Hidalgo revolt was breaking down. On March 21, royalists led by Igancio Elizondo captured Hidalgo at Baján, Coahuila. The next day, Commandant General Nemesio de Salcedo escorted Hidalgo and other captured insurgents to Chihuahua, where they stood trial for treason. Salcedo was given the honor of commanding the firing squad at Hidalgo's execution. The actions of Ruiz and other royalist counter-revolutionaries in Texas and the Eastern Interior Provinces thus indirectly led to the capture of Hidalgo and a royalist victory in the first phase of the Mexican War for Independence.[27]

As part of the military reorganization under the counter-revolutionary junta, the militia company from Coahuila was dissolved for supporting rebels, as was the company from Nuevo Santander, in which Casas had served and received much support. The remaining companies were strengthened with royalist officers. Salcedo appointed José Francisco Ruiz to the rank of lieutenant, making him second-in-command for the company of Captain Mariano Rodríguez, the militia of the presidio of Texas.[28] His appointment was largely political and a consequence of his royalist sentiments.[29] His duty was that of quartermaster (*abilitado*), in charge of the provisions of the military and the four new militia companies.[30] Ruiz's profession as a merchant, his prior experience inspecting the presidio's beef supply, and his family connections to the largest merchant houses of Béxar, those of Veramendi and Navarro, made this assignment a natural fit. He reported often to the general headquarters in Chihuahua regarding the needs of the various militia companies stationed in Béxar.[31] Shortly thereafter, an additional military reorganization by the commandant general transformed Ruiz's company into the Second Militia Cavalry Company of Texas of Don Mariano Rodríguez.

On March 9, one week after the counter-revolution, Ruiz issued a report to Juan Manuel Zambrano, president of the governing junta, on the search for clothing needed by the new militia companies. Ruiz stated that he had purchased clothing from the stores of Francisco José Pereira and

Juan Martín de Veramendi, but these were not sufficient. He had gone into the Governor's Palace to see if any supplies remained there and found some *bretañas y paños* (linen and woolens). He ended his report with a request to use the clothing he had discovered to complete equipping the militia with uniforms.[32]

Ruiz's hasty search for supplies became even more difficult when the junta ordered an expedition to recapture Laredo for the royalists. Five hundred soldiers quickly mobilized but logistical issues, primarily a lack of supplies, caused delays. Once under way, Father Sálazar and Ignacio Aldama began plotting against the royalist junta but were discovered before they could exploit the absence of the militia. The Laredo expedition proved to be unnecessary because the capture of Hidalgo and the leaders of the revolution put an end to the revolution in northern New Spain. Over the next year, Ruiz issued a series of reports and requests as part of his quartermaster duties in the militia.[33]

This period saw a rapid militarization of Béxar as additional militia companies reinforced the Texas garrisons. Over the next year, quartermaster Ruiz issued a series of reports and requests as part of his duties in the militia.[34] Immediately following reestablishment of royalist authority, Indian hostilities escalated. A series of attacks and counter-attacks marked 1811 and 1812.[35] In February 1812, the governing junta ordered construction of better defenses following a Comanche attack on the Barrio de Valero. The junta also ordered the reconstruction of the guardhouse and quarters for the soldiers.[36]

Additionally, Spanish authorities had great concerns regarding Texas's border with the United States. The once huge distance of the United States from Texas was removed with the Louisiana Purchase of 1803. Spain and the United states disputed the boundaries of Louisiana, however, which led to the creation of the Neutral Ground, a strip of land between the Sabine River and the Calcasieu River in present-day western Louisiana claimed by both Spain and the United States. In order to avoid military conflict, it was agreed to designate the area as "neutral ground." Both countries thenceforth had no official presence until the two governments settled the boundary. (The boundaries were not settled until the Adams–Onís Treaty of 1819.) The area became infamous for its mix of squatters, refugees, runaway slaves, bandits, and others seeking the sanctuary of a land with no government. It also gained a deserved reputation as a staging ground for the invasion of Texas.

Rumors of filibustering expeditions coming from the Neutral Ground swirled around Béxar, even as war between the United States and Britain loomed. Governor Salcedo ordered an end to all communications with Louisiana, and in return the United States issued a trade embargo against Spain, which was specifically enforced at Natchitoches.[37] The concerns of the Spanish were merited. Their spy network, which included the pirate Pierre Lafitte and the trader Samuel Davenport, relayed news of an army being organized at Natchitoches by Bernardo Gutiérrez de Lara, who had recruited for the rebellion along the Río Grande and continued to pursue the goals Hidalgo's revolution.[38]

After the Casas revolt, Gutiérrez de Lara traveled to the United States to solicit support for Hidalgo's movement. He left Saltillo in March 1811 and arrived in Natchitoches, Louisiana, during August of the same year, barely escaping capture in the Neutral Ground. In Louisiana he learned of Hidalgo's capture and death but continued on his mission, arriving in Washington, D.C., in December 1811. There he met Secretary of State James Monroe and shared his plan to establish a republican government in Texas and use it as a base to liberate the rest of Mexico from Spain's control. Gutiérrez de Lara was unable to secure the open support of the Americans, but he received tacit approval to recruit an army in Louisiana and invade Texas across the Neutral Ground.[39] Back in Natchitoches, Gutierrez de Lara recruited Augustus Magee, a graduate of West Point serving as a lieutenant in the United States Army, to be the military leader of the expedition.[40] They also recruited one hundred and thirty land-seeking American adventurers.[41]

Gutiérrez de Lara began preparations for the invasion of Texas by launching a propaganda campaign. He had brought a printing press with him from the United States, and he printed hundreds of letters and political writings calling for people to support rebellion, criticizing the royal administration, and explaining the goals of the invading army, and shipped them to Texas.[42] In Béxar, Governor Manuel María de Salcedo banned these materials, as well as the discussion of the ideas they contained.[43] The ban was ineffective, and Gutiérrez de Lara continued to speak to the people of Béxar from afar.[44] A deserter known only as "Bagens" from the presidio of Nacogdoches became an agent of Gutiérrez de Lara and delivered a heavy bundle of subversive literature that he distributed before returning to Natchitoches.[45] Several persons were arrested for possession of writings by Gutiérrez de Lara and for seditious speech.[46] One intelligence report found in the Bexar Archives claimed that Gutiérrez de Lara used Indian allies to smuggle his propaganda into Béxar.[47] The results were encouraging; hundreds of men, Tejanos, Americans, Apache and Tonkawa, joined the fledgling army.[48] One smuggled letter reads:

> Soldiers and citizens of San Antonio de Béxar: It is more than a year since I left my country, during which time I have labored indefatigably for our good. I have overcome many difficulties, have made friends, and have obtained means to aid us in throwing off the insulting yoke of the insolent despotism. Rise en masse, soldiers and citizens; unite in the holy cause of our country! I am now marching to your succor with a respectable force of American volunteers who have left their homes and families to take up our cause, to fight for our liberty. They are the free descendants of the men who fought for the independence of the United States; and as brothers and inhabitants of the same continent they have drawn their swords with a hearty good will in the defense of the cause of humanity; and in order to drive the tyrannous Europeans beyond the Atlantic.[49]

Despite the exceptional political and military events of the time, personal and family events in Béxar continued as usual. José Francisco experienced a great deal of joy and pain in 1812. On February 13, his brother, José Antonio Francisco Victoriano, died and was buried in the *camposanto* (church graveyard) of Béxar.[50] José Antonio owned a ranch named Santa Bárbara Río Hondo in the Neutral Ground near Bayou Pierre in Louisiana, which his mother inherited upon his death.[51] He had acquired it during his service in the Béxar Company, which was sent to fortify Bayou Pierre following the Louisiana Purchase tensions and boundary dispute of 1805.[52] Later in 1812, María Josefa gave birth to a son, Francisco Antonio Ruiz, who they named after José Francisco's recently deceased brother.[53] On September 22, José Francisco and his wife, Josefa, served as godparents at the wedding of José Sipriano and María Candelaria Vidaurri.[54] But politics and military affairs intervened once more, brought by the machinations of Gutierrez de Lara. By 1813, the ranch established by José Antonio had become José Francisco's home while he was in exile after yet another revolt in Béxar had put him on the losing side of rebellion.

CHAPTER IV

Revolutionary

I spent the flower of my life and freely shed my blood for the
Independence of Mexico, and I would willingly do so again.
—José Francisco Ruiz, 1835[1]

J osé Francisco's revolutionary career began in 1812, not with arms, but
through a philosophical correspondence across enemy lines with the
rebel leader, Bernardo Gutiérrez de Lara, who represented a link to
Hidalgo's revolt. Eventually, Ruiz joined the rebel army and helped negotiate its peaceful entry into Béxar. However, intrigue, rivalry, and international politics resulted in personal disaster for José Francisco, who ended
up exiled, stateless, and separated from his family.

Throughout 1812, José Francisco Ruiz remained in the royalist Bexareño militia. For his loyalty and service in putting down the Casas revolt, he
was rewarded with a military appointment. However, Ruiz's political leanings underwent a dramatic shift in 1812, as the social order and institutions
that he had supported for his entire adult life dissolved around him. His
conservatism stemmed from his upbringing and social status within the
Spanish colonial system. His early legal and political careers were tied to
the established Spanish order and, like most merchant elites, his economic
prospects depended on relative stability.

Beginning with Manuel Hidalgo's failed revolution, social stability deteriorated and the old powers and institutions began to weaken. As the
Spanish military exerted draconian power over his fellow Bexareños, Ruiz
began to embrace the political philosophy of the Spanish liberals. By 1813,
he was a military and political leader of the so-called "Green Flag" rebellion in Béxar and an ardent supporter of a new political system.

The word "liberal" is highly contextual and has been used by many
political movements throughout history. It is particularly important to de-

fine the liberalism to which Ruiz adhered to beginning in 1813, given that it differs from the use of the term in the modern United States. Nineteenth-century Spanish American liberalism emphasized the freedom of the individual and called for limiting the power of the government and the Catholic Church. Tejano liberals supported policies such as statehood for Texas, a generous system of land grants, open immigration policies, free trade, coastal ports, and the development of a cotton industry. The political liberalism Ruiz espoused was based upon the principles of provincial autonomy, municipalism, secular politics, the divine authority of the Catholic Church, rule by consent, and a distinct American (New World) identity.[2]

Ruiz was first introduced to such principles through his father, who was educated in San Luis de la Paz, a center of Jesuit Enlightenment thinking.[3] Active in politics and a participant in the political debates of Béxar, the younger Ruiz was further shaped by the publications of later Scholastic thinkers and the polemical writings of Hidalgo, his revolutionary heir, Father José María Morelos, and even Bernardo Gutiérrez de Lara. New Spain was largely an illiterate society, and the writings of these intellectuals were accessible to only a few Mexican elites. Their ideas diffused among the population mostly by private conversations, debating societies, and brief tracts, which were often read aloud. All of these works were known to have reached Béxar, often as contraband smuggled from Louisiana.[4]

José Francisco and other Tejanos were influenced by Catholic political thought. Catholic political philosophy developed both conservative and liberal traditions. While the conservatives adhered to the doctrine of the divine right of kings, liberals, such as Ruiz, adhered to the Spanish Jesuit political theorists, such as the Salamanca School, who supported a secular state. During the sixteenth century, the political doctrine of the divine right of kings had developed throughout Protestant northern Europe, and it also took deep roots in Catholic France. Conservative monarchs claimed for themselves divine sovereignty just as the Church had claimed divine moral authority, resulting in a divinization of the state in which monarchs claimed to be answerable to neither church nor subjects, but only to God alone. A leading Jesuit of the Salamanca School, Francisco Suárez, believed no monarch could possess sacred attributes because the Church was the only institution established through divine intervention. Given the primacy of the spiritual over the temporal, the Church was thus superior to the state.[5] Suárez argued further that human beings have a natural social nature bestowed upon them by God, and this included the potential to make laws. When a political society was formed, the authority of the state was of human, not divine, origin, therefore its nature was determined by the people involved, and their natural legislative power was given to the ruler. Because legislative power was given by the people, they had the right to take it back. José Francisco and his fellow Tejano liberals implemented this theory in the various local juntas they established during times of political revolt and transition.[6] Upon these philosophical and political foundations, Ruiz developed his liberal worldview.

The philosophical foundation of Spanish liberalism was the revival of scholasticism during the Catholic Reformation. The scholastics believed that meaning could be found in contemplating the natural order and God's reflection in it. They originated natural law theory and were among the first Europeans to author discourses on international law and justice. The scholastic world view also supported an enchanted reality where the Divine could be found everywhere, including the received word and teachings of the Church, but also via the contemplation of relics, religious art, community processions, and the order of nature.[7]

A particularly influential text in bringing together the ideas of Scholasticism with the more secular ideas that emerged out of the Protestant Reformation was François Jacquier's *Instituciones*. It was this book, not the Northern European Protestant philosophers, which had the greatest impact in bringing Spanish America to modernity. During the colonial era, print media was tightly controlled by the monarchy and news or discussion of Northern European philosophers or the American Declaration of Independence was highly restricted. Jacquier's text was nearly unheard of in Northern Europe and America, but it was published in five editions over the course of the eighteenth century, each in Latin and one in Spanish. It provided a modern Catholic philosophical framework that differed from the secular Protestant Northern European-American framework. This Catholic philosophy taught its students to question master narratives, to use skepticism and rationalism to ask particular questions about the local, or parts of things, without questioning how the whole came together. For example, this modern philosophy led educated criollos to begin questioning the practice of appointing only peninsualar administrative officials, who lacked an understanding of the local conditions and denied them access to these positions based upon the location of their birth in the Americas.[8]

Not only were José Francisco's political views in 1812 heavily influenced by Spanish liberalism, but also demonstrated a distinctly regional application, characterized primarily by loyalty to Texas and the *municipio* of Béxar in the face of uncertainty at the top of the political hierarchy.[9] Time and again, when distant governments failed to uphold their promise of good government, Ruiz acted in a manner he felt was best for Texas and specifically Béxar. Each time that Ruiz joined in revolutionary activity, he gave greater weight to local concerns over national.

Early Mexican liberals, such as José Francisco, were influenced by the Iberian traditions of provincial autonomy and political municipalism. Spanish political theory of the time did not view the empire as a singular entity ruled by a single monarchy, but rather a plurality of provinces ruled by a unified monarchy. Thus each province was politically autonomous, but shared a common monarch. Political identity was commonly viewed as a pyramid of communities with overlapping authority: city, province, and monarch. Only in a cultural sense was it "Spanish." Exemplification of this political theory can be found in the shortened unofficial style of the king: "Rey de las Españas y las Indias," in which the use of plural names clearly illustrates the political nature of the realm. The removal of the Spanish monarch by Napoleon cast open a natural inquiry by Mexicans to answer the challenge of where to find sovereign authority in the absence of a king. The answers spanned the political spectrum from a restoration of an absolutist monarch, to a reformed monarchy, to a liberal republic. Hidalgo's revolt sought the middle path of a reformed monarchy, as illustrated by its goal to restore the monarchy and reclaim criollo and ecclesiastical rights under the monarchical structure.

In Spanish political municipalism, sovereignty was temporarily held in the person of the king, but in his absence, sovereignty reverted to the existing political corporations to represent the people. The ayuntamiento (town council) formed the basic political unit of Spanish-American political society. Therefore, the municipalities and not the people held ultimate sovereignty. Political municipalism also held that in the absence of a legitimate ayuntamiento, such authority could be restored by the formation of a temporary municipal structure known as the junta. These governing juntas were organized for the purpose of providing legitimate government in the

absence of municipal, provincial, or imperial authority or in response to
authorities perceived as illegitimate. Junta members were typically drawn
from among local leaders of the church, military, and civilian classes. Ruiz
joined three juntas, during his revolutionary career, including arguably the
convention at Washington-on-the-Brazos in 1836.

Ruiz's full conversion to liberal principles still lay in the future when
Bernardo Gutiérrez de Lara crossed the Sabine River into Texas with
about one hundred and thirty men in the Republican Army of the North,
on August 8, 1812, under the command of Augustus Magee and met little
resistance. The invading army grew to three hundred and set its sights on
the settlement of Trinidad, which it took in September 1812.[10] Governor
Salcedo responded to the invasion by ordering Béxar's troops to march to
the Guadalupe River. Learning of Salcedo's reaction, Gutiérrez de Lara
shifted his focus from Béxar to La Bahía, which fell with little opposition.
Salcedo pursued the rebel army and besieged La Bahía. Ruiz's company,
the Second Militia Cavalry Company of Texas, was among those that participated in the siege, which began on November 7, 1812.[11]

An attack by Salcedo on La Bahía failed, but a prolonged siege depleted his enemy's supplies. Hunger and thirst ground at the rebels' resolve.
A month later the strategy seemed to have worked, and the governor met
with Magee to discuss terms of surrender. Magee returned to La Bahía in
exchange for a safe return across the Sabine River and for the surrender of
La Bahía and delivery of the Tejano rebels to Salcedo. Gutiérrez de Lara
was incensed, and the army rejected the offer. Magee died in February
1813 of an undocumented disease, possibly consumption or malaria.[12] After
Magee's death, Lieutenant Colonel Samuel Kemper took charge of the
rebel army.[13]

According to a report submitted after the Battle of Medina by Juan
Ignacio Pérez, insurgents injured José Francisco Ruiz during the siege of
La Bahía.[14] Perez offered no information on the extent of these injuries;
however, they did not inhibit Ruiz from continuing his military duties.
Pérez did state that Ruiz served as a *teniente habilitado,* or lieutenant quartermaster, and kept a detailed list of the debts incurred by Salcedo's forces
during the siege. Unbeknownst to Pérez and other royal officers, Ruiz corresponded with Gutiérrez de Lara throughout the siege, discussing "matters of independence."[15]

On February 19, 1813, Governor Salcedo ordered a retreat to Béxar, at
which point many royalist soldiers defected to the rebel cause.[16] Ruiz re-

mained with his militia company and returned to Béxar, but by this time he was working as an informant for the rebels. As a military quartermaster, Ruiz had contacts with lawful traders and illicit smugglers alike, including Miguel Menchaca, who smuggled propaganda into Béxar for Gutiérrez de Lara.[17] A letter dated March 22, 1813, from Ruiz to Menchaca, then serving as second in command of the rebels, discusses an upcoming negotiation with the commander of the Spanish forces, Simón de Herrera.[18] Ruiz advised the rebels not to attend the meeting because Herrera would only maintain his hardline position. Ruiz also revealed the exceptional nature of the correspondence when he wrote, "I am writing very hastily at night."[19]

At this early stage in his revolutionary career, José Francisco showed the maturity of thought he would demonstrate in the later war for Texas independence. He told Menchaca to be patient with those who continued to support the Spanish because he believed they would rally to the republican cause if left unmolested: "when the time arrives that they shall think otherwise, there will be many who espouse our cause. As a friend, I tell you that all we can avoid that which is detrimental to our fatherland (*nuestra patria*), will be advantageous to us, since we must not only think of the present, but also of the future."[20] He continued with a statement which characterized his later actions on behalf of all Texans, whether Indians, Anglos, or Tejanos. He wrote to Menchaca, "I speak with the greatest sincerity, I have never been a flatterer and I love all of the people of my country." Here Ruiz expressed his provincial worldview. In using the term "my country," literally "*mi país*," he clearly referred to the province of Texas and more specifically the community of Béxar.[21]

Gutiérrez de Lara strengthened the rebel forces at La Bahía with Indian allies, as well as reinforcements from Louisiana and marched on Béxar. The rebels next clashed with the Spanish in the Battle of Rosillo on March 29, 1813. It is unclear if José Francisco participated in this battle. He did not list it in his Texas military pension application like he did the battles of Alazán Creek and Medina. He may have still been recovering from the injuries he received at the siege of La Bahía, or he may have purposefully omitted his participation because he was still in Spanish service. What is certain is that he secretly corresponded with Gutiérrez de Lara prior to the battle, as he had since February 1813.[22]

Ruiz may have helped Gutiérrez de Lara avoid a surprise attack by royalist troops. Salcedo and Herrera attempted to surprise the rebels at a bridge over Salado Creek at a place called Rosillo, but the rebels were not caught off guard. The battle became a rout. Indian rebels pursued and scalped the fallen.[23] Salcedo and Herrera refused to surrender, so the fighting drifted into Béxar and continued for several days. On April 1, 1813, the Spanish formally surrendered. The terms included the protection of residents and their property, while army officers were allowed to retire with honor and leave Béxar with their property unmolested.[24]

Gutiérrez de Lara charged Salcedo, Herrera, and other Spanish officials with treason and "bribing Ignacio Elizondo to betray Hidalgo and the leaders of the Revolution." Two days later Gutiérrez de Lara created a junta to try the accused. The men were quickly convicted and sentenced to death.[25] Due to protests by several American officers, Gutiérrez de Lara agreed to imprison the condemned away from Béxar, possibly as far as New Orleans. Under this pretext, the condemned men were imprisoned in the Alamo. Later that night Captain Antonio Delgado, a rebel commander of around sixty Mexican soldiers and others, such as Pedro Prado and José Francisco Ruiz, forcibly seized fourteen prisoners, including Salcedo and Herrera. They led them down the La Bahía Road to a point six miles outside of town, where they were ordered to dismount. The prisoners were bound to trees and stripped. Finally, their throats were cut, and their bodies were refused burial and left to the wild animals. Governor Salcedo was granted one request, to die in a manner worthy of a man of his position, and he was shot before his throat was cut.[26]

Accounts differed between Gutiérrez de Lara and the American volunteers as to the nature of the incident. American Agent William Shaler wrote to Secretary of State James Monroe, describing the incident as "murder" and the result of "Mexican cruelty and barbarism." This report was effective in souring what American government support there was for Gutiérrez de Lara's leadership of the filibuster.[27] Gutiérrez de Lara later wrote that the mob was instigated by agents of Shaler and Toledo to thwart his leadership.[28] However, the sole surviving Spanish soldier, Guillermo Navarro, who escaped and fled to Laredo, reported that the group was "composed of Americans and troops from La Bahía, Álamo [de Parras], and Béxar [companies]," and that the expedited executions of the already condemned men were the consequence of mob rule and not official orders.[29] The alleged leader, Antonio Delgado, was court-martialed by American officers who were horrified by the incident.

A sensational account of the Delgado trial in the *Niles Weekly Register* reported that "the young Creole officer Delgado had witnessed many cruelties of Salcedo, and among them the beheading of his father, at which his mother was compelled to be present, and 'by order of Salcedo the blood from the bleeding head of his father was sprinkled over his unfortunate mother.'" The writer added that the executioners denied Salcedo access to a priest.[30] As sensational as this accusation is, the historical record does not support it. Salcedo and Herrera's swift trial, condemnation, and execution for treason mirror the one for Miguel Hidalgo, which Governor Salcedo participated in himself.

However justified, the hasty executions threatened to divide the Republican Army of the North. Captain James Taylor Gains, ordered to explain the incident to the American volunteers, wrote a clumsy letter claiming that the Spanish had a tradition of executing officers who surrendered rather than retreated.[31] This did not satisfy other American officers, who ordered Gutiérrez de Lara and Delgado arrested, imprisoned in the Alamo, and court-martialed. The makeshift trial resulted in their acquittal. Colonel William McLane explained in his diary that, "on further investigation, the Americans found so many Mexicans justifying the act; they had no alternative but to submit."[32] Gutiérrez de Lara, however, was temporarily removed from command for allowing the affair to occur.

Ruiz's participation cannot be taken lightly or attributed to following a mob. He was clearly implicated as a leader or instigator of the group that executed the condemned prisoners, a fact which resulted in him being one of a handful of rebels who was refused pardon after the restoration of Spanish authority in Texas. He, Gutiérrez de Lara, and other revolutionaries blamed Salcedo and Herrera for the capture and execution of Hidalgo. Ironically, just a couple of years prior, Ruiz had been a loyal officer of the ayuntamiento, serving under Salcedo and rewarded for his loyalty with a military appointment. Salcedo and Herrera came to exemplify the colonial government that Ruiz now opposed. Ruiz would not have taken such actions lightly; only a week prior he had written Menchaca about moderation, humaneness, and reason. He added, "when I cannot do the greatest good, I shall do no harm."[33] José Francisco was clearly thinking in moral terms and felt justified in the swift execution of both Salcedo and Herrera. Not two years earlier, he and other Bexareños had witnessed Salcedo and Herrera's ability to escape imprisonment and cripple the rebellion. From the perspective of the liberal Mexican revolutionaries and the Bexareños who had witnessed the swift execution of their leaders at Chihuahua, the executions were morally justified. From the perspective of the filibustering

Americans, who had differing military traditions, they were not. Béxar was
once again in rebel hands, and Ruiz officially joined the insurgent army
along with most of his company.

Ruiz, who had come to reconsider his allegiance to the royalist cause,
and his fellow Tejano revolutionaries viewed their efforts as a continuation of Hidalgo's revolution, and they set about organizing Texas in that
light, to the disdain and frustration of the Americans. Gutiérrez de Lara,
assuming control of the province of Texas, issued a declaration of independence.[34] It declared, "The bonds that kept us bound to the dominion
of Spain have been severed forever; we are free and independent and have
the right to establish our own government. In the future, all legitimate
authority emanates from the people where it rightly resides. From this day
forward, we are free from all foreign domination." To Gutiérrez de Lara,
"foreign domination" included that of the United States. His government
would be composed of Texans, meaning the residents of Texas, and based
on Spanish, not United States, political models.[35]

On April 6, 1813, Ruiz took an oath of independence in the Plaza de
Armas after hearing the declaration read. Gutiérrez de Lara next issued
a constitution that was firmly rooted in the Spanish liberal tradition. It
defined Texas as an independent state within a Mexican republic and guaranteed the primacy of the Catholic faith.[36] Since a national government
had not yet been achieved, the constitution organized a provisional junta,
naming Gutiérrez de Lara as its executive head with the title of president-
protector. The junta was composed of seven men, including Francisco
Arocha as president and Mariano Rodríguez as secretary.[37] Two members
were actually foreign-born, a Frenchman named Louis Massiot and an
American named Hale.

Fissures were developing among the rebels just as the new government
formed. Along with the frustration over the executions of Salcedo and
Herrera, the lack of American representation in the newly formed government disheartened many volunteers from the United States. Nearly
one hundred American volunteers and officers requested furloughs and
returned to Louisiana, thus quitting the project.[38]

Meanwhile, the Spanish responded resolutely to Gutiérrez de Lara's
invasion of Texas.[39] Spanish Colonel Joaquín de Arredondo, Governor of
Nuevo Santander, first learned of the invasion of Texas in January of 1813,
while in far southern Nuevo Santander in Valle de Maíz, putting down an-

other remnant of Hidalgo's rebellion. He wrote to the viceroy stating that he would abandon his current mission and immediately march on Texas with or without his approval. The presence of Americans among the Texas insurgents was far too dangerous and there was little prestige in defeating the remaining rebels in Nuevo Santander. He left his successor in charge of his post and left to raise an army to retake Texas.[40]

News of Arredondo's disobedience reached the viceroy as he was preparing to leave his post. The incoming viceroy was Félix María Calleja del Rey, a general who had helped Arredondo fight the insurgency in the northeastern provinces. Rather than reprimand Arredondo for abandoning his post, he promoted him and endorsed his plan. He ordered 1,000 veteran troops sent north by sea to Tampico. Arredondo methodically began preparations by calling up provincial militias, gathering supplies, and sending advanced units to capture Gutiérrez de Lara's family at Revilla. Volunteers and supplies flooded into his army.[41] He promised the viceroy a professional and well-planned attack, explaining that he would not risk success for the sake of haste. He instituted a propaganda campaign to counter that of Gutiérrez de Lara, warning Tejanos that the rebel would only lead them into the hands of the Americans, who had secret designs to annex Texas and all of the Internal Provinces.[42] Arredondo prophetically threatened any town supporting the rebels would "be put to fire and sword and nothing will remain of it but ruins to serve as a lesson for the future and a warning to malicious rebels."[43]

Such threats were effective. When Gutiérrez de Lara wrote to Ignacio Elizondo in Coahuila, who had once supported the revolution, asking for his support, he received an angry reply, notable for its imagery. After branding Gutiérrez de Lara a traitor, Elizondo swore that he would personally come to burn him and his "Protestant and heretical" followers "were you to hide in hell itself as the last refuge, from there will I drag you by the hair, cast you into the flames, and when you are burnt to ashes, scatter your remains to the four winds."[44]

Spanish forces under Joaquín de Arredondo had reached Laredo by June 1813. Arredondo had earned a reputation as an effective and ruthless officer for his role in suppressing the Hidalgo revolt in Nuevo Santander. At Laredo, Arredondo learned he had been promoted to Comandante de las Provincias Internas del Este (Commandant of the Eastern Interior Provinces), replacing Nemecio de Salcedo. Arredondo threatened that any town supporting the rebels would "be put to fire and sword and nothing will remain of it but ruins to serve as a lesson for the future and a warning to malicious rebels."[45]

Arredondo soon learned from deserters of the discord within the rebel army and the withdrawal of some American officers. While he waited for the arrival of the veterans, he ordered Ignacio Elizondo to assemble the troops at Presidio San Juan Bautista del Río Grande, advance to the Frio River, and establish a post. Elizondo was told to wait there for the arrival of the main force, but he clearly saw an opportunity to repeat his acclaimed actions at Baján, where he advanced before the regular army and captured Hidalgo and the insurgent leadership. Elizondo left Laredo on June 19 and ignored his orders to stop at the Frio. Six days later he wrote to Arredondo that he was on the outskirts of Béxar and had sent an offer of pardon to the community for all but twelve leaders, hoping this would avoid bloodshed. Upon receiving the letter, Arredondo was furious.[46]

In fact, the news of Elizondo's approach was received with panic in Béxar. The Republican Army of the North organized a council. Major Rueben Ross, commander of the American troops, argued for a retreat to Louisiana and eventually did just that himself. Major Henry Perry then took command of the American forces and with Gutiérrez de Lara reorganized the army, placing Miguel Menchaca in command. The new command structure tried to reconcile racial divisions by reorganizing units so that each had American, Tejano, and Indian members. Menchaca was ordered to prepare for a surprise attack on Elizondo's troops, in an operation known as the Battle of Alazán Creek.[47]

The rebels left Béxar by cover of night and surrounded the enemy camp, which was near Alazán Creek, taking advantage of their knowledge of the terrain. At dawn on June 20, 1813, as Elizondo's soldiers, their wives, and children knelt for morning mass, the rebels quietly approached and fired cannon shot into the assembly, killing indiscriminately, and scattering them in all directions.[48] The rebel cavalry then rushed at the survivors. Ruiz's nephew, eighteen-year-old José Antonio Navarro, watched the thunderous battle from atop the tower of San Fernando Church.[49] Gutiérrez de Lara turned his back from the scene as the Apache soldiers in his army scalped the unlucky survivors who were not able to reach their horses.[50] Elizondo had two horses shot out from under him, but he eventually escaped with his life. The rebel victory was sweetened with the capture of many Spanish supplies, including "4,000 pounds of biscuits, forty mule loads of flour, 2,000 horses and mules, 300 guns and muskets, 5,000 pounds of powder, $28,000 worth of goods and clothing, $7,000 in cash, hundreds of saddles, liquor, cigars, coffee, and other luxuries."[51] The Republican casualty estimates ranged from five to nine, including Louis Massiot, a member of the provincial junta. Royalist losses were reported to be three hundred and fifty killed and one hundred and fifty taken prisoner. Ruiz, who had previously served as quartermaster, received his first field command for this battle, about which he proudly boasted in his pension application.[52]

Elizondo and his remaining troops fled to Cañada de Caballos, where Arredondo's wrath awaited them. Those men who were first to flee were made to wear a white armband with the letter "C" for *cobarde*, or coward, which would only be removed once they had proven themselves in battle.[53] Viceroy Calleja del Rey responded to Elizondo's loss at Alazán by sending an additional 1,200 veteran infantrymen, ordering Arredondo to await their arrival and not risk another defeat.[54]

Once again, the euphoria of rebel victory was muted by dissension in the ranks. The American volunteers were increasingly unhappy with Gutiérrez de Lara and his direction of the expedition, so they moved to replace him with José Álvarez de Toledo, a Spaniard from Cuba who had been an outspoken liberal member of the Spanish Cortes of 1810–11. Initially a friend and confidant of Gutiérrez de Lara, Toledo took advantage of the dissatisfaction of the American volunteers to undermine Gutiérrez de Lara's leadership. He attacked first with the press. From Natchitoches he began printing a weekly bilingual newspaper called *El Mexicano,* which covered the revolution. Toledo viciously attacked Gutiérrez de Lara in the pages of *El Mexicano,* the first issue of which reached Béxar a few days after the victory at Alazán Creek.[55] In June an advanced group was sent from Natchitoches to Béxar; among the arrivals was Henry Adams Bullard, a lawyer. Although Gutiérrez de Lara gave Bullard a position on Béxar's revolutionary junta, the lawyer gave public speeches against Gutiérrez de Lara and claimed that Toledo had the support of the United States and would be able to deliver on promises of money, reinforcements, and supplies. Bullard warned that unless Toledo was allowed to come safely to Béxar, the American volunteers would return to Louisiana.[56]

Bullard and Perry approached Miguel Menchaca and José Francisco Ruiz, both of whom they believed supported Toledo. In exchange for continued American support of Menchaca as commander, Ruiz and Menchaca agreed to "speak out boldly." James Wilkinson, who had plotted with several factions in the Spanish borderlands as a United States Army officer, wrote to Shaler that Menchaca and Ruiz would be very effective "for they carry with them the voice of the people and the army."[57]

The plan was successful and the provisional junta voted to call for Toledo, but placed conditions: Toledo was to serve under the command of Gutiérrez de Lara, American volunteers would eventually become Mexican citizens or return to Louisiana, the Catholic Church would remain the only approved religion, and freemasonry would not be introduced. Obviously, José Francisco Ruiz and his colleagues, although they rejected the authority of the Spanish officials seeking to quash their rebellion, remained very mindful of the potential threat of the Americans to their traditional values and newly claimed Mexican sovereignty.[58]

Toledo received the news at Nacogdoches on July 3, 1813, and immediately set out for Béxar, where he arrived on August 1. The provisional junta installed him as a member immediately. Tensions quickly arose as the Americans demanded that Gutiérrez de Lara be exiled and Toledo be made commander-in-chief, while Ruiz and his fellow Tejanos argued that the original agreement should be followed. News that Arredondo was approaching exacerbated the debate. The Americans pressed until the provisional junta capitulated. When Gutiérrez de Lara resigned and left for Louisiana, the sole thread of legitimacy that connected the Republican Army of the North at Béxar to Hidalgo was cut.[59]

The Tejanos of Béxar and the militia were outraged. Ruiz and Miguel Menchaca, who had argued for Toledo before the provisional junta, felt betrayed. American meddling had undermined their revolutionary leader. Discontent among the Tejanos was so strong that Toledo wrote that if not for the imminent arrival of Arredondo, he would purge the military of Tejano officers. Distrust of Toledo and the Americans undoubtedly spread throughout the militia. Gutiérrez de Lara had proven his worth to them as a leader, and furthermore he was a fellow *norteño* who had been unjustly ousted by a foreigner, a Spaniard, no less. Tejanos remained in the army to ensure the protection of their homes and families, but they seem to have had little faith in their new commander.[60]

Tensions were so high that Toledo decided to restructure the army again, in some degree a move that advanced José Francisco Ruiz's status. To isolate the angry Tejanos, he segregated his forces along ethnic lines, creating two divisions. The first was comprised of Tejano and Indian companies under Menchaca and the second of Americans under Major Henry Perry. Exact numbers are unknown, but clearly Menchaca had about twice as many troops as Perry. Historian Ted Schwarz has concluded that there were probably three hundred to four hundred Americans under Perry, and eight hundred to nine hundred Tejanos, plus one hundred Indians (mostly Lipan Apaches), with Menchaca. The total strength was between 1,200 and 1,400 troops, not counting packmen, mule drivers, and camp followers. José Francisco was promoted to the rank of lieutenant colonel and served as second-in-command under Menchaca.[61]

Arredondo left Laredo on August 1, the same day that Todelo arrived in Béxar. Elizondo was ordered to resupply and meet him at Cañada de Caballos. There the two armies merged, and Arredondo drilled the troops for several days. Elizondo received a harsh verbal reprimand for his disobedience before the Battle of Alazán Creek, but Arredondo needed his services and so his indiscretion was largely forgiven. From there the royalists, now numbering 1,830 men, consisting of 635 calvary and 1,195 infantry, marched to Rancherías (present-day Pleasanton), and then to Campo del Atascoso (possibly present-day Rutledge Hollow in northern Atascosa County), where they camped.[62] At Campo del Atascoso, Arredondo sent scouts to locate the enemy, but none were found and the royalists incorrectly presumed that the rebels were still in Béxar.[63]

The reason Toledo ordered his army to leave the security of Béxar to meet the Spanish south of town has been hotly debated by historians. It may have been that the Tejanos objected to fighting in the city, among their families and homes, or perhaps it was done to gain the advantage of surprise, as had happened at Alazán Creek. Menchaca responded by calling a court-martial of Toledo, in which he accused his commander of planning to deliver the rebel army to the royalists. The provisional junta took action by removing two hundred men from Toledo's command. Even some Americans seemed reluctant to follow their new leader. Perry failed to move out as ordered. When the news arrived that Arredondo and Elizondo had merged armies and were advancing on Béxar, attitudes changed and the rebels united to meet them.[64]

Ruiz and the Republican Army of the North marched out of Béxar to cheers and martial music. The men sang an expletive-filled song about what they planned to do to the "one-eyed" Arredondo.[65] The column was led by the Washington Regiment of American Volunteers, followed by four hundred Mexican infantrymen. The Madison Regiment was next, followed by two pieces of artillery. An advance guard of twenty Americans and Tejanos kept two hundred paces ahead of the column. Behind the main column was the munitions train, escorted by more artillery.[66] On the first day, the rebel army reached Arroyo de la Piedra, a creek whose location is no longer remembered but is likely near Mission San José. The next day Toledo chose a nearby ford of the Medina River to cross, most likely the Laredo Road crossing on the Pérez Ranch. There, on the southwest side of the river, was Rodeo de la Espada, a part of the old Mission Espada Ranch. Here the army camped for two days as they scouted the area.[67] On August 17, Toledo received news from his scouts that Arredondo was camped nine miles to the south on the "great road." Toledo wished to engage the enemy from the high ground and on the morning of August 18 marched his army to a hill overlooking the Laredo Road, where he hoped to ambush the royalists.[68]

Arredondo, notified of the rebels' approach, placed his vanguard troops in an oak grove, and positioned an exposed line of men across a sandy clearing that stretched along both sides of the Laredo Road. He hoped to lure the rebels into a trap, whereby the rebels would pursue the exposed troops and he would flank them.[69] Elizondo advanced with one hundred and eighty soldiers along the Laredo Road scouting for the rebels. One of Elizondo's men, Ensign Francisco López, got separated from his company and accidently wandered into the rebel ranks. Menchaca, fearing this wayward soldier would reveal their location, ordered his men to fire on him. He turned at full gallop as shots whizzed past him, and Elizondo advanced to his aid. Realizing that he had found the rebel army much sooner than expected, Elizondo retreated with his foes in full pursuit. His orders had been to lure the rebels toward the Spanish line, so he engaged them again briefly and sent couriers to Arredondo, warning him of their position. Arredondo sent another detachment of one hundred and eighty men, led by Lieutenant Colonel Juan Manuel Zambrano, who had led the counter-revolt against Casas, to join Elizondo and continue luring the rebels south.[70]

The combined forces of Elizondo and Zambrano advanced again, this time with two small cannons, and the Tejano cavalry engaged what they believed was Arredondo's main column. The sun was brutally hot, and the sandy oak groves south of Béxar had few places to water horses or men. The rebels captured the two enemy guns and the royalists retreated into the oaks. However, the sand slowed the ability of the rebels to pursue and they abandoned two cannons, stuck in the sands.[71]

When Toledo ordered his men to return to their original position, Menchaca and Kemper challenged his command, demanding that they pursue the enemy further. When all of the Tejano officers supported Menchaca, Toledo capitulated and ordered the army to pursue. The rebels advanced across Galván Creek in pursuit of Elizondo and Zambrano, thinking they were the main army of Arredondo. When Toledo ordered Menchaca to make a maneuver to scatter the Spanish horses, Menchaca again disobeyed. Instead, Tejano cavalry under Menchaca pursued the retreating Elizondo and Zambrano into the oak grove where Arredondo had placed his line of soldiers and artillery in a V-formation facing north, with artillery along its flanks.[72]

Elizondo and Zambrano retreated into the middle of the open V, luring the rebels into position to take fire from multiple angles. When the surprised rebels encountered the Spanish formation at a distance of only forty yards, the royalists opened fire. The rebel army fell into the trap. The Apache and Tonkawa Indian rebels fled the scene after the Spanish opened fire, raining down cannonballs, shot, and shrapnel on the rebel army. Ruiz and Menchaca survived the initial barrage and rallied their men for a direct charge at the Spanish lines. Menchaca fell, hit in the neck with grapeshot from a Spanish cannon, and died on the battlefield. Ruiz assumed command of the Tejano cavalry. Under his direction, the troopers made two furious charges against Arredondo.[73]

Toledo planned a flanking maneuver designed to capture Arredondo on the field. During the fighting a rebel sharpshooter had his sights on Arredondo, but the general was warned at the last second by an observant Spanish corporal and his life was spared.[74] The Spanish were able to hold their line and inflicted heavy casualties on the rebels. Toledo and his remaining cavalry fled the battle in the direction of Louisiana. Arredondo then ordered the infantry to close the V-formation in a pincer-like movement to trap the surviving exhausted infantrymen who could not reach a horse or were too tired to flee. Remembering how the rebels had executed Salcedo and Herrera and fired upon unsuspecting women and children in prayer, no quarter was given.[75] The battle was over. Nearly six hundred men lay dead on the field of battle, including Menchaca, leaving Ruiz as the highest-ranking surviving Tejano officer.

After the battle, Arredondo ordered the execution of one hundred prisoners and sent Elizondo with two hundred troops to pursue the retreating rebels into Béxar. Accompanying Elizondo in his pursuit of rebels was

Captain Juan Ignacio Pérez, brother-in-law and compadre of José Francisco. More than half of the Americans who retreated from the field at Medina were overtaken and killed. Elizondo took no prisoners; instead, he quartered those who were captured, hanging body parts in trees and heads on pikes.[76] When word reached Béxar of the defeat of the rebel army, nearly three hundred families fled for Louisiana, having previously prepared for a possible flight. Some Béxareños turned on the revolutionaries. When fifty American stragglers reached the town, they were imprisoned and turned over to Elizondo who promptly executed them.[77]

A door-to-door search was conducted in Béxar for rebels and rebel sympathizers. More than seven hundred Tejanos and eight to fifteen Americans were rounded up. Most were imprisoned in the guardhouse, but two hundred were packed into the priest's quarters at San Fernando Church. The heat was sweltering, and eighteen died of suffocation that night. José Antonio Menchaca recalled in his memoirs that Arredondo selected a number of Bexareño rebels for hard labor and forty for execution: "Of the forty who were selected to die, every third day they would shoot three, opposite the Plaza House, until the entire number were disposed of."[78] After execution, their bodies were then dragged in the plaza, and their arms and heads were cut off and displayed in public places. José Antonio Navarro recalled the piercing silence that enveloped Béxar during this time, "in that time of daily executions nothing was heard except the laments of the dying."[79] The number of executed rebels eventually far exceeded forty: Arredondo himself estimated that he had two hundred and fifteen men executed in Béxar, mostly Tejanos. Those not chosen for execution were chained and used as forced labor repairing the streets of San Antonio.[80]

The women of Béxar suffered greatly. Those suspected of aiding the rebels or having rebel family members were arrested and held in the *quinta*, a building originally designed to warehouse goods for the Indian trade. They suffered daily abuses, including rape and public whippings.[81] After nearly two months the women of Béxar were finally released; most were entirely destitute having lost husbands, property, and dignity.

José Francisco and many surviving Tejano insurgents, including José Antonio Navarro, initially retreated to La Bahía, where they regrouped.[82] A few days later they received news of the atrocities committed in Béxar after the battle and decided to leave for Louisiana.[83] Among those who joined them there was José Ángel Navarro, the oldest son of Ruiz's late uncle and mentor, who had been removed as a lieutenant in the royalist forces and exiled by Arredondo because of the actions of his relatives.[84] His younger brother, José Antonio Navarro, recalled his "venerable uncle Francisco Ruiz and my brother-in-law Juan Martín de Veramendi leaving Béxar fugitives from their families, as insurgents, whom Arredondo desired to have shot as the principal ring leaders of the revolutionists of Béxar."[85]

Accompanying Elizondo in his pursuit of rebels was Captain Juan Ignacio Pérez, brother-in-law and compadre of José Francisco. When they reached the Trinity River, three-hundred rebel sympathizers, who had fled Béxar, were trapped on the western bank of the river due to flooding and taken into custody.[86] Elizondo then ordered his men to cross the Trinity at a different point and continue their pursuit, but they were repeatedly tuned back by a barrage of arrows fired by Indian allies of the rebels. This allowed Ruiz and the soldiers remaining under his command to escape to Louisiana. On his return to Béxar, Elizondo was stabbed in the torso by Miguel Serrano, a royalist soldier under his command, who was sickened by the atrocities he had witnessed. Elizondo died of his injuries before reaching Béxar and was buried on the banks of the San Marcos River.[87]

Following the Battle of Medina, Arredondo ordered every ranch to be abandoned and their workers enlisted into militia. The result was devastating for Texas. Food scarcities resulted, as most of the available male labor was enlisted in the military and unable to tend to fields and flocks. The unattended ranches became prime targets of raiding parties, further depleting the food supply.[88]

Over the next two months, Arredondo had his soldiers confiscate rebel property. The Medina River ranch owned by the Ruiz family was among those confiscated. When Captain Pérez returned to Béxar, Arredondo tasked him with looking after the rebels' confiscated property, including the Ruiz ranch that adjoined his own ranch. A total of 62,642 pesos worth of property was taken without trial, or even charges.[89]

The terror in Béxar ended on October 14, 1813, the birthday of King Ferdinand VII, when Arredondo issued a general pardon, which excluded Ruiz by name.[90] José Francisco's family escaped the worst of the violence, however, most likely due to the protection of his in-law and compadre Pérez. José Antonio Navarro later wrote to Mirabeau B. Lamar, "During the three months tyrannies, very few families escaped. The family of Lieutenant Colonel Ruis, Navarros, Veramend[i], etc. were on this occasion respected although their husbands' relations were insurgents, and why the *Caligula* Arredondo hid from these his sanguinary hand was unknown."[91]

Though they escaped the terrors of the quinta, the Ruiz and Navarro women were left destitute and without husbands. Ruiz's wife, María Josefa Hernández, had to care for two children, which she did by taking in boarders. In the 1817 census, María Josefa was listed as living in the Ruiz home in Barrio del Sur with her children Antonia (age eight) and Francisco (age six), her nephew Fernando Ruiz (age two), and two women, Ingina Castro (age thirty-four) and Nasaria Martínez (age sixteen). Three years later, by the census of 1820, a completely different set of boarders lived in the home.[92]

Though separated by what was then an immense distance, María Josefa remained suspect of maintaining contact with her husband. In November 1816, the governor ordered Juan Ignacio Pérez to search Josefa's home for correspondence.[93] He dutifully did so, but found nothing. Meanwhile, José Francisco's mother, Manuela de la Peña, went to live with her widowed daughter, María Josefa Ruiz de Navarro, and her four remaining children. Three years later, when María Josefa Ruiz de Navarro's son José Antonio Navarro returned from exile, he found his family destitute, driven from their home, and their businesses abandoned.

CHAPTER V

Exile

The names of Ruiz, Veramendi and Navarro were the mark of
ignominy, the alarm of treason, and of all evil that could be
invoked against the holy Cause and the Rights of the King of
Spain—In Augt. 1813 [we] fled to the United States at the time
... the Battle of Medina was lost, and with it the last hope of the
Mexican Patriots.

—José Antonio Navarro, 1841[1]

José Francisco Ruiz arrived in the Neutral Ground on September 3,
1813.[2] This strip of land between the Sabine River and the Calcasieu
River in present-day western Louisiana was disputed by Spain and
the United States and was designated as "neutral ground" in which neither
government had an official presence. Those who settled on this land were
a mix of squatters, refugees, runaway slaves, bandits, and others seeking
the sanctuary of a land with no government. It also served as a sanctuary for Ruiz and his fellow Tejano rebels, including Juan Martín de Veramendi.[3] The Tejano rebels' camp was most likely located at Santa Bárbara
Río Hondo, a six hundred forty acre ranch established by Ruiz's brother,
José Antonio Ruiz, who died in 1812.[4] This settlement became a center for
smuggling, especially cattle from Texas to Louisiana.

Ruiz's rebel encampment is often identified in contemporaneous Spanish records as "*Ballupier*" (Bayou Pierre).[5] However, the Tejano rebel camp
was not the same place as the nearby settlement of Bayou Pierre.[6] Life in
the Neutral Ground was not easy for Ruiz and the other fugitives. Natchitoches Parish records show that an epidemic swept through the Tejano
camp immediately upon their arrival. The first victim was Francisco Treviño, who died on September 11, 1813, of "a fever." A few days later Juan José
Vela died "suddenly of a fever." Fernando Menchaca died on October 20.

José Francisco's nephew, Ignacio de la Peña, died next without sacraments or a final confession because he was "unconscious with a putrid fever."[7] While it is impossible to find the exact cause of the epidemic, the victims were described as having a fever, abdominal pain, unconsciousness, and sudden death, all of which could be attributed to typhoid fever. Ruiz's brother-in-law, Francisco Rodríguez, died suddenly of a pain on March 22, 1814.[8] Over a dozen other rebels succumbed to the epidemic, which subsided only in April of 1814.[9]

On October 15, 1813, Francisco Martínez of the Spanish consulate in New Orleans, proclaimed a royal pardon to insurgents in the Neutral Ground who presented themselves at Nacogdoches.[10] It excepted "as not worthy of obtaining any consideration whatsoever, the accused leaders, Bernardo Gutiérrez de Lara, José Álvarez de Toledo, Francisco Arocha, José Francisco Ruiz, Juan Beramendi [Veramendi], Vicente Travieso, and the infamous blood thirsty Pedro Prado, who committed the atrocious crime of leading to the slaughter Colonel Don Simón de Herrera, Lieutenant Colonel Don Manuel Salcedo, and the other helpless victims of the inhuman monsters who sacrificed them." His order offered a reward of two hundred and fifty pesos to anyone who killed Ruiz or any of the other named "bandits" and an additional reward if captured alive.[11] Ruiz's options were thus limited. With a hefty price on his head, he risked capture either by entering the United States or Texas. Instead, he stayed in the Neutral Ground, where he lived among pirates, bandits, and smugglers.[12]

A sumaria filed against Ruiz in October 1815 provides over a dozen testimonies about him and his activities while he was in exile. One witness testified that the refugee Ruiz lived near Bayou Pierre in a "casa del campo" (farm house), was engaged in subsistence farming with a partner, Vicente Tarín, and that he hoped for a pardon. Nearly all others testified that he was trading with Americans or enemy Indians.[13] Wanted and without the ability to provide any more than a subsistence living for themselves while farming at Bayou Pierre, Ruiz and other insurgents in fact did engage in smuggling, selling goods and arms to the Indians on the upper Red River, primarily the eastern Comanches. Juan Antonio Padilla, in a report on Texas Indians, noted the role of the Tejano rebels in supplying the Comanches:

[U]p to the year 1811, the Comanche were not so well armed, nor so war-like, nor had they penetrated into places where they are now seen

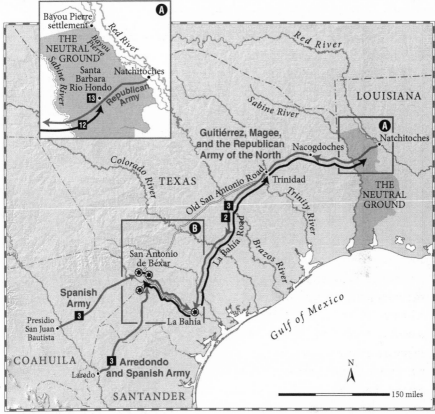

1. **1812** Ruiz serves as quartermaster of the militia of the Presidio of San Antonio de Béxar.

2. **1812–1813** Revolutionary literature flows south.

3. Republican Army of the North moves south; Spanish Army approaches from south.

4. **Feb. 19, 1813** Ruiz wounded during Seige of La Bahía.

5. **February to March 1813** Ruiz corresponds with Gutierrez and Menchaca about revolutionary matters.

6. **March 29, 1813** Battle of Rosillo. Ruiz does not participate due to injuries.

7. **April 3, 1813** Salcedo and Herrera executed on La Bahía Road

8. **April 6, 1813** Ruiz takes Oath of Independence in Plaza de Armas.

9. **June 20, 1813** Battle of Alazán Creek. Ruiz's first field command.

10. **Aug. 18, 1813** Battle of Medina. Ruiz takes command of Tejano forces.

11. **Aug. 19, 1813** Ruiz and remaining Tejano forces retreat to La Bahía.

12. **Sept. 3, 1813** Ruiz arrives in the Neutral Strip.

13. Ruiz settles at Santa Barbara Rio Hondo ranch.

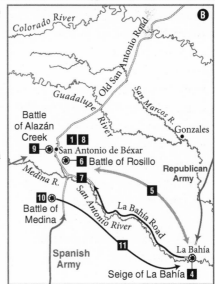

Carol Zuber-Mallison / ZMGraphics.com

Ruiz during the Gutiérrez-Magee Expedition and aftermath, 1812–13.

. . . The revolution which broke out in the center of the kingdom at that time, came to the ears of the Indians . . . they took advantage of the situation . . . and hastened to make war . . . at the same time that the Indians [the Comanches] laid waste the haciendas and ranches, the foreigners and various rebel Spaniards, who escaped from the victorious army of our sovereign at Medina, introduced munitions and other things in exchange for animals, making a well worn road through the unsettled regions toward Natchitoches.[14]

Spanish officials frequently noted that "revolutionaries" lived with Comanches, clearly a reference to Tejano exiles in the Neutral Ground.[15] Not only did José Francisco trade with the Comanches on the Red River, he lived among them for extensive periods. His later writings about the culture, religion, and politics of the Comanches possessed a deep level of understanding, unrivaled among his contemporaries. Anthropologist Thomas W. Kavanagh writes, "José Francisco Ruiz lived with the Comanches from at least 1812, if not earlier, and between 1821 and 1835 he was often in more or less constant contact with them. Thus, his descriptions have an authority unsurpassed by any other historical writer."[16]

José Francisco's involvement with the Comanches came during a time when their relationship with the Spanish was changing dramatically. Trade policies had a significant effect on the balance of power on the frontier. After the arrival of Europeans, access to manufactured goods became one of the dominant economic drivers for Texas Indians. European trade goods dramatically altered traditional lifeways by providing superior tools that replaced or enhanced native-produced items. Steel hatchets, tomahawks and hunting knives replaced the stone weapons used in the past. Cotton, linen, or woolen clothing and blankets replaced those made of animal hides. Scissors, awls, picks, and flints for starting fires were labor-saving devises. Beads, mirrors, combs and copper bracelets added to native selection of vanity items. Guns, powder, and ammunition introduced more efficient methods of hunting and superior weapons for warfare.[17] Horses were particularly prized by the Comanches, and the Tejano rebels aided them in acquiring them. Ruiz noted the integral role horses played in Comanche society: "They are very dexterous horsemen being accustomed to it from their infancy, their parents rigging out with bow, arrows, shield and even before they can walk, trying them to the saddle."[18]

The Comanches had a highly decentralized leadership that was intimately personal. Thus, there was no single chief or elder who could speak for all Comanches. War parties would elect a war chief solely for the duration of their campaign. With no clear hierarchy, the divisions and grouping among the Comanches was ever shifting. Ruiz observed, "[The Comanches] are comprised of various small tribes . . . in every [Comanche] town there is a chief who has the management of affairs, who is always an old man."[19] One clear cultural division was between Western and Eastern Comanches. Western Comanches, sometimes referred to as "Yamparikas," established trade with New Mexicans despite prohibitions by the Spanish.[20] Ruiz became particularly close to a band of Eastern Comanches known as the "Tenewah."[21]

At the beginning of 1810, the Spanish enjoyed peace with the Comanches in both Texas and New Mexico, but it did not last. That summer, the Spanish and Yamparikas engaged in a joint campaign against the Apaches, led by Comanche elders Cordero and Quegüe and New Mexico governor José Manrique. While this expedition was fighting Apaches, Eastern Comanches swept through Texas raiding ranches, stealing hundreds of horses from La Bahía, and then headed south, sacking Monclova in Coahuila. The evidence implicated Comanche bands led by El Sordo and Pisinampe. El Sordo was known to be hostile to Béxar after confronting Texas Governor Nemesio de Salcedo earlier that year, while Pisinampe was accused of selling horses to Americans on the Colorado River. Coahuila Governor Manuel Cordero y Bustamante appealed to two Yamparika leaders for assistance, Cordero and Parauquita. At the latter's instigation, El Sordo returned to Béxar to report pending hostilities by the Taovayas and Tawakonis, two tribes of Wichita Indians. He entered Béxar unarmed as a sign of good faith, but rather than accept this peace offering, the Spanish arrested him. This was a gross violation of Comanche etiquette. In response, Parauquita led a group of Comanche leaders, including Cordero, Pisinampe, and Yzazat, to Béxar to demand an explanation for El Sordo's arrest. Salcedo, having just survived the Casas revolt, met the Comanches with six hundred soldiers, including Ruiz, on April 8, 1812. Confronted by the largest Spanish force ever assembled against them, the Comanches left with El Sordo still in jail, but this marked the end of their good relations with the Spanish.[22]

El Sordo's arrest pushed most Comanche leaders, including Cordero, to abandon their pro-Spanish position and seek closer ties to American traders in Louisiana. The Wichita Indians had for many years acted as intermediaries between the Comanches and Americans, but by 1812, the Wichitas were in disarray due to a succession crisis. This allowed the Eastern Comanches to expand their trade with Natchitoches at the same time that their relations with the Spanish dissolved over El Sordo's arrest. By 1814, Texas Governor Antonio Martínez wrote, "the traffic between the Comanche and the traders from the interior continues without interruption, . . . arms, munitions, and other war supplies are being brought in."[23]

Ruiz and other Tejano exiles arrived in the Neutral Ground precisely at the time that eastern trade was shifting. Furthermore, they fully understood the weakness of the Spanish. Historian Pekka Hämäläinen wrote that the new arrivals in the Natchitoches area quickly transformed the "frontier outpost into a quasi-autonomous political entity on the Comanche-Texas borderlands." Hämäläinen further agues, "Still determined to fight the Spanish regime, the refugee rebels began operating as middlemen between the Comanches and the American merchants, carrying guns, munitions, and powder to the west and horses and mules to the east." In 1813, Nemesio de Salcedo lamented that the refugee trade was undermining Spain's commerce in Texas, but there was nothing he could do about it.[24]

The devastation inflicted upon Béxareños by the Spanish after the Battle of Medina also contributed to the Comanches' abandonment of trade with Béxar. Following the Battle of Medina, Arredondo ordered all ranches to be abandoned and their workers enlisted into militia. The result was devastating for Texas. Food became scarce as most of the available male labor was enlisted in the military and thus unable to tend to fields and flocks. With no one tending to the ranches, they became prime targets of raiding parties further depleting the food supply. Frankly, there was little left for the Spanish to trade.[25]

Records of Ruiz's trading activity are scant, but enough exist to paint a picture of his operations. His base of operations was Natchitoches, a town built by tradesmen. Among the amenities it provided were numerous warehouses to store and deliver trade goods. The Red River provided water access to New Orleans.[26] Ruiz had accounts at the Natchitoches warehouse, where he stored trade goods. A February 18, 1819, inventory showed Ruiz's personal account owed $227.43.3/4. A second joint account for Vicente Tarín and Francisco Ruiz owed $889.43.3/4. Both accounts received a credit rating of *bon* (good), the highest available.[27] Records of a trading party led by John Ross that visited the Comanches in 1815 indicate that the members included José Francisco Ruiz, Bernardo Gutiérrez de

Lara, and Peter Ellis Bean.[28] The party moved sixteen mule loads of goods west that summer, including guns and ammunition, as well as blankets and kettles.[29] Ruiz's trading extended beyond the Comanches. He also traded with Lipan Apaches in places as far as West Texas and eastern New Mexico. Arredondo, in 1814, estimated that illegal goods from the United States cost, on average, 400 percent less than goods legally traded in New Spain.[30] This margin fueled illicit trade and created tremendous opportunity for Ruiz.

The Comanches used the arms and ammunition that Ruiz and other traders provided against settlements, which is why the Spanish continued to view the Tejano exiles as a threat. Ruiz described the arms used by the Comanches as "firearms, bows and arrows and lances, and some of them tomahawks and a species of warclub with a large head of stone a blow from which is generally fatal."[31] Padilla believed that Béxar exiles even guided the Comanches: "There were not lacking some Spaniards . . . who led them and incited them to kill and burn whatever came in their way. With such guides, they penetrated to the Villa[s] del Norte de la Colonia where these Indians never had set foot before."[32] Joaquín de Arredondo believed that "bad Spaniards and some Americans formed a new plan to destroy the provinces." He argued that rather than fight the Spanish military in a battle they would certainly lose, they fight by supplying the Comanches with firearms and encouraging them to attack soft targets such as farmers and mail carriers.[33]

By 1814, Texas was nearly depleted of livestock.[34] The Comanches had to seek new sources of Spanish horses and mules, so in 1816 they negotiated a truce with the Lipan Apaches under El Cojo. Together they raided the Río Grande villas and other southern settlements. Ruiz himself later wrote, "Possessing a thorough knowledge of the terrain, [the Lipan Apaches] served as guides to the Comanches, with whom they were at peace."[35] In truth, Ruiz and other Tejano insurgents facilitated this through arms smuggling and supplying the Eastern Comanches, as well as the Lipan Apaches. Food became scarce and settlers began to flee the colony. In 1818 Governor Antonio Martínez wrote, "not a single day passes without their [the Comanches] making some depredation or attack." He complained again the next year, "this province will be destroyed unwittingly by lack of inhabitants . . . because no one wishes to live in the province for fear and danger and because the few inhabitants now existing are being killed gradually by the savages."[36]

Despite their suspected role in aiding the Comanches, some of the Neutral Ground exiles were welcomed back to Béxar. Juan Martín de Veramendi and José Antonio Navarro, Ruiz's brother-in-law and nephew respectively, received pardons and returned to Béxar.[37] The terms of their pardons excluded the return of their confiscated property and required they be placed under surveillance.[38] Veramendi's loss of property was upward of $30,000.00.[39] Upon his return he immediately set out to regain his house and reputation. He sought and was granted an audience with General Arredondo, who had left Texas in March of 1814 for Monterrey, the new capital of the Provincias Internas del Este.[40] Showing the political skills that would elevate him to the governorship of Texas, Veramendi returned with an order to return his home, to dismiss all charges that he had been a revolutionary and to not molest him any further.[41]

In 1818 Veramendi and José Angel Navarro joined a Spanish expedition sent from Béxar to investigate reports of piracy on the Texas coast, but they also seem to have returned to the Neutral Ground. It is unknown if they visited with Ruiz or the other Tejano exiles, but since both Veramendi and Navarro had recently been exiles themselves and lived with Ruiz near Bayou Pierre, it was likely that they sought to make contact with him. Veramendi may have had other reasons to visit the Neutral Ground; he had long engaged in illicit trade. Records indicate that he had even loaned money to the infamous pirates Jean and Pierre Lafitte.[42] Governor Martínez was angered by the side trip and officially charged them with illicit trade and going to Natchitoches to meet with agents of the United States. The charges were never prosecuted.[43]

Between 1814 and 1821, official reports of illegal trade from Louisiana became increasingly common. In 1820 alone, one Spanish estimate claimed that $90,000 worth of illicit goods passed through Nacogdoches, mostly "arms of good quality, double barreled shotguns, lances, and a great amount of ammunition."[44] The items were acquired in New Orleans or Natchitoches, where the Tejano rebels, who had become known as the "Old Comanche Traders" by local Americans, developed relations with merchant houses and purchasing agents in both cities.[45]

During his time in exile, Ruiz developed a business relationship with New Orleans merchant José Cassiano, who was born Giuseppe Cassini in San Remo, Genoa (now Italy), in 1791.[46] Cassiano moved to New Orleans in 1816 and became a successful merchant. Steamboat service to Natchitoches connected it with New Orleans merchants such as Cassiano, who

Ruiz's trade network while in Exile, 1813–21.

supplied Ruiz with goods for his Comanche trade.[47] Following Mexican independence in 1821, Cassiano relocated to Béxar, where he married Ruiz's niece, Gertrudis Pérez de Cordero, the widow of Texas Governor Manuel Antonio Cordero y Bustamante. In Béxar, Cassiano continued his business relations with Ruiz.[48] Their relationship was so close that it endured for several generations. Well into the 1890s, the Cassiano family leased Ruiz's former home as the location for A. Cassiano & Bro. Groceries.[49]

During José Francisco's years of exile in the Neutral Ground, his wife María Josefa Hernández led the household in Béxar, making ends meet by taking in boarders, a common practice at the time. Due to the devastation following the Battle of Medina, the city contained a large number of households headed by one or more women, including many widows.[50] In the 1820 census, María's two children lived in the home, but her nephew Fernando no longer resided with her. Two rebel families also lived in the Ruiz household.[51] Refugia San Miguel, age twenty, the wife of rebel Juan José Arocha and daughter of rebel Nepomuceno San Miguel, lived there with her sister Antonia, age ten, her brother Mauricio, age eight, and her son Juan José Arocha, age one.[52] Nepomuceno San Miguel had his home in the Barrio de Valero confiscated by the Spanish government in 1813.[53] Ana de Luna, wife of rebel Francisco Travieso, also lived in the Ruiz household, as did two servants, Ignacia Almanze and Trinidad Santa Cruz.[54] The presence of servants in the Ruiz home was not necessarily an indication of the family's relative wealth or success, but of its social status.

Stateless, separated from his family, and with a reward for his capture, dead or alive, Ruiz chose to do business with all comers, including the Comanches. In doing so he remained intimately involved in the tangled politics of the Texas frontier during an era of important transition. Spanish influence was in decline, the American presence was emerging, and Comanche dominance was firmly established. The eight years Ruiz spent working with Comanches and Americans resulted in long lasting relationships and insights that would be constant influences during the remaining twenty years of his life.

CHAPTER VI

Indian Agent

We must all live with the same quietness and safety as the birds
of beautiful plumage that fly through the air, bringing joy to the
countryside, and we must put an end to the birds of prey that
disturb them.

> —José Francisco Ruiz, Comanche Treaty of 1823[1]

In 1820, the ayuntamiento at Béxar officially complained to Governor
Antonio Martínez and the provincial deputation about the ravages of
"the two nations, the Comanches and the Lipans, who have occasioned
so many evils in this province during the last years," asking that they "be
followed until they are exterminated or forced to an inviolable and lasting
peace." The ayuntamiento members even suggested the type of men who
should be selected to undertake the pacification of the Indians: "officials
hardened to an active life, familiar with the country and experienced in the
methods of making war against this kind of enemy."[2]

Despite the pleas from Texas, Joaquín de Arredondo, the commandant
of the Eastern Internal Provinces, no longer favored a policy of military response, which had proven ineffective over the previous decade.[3] He turned
instead to a policy of pacification of the so-called *indios bárbaros* through
trade and diplomatic negotiations. A plan for pacification through diplomacy had been originally proposed by Juan Cortés, a merchant at Natchitoches.[4] Cortés suggested that the exiled rebels who lived near Natchitoches, in particular José Francisco Ruiz, were best suited for pacifying
the indios bárbaros because they "spent several years with the tribes." He
added that only Ruiz's experience with Comanches was well known.[5] In
the spring of 1821, Arredondo, the same man who had defeated the Texans
at Medina, forced Ruiz into exile, and had for years refused to pardon him,
finally offered him a full pardon.[6] Under the terms of the pardon, Ruiz

agreed to lead a peace expedition to the Comanches and Lipan Apaches and end his rebellion against Spain.[7] He accepted and began planning the expedition. Sensing that political change was eminent, other Texas exiles appealed to Governor Martínez for pardons, which he granted.[8]

Ruiz's pardon took place as the independence movement in Mexico regained momentum. As the movement for independence spread northward, Arredondo met with the ayuntamiento in Monterrey and concluded that the people favored independence, which seemed inevitable. A vote occurred and he declared support for Mexican independence on July 4, 1821. Governor Martínez was convinced by a note from the chaplain of the cathedral of Monterrey that support for independence was widespread. He too opted for a peaceful transition of government in Texas and met with the newly elected alcalde of Béxar, José Ángel Navarro, to plan a ceremony for the transition of government. In the midst of this unprecedented political change, Martínez followed the Spanish political tradition that the ayuntamiento remained the legitimate representative of the people in the absence of higher legitimate authority. On July 18, 1821, in the Plaza de Armas, Navarro publicly announced the independence of Mexico and lowered the Spanish flag there for the last time.[9] A few weeks later, on August 24, the Spanish viceroy of New Spain signed the Treaty of Córdoba, securing Mexican independence.[10]

Just prior to independence from Spain, on June 30, 1821, Juan Cortés wrote that funds for the Ruiz expedition had been received and that Ruiz was in Natchitoches gathering supplies and presents for his meetings with the Comanches and Lipans.[11] He did not provide a complete list of supplies, but they included "tobacco and other articles in common use among them."[12] Cortés's correspondence notes that Ruiz obtained "12 bolts of colorful cloth with blue bows" that were indispensable as presents to the principal chiefs, and that *bujerias* (knick-knacks) were essential to the success of the mission.[13] Other lists of Comanche presents included items such as blankets, guns, powder, balls, flints, fire steels, knives, Tomahawk pipes, vermillion, braggys (apron-like loincloths), bells, tin cups, scissors, calico, looking glasses, combs, hats, *piloncillos*, gold braid, thread, metal buttons, ribbon, and tobacco.[14]

On July 21, 1821, Martínez, who continued to serve as governor, informed Gaspár López, who succeeded Arredondo as commandant general, of the ayuntamiento's desire to continue with the plan for Ruiz to lead a pacification expedition.[15] On August 21, López wrote to Ruiz at Natchitoches to reassure him that "it gives me great satisfaction and the greatest impression that you have agreed to cooperate with the pacification of the Indian Nations that live on the frontier lands." He addressed the peculiar circumstances in which they found themselves as former enemies, offering an olive branch: "in the Capital and in all quarters of the Provinces an era of awakening has begun towards the patriotic sentiments you manifested in another time ... now we are one country and family." López asked Ruiz to "use all of your influence with those Nations to negotiate a peace with all of the bands of this Province, free all of the captives that you are able ... be certain that this Supreme Government forgets all the past offences and seeks union and peace."[16]

Ruiz reported to Martínez on October 15, 1821, that he had finally received his orders and was preparing to visit the Comanches in their villages on the frontier. He declared the goals of his expedition were "to persuade the Comanches of the benefits of peace, to persuade them to give up their captives, and to get them to visit the capital."[17] Ruiz planned to depart Natchitoches on November 1, but delays prevented him from leaving until December 3.[18] José Francisco was accompanied by fellow exile Vicente Tarín and a *compañía* (company) of porters carrying supplies and trade goods.[19]

Ruiz's expedition entered Texas from Louisiana on December 3, 1822, and arrived at Waco Village on the upper Brazos in January.[20] The village consisted of sixty houses and contained approximately nine hundred residents on the west bank of the Brazos in what today is downtown Waco. The settlement was surrounded with earthworks several feet high and had five underground shelters where villagers could take refuge during an attack. Around the village were four hundred acres of corn, beans, pumpkins, and melons.[21.]

The Wacos were a division of the Tawakoni people within the Wichita confederation who would establish their own independence in the late 1820s. The Wichitas were divided into the Taovayas and Tawakonis; at the time of Ruiz's visit, the Wacos were still allied with the Tawakonis and their village was very near three Tawakoni settlements on the Brazos and Navasota Rivers. With the loss of their French trading partners following the Louisiana Purchase and increased competition from the Tenewah Comanches for trade with the Americans at Natchitoches, the Wichitas had begun raiding Béxar and La Bahía. They focused primarily on taking livestock to barter for firearms, ammunition, and other items from traders like Ruiz, who brought goods up the Red River and ventured further into Wichita territory to trade.[22]

Visitors often noted the presence of other Indian groups in the Waco Village, including other Wichitas (Taovayas and Tawakonis), Kichais (a Wichita-related tribe), and Comanches. When Ruiz arrived, he found that a recent bout of hostilities with an expedition under the leadership of former Béxar alcalde by Juan Manuel Barrera had poisoned the mood for further negotiation, particularly among the Comanches. López reported that "Ruiz found it very difficult to dissuade them from the idea . . . that they had formed of Barrera, and which reflected upon the government for having selected him for its agent in the matter."[23]

Unable to negotiate a peace at the Waco Village, Ruiz turned his attention to the Lipan Apaches. To meet with the Lipans, Ruiz traveled from the Waco Village to the town of San Fernando de Austria (now Zaragoza) in Coahuila. On April 3, 1822, he wrote to the ayuntamiento of Béxar to note that his negotiations with the Lipan leaders Cuelgas de Castro and Yolcha Poca Ropa had been an immediate success. Both promised to obey the laws of the Mexican government, to release all Tejano captives in their possession, to establish definite limits of their territories, and to provide warriors for campaigns against hostile tribes. The Mexicans in turn promised to provide the Lipans with protection against their enemies, to grant them lands along with rights to water and pasturage, to make annual gifts of gunpowder and corn, to release Lipan prisoners, and to permit Lipan bands to catch and sell wild horses.[24]

Ruiz next led his expedition to the Red River Valley. The ensuing negotiations were difficult, due in large part to the lack of funds available for trade. A series of letters between Ruiz and López between January and April of 1822 outlined their frustration, but there was little that could be done because the Mexican imperial government lacked financial resources.[25] Through his Tenewah connections, Ruiz was able to call a three-day council attended by five thousand people, including "principal chiefs, captains, and elders."[26] The "principal chiefs" named by Ruiz in his report were Pisinampe, Paruakevitsi, Guonique, Barbarquita, and Temanca.[27]

The group discussed matters for three days and resolved, by unanimous vote, that, "assuming that [the] Spanish government had come to an end, and since those who were governing the Mexican Nation were not Spaniards, but an Emperor [Agustín de Iturbide] who was a native of the country and who had the virtues which had been described . . . by

Ruiz, one of their principal chiefs should go forward to negotiate for peace under the terms that he might find most appropriate and useful for the Comanche nation, and principally so that they, united with the Mexican Nation would not permit Spain, or any other power whatsoever, to take any part of the territories which they now occupy."[28] In July 1822, Ruiz and a party of Comanches, led by Pisinampe, traveled to Béxar to negotiate a formal treaty.

Negotiations at Béxar progressed until stalling on the Mexican demand for the return of all prisoners without ransom. The sides agreed to sign a truce and defer the issue for discussion with authorities in Mexico City.[29] The formal truce was signed on July 11, 1822, by Governor Martínez, the ayuntamiento of Béxar, and the Comanches under Pisinampe.[30] Ruiz, who was certainly present at the signing, was appointed interpreter and peace commissioner to the Comanches. It would be his responsibility to lead the Comanche delegation selected by Pisinampe to the Mexican capital to settle the issues surrounding captives.[31]

The next day, Martínez reinstated Ruiz's commission at the rank of lieutenant in the Mounted Militia Company of Texas, and preparations began for the journey to Mexico City.[32] According to the passport issued to Ruiz, the Comanche delegation consisted of thirteen individuals, including a chief captain (*capitán mayor*), as well as eight braves (*gandules*) and four women. No names were listed in the margin of the passport found in the Bexar Archives. From other records the chief captain can be identified as Guonique and another member was likely named Paruakevitsi.[33] Ruiz had three soldier escorts (*soldados de escolta*) at his disposal.[34] The party departed Béxar on or near the planned date of September 4, 1822, and arrived in the capital city in November of the same year.[35]

The negotiators, with Ruiz serving as interpreter, reached agreement on December 13, 1822, and Emperor Iturbide signed the treaty the following day.[36] It recognized the Comanches as a sovereign nation within the Mexican empire. The Comanches received Mexican citizenship, and both sides agreed to forget all hostilities that had occurred under Spanish rule. The Comanches agreed to recognize the United States–Mexican border as defined under the Adams–Onís Treaty of 1819 and to defend that border against invasions by hostile tribes. They also agreed to not allow hostile tribes, Europeans, or Americans to pass through their lands. Both sides agreed to pass through each other's lands only via public roads and with passports. Trade was to be conducted only at Béxar, where it would be

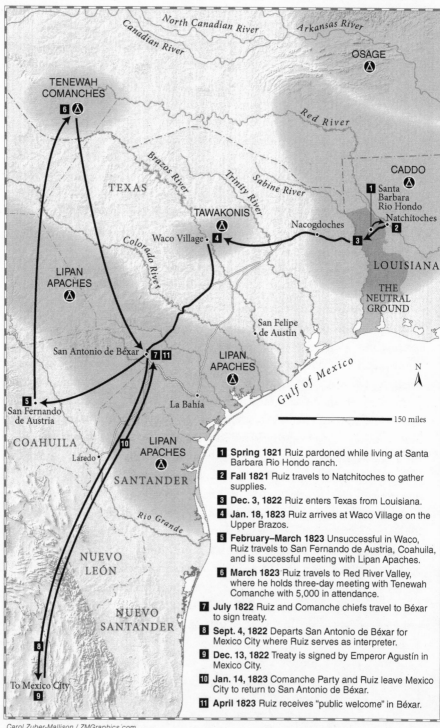

1 Spring 1821 Ruiz pardoned while living at Santa
Barbara Rio Hondo ranch.

2 Fall 1821 Ruiz travels to Natchitoches to gather
supplies.

3 Dec. 3, 1822 Ruiz enters Texas from Louisiana.

4 Jan. 18, 1823 Ruiz arrives at Waco Village on the
Upper Brazos.

5 February–March 1823 Unsuccessful in Waco,
Ruiz travels to San Fernando de Austria, Coahuila,
and is successful meeting with Lipan Apaches.

6 March 1823 Ruiz travels to Red River Valley,
where he holds three-day meeting with Tenewah
Comanche with 5,000 in attendance.

7 July 1822 Ruiz and Comanche chiefs travel to Béxar
to sign treaty.

8 Sept. 4, 1822 Departs San Antonio de Béxar for
Mexico City where Ruiz serves as interpreter.

9 Dec. 13, 1822 Treaty is signed by Emperor Agustín in
Mexico City.

10 Jan. 14, 1823 Comanche Party and Ruiz leave Mexico
City to return to San Antonio de Béxar.

11 April 1823 Ruiz receives "public welcome" in Béxar.

Carol Zuber-Mallison / ZMGraphics.com

Ruiz's peace negotiations, 1821–23.

duty free except for mustangs, for which a percentage caught would be given to the government at Béxar. The treaty also provided for twelve Comanche youths to be sent annually to Mexico City for schooling and for a permanent Comanche representative to be stationed at Béxar to provide translation and facilitate direct dealing with the Mexican authorities there. Finally, the Mexican government promised annual gifts in the amount of two thousand pesos.[37]

Happy with the results of his visit, Guonique was even willing to involve his tribe in national affairs. In December 1822, Mexico was at a crossroads. For nearly a year Emperor Iturbide had struggled with the Mexican Congress over the issue of centralized power, with the emperor increasingly determined to sideline the legislative body for the purpose of exercising sovereignty in the name of the people. As the government's finances deteriorated and Iturbide increased his crackdown on opponents by jailing congressmen and closing newspapers, even supporters in the military turned against him. In December, General Antonio López de Santa Anna and other leading figures declared their opposition to Iturbide, which eventually led to outright rebellion and an end to the first Mexican Empire in March 1823.[38] Guonique, upon learning of the revolt, offered his assistance as Iturbide's ally. The *Gaceta del Gobierno Imperial de Mexico* recorded the offer, "If needed to prevent a return of the Spanish, he and Paruakevitsi would station four thousand armed warriors on the border and in six months could raise 27,000 men."[39] Apparently, the embattled emperor declined the offer, so the Ruiz party left Mexico City on January 14, 1823.[40]

Ruiz arrived at Béxar by April and rejoined his family. His children, Francisco Antonio and María Antonia, had been four and eight years of age respectively when he fled into exile. When he returned, they were youths aged thirteen and seventeen. With the Indian question temporarily resolved, Ruiz prepared to reengage with the development of his homeland and the fortunes of his family.

CHAPTER VII

Restoration

I will continue to proclaim the advantages that in my opinion,
will result by admitting hard working and honest people, no matter what nation they are from . . . even hell itself.

—José Francisco Ruiz, 1830[1]

Mexican independence brought about a restoration of status and political influence for the extended Ruiz-Veramendi-Navarro family. In Béxar, Governor Antonio Martínez called for elections to form a new ayuntamiento, and José Ángel Navarro assumed the duties of alcalde from Erasmo Seguín. Navarro had participated in the transfer of power from Spain to an independent Mexico and celebrated the transition in the municipio with a public ceremony designed by Martínez to ensure a peaceful transition.[2] In December 1821, José Francisco Ruiz's nephew and fellow exile, José Antonio Navarro, younger brother of José Ángel, was elected to the ayuntamiento. The members immediately took up the issue of property confiscated in 1813 and determined that it had been illegal under the 1812 Spanish Constitution and ordered the property returned.[3] This included Ruiz's Medina River ranch. José Antonio Navarro also resumed operating the family mercantile business. When news of independence reached New Orleans, trade goods began to flow into Texas towns such as La Bahía, where Juan Martín de Veramendi was appointed customs agent. This allowed the families to have advantageous access to revived commerce under favorable terms.[4] Ruiz, for his part, was serving as an agent to the Comanches under the treaty he had helped to negotiate. The Ruiz-Veramendi-Navarro family was thus well placed to benefit from their political positions to reestablish their mercantile and political network if political and economic stability could be established.

Ruiz could not be faulted for wondering if such stability was possible.

The disturbances led by Santa Anna, which had begun while Ruiz was in Mexico City with the Comanche delegation, rapidly continued to develop into outright revolt. In February 1823, generals Santa Anna and Guadalupe Victoria signed the Plan de Casa Mata, which called for the overthrow of Emperor Agustín de Iturbide and the creation of a republican government. Initially, Martínez and the ayuntamiento of Béxar rejected Santa Anna's plan, but they soon realized their loyalty to the emperor placed them at odds with the rest of the nation. Iturbide's collapse came quickly as Santa Anna consolidated power, and Ruiz certainly heard the news on the road back to Béxar.[5]

Ruiz arrived home in Béxar in early April 1823. He was received as a hero, and the town gave him "a public welcome."[6] That month he also participated in religious services that reinforced the network of the Ruiz-Veramendi-Navarro family. On April 11, 1823, he was the official witness for the marriage of José Luciano Navarro and Teodora Carbajal.[7] Eight days later, he served as godfather to Juan Martín, the son of Juan Martín de Veramendi and Josefa Navarro.[8]

While tending to family matters, Ruiz again found himself in a political firestorm. Governor José Félix Trespalacios resigned as governor of Texas and a *junta gubernativa* was organized to govern during the vacancy.[9] Those chosen to serve were Trespalacios, Ruiz, Baron de Bastrop, Erasmo Seguín, Juan de Castañeda, Francisco Roxo, and Juan Manuel Zambrano.[10] Other Texas municipalities were invited to send representatives to sit on the junta gubernativa, and José Antonio Navarro was selected by the municipio of La Bahía to represent it.[11] All the members save Zambrano immediately announced in favor of the Plan de Casa Mata and the creation of the new Mexican republic.[12]

On May 6, 1823, a letter from Santa Anna addressed to Trespalacios arrived in Béxar. It belatedly chastised local leaders for their loyalty to Emperor Iturbide: "Will your province refuse to yield to the general will [of the nation]? You well know the weakness of your province . . . and there is no possibility for you to resist the troops that I will speedily bring against you."[13] The general's threat illustrated two realities. First, because Texas lacked population, it was vulnerable to military attacks from Americans, Indians, or even other Mexicans. Second, the national leaders of Mexico had no concerns about treating Texas as a second-class province, such as using threats to compel obedience instead of using a peaceful approach. The junta gubernativa immediately drafted two memos explaining the pro-Iturbide actions of Béxar. The first, to Santa Anna, accused him of overreacting and explained that the cause of Béxar's previous sentiment was simply a lack of information. The junta gubernativa then sent a second memo to the provincial deputation at Monterrey. It explained the strong liberal tradition in Béxar and blamed earlier support for Emperor Iturbide on the peculiar concerns of frontier provinces, namely a need for physical security.[14]

The transition from empire to republic proved to be relatively peaceful in Texas, as elsewhere in Mexico. Congress initially named a military junta to act as the executive branch while it drafted a constitution. On July 1, 1823, the provinces of Honduras, El Salvador, Guatemala, Nicaragua, and Costa Rica separated peacefully from Mexico to form the United Provinces of Central America. Representatives of the other provinces gathered in Mexico City to debate the structure for the new national government. The idea of monarchy was dead and liberals, such as Lorenzo de Zavala, favored a federalist republic. Conservatives favored a strong central government with concentrated power, resembling a monarchy. The junta gubernativa at Béxar ruled Texas until July 8, 1823, when orders came from Mexico City to disband and transfer authority to Lieutenant Colonel Luciano García as the interim governor of Texas. Veramendi wrote to García that same day on behalf of the junta gubernativa and acknowledged the transition of power.[15]

García's term as governor of Texas was short, less than two months. In September 1823, he received instructions that civil and military government were to be separated in all the provinces, and so he transferred his civil powers to a new Provincial Deputation.[16] Texas thus became in effect an independent province, at least temporarily, in the proposed Mexican republic. Erasmo Seguín, elected as the Texas representative to the Constitutional Congress in 1823, received a slate of instructions from the electoral junta. He was to ensure that the Roman Catholic Church remained supreme in Mexico, support a federal form of government, establish ports at Galveston, Matagorda, and Aransas, create a colonization plan with land grants for settlement, reform the presidio companies, and sell mission lands to pay the retired military in Texas.[17]

Federalists outnumbered centralists seventy to ten, and the new Constitution of 1824 featured strong state governments and limited central government. It borrowed heavily from the Spanish Constitution of 1812 and structurally resembled the United States Constitution. It provided for three branches of government, a bicameral congress, and a president and vice president elected to four-year terms.[18]

Of great concern for Tejanos was the status of Texas in the new republic. Would it remain an independent state, unite with the province of Coahuila, or become a federal territory? In January 1824, the Mexican Congress created the "Interior State of the East," composed of Coahuila, Texas, and Nuevo León. The Texas provincial deputation responded with a statement explaining its desire for Texas to be an independent state and rejecting union with Coahuila except under certain conditions.[19] Texas's case for statehood was weakened by the fact that it had a modest population compared to that of Coahuila. In the first census of the new republic, there were 4,824 residents of Texas, compared with 66,131 in Coahuila.[20]

On May 7, 1824, Nuevo León was granted independent statehood and Texas was joined to Coahuila. Texas thus became the only former province that did not retain its status, and Texans found themselves in a new political context as an extreme minority. The Tejanos were shocked, and the provincial deputation attempted nullification by decree. Mexico's secretary of state sent a stern reply insisting that Texas comply with the law and elect a deputy to the new state legislature. The delay caused by the nullification standoff resulted in several unfavorable actions by the new legislature of the state of Coahuila y Texas. Without any Tejano representatives present, it stripped Texas of political autonomy by abolishing the office of *jefe político* (political chief) in Texas, dismissing the Texas provincial deputation and transferring its archives to Saltillo, reducing the size of the ayuntamiento of Béxar, and calling for the election of a new congressional deputy for Texas.[21]

The Texas provincial deputation stood its ground, suspending action on that decree until Congress acted on its renewed request for statehood. The ayuntamiento of Béxar was not as willing to maintain the nullification standoff, as it favored unification with Coahuila. The standoff ended the next day when the members of the provincial deputation conceded, in order to "to conserve the peace and public tranquility." The nullification crisis was over. Politically, the new state of Coahuila y Texas was divided at the Medina River into the Department of Texas and the Department of Coahuila, but Tejanos understood that having similar titles did not mean that it was a union of equals.[22]

The private letters of Erasmo Seguín reveal that he and Ruiz favored unification with Coahuila. Seguín wrote plainly, "I have been in favor of the union of these two provinces." Seguín believed that if Texas had pursued its challenge for statehood, Congress would have made it a federal territory due to its extremely low population. Under that scenario, its public lands would have become the property of the national government. Seguín, Ruiz, and others believed that colonization was essential to bring about frontier security and prosperity. Under unified statehood with Coahuila, the vast unallocated lands of Texas would remain in the control of the state, and Tejanos could maintain greater influence over land policy. Seguín in fact did not oppose the dismissal of the Texas provincial deputation because they were "men of little enlightenment" and were in his view not nearly as wise as the men of the Navarro and Ruiz families or the members of the ayuntamiento of Béxar.[23]

The unequal union of Texas with Coahuila did result in the emergence of a new Tejano political identity that was politically liberal and sought economic growth through colonization. The Tejano desire for eventual independence from Coahuila and statehood fueled their support for American and European settlement. This aspiration diverged from the rest of the Mexican nation and resulted in the development of a more protective attitude towards Anglo American settlers, which eventually alienated Tejano leaders from the authorities in Mexico City.[24]

Ruiz remained a leader of the frontier federalists, among whom were José Antonio Navarro, Erasmo Seguín, and Juan Martín de Veramendi. They allied themselves politically with other liberals in state government such as José María Viesca, his brother Victor Viesca, and Victor Blanco. Nationally, they supported liberal heroes such as Lorenzo de Zavala, Guadalupe Victoria, and Vicente Guerrero.[25] The Tejanos elected the Baron de Bastrop to represent Texas in the state legislature, and he became an effective advocate for colonization.

While Mexico and Texas struggled with the issues of establishing a republic in the wake of the collapse of the short-lived imperial experiment, Ruiz prepared for his duties as an Indian agent in Béxar. On January 6, 1823, while still in Mexico City, he received a promotion to the rank of "Capitán, unassigned, with the rank of Lieutenant Colonel," which meant that he actually served at the rank of captain, but held the honorary rank of lieutenant colonel due to his prior service at that rank.[26] This entitled him to the title, salary, and retirement pay of a lieutenant colonel, which was not unusual for the period. After the Wars for Mexican Independence, the army was greatly reduced, requiring many officers to serve at lower ranks.

Ruiz was designated as "unassigned" because he did not have a specific post or command within the army due to his special assignment as Indian negotiator and Comanche agent. Upon his arrival in Béxar, Ruiz received confirmation from the governor, José Félix Trespalacios, of his appointment as agent to the Comanches with a budget of one thousand pesos per year backdated to April 4, 1821.[27] This was a large sum, considering the tax revenue for Béxar that year was just 161 pesos and municipal expenditures were 136 pesos.[28]

Ruiz resumed his duties as agent to the Comanches after the arrival of interim governor Luciano García. On August 10, 1823, Ruiz wrote to García from Arroyo de las Vacas about the impending arrival of Comanche leader Paruakevitsi, who was traveling to Béxar on his way to "corral mesteños and search for Lipan."[29] Ruiz asked García to treat Paruakevitsi well for the sake of the province.[30] Ruiz also repeatedly petitioned for the provisions required under the Comanche treaty of 1823. On February 26, 1824, one such request reached Mexico City, but the turbulent transition of government prevented its consideration.[31] On June 1, he received word that the new congress had nullified his treaty because the imperial government had authorized it.[32] Ruiz understood that much of the value of the treaty lay in the protection it provided for Béxar, and he was reappointed Indian agent by the new government in October 1824.[33] He made a final appeal for support to the ayuntamiento of Béxar on November 27, but they lacked the resources to act upon it, and Comanche raids once again became a constant threat.[34]

The ayuntamiento of Béxar understood well what Ruiz had tried to do for them. In what may have been a gesture of gratitude, Alcalde Juan Martín de Veramendi recommended him for an award of valor for his sacrifices during the War for Mexican Independence.[35] The recommendation was approved in March 1825 and was noted in Ruiz's military record.[36] The feelings of gratitude expressed by civil authorities at Béxar, among whom of course were his political allies and members of his extended family, were not shared by all of Ruiz's military compatriots. Some of them had suffered greatly as a result of his arms smuggling. Ruiz's commanders limited his activities, and the tension was notable. His many petitions for military promotion and assignment went unanswered for several years.

Ruiz's work as Indian agent was also complicated by changing Indian policy in the United States, which contributed to increasingly complex conditions in Texas. In the 1820s and 1830s, the Indian removal policies of the United States led to escalating violence among tribes on the Texas border. In the late 1820s, President Andrew Jackson dramatically changed federal policy. The United States convinced some Indians and coerced others to accept land west of the Mississippi in exchange for their ancestral lands in the east. This led to the Indian Removal Act of 1830, which targeted Chickasaws, Choctaws, Creeks, Seminoles, and Cherokees, all of whom posed legal and physical barriers to further white settlement in the American South. In the Ohio River Valley, groups such as the Kickapoos, Shawnees, Pawnees, and Delawares were pushed westward following their military losses in the War of 1812. Many reached the Red River and crossed into Texas.[37]

Collectively, these immigrant Indians had a clear impact on Texas, and Ruiz sometimes found himself at the center of the turmoil. For Mexican officials, the arrival of "civilized" Indians seemed to provide new allies in their ongoing conflicts with Comanches, Lipan Apaches, and Wichitas. The newcomers in turn sought recognition and land grants to settle in Texas and permanently rid themselves of the white settlers. Cherokees under Chief Bowles crossed the Red River into Texas in 1820 and sought a land grant from the imperial Mexican government through their agent Richard Fields in 1823.[38] In October 1824, a band of Shawnees comprising two hundred and seventy families, or nearly two thousand people, petitioned the newly formed state of Coahuila y Texas for a grant of land on which to settle. The state government asked Ruiz to provide an opinion, so he visited the Shawnee settlement to investigate. During this expedition, Ruiz visited a Comanche war council that numbered 2,300 tents.[39] They were planning a campaign against their longtime foes, the Osages, who lived north of the Red River and were at war with the Cherokees. Seeing the advantage of the Shawnees as a buffer, Ruiz recommended granting them land, which was approved. The Shawnees subsequently settled in Texas on the Red River, although their grant was never confirmed.[40] As the Shawnees, Cherokees, and others were to discover, the confused state of land settlement in eastern Texas meant that lands requested had often been already claimed or promised to others, including settlers from the United States.

Part of the problem was that Ruiz was among only a very small number of people able to see past cultural barriers and envision a Texas shared by both Indians and the descendants of Europeans. By 1823, Stephen F. Austin and other American empresarios began lobbying against such grants due to the transplanted tension that existed between the settlers from the American South and the immigrant Indians. Anglo Texans came to fear the intentions and alliances made by the immigrant Indian tribes, due to their previous encounters with them in the United States.[41]

Austin was already familiar with Spanish culture and colonization in the region when he became involved in the province's development. His father, Moses Austin, had been a Spanish subject in Upper Louisiana during the last years of Spanish rule and established a mining settlement in modern-day Missouri. When this and other financial ventures failed, Moses sought a new opportunity in Spanish Texas in 1820. His intent was to be the empresario of a frontier settlement that traded with the United States. In Béxar, he negotiated for a location that was three-days' sailing distance from New Orleans on the lower Colorado River. Despite orders to not allow American immigration, Commandant Joaquín de Arredondo approved the colony and gave Moses Austin permission to settle three hundred families.[42]

Stephen F. Austin was in New Orleans, pursuing a legal career, when he received word in 1821 that his father, Moses, was ailing and required his assistance to complete the Texas project. Stephen traveled to Natchitoches, where with the help of Erasmo Seguín and Juan Martín de Veramendi, he gathered supplies and departed for Béxar.[43] José Francisco Ruiz was also in Natchitoches at that time preparing for his Comanche expedition, so he almost certainly visited with Seguín, Veramendi, and Austin. Thus, from his earliest days in Texas, Austin and the Ruiz-Navarro-Veramendi family were intertwined in the development of Texas.[44]

Following the issuance of Austin's contract, the Mexican government formalized the process of colonization contracts with the National Colonization Law of 1824, which transferred control of both immigration policies and the public domain to the states. The American immigration policy thus shifted to the legislature of Coahuila y Texas. There the Baron de Bastrop served on the important Colonization Committee.[45]

Like the Tejano electors who voted for him, Baron de Bastrop remained a strong proponent of American immigration. A new Tejano political identity emerged within this context that was different from other Mexicans or the Anglo newcomers.[46] Ruiz exemplified the views of the leading families of Béxar when he wrote to Austin in November 1830, "I will continue to proclaim the advantages that in my opinion, will result by admitting hard working and honest people, no matter what nation they are

from . . . even hell itself."[47] The Tejano desire for eventual independence
from Coahuila and statehood fueled their support for American and European
settlements. These aspirations diverged from the rest of the Mexican
nation and resulted in the development of a more protective attitude
towards Anglo American settlers that eventually alienated Tejano leaders
from the authorities in Mexico City.

Tejanos came to accept Austin's belief that the establishment of a cotton
industry in Texas was the surest way to bring prosperity to the region.
The slight rolling hills and coastal plains of Central and East Texas were
ideal for the cultivation of cotton. Abundant rivers and natural ports rendered
transportation of the heavy bales by ship relatively easy. But cultivating
cotton in large quantities for market required lots of labor, and immigrants
from the southern United States brought slaves to meet that need.
The political agenda of Tejano leaders thus shifted to support what they
realized were the two necessities for cotton cultivation: land grants and
slavery. Guaranteeing the continuation of slavery in Texas required intricate
legal maneuvering around federal and state prohibitions.[48] Congress
on July 13, 1824, abolished the slave trade and in effect made all persons in
Mexico free.[49] Article 13 of the state constitution stated that no one could
be born a slave in Coahuila y Texas.[50] The Baron de Bastrop led efforts
to weaken the prohibition against slavery in the state colonization law to
allow for the import of slaves from the United States.[51] He was initially
successful, but the battle continued.

In 1827, the first legislature of Coahuila y Texas met under their new
state constitution, and from the beginning the Texas delegates were on the
defensive. The two representatives from Texas were José Miguel Arciniega
and José Antonio Navarro, who had to keep in mind the interests of the
new settlers from the United States.[52] They entered the legislative session
in Saltillo knowing there was strong opposition to slavery within both the
liberal and conservative factions. A bill was immediately filed to end the
slave trade. It eventually passed as Decree No. 18, which required owners
to enumerate and educate their slaves and declared the end of slave trading
within six months after its passage. Navarro countered with a proposal
legalizing indentured servitude. His fellow legislators were familiar with
service contracts for peons and saw no threat in the bill, which passed with
little notice during a period of intense debate over another bill, one filed
by conservatives to centralize the power of the governor. Navarro thus

stealthily provided legal sanction for Anglo Americans to bring slaves into Texas under lifetime servitude contracts.[53]

Although Ruiz does not appear to have ever owned or trafficked in slaves, he appears to have supported the continuation of the institution, which had remained legal in the years immediately following independence. At his death, José Francisco held Anselmo Prú under a peonage contract (*peón sirviente*), so he must also have been comfortable with Navarro's solution to the elimination of overt slavery under Coahuila y Texas law.[54] Several members of his family and close associates did own slaves: Ángel Navarro, his brother-in-law with whom he lived after his father died, had three slaves in 1795 and still owned at least one female slave in 1804; and, Angel's son José Antonio, Ruiz's nephew and political ally, eventually owned as many as seven.[55] Ruiz's co-conspirator in 1811, Juan Manuel Zambrano, had two slaves and thirty-two servants in the census that same year.[56]

Further indication of Ruiz's attitude toward slavery is seen in his opposition to the article in the state constitution for Coahuila y Texas that provided for the eventual abolition of slavery, an issue on which he wrote to Austin expressing his concern. When he had the opportunity to assist in the emancipation of a slave, he declined. On September 13, 1831, a runaway slave presented himself to Ruiz at Tenoxtitlán, claiming to have fled from the United States. Rather than free him as prescribed under Mexican law, Ruiz returned him in chains to San Felipe de Austin, where he believed the true owner resided.[57] In sum, Ruiz not only did not oppose slavery, he surely regarded Navarro's efforts to block abolition as good for the future of Texas.

A system of generous land grants and legal protections was the other political goal of the Tejanos in the state legislature. Ruiz would eventually profit greatly from its passage. The legislators authorized a grant of one league and a labor for military service or settlement on the frontier and a system of *denuncios* whereby settlers could stake a claim to land and then force the government to sell it to them. The latter was similar to several preemption bills passed by the United States Congress before the Homestead Act was approved in 1862. A homestead law provided protection against creditors seizing land for payment of debts. This legislation was of great interest to American colonists, many of whom left the United States to escape debt. Its origins lay with the Catholic Monarchs, Ferdinand and

Isabella of Spain, who decreed that a man's tools and work animals could not be seized for payment of debt. In Coahuila y Texas, this was expanded to include land.[58]

While the arguments over slavery and land in the legislature would have a great impact on Ruiz's future, he did not participate directly in the debate. Instead, after the cancellation of the Comanche treaty, Ruiz attended to his military career and his law practice.[59] In November 1825 he was ordered to travel to Soto la Marina, in the state of Tamaulipas, and return with money to pay the Texas troops.[60] This was an important, dangerous and laborious task. He left Béxar in November with Sergeant José María Sánchez, Corporal Tomás Mungia, and two unnamed soldiers.[61] He arrived at San Carlos, Tamaulipas, on December 1 after being delayed by high water.[62] At this time, Comanches were raiding both Tamaulipas and Coahuila. Colonel Mateo Ahumada wrote to Bernardo Gutiérrez de Lara at San Carlos and requested that he raise thirty men to escort Ruiz.[63] The rains persisted, as did the Comanche raids, and Ruiz finally returned to Béxar, apparently without getting an escort or reaching Soto la Marina.[64]

On February 9, 1826, Ahumada again ordered Ruiz and Francisco Roxo, captain of the Presidio Company at Béxar, to return to Soto la Marina to receive money for the Texas troops, and to appear in Laredo by March 1.[65] Ruiz transferred the court cases under his care and prepared to leave once again for Soto la Marina.[66] Legal matters delayed his departure while the rest of the company left ahead of him.[67] Ruiz arrived on the Frio River on March 25 while Roxo waited for him at Revilla, Tamaulipas.[68] Ruiz eventually arrived in Soto la Marina on April 16, and collected 46,300 pesos, a very large sum. He requested an escort of thirty men from Bernardo Gutiérrez de Lara due to new reports of Comanches raiding at Tampico and on the Río Grande.[69] Historian James C. Milligan noted that this time the commander at San Carlos provided troops as requested, having been told about "a band of more than a thousand warriors somewhere in the vicinity of San Ambrosio on the Río Grande." Milligan added that "the size of the war parties was probably exaggerated, but not the frequency of their raids."[70] Arriving in San Carlos on April 21, Ruiz was joined by a detachment of soldiers that accompanied him to Laredo and onward to the Nueces River, where Ahumada met the expedition and escorted Ruiz home to Béxar.[71]

Ruiz attended a commissary review in Béxar on May 3, 1826, then returned to private life and resumed his law practice once more.[72] He remained anxious for military promotion, however, and a meaningful assignment. He wrote letters to many of his superiors, ultimately writing to President Guadalupe Victoria personally requesting a military promotion and assignment.[73] While he was certainly glad to be home from exile with his family, pardoned and reinstated in the economic and social hierarchy with which he was familiar, he wanted more.

Texas Historical Commission historical marker commemorating the life of José Francisco Ruiz. Photograph by Art Martínez de Vara.

Signature of José Francisco Ruiz. UTSA Special Collections, General Photograph Collection, 068-0500, https://digital.utsa.edu/digital/collection/p9020coll008/id/5500/rec/50 [Accessed March 11, 2020].

The Ruiz home with hay wagons in front, c. 1883. UTSA Special Collections, General Photograph Collection, 079-0107, Hay wagons on Military Plaza, San Antonio, Texas, 1883, https://digital.utsa.edu/digital/collection/p9020coll008/id/1615/rec/162 [Accessed March 11, 2020].

Francisco Antonio Ruiz, the son of José Francisco Ruiz. UTSA Special Collections, General Photograph Collection, 086-0091, https://digital.utsa.edu/digital/collection/p9020coll008/id/9752 rec/26 [Accessed March 11, 2020].

María Antonia Ruiz de Herrera, the daughter of José Francisco Ruiz. UTSA Special Collections, General Photograph Collection, SC115461.

Blas María Herrera, the son-in-law of José Francisco Ruiz. UTSA Special Collections, General Photograph Collection, 089-0620, Blas Herrera, 1860–1869, https://digital.utsa.edu/digital/collection/p9020coll008/id/3602/rec/8 [Accessed March 11, 2020].

sé Antonio Navarro, phew of José Francisco iz and fellow Texas revolu-nary. The only other native xan signer of the Texas claration of Independence. SA Special Collections, neral Photograph Collec-n, SC96.247.

Stephen F. Austin, friend and confidant of José Francisco Ruiz; fellow Texas revolutionary. UTSA Special Collections, General Photograph Collection, SC95.007.

Grave of Col. José Francisco Ruiz. Photograph by Art Martínez de Vara.

CHAPTER VIII

Redemption

Ruiz knew the Western Indians well, but had been tainted by his
earlier gun-running activities in West Texas. It took the crises of
Fredonia for state officials to finally turn to him.

—Gary Clayton Anderson, 2005[1]

The mid to late 1820s were troubled times in Texas. Among the
major challenges that men like Ruiz and other Tejano leaders
faced was trying to maintain command of conditions in the face
of both uncontrolled immigration of Indians and Anglo Americans on the
one hand and the diminished political power for Texas in its union with
Coahuila in the far-off capital of Saltillo. These circumstances first came
to a head together in the Fredonian Rebellion. The alliance of at least one
group of Anglos with Indians in a rebellion against Mexico shocked frontier officials and their superiors alike. José Francisco Ruiz was among those
who were asked to cope with this unexpected challenge.

The peculiar alliance of Anglos and Indians arose in East Texas. Haden
Edwards, a colonist from the United States, received an empresario contract to settle eight hundred families in the area around Nacogdoches in
April 1825.[2] Tensions quickly rose when Haden and his brother Benjamin demanded legal titles from existing settlers within their grant area or
demanded they pay him a fee to gain title. Demands for the removal of
the so-called squatters resulted in a flood of complaints to authorities in
Béxar.[3] Three factions quickly arose in the area: established Mexicans who
opposed Edwards, Anglos who at first favored Edwards, and Indians who
initially did not take sides.[4]

Austin attempted to mediate, but feared a reaction by Mexican officials that would hinder or prohibit future Anglo American immigration.[5]
On October 2, 1826, Mexican authorities nullified the Edwards grant and

ordered the brothers expelled from Texas, thereby placing the land titles of Anglo newcomers to the Edwards colony in question.⁶ Edwards then declared the independence of the Republic of Fredonia. The rebels' "Committee of Independence" sought an alliance with a group of Cherokees who had settled north of Nacogdoches.⁷ Austin appealed for calm from both the rebels and the Mexican government. He wrote to Béxar jefe político José Antonio Saucedo to explain that Haden Edwards was not a typical American settler and that his actions were rash.⁸ He also wrote to Edwards advising that the Fredonians disband and reaffirm their loyalty to Mexico.⁹ Efforts by the rebels to ally with the Cherokees further alienated Austin and other Anglos. Fredonia had lost its chance for broader support.¹⁰

In Béxar, Saucedo vowed to "make the rebels feel the power of the law."¹¹ He accompanied Lieutenant Colonel Mateo Ahumada with troops to Nacogdoches.¹² José Francisco Ruiz served on the campaign as a captain of infantry. They departed Béxar on December 13, 1826, and on January 2, 1827, reached San Felipe, the capital of the Austin Colony, where they waited due to heavy rains and flooding.¹³ Ruiz and his fellow Mexican troops remained in San Felipe for three weeks. The rains were incessant. Saucedo wrote to his superior requesting assistance, estimating that his enemy numbered two hundred and had nine hundred Indian allies. This report went to Mexico City, where officials authorized the expenditure of 500,000 pesos, the movement of regular army units from Nuevo León, Coahuila, and Tamaulipas to Texas, and a draft of 4,000 militia. Saucedo was ordered to secure Béxar, La Bahía, and San Felipe, then await reinforcements before approaching Nacogdoches. Mexican officials did not want to risk the loss of Texas to a small rebel group. Saucedo wrote to Edwards offering a full pardon if he laid down his arms and quit his "hostile ideas." Peter Ellis Bean, the Indian agent stationed at Nacogdoches, sent a separate letter to Edwards, suggesting that he accept the offer. Saucedo also contacted the Cherokees, warning them against the folly of supporting the rebels and offering them pardons as well. As the rains subsided, the Mexican forces at San Felipe, including Ruiz, set out for Nacogdoches on January 24, 1827. Austin and his mounted militia left a few days later to reinforce the main column. Meanwhile, American settlers, including Fredonians, fled the area. Finally, on January 28, 1827, the rebellion collapsed and the remaining Fredonians fled without ever engaging the Mexican army.¹⁴ Saucedo entered Nacogdoches, and Ahumada arranged a ceremony of loyalty in which Choc-

taws, Creeks, Shawnees, Delawares, and Cherokees participated. Cherokee Chiefs Bowles and Big Mush traveled to Nacogdoches to meet with
Saucedo and promised to live in peace and deliver to Mexican authorities
any rebels found among them. Saucedo and Ahumada worked quickly to
reestablish order. By March 30 they received orders that state officials were
satisfied and that they could return to Béxar. Ruiz was left in Nacogdoches
in command of the Twelfth Permanent Battalion with one hundred and
twenty-nine soldiers and nine officers.[15] Ruiz, along with Austin, were
recommended for awards for their conduct during the campaign.[16]

The Fredonian Rebellion convinced many Mexican officials that the
Anglo and Indian newcomers alike could not be trusted, which made
Ruiz's role in Nacogdoches more complicated. Part of the problem was
that Fredonian activity did not immediately cease. Rumors of their re-
grouping in Louisiana spread wildly.[17] A poster mysteriously appeared in
May 1827 calling on Fredonians to gather at Nacogdoches to discuss land
titles on July 4, prompting Ruiz to request reinforcements.[18] The rumors
proved false, and, although the Fredonians were not heard from again,
suspicions persisted.

The aftereffects of Fredonian Rebellion continued to cause problems
for Ruiz months after its collapse. Cherokees arrived in May and informed
Ruiz that they had killed diplomatic chief Richard Fields, who had tried to
forge an alliance between them and the Fredonians, as a traitor and a rebel.
They appealed to Ruiz for the welfare of Field's widow and her seven
children, fearing that the dead man's creditors would take his property and
leave them destitute.[19] Ruiz agreed to suspend debt collections temporarily
and forwarded the request to his superiors in Béxar.[20]

Ruiz's involvement in Cherokee affairs infuriated Peter Ellis Bean,
who regarded himself as the only valid Indian agent in the area. This may
have troubled Ruiz on two levels. First, Bean had strong connections to
President Guadalupe Victoria, with whom he had served in the independence movement led by José María Morelos. Victoria had given him the
rank of colonel and arranged for his empresario grant and original assignment to Nacogdoches as an Indian agent. Second, Bean and Ruiz were old
allies, having met when Bean first came to the Neutral Ground in 1813 to
try to convince Ruiz and other exiles to attack again in Texas. This alliance
had strengthened when the two worked together to smuggle arms to the
Comanches as part of a proxy war against the Spanish. Bean's assertion
that his authority superseded Ruiz's prompted a flurry of letters request-

ing clarification from President Victoria. The president declared that they should use Bean in any capacity for which he was deemed fit. By the time this response reached Texas, Ruiz had left Nacogdoches on another Indian-related government errand and the issue was moot.[21] But this would not be the last time Ruiz would run afoul of Bean.

After the Fredonian Rebellion, the Cherokees requested Mexican support for a campaign against the Comanches and their allies, with the goal of allowing the Cherokees to settle on the Trinity River. On April 7, 1827, Commandant General Anastacio Bustamante ordered Lieutenant Colonel Ahumada at Béxar to prepare for a joint operation against the Comanche alliance. Alluding to the Comanches' warlike disposition, Bustamante noted in his instructions, "it is thus necessary to fight them in their own villages with an energy equivalent to the perfidy and cruelty of their outrages." The general also thought it wise to conduct the campaign after the friendly tribes had worked their fields.[22] The delay allowed Ruiz to demonstrate again his abilities as a peace negotiator.

When reports of Bustamante's plans spread among the Indians, several tribes determined to make peace. Ruiz spearheaded that effort. As early as February 1827, he had sent letters to Tawakoni and Waco leaders, inviting them to come to Nacogdoches to make a peace treaty.[23] Rather than await a response, Colonel Ahumada proposed the formation of a junta composed of himself, Ruiz, and Benjamin R. Milam to handle Indian affairs and seek peace treaties with friendly tribes.[24] Leaving Captain Mariano Cosío in charge of the troops in Nacogdoches during his absence, Ruiz, with Bean, left on April 14, 1827, for a Kichai village on the Trinity River near present-day Palestine.[25] Their purpose was to prevent a war with the Wacos and Tawakonis. The latter sent two headmen to the Kichai village to meet Ruiz and tell him that neither the Tawakonis nor the Wacos had been involved with the raids on Austin's colony and that they were willing to make peace with Mexico.[26] Recalling the meeting in a letter to Austin, Ruiz wrote the following:

I had an interview in the Quicha [Kichai] Village with two Tahuacano [Tawakoni] Indians whom I found there. These assured me that both the Hueco [Waco] Village and the Quicha Tahuacano Village were in the best possible humor and anxious to make peace with our government. The same Indians told me that it had been a long time since they went down to make war on the new [American] colonies, and that the

Chiefs of the said villages had agreed not to cause any more harm, in order that they might be admitted to the peace which they desire . . . I send them to their villages with the object of telling their Chiefs that they could come without any fear whatsoever to present themselves in peace, and so that we might confirm to them what Mr. Ahumada, you, and I had already said in letters which we sent by the first envoy.[27]

Ruiz returned to Nacogdoches with more than forty Wichitas who wanted to go with him to Béxar to sign an official peace treaty.[28]

Ruiz's success produced an abrupt about-face from the government. Having received orders from Ahumada to return to Béxar from Nacogdoches to attend meetings designed to plan a campaign against the Comanches and their allies, Ruiz had been preparing to leave as soon as Milam returned from his own visit with the Indians.[29] Upon learning of Ruiz's success with the Wichitas, however, Ahumada ordered Ruiz to remain in Nacogdoches to finish his peace efforts.[30]

On June 2, Ruiz wrote to Austin that Menchaca, a Waco leader, and a large number of Wacos and Tawakonis had appeared in Nacogdoches to make peace:

Just yesterday the Chiefs of the Tahuacanos and Huecos presented themselves to me, with a number of braves and squaws. They have offered to make a true peace with our government, and that they will never again go on the warpath anywhere, especially in that colony of yours, along the Colorado, etc. You may communicate such pleasant news to all of your friends, with the understanding that, in order to consolidate it more, they will pass on to Béjar as soon as they return from here, to present themselves to the Most Excellent Commandant General . . . The same Indians have told me that the Comanches are in a mood to do the same, and that they want me to give them information, or so they can talk about peace, which has encouraged me all the more to go without orders, as I have said, but I am confident that they will approve this measure for me, in view of the interest and desires which the Most Excellent Commandant General has for tranquility.[31]

Unfortunately for Ruiz and his plans for future negotiations, Austin did not mention Bean, who was becoming increasingly jealous of his colleague after his exclusion from General Bustamante's junta on Indian Affairs.[32] Bean believed his appointment as the Indian agent in Nacogdoches required his inclusion in all negotiations concerning the region. As a full colonel, he also outranked Ruiz, a lieutenant colonel. Bean sent his own letter to Austin claiming all credit for successful negotiations with the Wacos and Tawakonis. He failed to mention Ruiz or the Wichitas' unwillingness to march with him alone:

> Dear Sir, I am happy to inform you that yesterday I have maid Pease with the Waco Nesion and tawacanys also the chiefs of Both nasions is now in this Plase you can treat them as friends and can let your uper setelment now it tomorrow I shall start with them to meet the Comanches and gow with them to Sn. Antonio to Settel all in this thare is nothing worth your notis to Right you all is quiot.[33]

Ruiz, clearly irritated by Bean's brashness, attempted to blunt his efforts to take sole credit. He wrote to Ahumada the following day in an uncharacteristically self-promoting tone, noting that the Indians had asked that he ride with them to meet the Comanches because "of the knowledge, esteem, and influence that no one else has in said Nations," except, of course, Ruiz. He strongly opposed the suggestion by Ahumada that Bean ride along, adding, "neither these tribes nor the Comanches [have] knowledge of Bean."[34]

Confident in his ability to produce good results, in June 1827 Ruiz left Nacogdoches and returned to the Wichita villages on the Brazos and Trinity, which were fortified with palisades to protect them from Austin's militia, which had set off a wave of far-reaching reprisals when it tried to remove the Wichitas from the Austin's colony land grant in the summer of 1826.[35] The Wichita leaders trusted Ruiz, whom they had known for many years, and welcomed him into the village. He persuaded nine of their leaders to travel to Béxar to sign a peace treaty. When Ruiz and the Wichitas arrived in Béxar they found representatives of three Comanche bands, who were allied with the Wichitas against Austin's militia, had also come to make peace. While Ruiz had been on his mission to the Wichitas, Captain Nicasio Sánchez had defeated a band of Tenewah Comanches in a battle on the Agua Fria River in Coahuila. The remaining leaders of this band, Incoroy, Quellunes, and Quellucare, learning of Bustamante's plans for a war of extermination, had come to Béxar to agree on a "suspension of arms" until their leader, Paruakevitsi, returned from his campaign against the Osages.[36]

At Béxar in the summer of 1827, Ruiz, along with Bean, Bustamante, Ahumada, and Saucedo, met with Caddos, Wichitas, Wacos, Tawakonis, and minor Comanche leaders. Bustamante gave beads and tobacco to the Tawakonis and Wacos, then afterwards they signed a treaty.[37] Those who signed included José María for the western Caddos, Menchaca for the Waco Wichitas, Cíbolo Tonto for the Tawakoni Wichitas, and Quellunes and Incoroy for the Tenewah Comanches.[38] Notably missing were nearly all of the major Comanche bands and the Taovayas (Red River Wichitas), who were away fighting the Osages.[39]

State officials of Coahuila y Texas drafted the treaty, but Ruiz's influence on the treaty can be seen in certain terms used in the text. The treaty required Indians to have passports to visit Mexican towns, as would Mexicans or Anglos wishing to trade with the Indians.[40] The Wichitas promised to "be responsible for robberies . . . castigating the evildoers and delivering up the robbed material," but the terms failed to mention the northward expansion of Anglos along the Brazos or the conduct of Austin's militia. The treaty used the ethnonym "Tanemues," which is a term attributed solely to Ruiz and used to describe the eastern Comanches along the Red River and in North Central Texas with whom he had traded and lived during exile. All other known uses of this term in the historical record were by Ruiz or could be traced to him as a source.[41]

The Comanche problem was exacerbated by the diffuse nature of Comanche political organization. Paruakevitsi of the Tenewahs finally arrived in Béxar in August 1827. He was the most prominent Comanche in Mexican Texas at the time and all other Comanche leaders in Texas deferred to his authority.[42] The main point of concern remained the "suspension of arms" agreement of the minor leaders, which was honored only by the Comanche bands near Béxar. Raiding had not ceased on the upper Rio Grande, around El Paso, or in New Mexico. Western Comanches, referred to by Ruiz and others as Yamparikas, conducted these hostilities and had not signed the recent treaty.[43] Ruiz understood that peace with the Comanches required painstaking efforts with each branch of the greater Comanche nation.

Ruiz traveled to New Mexico with Paruakevitsi to negotiate with the Kotsotekas (literally "Buffalo-Eaters").[44] These Indians were an indepen-

dent band of Comanches that had separated from the Yamparikas in the
1750s. They lived on the Llano Estacado, south of the Cimmaron River
Valley in modern-day northeastern New Mexico and the Texas Panhandle.
Along with the commandant general of New Mexico, Juan José Arocha,
Ruiz met with six hundred Kotsotekas on the Gallinas River near San
Miguel to negotiate an agreement to stop their raids around El Paso and
San Elizondo.[45] After listening to a translation of a treaty signed in Chi-
huahua in 1826, the Kotsotekas agreed to the terms of peace and friendship,
and even promised not to let other Comanches raid the same settlements.
Arocha, to confirm the arrangement, presented a small assortment of gifts,
including a medal and silver-headed cane to the Kotsoteka leader.[46]

Ruiz's success was apparent in the optimistic tone adopted by both
Comanches and Mexicans. Upon their return to Béxar in October 1827,
Paruakevitsi declared that he had "examined the intentions of the different
tribes of his nation" and determined that all wanted peace.[47]

Following the signing of the Peace Treaty of 1827, Tenewah warriors
began working as scouts for Mexican authorities, primarily chasing Waco
and Tawakoni horse thieves. Both of these Indian groups broke the treaty
and resumed their attacks within a year, likely to Ruiz's considerable frustration. In the winter of 1828, a mixed group of Wacos and Tawakonis attacked a Mexican resident of the Austin's colony on the Colorado River. A
few months later, they raided around Béxar and La Bahía, stealing horses
and mules. Paruakevitsi recovered thirty of these animals from the Wacos
and returned them to the Bexareños, an action repeated numerous times
over the following years.[48]

Unfortunately for the prospect of lasting peace, Ruiz's bond with Paruakevitsi was the only thing that held the treaty between Comanches
and Mexicans together. When Paruakevitsi was killed in 1831 while among
the Tawakonis, the treaty regime broke down. Ruiz's personal bond with
Paruakevitsi and the Tenewahs in general was central to the effort to facilitate peace and maintain a tenuous alliance between the Mexicans and
Comanches. With the powerful Comanche leader gone, Ruiz's influence
waned.[49]

Between chasing rebels in Nacogdoches and signing treaties with Indians all over Texas, Ruiz served in another official capacity in Béxar. He was
assigned to dispose of the remaining property of the old Spanish missions
at auction.[50] When the Tejanos at Béxar elected Refugio de la Garza to
the first Constitutional Congress in 1822, they sent him with instructions

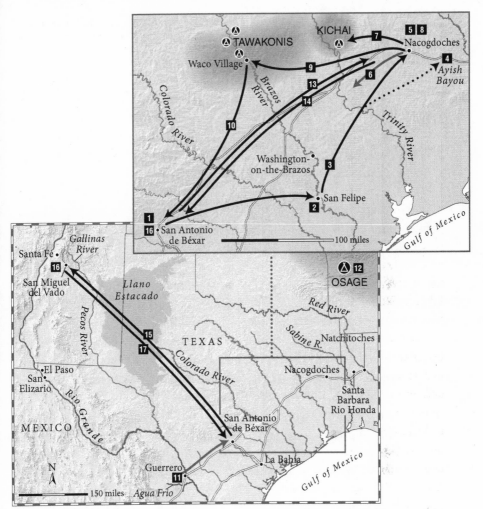

1 **Dec. 13, 1826** Ruiz departs San Antonio de Béxar as captain of infantry under command of Lt. Col. Ahumada and Gov. Saucedo.

2 **Jan. 2, 1827** Ruiz reaches San Felipe.

3 **Jan. 24, 1827** Ruiz sets out for Nacogdoches.

4 **Jan. 26, 1827** Ruiz's company searches up Ayish Bayou.

5 **Jan. 31, 1827** Ruiz arrives at Nacogdoches, attends peace meeting with Choctaws, Creeks, Shawnees, Delawares, and Cherokees.

6 **March 30, 1827** Mexican Army departs, leaving Ruiz in command at Nacogdoches.

7 **April 14, 1827** Ruiz leaves Nacogdoches for Kichai village on Trinity River.

8 **June 2, 1827** Ruiz meets with Wacos and Tawakonis at Nacogdoches.

9 **June 1827** Ruiz leaves Nacogdoches and returns to Wichita villages on Brazos and Trinity.

10 **June 1827** Ruiz travels to San Antonio de Béxar with Wichita to sign peace treaty.

11 **Summer 1827** Tenwah Comanche defeated. Surviving leaders, Incoroy, Quellunes, and Quellucare travel to San Antonio de Béxar to meet with Ruiz.

12 **Summer 1827** Paruakevitsi warring with Osage, absent from peace talks.

13 **June 1827** Ruiz returns to Nacogdoches, where he meets with Caddo, Waco Wichita, and minor Comanche.

14 **Aug. 8, 1827** Ruiz travels to San Antonio de Béxar. Paruakevitsi of Tenewahs signs peace treaty.

15 **August 1827** Ruiz travels to New Mexico to meet with Kotsotekas Comanche.

16 **August 1827** Ruiz and commandant general of New Mexico, Juan José Arocha, meet with 600 Kotsotekas on Gallinas River to negotiate agreement to stop raids around El Paso and San Elizario.

17 **October 1827** Ruiz returns to San Antonio de Béxar.

Carol Zuber-Mallison / ZMGraphics.com

Ruiz and Indian affairs, 1826–27.

to support the sale of mission lands. The process of secularization had begun in 1793, but it had proceeded slowly. Closure was finally achieved by passage of the Secularization Decree of 1824, which ordered inventories of the missions followed by the disposal of their fixtures, buildings, and land. A land rush ensued. The most desirable properties at Béxar were those of Missions Concepción and San José. Both were close to town, but San José was particularly appealing due to the spaciousness of its buildings. Applications were filed with the jefe político of Béxar, who assessed the merit of each request and, with the approval of the ayuntamiento, approved land grants. Along with written deeds, a ceremony made the transfer of ownership official.[51]

The Ruiz-Veramendi-Navarro family was well positioned to receive a land grant due to their support for Mexican independence, their resources, and their political ties. In 1824, José Antonio Navarro and Juan Martín de Veramendi petitioned the jefe político, José Antonio Saucedo, for water rights and land from Mission San José for themselves and on behalf of José Francisco Ruiz, then in Nacogdoches. All three men got grants; Ruiz received two *dulas* of water[52] and two corresponding lots of one hundred varas each bordered on the west by the river, on the north by the lands of Ignacio Lara, on the east by the San José Acequia Madre, and on the south by the still public land. Ruiz later purchased at auction "one stone room with thirteen varas in length; one stone room with 6 ¼ varas, and one mural wall of 14 ½ varas in length located on the northern section of the Mission . . . it was bounded on the west by the house of Antonio Huizar, previously known as 'El Troje.'" For these rooms within the San José Mission compound, Ruiz paid 236 pesos through a lien.[53]

Ruiz oversaw the final auctions of mission property in Béxar, which focused on San Antonio de Valero, better known as the Alamo. The process began on July 16, 1827, when Saucedo received instructions from the legislature at Saltillo to sell any real property at Valero that might help pay for the improvements to the town's military facilities, since the legislature lacked the means to pay for them.[54] Ruiz conducted the auction and sought reimbursement for the expenses he paid, which amounted to 328 pesos.[55] He also may have bought a few items. The Ruiz family ranch in southwest Bexar County housed a set of mission gates, now known as the Herrera Gates, that the family referred to as the "gates to the Alamo."[56] The gates quite possibly became the property of the Herrera family during the 1827 auction of the Alamo's lands and fixtures conducted by Ruiz.

A few months after the auction, Ruiz's daughter, María Antonia, married Blas María Herrera and moved to the Ruiz family ranch.

Having survived a busy year in which he finally shed the stigma of gun smuggler through good service as a military officer and diplomat to the Indians, Ruiz must have been satisfied with his political redemption. He had already re-established the family business and resumed his active social calendar before 1827, but that year proved to be when he redeemed himself as a useful military and political leader, despite the grumbles of former friends such as Bean. Ruiz's experience with Indians was of great value to Mexican officials struggling to keep the peace on the far northern frontier, and he took the opportunity to reassert himself as a key figure in negotiations. Having done that, Ruiz would find himself repeatedly called to serve in leadership roles as Mexico continued to struggle with administering its borderlands, although he would ultimately join those who became part of the problem for Mexico rather than the solution.

CHAPTER IX

Boundary Commission

[Ruiz's] descriptions have an authority unsurpassed by any other historical writer.

—Thomas W. Kavanagh, 1999[1]

In 1827, Mexican President Guadalupe Victoria ordered the formation of a boundary commission to survey the border between the United States and Mexico that had been defined in the Adams–Onís Treaty of 1819.[2] Since that time, no survey had been conducted to establish its key points.[3] Other pressing issues in Texas quickly expanded the objectives of the boundary commission. The arrival of Anglo Americans and immigrant Indians from the United States alarmed Mexican officials, mainly because they knew so little about them. Would they be a hostile disrupting force or a stabilizing force for settlement? How many of the immigrants had entered legally? Were the empresarios conforming to their contracts by bringing respectable loyal citizens who promised to learn Spanish and practice the Catholic faith? Were Catholic immigrants from Europe preferable to Protestant immigrants from the United States? Lastly, the natural resources of Texas were unknown, including its agricultural, mining, and commercial potential. The boundary commission was asked to investigate all of these issues and report its findings.[4]

General Manuel de Mier y Terán, an engineer in charge of Mexico's artillery school, was assigned to lead the boundary commission. Accompanying him were two lieutenant colonels, José Batres and Constantino Tarnava, who recorded geographic and military observations. José María Sánchez y Tapia, a sub-lieutenant of the artillery corps, was the commission's draftsman. Rafael Chovell, a student at the College of Mines, was the mineralogist. Jean Louis Berlandier, a native of France, served as the botanist and zoologist.[5] José Francisco Ruiz's knowledge of the Indians of

Texas became a valuable resource for the commission. His contributions formed the basis of both the official report submitted by the commission and several works published by Berlandier.[6]

The expedition departed Mexico City on November 10, 1827, and arrived at Laredo on February 1, 1828. There its members remained for three weeks as the guests of General Anastasio Bustamante, comandante general of the Eastern Interior Provinces, and learned firsthand about the military expedition against the Fredonian rebels and the Indian diplomacy that followed. Their journey to Béxar from Laredo took eleven days. The expedition reached Béxar on March 1, 1828. Mier y Terán remained there for six weeks, where he met with the new military commander for Texas, Colonel Antonio Elosúa, who replaced Colonel Mateo Ahumada.[7]

At Béxar, Ruiz joined the boundary commission as an interpreter, guide, and expert on Indians. During the preparations, Mier y Terán instructed Ruiz to prepare a report on the Indians of Texas, and letters written by Mier y Terán at this time employ data and statistics identical to that found in Ruiz's later writings, indicating that the general relied heavily on Ruiz's report in his own correspondence.[8] After the commission left Béxar on April 13, 1828, several members fell ill with fever and suffered greatly until they reached the Trinity River on May 25. Mier y Terán decided to proceed only with Sánchez and Ruiz to Nacogdoches and sent the others back to Béxar to recover.[9]

To inspect the border the expedition next visited Nacogdoches, which they reached on June 3 and where Mier y Terán examined the Anglo colonies and met with the immigrant Indians. While there, Ruiz and Peter Ellis Bean sent messages to the Cherokees, Shawnees, Kickapoos, and Delawares to meet them at Nacogdoches. Following meetings with various groups, Mier y Terán was more impressed with the Indians than with the American settlers, suggesting in his official report that granting land to the Native peoples would be a positive check against Anglo domination of the area. As Mier y Terán prepared to return to Mexico City he met, in an elaborate ceremony, with leaders of the Cherokees, Shawnees, Delawares, Kickapoos, Alabamas, Coushattas, and Caddos, all of whom pledged allegiance to Mexico. He presented a baton, medal, and pipe to Big Mush of the Cherokees to symbolize his ascendency as spokesperson for the immigrant Indians. When he returned to Mexico City, he filed a report in which he called for the containment of Anglo American immigration, which threatened to swamp the frontier and lead to the loss of

Texas. His recommendations would be at the heart of the Law of April 6, 1830, which precipitated the long slide toward the separation of Texas from the Mexican nation.[10]

Ruiz had a very different opinion on the situation along the border, as he detailed in a letter to Stephen F. Austin in July 1829:

> As for the emigration of the barbarians from the North, I have said a great deal, and to the government itself, or, to be more specific, to the Commandant General of these States [General Bustamante]. On repeated occasions I have expressed my opinion to him, which is: namely, that, if not very soon, then someday so many tribes are going to be harmful to us, and all the more so if they, as may be expected, band together with those already in this Department, but, my friend, the ailment is in the liver, and death alone (as they say) will cure it. I believe that all too late our Government will recognize this evil, and perhaps when it is already too late, when it could have been cut off if action had been taken at the proper time.[11]

Ruiz also submitted his own report on what he observed as a member of the commission, a document lauded by many scholars as the most authentic and insightful account of Indian cultures in Texas from his era. Ruiz's own contemporaries frequently noted his superior knowledge of Indian culture. Even Native people apparently held Ruiz in high esteem. An 1829 letter from Thomas McKinney of Nacogdoches to Austin remarked, "the Shawnees have talked of going for some time to see a big man in St. Antonio who they say is a good man no lie and a good friend to the Indians, Ruis."[12] Unlike other contemporaries, Ruiz's years living among the Tenewah Comanches as a stateless exile allowed him the time and circumstance to understand various Native cultures without the rigid preconceptions of most Anglo and even Mexican observers in Texas.[13]

Ruiz's report was the result of personal observations and reflected the location and time in which he made observations. For example, he divided the Comanches into two groups, the western Comanches, or Yamparikas, and the eastern Comanches, or Tenewahs.[14] This clear distinction lasted only a short period, from the time that Ruiz spent in exile until the death of Paruakevitsi in 1831. After that, the Comanches in Texas experienced a realignment in leadership. Ruiz's report is also very critical of the Lipan Apaches; he describes them as "very cruel" and "having a tendency to steal."[15] This negative opinion may be reflective of his intimate ties to the Comanches, who were often at war with the Lipans.[16] Among the cultural insights provided by Ruiz in his report were the earliest known description of the no-flight warrior society that existed within Comanche society:

> The Lobos, an elite group of warriors . . . are not allowed to retreat from the scene of battle, not even when they are vastly outnumbered. It is their duty to die rather than surrender their ground, although the other warriors may be in full retreat. Even if their chief orders them to turn back, it is a sign of great courage to disobey such orders and to continue to fight. This kind of courage is admired greatly by the women. The Lobos who survive a fierce battle in which many of their number have lost their lives are forced to leave the *ranchería* [village] and find a new one which has no connection with the warriors who have died. The dead Lobos's surviving kin will pursue and slay any Lobo who has escaped alive. This has happened before. Everyone respects the Lobos for their courage and dignity. When they ride through a ranchería their horses may trample on animal skins, meat, or other objects on the ground. They are allowed to take all the meat they desire and eat whatever they wish without anyone hindering them.[17]

Ruiz's explanation of the Comanches understanding of the afterlife gave greater insights into their warrior culture:

> It is believed that the dead go to three places which are reached by three different roads. The ones who die of natural causes go to one place, the road to which has the trappings of mourning along its path. The Comanches imagine adornments reminiscent of funerals. The ones who die bewitched are believed to follow a second road which is strewn with ashes and bordered by profuse and twisted vegetation and brambles. The bewitched never reach a place of rest, they just keep wandering along this road. The third road is supposed to go between the two others. This is the road of the Comanches who die in battle. The entire length of it is believed to be pleasant, full of amenities, and beautiful rivers flow by, bordered by lush vegetation. There are meadows abounding in fat buffaloes. The horses which are killed at the warrior's funeral rites are also on this road, and so are their weapons, and other war adornments. This road supposedly leads to the place where the sun

sits surrounded by all those who died in wars. Warriors are received in
this paradise as sons. War heroes who die fighting become children of
the sun and are to enjoy eternal happiness in its presence.[18]

Certainly anyone, Tejano or Anglo, who had to take the field against the
Comanches and read Ruiz's explanation of their perspective on the death
of a warrior drew scant comfort from his words.

Ruiz was also the first to write about the Comanches' sun-based religion. He explained, "The whole Comanche nation believes in the existence of a supreme being which is the sun. They call it 'the father of the
universe.' All their religious rites center on the worship of the sun. The
doors of their homes or tents face east so that the rising sun can shine
upon them and they can adore it."[19] In a later report to Texas president
Mirabeau B. Lamar, Ruiz expounds on the individual practice of this sun
based religion, "Notwithstanding they worship the sun and the earth, each
one, like the Catholics, has his particular inferior deity, such as the Buffalo,
the Common Bull, the panther, the bear, the alligator, the eagle, etc, which
they paint upon the center of their shields, believing that they will have the
effect to avert the weapons of their enemies."[20]

The boundary commission was not the only significant event in Ruiz's
life in 1828. On November 9, 1828, José Francisco adopted a six-day-old
son and had him baptized as José María de Jesús Ruiz at the San Fernando
Church. It was likely that this adopted son did not live to adulthood because no other record of him has been found and he was not named as an
heir to Ruiz's estate in 1840. The child was possibly a captive recovered by
a Comanche party and returned to Ruiz. That same day, Ruiz's grandson,
Francisco Antonio Herrera, was also baptized at San Fernando Church,
with Juan Martín and Ursula de Veramendi serving as godparents.[21]

That winter Ruiz also led a hunting expedition to stock up on the
winter meat supply. The party consisted of thirty Mexican dragoons, a
Comanche trading party and Jean Louis Berlandier, the naturalist from
of the Boundary Commission who kept a detailed diary of the hunt. On
November 18, the party set out and traveled as far as Uvalde. Berlandier
noted Ruiz's bravery hunting bison at close range, "Sr. Ruiz, having posted
himself behind a tree, wounded one in the shoulder blade, but it was impossible to follow it because of the clouds and the bad roads. When one
thus shoots one of these animals at so close a range, it is necessary to take

refuge behind a tree; for, if the bison is only wounded and if it has seen the fire, it charges the spot where it believes to have discovered its adversary."[22] Berlandier also noted Ruiz's ability to track mustangs and longhorns hiding in the Texas hill country gorges, "A skilled hunter can also distinguish the tracks of bison from those of wild cattle, over dry or rocky terrain where no imprint can be found."[23] They party arrived back in Béxar after thirty days in the Texas wilderness. They had been gone so long that a rescue party was being organized.

With Indian hostilities in a lull, Ruiz then found time to engage in the family business. In April 1829, he delivered trade goods to Presidio San Juan Bautista del Río Grande from the merchant house of Veramendi. The entire delivery was valued at three hundred pesos and included bolts of cotton fabric and English dinnerware. Goods not purchased by the presidio garrison were sold in the civil markets of the town.[24]

Peace did not last long, and Ruiz resumed his duties as an Indian agent when Wichita hostilities erupted again. In the spring of 1829, as Mier y Terán left Texas, General Bustamante decided to campaign against the Taovaya Wichitas. In March 1829, Indian raiders had sacked empresario Green DeWitt's colony. Tenewah leader Paruakevitsi provided intelligence that northern Wichitas had joined with Yamparikas to raid South Texas. This confirmed Bustamante's suspicions of Taovaya involvement. He ordered the destruction of their village: "since the Tahuayases [Taovayas] are committing frequent thefts and assassinations in the vicinity of Bejar and the other frontier establishments, despite the fact that they have been invited to make peace, it has become indispensable to destroy that perverse tribe by attacking their own village and annihilating it." Bustamante told Colonel Antonio Elosúa, as commander of the troops in Texas, to plan the expedition with Austin and Indian agents Ruiz and Peter Ellis Bean: "the time, method, and conditions under which this expedition is to be carried out shall be the result of an agreement by you with Citizens Bean and Austin, with the advice of Lieutenant Colonel Ruiz, because of the information these Chiefs possess."[25]

Elosúa prepared carefully for his expedition. He cautioned Bustamante that in attacking the Taovayas, great care should be made not to upset the parties to the treaty of 1827: the Tenewah Comanches, Wacos, and Tawakonis, who were ethnically Wichitas. He ordered Bean to raise a force of immigrant Indians to approach the Tawakoni village, inform them of his intentions, and invite them to join the expedition. He instructed Ruiz to meet with rangers from Austin's colony and approach the Waco village upstream from there in the same manner.[26]

Ruiz, with two dozen Anglo rangers, traveled to the village on the upper Brazos but found it nearly deserted in May 1829, with only a few dozen Wacos present. The Anglos wished to kill the inhabitants of the village, but Ruiz prevented them from doing so, respecting the peace treaty that he had negotiated in 1827. His refusal to destroy the settlement outraged the Anglos, who left. In fact, Ruiz had intelligence that those at fault for the raids were in fact the Taovayas, and he argued that the best strategy against these northern Indians was to attack in the fall "when they returned to their towns to harvest their crops." Historian Gary Clayton Anderson has remarked that Ruiz's "advice, while rejected at the time by Austin's troops, would become standard ranger tactics in the future."[27] At that time, however, Ruiz's counsel helped Elosúa keep a conflict with some Indians in Texas from becoming a general war.

In the meantime, Elosúa prepared for a fall expedition against Tawakonis and Wacos after an incident in which Tawakonis killed Mexican officials who removed stolen animals from a village.[28] Preparations for a September campaign included a call for militia from the Anglo colonies. More incidents involving Wacos and Tawakonis pushed tensions to a breaking point. In a final attempt to maintain the peace of 1827, more than one hundred Tenewah Comanches and Wacos came to Béxar in the summer of 1829 to meet with Elosúa to argue that the raiding was conducted by Taovayas and other Comanches. Elosúa smoked a peace pipe with the leaders, solemnly sealing his promise for peace, then proceeded to order the destruction of the Wacos' village.[29] Two weeks later, two hundred rangers from Austin's colony attacked the Wacos near Bastrop.[30] These hostilities resulted in the final break of the peace of 1827. War raged for the next several years between the Wacos and Tawakonis on one side and the Mexicans, Anglos, and their Indian allies on the other.

During his time as an Indian agent from 1826–29, Ruiz worked without a salary and even paid for campaign expenses and Indian gifts from his own accounts. Reimbursement came in one big payment on October 30, 1829, of 7,879 pesos, of which 6,328 reimbursed his expenses.[31] Ruiz also applied for and was granted two leagues of land on the San Antonio River adjacent to that of Erasmo Seguín's in an area known as *el paso de la mora* and later described as San Simón de Capote.[32] He retained this ranch until his death, when it passed to his surviving children.[33]

Having been amply compensated for his services, Ruiz requested leave to travel to Matamoros on "personal business."[34] It was granted and he left on December 12, 1829.[35] Details of the trip do not survive, but some records indicate he traded foreign goods. In both February and March 1830, Ruiz as a *comerciante* (merchant) filed a summary of foreign goods sold with the alcalde of Béxar, presumably for tax purposes.[36] Also, in a private letter to Austin, he discussed sending his son, Francisco Antonio Ruiz, to sell cows in Durango and New Orleans.[37] Once again, though, Ruiz put family business and personal finances aside as he was called into public service for Texas.

CHAPTER X

Tenoxtitlán

Your Lordship will please arrange . . . for the Álamo [de Parras]
Company to march under the immediate orders of Lieutenant
Colonel Francisco Ruiz to take up a position at the upper cross-
ing of the Brazos.
— *Comandante General* Manuel de Mier y Terán, 1830[1]

In 1829, General Manuel de Mier y Terán issued his report on conditions in Texas, which led directly to the Law of April 6, 1830. The law
explicitly banned any further immigration from the United States to
Texas. Settlement contracts were brought under federal rather than state
control, and colonies that did not have at least 150 grantees were to be canceled. The further importation of slaves into Texas was expressly banned.
Provisions of the law were also designed to encourage Mexican citizens to
move from the interior to Texas. Mexicans who agreed to relocate would
get good land, free transportation to Texas, and financial assistance. Con-
victs would be sent to Texas to build fortifications and roads to stimulate
trade. Finally, the legislation authorized spending "up to the sum of five
hundred thousand dollars on the construction of fortifications and settlements on the frontier" in Texas.[2]

To strengthen Mexico's presence in Texas, Mier y Terán selected José
Francisco Ruiz for an important task: building a presidio on the Camino
Real, the road that ran from Béxar to Nacogdoches, at the point where
it crossed the Brazos River. Ruiz was told to take the Álamo de Parras
Company and choose an elevated site with access to good drinking water
and farmlands, on which the troops would raise crops. Of course, any empresario who had any previous claims to the location would be asked to
give his permission. Anticipating that the post would become the focus of
a settlement, Mier y Terán explained that while no families could go with
the soldiers initially, the men could later build cabins, apply for ownership

of the land, and send for their wives and children if they succeeded as farmers and secured the area from Indian attacks. Ruiz was to do his best to keep his soldiers from clashing with either Indians or settlers.[3] Apparently Mier y Terán anticipated that this new outpost might serve as a new capital for Texas once it became a settlement.[4]

The historic Álamo de Parras Company that Ruiz now commanded had originated in the town of San José y Santiago del Álamo, in Coahuila. It subsequently had transferred to San Carlos de Parras, also in Coahuila, and then in 1803 to Béxar, where it was posted at San Antonio de Valero, the former mission that had been secularized in 1793. This is how the former mission came to be known as the "Alamo," in reference to the company stationed there.[5]

Ruiz received his orders on May 7, 1830, to lead the expedition, which clearly combined military objectives with civilian colonization efforts. Lieutenant Colonel Ruiz reassured his commander, Colonel Antonio Elosúa, "I am ready to march as you order me to do, and . . . I shall omit nothing within my power to accomplish everything contained in your aforementioned letter."[6] The same day Elosúa ordered Severo Ruiz, captain of the Álamo de Parras Company, to prepare his troops to march. He served directly under the command of José Francisco Ruiz, apparently of no relation.[7] The jefe político of Béxar, Ramón Múzquiz, wrote to Stephen F. Austin, telling him that the main goal of the project was to create a line of defense against the Indians: "It would be a good idea for you to encourage your settlers to aid them with provisions."[8]

Preparations for the relocation of the company in 1830 included an inspection, inventory, and financial audit. The muster roll submitted after the inspection listed one armorer, two sergeants, one bugler, six corporals, three carbineers, one cadet, and fifty privates. With Captain Ruiz and Lieutenant Colonel Ruiz, the total unit strength was sixty-six. The inventory revealed the company was poorly provisioned, which would cause considerable frustration for José Francisco. It had seventy-two horses and four mules, but many saddles were merely a piece of buffalo hide or other skin without any iron rings. Apparently only four men had spurs. The soldiers generally had only one suit of clothing, and more than half did not have scabbards to protect their weapons from the elements. The total armament consisted of ten muskets, fifty-three carbines, fifty-six swords, and six lances, 1,890 cartridges, and 125 flints.[9] (A list of Álamo de Parras company members is shown in Appendix 1.)

Before the troops left Béxar, a financial report indicated that Lieutenant Francisco de Castañeda, the paymaster for the Álamo de Parras Company, "has been found short 901 pesos, 7 reales, 1½ granos on turning over the accounts covering funds which were under his supervision," a large sum.[10] In comparison, an enlisted man of the Álamo de Parras Company earned 300 pesos per year and its captain 1,404 pesos per year.[11] Castañeda was placed under arrest and José Francisco Ruiz, a former prosecutor, was ordered to "proceed immediately to draw up the corresponding record of information concerning the case, after you have carried out all the appropriate investigations . . . [and then] file against Castañeda such charges as may result therefrom."[12] In a ninety-eight-page sumaria, Ruiz concluded that not only was Castañeda guilty, but Captain Ruiz was equally guilty. He forwarded the case to Mier y Terán in Matamoros with the recommendation that Ruiz's punishment be service on the frontier, which was ironic considering it was the same as his current assignment.[13]

On June 23, 1830, a company from Laredo arrived in Béxar to replace the Álamo de Parras Company and Ruiz received his orders to march on June 25.[14] Before leaving, José Francisco Ruiz and his wife again reinforced the kinship bonds that were so important to family survival and prosperity. They became godparents to Teresa de los Ángeles de Veramendi, the daughter of Juan Martín de Veramendi and Josefa Navarro, at San Fernando Church.[15] Having once more tended to family matters, Lieutenant Colonel Ruiz led the Álamo de Parras Company out of Béxar as ordered on June 25, 1830.[16] As no response had yet been received from Mier y Terán regarding the missing funds, Elosúa and José Francisco Ruiz decided to allow Severo Ruiz to march with his troops, but they detained Castañeda in Béxar.[17] Non-payment of salaries was a highly contentious issue, especially when soldiers were being marched into the wilderness and separated from their dependents in Béxar. In order to restore some confidence that their families would be paid in a timely manner, Sergeant Francisco Meza of the Álamo de Parras Company also remained in Béxar as a trustworthy substitute paymaster.[18]

Ruiz kept a diary of the march that noted daily movements. Because he was very familiar with the terrain, the entries were very brief and typically designated the location of camps. The only incident of note was the capture of an unnamed deserter on the third day of the march near Cíbolo Creek.[19] They arrived on the Brazos on July 13, eighteen days after leaving Béxar.[20] José Francisco wrote a more detailed account to Elosúa a few days later. He explained that even the quartermaster requested a slow and "prolonged march" to ensure that supplies and carts would arrive in good condition. This objective also required the clearing of more than two miles of brush along the overgrown road. After their arrival, Ruiz reported that he searched for three days on both sides of the river for a suitable location for the outpost but was unable to find one. He therefore established a temporary camp for his company "on the east side of the Brazos River on the Upper Crossing, about a quarter of a league downstream and on the banks of the river."[21]

The location Ruiz chose was within the upper portion of Austin's colony. He soon encountered two American immigrant families who resided near the site he had selected. He noted, "neither one of them, in my opinion, has possessed [their land] with a valid title."[22] Considering that the purpose of the expedition was to establish a presidio for enforcing a law prohibiting Anglo immigration, it was an auspicious beginning, but he did later learn that his neighbors had valid titles. Ruiz did not yet know this, but he nonetheless, in a demonstration of good will, requested and received permission from them to remain. The soldiers, Ruiz reported, "are camped under good brush arbors which are quite comfortable, and they have maintained the greatest harmony with the foreign colonists, having, in addition, a good supply of provisions at comfortable prices, and they pay cash for them."[23]

Communication with the settlers was hampered by the fact that they did not speak Spanish and no one in the Álamo de Parras Company spoke English. Ruiz tried to obtain the local price for lumber, but his neighbors, probably recently arrived, were "completely ignorant of the prices of lumber." Ruiz decided to gather price information from Austin, who had promised to visit within a few days. At the same time, the American colonists became uneasy by the arrival of a Mexican company to enforce the Law of April 6, 1830. Austin wrote to Mier y Terán about their unease and his strategy of writing several "letters to the editor" in the Austin colony's newspaper, *The Gazette*, emphasizing that his company was only constructing a presidio to provide greater protection against Indian raids.[24]

Stephen F. Austin arrived on July 21 to assist Ruiz in finding the proper location for a permanent outpost.[25] He brought with him mail from Elosúa that included news from Peter Ellis Bean that the immigrant Indians of Nacogdoches had united and attacked the Waco and Tawakoni villages. Ruiz was very pleased with the success of the attack and discussed with

Austin the need to end the illicit trade from his colony that supported the Wacos and Tawakonis. Ruiz wrote, "the door for such [clandestine] trade will be closed to them as far as possible, for which purpose I have taken or made some observations which have seemed appropriate to me, and I have talked with Mr. Austin concerning this matter."[26] Despite Ruiz's efforts, illicit trade between Austin's colony and the Wacos and Tawakonis continued.

Ruiz and Austin located several appropriate sites on the Brazos. Austin, having stayed nearly a week, returned to San Felipe, leaving Ruiz to inspect one final location. Ruiz found this place, five leagues upstream on the west side of the river, to be the most suitable. He wrote, "there is a place which, in my opinion, is the best of all those I have seen since my arrival . . . it has the advantages of possessing many permanent springs of water . . . which can serve a large establishment." The location was inhabited by "three families of foreigners," i.e., illegal immigrants. Ruiz confirmed with them that "they have established themselves without the knowledge of any authority, with only the hope of being admitted as settlers." Nonetheless, Ruiz recommended paying the squatters for their wooden dwelling, which they had constructed for the price of forty pesos.[27]

Ruiz clearly missed the comforts of home. Among the mail he sent to San Felipe on July 23, 1830, was a note to Samuel May Williams, Austin's business partner and a trading partner of Ruiz's. He reminded Williams about some wool that he had sent to San Felipe with his son, Francisco Antonio Ruiz, in April of that year, which he had been unable to sell. Ruiz asked Williams to sell the wool at any price and send his half of the profits to him in coffee and sugar. Williams responded by immediately sending Ruiz five pounds of coffee and a box of *pan dulce* (sweet bread), and he offered to send another fifty pounds of coffee on credit. These letters were revealing. For the first time Ruiz, who was 47 years old, wrote of being "slightly ill," and of his weariness concerning national politics: "it seems to me that the heads of the Mexicans are going to settle down. Time will tell how it will all end."[28] On August 21, Ruiz sent Private Zeferino Villa to San Felipe to purchase twenty pounds of coffee, one *arroba* (25 pounds) of sugar, and "a little hardtack."[29] On October 16, Ruiz sent Williams ten pesos to buy "a reticule of a nature which will be described for you orally by the said bearer."[30]

Upon the request of his troops, Ruiz allowed some families to travel with the mail carrier, reunite with their soldiers, and become the first civilian settlers of the new fort. He understood the importance of family reunification for the morale of his troops, and so he wrote Elosúa to thank him "relative to the families of the troops which you were pleased to permit to march with Alférez Don Santiago Navayra to this post, which measure, in my opinion, was a very good idea, and for that I wish to express my appreciation to Your Lordship."[31] The arrival of these family members spurred others to request the same.[32]

On August 7, 1830, what was to that point known as the "Establishment on the Brazos" was christened "Tenoxtitlán."[33] The name was not even Spanish but Nahuatl, the language of the Aztecs, which meant "place of the prickly pear," and was the name of the Aztec capital that became Mexico City after the Spanish conquest. Mier y Terán chose the name for Ruiz's post, and other clearly indigenous names for the other presidios established under his plan (Lipanitlán and Anáhuac), to symbolize his efforts to re-Mexicanize Texas.[34] To ensure that the name would be used by his troops, Ruiz had it announced to the Álamo de Parras Company on three successive days.[35]

Ruiz established a temporary camp at the new location while he waited for approval to begin building. Tenoxtitlán's military use began immediately. Ruiz received orders for the outpost to serve as a relief station for military escorts en route from Béxar to Nacogdoches. He responded that day, "I have been informed that, whenever the occasion arises, the escort that conducts them from Béxar will be relieved at this point, and that the escort from this post will conduct them to the Trinity River Crossing, all of which will be duly obeyed."[36]

Just a week later, José Francisco was confronted by the first demand on his post's resources when he received a report from Elosúa that a group of Tawakonis had raided Béxar, stealing more than twenty animals. Elosúa ordered a punitive expedition against the raiders, led by Captain Nicasio Sánchez with no less than 125 soldiers. Sánchez was told to march to Tenoxtitlán to confer with Ruiz and get reinforcements if necessary.[37] When Sánchez arrived on August 28, Severo Ruiz gave him six hundred cartridges under the condition that they would be replaced.[38] José Francisco Ruiz reported, "I had an interview with [Sánchez] on the 27th of said August on Nuncio Creek, from which place he continued his march to this camp, and on the 28th he departed from this post." He added, "I, for my part, gave him all the information that I had."[39]

Due to the eruption of hostilities and probably because of José Fran-

cisco's description of conditions at Tenoxtitlán, Elosúa became concerned
with vacancies in the Álamo de Parras Company. He called for fifty-eight
volunteers from the Béxar Company to march with Santiago Navayra to
Tenoxtitlán. Hardly more than ten agreed to go. Elosúa responded to this
unsuccessful roundup by transferring forty soldiers of the Béxar Company
to Tenoxtitlán, where they arrived on October 30, 1830.[40]

It was becoming clear that Tenoxtitlán, more than simply a post from
which to keep an eye on the Anglo American settlers, was to serve as an
advance station for the campaigns against the Wacos and Tawakonis that
fall. The expeditions led by Sánchez and Gaspar Flores de Abrego relied
on the post for supplies, knowledge of the enemy, rest, and transfer of
deserters and wounded.[41] As desertions mounted, the company brig grew.

Despite Tenoxtitlán becoming a useful military base, construction of
more permanent facilities was delayed. On September 20, 1830, Mier y
Terán approved the site chosen by Ruiz and ordered the immediate building of a road in the direction of Nacogdoches. He also told Elosúa and
Erasmo Seguín to select "a military individual" who would direct construction "under the supervision of Citizen Lieutenant Colonel Ruiz."[42]
They chose Santiago Navayra to oversee the construction of the presidio.
Navayra deferred greatly to Ruiz in a letter dated October 10, 1830, ac-
knowledging that he was "limited in knowledge for executing properly the
performance of a commission of such a nature."[43] This marked the beginning of a never-ending bureaucratic struggle to finalize plans, find funds,
and construct the fort.

As Ruiz began work on the road, he wrote to Elosúa recommending
that the fort be constructed of wood because stone and mortar were not
available in the area. He also requested architectural plans in order to estimate the cost of materials. Ruiz then moved his company to the approved
permanent site, where they arrived on October 17, 1830.[44] He wrote from
there to Elosúa and was clearly frustrated at the incredibly slow pace of
producing plans for a fort: "the troops are camping out now as best they
can until we receive the plan from His Excellency so that we can know
more definitely how to locate it in its permanent position." On October 26,
perhaps to boost morale, Ruiz allowed thirteen of his soldiers to join their
dependents in Béxar. The reunited families subsequently left Béxar for
Tenoxtitlán in a convoy on November 10.[45] This left just fifteen men of the
Álamo de Parras Company available for duty with Ruiz. In addition to the
fifteen soldiers absent with their families, seven men were on guard duty,

six were herding horses, one was in Tamaulipas, one was in Nacogdoches, one was carrying mail to San Felipe, one was a prisoner in Matamoros, one was a prisoner in Presidio San Juan Bautisa del Río Grande, nine were sick, and three were prisoners at Tenoxtitlán. There was no chaplain, so Mier y Terán assigned a priest, Juan Nepomuceno Ayala from Nacogdoches, to Tenoxtitlán to organize a parish.[46] Ayala replied that while he truly desired to go to his new post, he was prevented for two reasons: poverty and venereal disease. The priest argued that the former prevented him from buying food for the journey, while the latter kept him from riding a horse.[47] Upon being reassured that he would be paid, Ayala traveled to Tenoxtitlán in time to appear on the roll as chaplain on December 1, 1830.[48]

The construction of Tenoxtitlán proved a frustrating and impossible assignment for Ruiz. Plans for the fort arrived in early November, but without the model. When it did arrive, Ruiz sent it to San Felipe to have the specifications translated into English because the bidders on the project were residents of Austin's colony who did not speak Spanish. Historian Malcolm McLean has noted the irony that "the materials for the fort to keep out Anglo Americans were to be supplied by Anglo Americans."[49] In January 1831, Ruiz sent the plans and model back to Béxar because he did not have anyone with enough experience to direct the construction of the fort. He asked Elosúa to request professional assistance from Mier y Terán.[50] By April 29, 1831, Ruiz received orders to construct the fortification out of wood. He reported that his men had already built "rustic lodgings made of wood," a chapel, and two rooms for the paymaster and on-duty guards.[51] When Mier y Terán took leave from his post in June 1831, Ruiz wrote to Samuel May Williams about his frustration, "I have learned . . . that General Terán is absenting himself from Matamoros for other points. Who knows whether we shall ever see him around here again, and then goodbye, Tenoxtitlán, in my opinion."[52]

On March 3, 1831, four soldiers from Tenoxtitlán, Juan José Reyes, a carbineer of the Álamo de Parras Company, and three soldiers of the Béxar Company, Blas Zamora, Francisco Calvillo, and Tomás Zúñiga, traveled to San Felipe de Austin to purchase corn. While in Austin's colony, they stole and slaughtered a calf from the Millican farm. A member of the Millican family came upon the soldiers with his weapon drawn, tied them up, and whipped the thieves. Ruiz had to deal with this embarrassing situation in a manner that preserved the authority of the Mexican military. He charged the four soldiers with theft and wrote to Williams, the alcalde of

San Felipe, asking him to have charges brought against Millican. At issue was law and order, and colonists' perception that they could take justice into their own hands. After much delay, the San Felipe ayuntamiento punished Millican by having him beaten with his own whip.[53]

Theft remained a vexing problem for Ruiz. Aside from Indian theft of livestock, particularly horses, he had to deal with larceny within his own ranks. In one report, he noted the theft of an ox by an unnamed soldier under his command. He pleaded with his superiors to handle the situation locally. Perhaps he wished to avoid the drama of the Millican affair, but he also wrote, "I believe that it is absolutely true, that nothing but a little bit of despotism, in some cases, accompanied by a club, will make them work . . . for I only desire to nip in the bud such harmful evils among the troops."[54] Ruiz obviously understood and was frustrated by the quality of the recruits he received, especially in the absence of adequate pay and working conditions.[55]

Difficulties also arose when Ruiz was confronted with recently arrived American settlers. On October 25, 1830, Sterling C. Robertson and six others arrived at Tenoxtitlán from Tennessee. Ruiz and Robertson would later serve together in the Texas Senate, but that day the empresario presented Ruiz with an 1825 contract from the government of Coahuila y Texas for the settlement of families on the Brazos or San Andrés Rivers (the San Andrés is present-day Little River). This was precisely the type of contract that the Law of April 6, 1830 declared void. Ruiz, faced with a duty to enforce an impractical mandate that he did not agree with issued by a distant government, responded in a manner that exemplifies the Spanish America tradition of "obedezco, pero no cumplo" ("I obey, but I do not comply"). Ruiz wrote to Elosúa for orders, noting, "Robertson and his party have conducted themselves very harmoniously with the Mexicans, and a doctor who came with them even cured some of our sick soldiers without charging them anything."[56]

Before Ruiz received a response, he wrote a second letter to Elosúa, informing him that Robertson had again visited Tenoxtitlán, this time with two more American settlers. Robertson also told Ruiz that more would arrive in a few days. In accord with orders he had received two days prior, on October 28, to not allow any foreign settlers without a passport issued in New Orleans or destined for Austin's colony, Ruiz detained Robertson and his comrades at Tenoxtitlán. Then, in a change of tone from military commander to that of a seasoned attorney, Ruiz questioned Elosúa about the liability the state could incur for "damages which will result to him [Robertson] if he is delayed for a long time, after such a long journey, and the expenditures which it will be necessary for him to make in order to support the families at that place."[57]

Clearly wishing to aid Robertson, Ruiz wrote to Williams asking for Austin's support: "I should appreciate it if our friend Don Stephen would write, immediately, something in favor of the aforementioned families, for to me the ones I have seen look like very good people, and this very day I am writing a letter . . . in favor of these individuals, for I think they deserve it."[58] Ruiz assisted Robertson further by drafting a letter for him in Spanish, explaining the history of his contract, and informing him that it dated to a much earlier colonization effort eventually approached by Stephen F. Austin.[59]

Robertson's business partner, Alexander Thompson, was already en route to meet Robertson with the first nine settler families. Detained at Nacogdoches, the authorities there informed him of an order prohibiting foreigners not destined for Austin's colony from entering without a passport. Colonel José de las Piedras made the families return to Natchitoches, Louisiana, but allowed Thompson and four others to proceed to Austin's colony to seek admittance. Believing they held a valid colonization contract and having risked everything to immigrate to Texas, the Anglo families left Nacogdoches but instead of heading to Natchitoches, they cut a new route around to the road to Béxar. This bypass of Nacogdoches came to be known as the "Tennesseans Road" and served as the main route used by unauthorized immigrants entering Texas from the United States at this time.[60] Ironically, when Thompson and the nine families reached the Brazos on November 12, they took shelter in the abandoned barracks that the Álamo de Parras Company had left four weeks prior when it marched to the new site approved for Tenoxtitlán.

Unfortunately for Thompson and the colonists, they encountered Peter Ellis Bean at the Trinity Crossing as he transported the mail. Less friendly toward the would-be settlers than Ruiz, Bean reported his sighting to Piedras at Nacogdoches, who flew into a rage. He fired off a series of letters to Elosúa and Austin that reported the settlers' deception and demanded their removal. Mier y Terán rejected Ruiz's appeal to allow the settlers to remain and ordered Ruiz to escort Robertson and his colonists to the east bank of the Sabine River.[61] Ruiz replied that he would do so as soon as Robertson presented himself to him. Robertson spent a few months signing contracts, selling land with questionable titles, and getting the promise of Austin, the newly elected state legislator from Texas, to take his case to the Coahuila y Texas legislature. Robertson then presented himself to Ruiz in Tenoxtitlán on February 16, 1831, and Ruiz carried out his removal from Texas. Robertson returned to Tennessee where he was wanted for murder; there he was tried, convicted, and sentenced to nine months in prison.[62] He and Ruiz would meet each other again, under better circumstances.

In addition to Ruiz's military role at Tenoxtitlán, he served as the representative of the Mexican government on the frontier. Ruiz used his position to maintain a delicate balance between Anglos, Tejanos, and Indian groups on the frontier. It took the full range and use of his acquired skills as a cultural broker and negotiator to balance so many competing interests.[63]

As little control as Ruiz had regarding the various groups contending for control of area, there were circumstances over which he had no control at all. Smallpox struck Ruiz's camp in late April 1831. Two soldiers were infected, but a cure was applied and it did not spread any further.[64] The outbreak then erupted among the Indians and reached the Wacos and Tawakonis. Ruiz received reports that twenty-two Tawakonis and seventeen Wacos had died. He noted spitefully, "May it be God's will that no trace shall remain of such a harmful family."[65]

Clearly, Ruiz's mood was taking a noticeable turn for the worse as the drudgery of his assignment dragged on throughout the summer. The first indication that melancholy had overtaken him appeared in a letter to his friend and confidant Williams. He wrote on October 30, 1830, "Ah, my friend, if you could but examine my heart, what sad ideas you would find in it! I no longer desire any power at all; I no longer aspire to anything except to devote my last days to silence. If only I could recover the tranquility which my spirit has lost. Patience, and let us leave it to time, for perhaps nature will bring things back into order."[66]

One month later, after the arrival of reinforcements from the Béxar Company in "pitiful condition," the dreary existence of the troops at Tenoxtitlán became too much for Ruiz to bear. He wrote to Elosúa that he needed supplies immediately to prevent his men from committing crimes, deserting, or staging a mutiny. Ruiz declared that his troops "do not have a thing to eat, and they are incapable of rendering any service whatsoever, being disposed to commit grave offenses, and even abandoning the camp." Because there was almost no money and no merchants nearby, the only recourse was to have supplies sent from Béxar, which had not been done.

Ruiz declared, "For these reasons from this day forward I remain free of any responsibility which I may be charged with in the future with respect to the security of this new establishment, the subordination and discipline appropriate for the military, for it is not within my power to achieve all the interesting objectives which have been entrusted to me, with subordinates who breathe nothing but the necessity which surrounds them on all sides." He concluded with a warning that if food and other necessities did not arrive in ten to twelve days, the Álamo de Parras Company, in whole or in part, would probably march home to Béxar, with or without Ruiz. Relief did come. Elosúa replied that Navayra would leave Béxar on December 7 with funds for Ruiz's troops and the recent reinforcements. Ruiz sent twelve men to escort the badly needed cargo, but even this did not satisfy some of the men as three from the Béxar Company deserted the same day. Elosúa later offered a reward for the capture of the deserters.[67]

Ruiz's letters continued to reflect his physical misery. In a February 15, 1831, note, he wrote "this very day it is snowing so hard that, since my house is just a shack, it is getting wet everywhere . . . it is very cold and I cannot write any more.[68] That winter, when José Francisco was visited by his son, Francisco Antonio, who he sent to Brazoria to buy provisions. The elder Ruiz wrote to Williams and asked him to send a letter of introduction ahead of the young Francisco Antonio because "he has no acquaintances there."[69]

It did not improve Ruiz's mood when he learned that his sumaria in the case against Lieutenant Castañeda and Captain Ruiz had resulted in the indictment of both. He was appointed *fiscal* (prosecutor) and ordered to conduct an investigation with the power to interview whomever he wanted. Elosúa ordered Castañeda transferred to Tenoxtitlán for easier access and assigned Ruiz a legal secretary, Alférez Tomás Porras, of the First Permanent Company of Troops.[70] Elosúa also ordered that Captain Ruiz be relieved of command. This added to Lieutenant Colonel Ruiz's heavy responsibilities; not only was he the commandant of the under-provisioned detachment at Tenoxtitlán responsible for the construction of the fortifications, but now he had to take personal command of the Álamo de Parras Company and conduct a trial at the same time.[71] Each of these duties was a full-time position by itself. An example of the burden faced by Ruiz at this point is his official correspondence; in order to comply with military protocol, each communication had to be handwritten in duplicate, one to be signed in his capacity as commandant of the Detachment at Tenoxtitlán and the other to be endorsed in his capacity as commander of the Álamo de Parras Company.

The trials of Lieutenant Castañeda and Captain Ruiz lasted a total of seventeen months. José Francisco Ruiz began with bond hearings. He set bond for the captain at 1,200 pesos, paid half in land and half in cash. Because Tenoxtitlán lacked a strong box, and both the incoming and outgoing paymasters were under investigation, Ruiz took personal possession of the bond. Castañeda's situation was different. He had been imprisoned at one-third pay for months and lacked any property of note, so Ruiz granted his bond without payment.[72] Ruiz personally conducted the first eight depositions. In a letter in February 1831, he complained about his exhaustion: "I am tired of my fate and I want, in order to see if it will improve, to be discharged from military service and live tranquilly, even though it may be in the wilderness."[73]

Ruiz found relief in the summer of 1831, when Castañeda filed a motion seeking his removal, arguing that because José Francisco Ruiz and Severo Ruiz shared the same last name, they were therefore relatives. Lieutenant Colonel Ruiz was relieved from his court duties on June 18, 1831, and replaced with Captain Nicolás Flores.[74] The case continued, uncovering more corruption and illicit trading by troops. Eventually Juan Martín de Veramendi and José Francisco Ruiz were questioned regarding their commercial activities. Ruiz, did in fact, engage in personal business while commanding the outpost, such as trading in bear skins, an important Texas export at the time.[75]

Ultimately, in August 1832, the investigation was suspended due to a lack of funds and so that Severo Ruiz could be tried. Castañeda was freed to participate in a campaign against the Tawakonis and performed so well that he received a medal for valor. He repaid the missing money in March 1833, redeeming himself.[76]

Although Ruiz made clear the harsh conditions at Tenoxtitlán, the government was not ready to give up on the outpost. At the end of June 1831 ten thousand pesos arrived in Béxar for the construction of the Tenoxtitlán presidio.[77] In July 1831, Ruiz tired of waiting for his money and fearing another winter without plans, organized his camp into a plaza:

I have already started to form a house of wood so that it can serve as the Office of the Military Commandant, and I am having all the houses that have been built up to now moved so as to form a plaza that will serve as a fortification, for it seems to me that the commissioner will be delayed for some time, and I do not want the winter to come and find us in disorder, or, better said, without being able to count on a base for support, because everything has been done in a provisional manner, each individual placing his house where he thought best, believing that soon a decision would be reached as to the form that should be given to this establishment. In short, I am planning to form my little plaza and, although informally, to designate the principal streets that are to go out from it . . . for little is to be lost by doing so, when we consider that all of the buildings are rustic and made of wood.[78]

Presumably, if the plans and money for building a fort ever arrived at Tenoxtitlán, Ruiz's flimsy buildings could be easily rearranged or even demolished.

As if matters were not bad enough, in August 1831 Ruiz contracted an illness that plagued him for the rest of his life. "I have been attacked by a multitude of pimples and big splotches of a rash which won't let me sit down for a single minute," he wrote.[79] The next day he observed, "for several days I have been pretty sick, and, although it is not serious, it makes me too uncomfortable to sit down or lie down, due to a multitude of pimples and blisters that have broken out all over my body . . . but it looks like I am getting better now."[80] Over time, Ruiz suffered periods of acute fatigue and "hydropsy," later known as edema, a disease related to failure of the heart, kidneys, or liver. Most likely, given Ruiz's symptoms, he suffered from an acute streptococcal disease caused by heart or kidney damage.[81]

While Ruiz's illness may have been caused by the rudimentary living conditions of Tenoxtitlan, his discomfort after contracting it was exacerbated by his crude quarters which, out of necessity and frustration, he later had completed with his own money.[82] But by October 16, 1831, Ruiz had enough and applied to Elosúa for retirement.[83] His formal request was written in the third person, "He would continue with pleasure in the glorious career in which he is engaged, if it were not for the fact that during the years that have passed his health has been somewhat impaired, and at this time he finds himself attacked by various and complicated infirmities from which he has been suffering since last July."[84]

Nearly a month later, Ruiz reconsidered. Although his health was broken, he had recovered enough to withdraw his application for retirement, writing that "my infirmities, which for some time had me quite concerned, have yielded to the strength of the medicines which I have taken. I think that I am out of danger." He was a bit deaf, his hair was "falling out at a rapid rate," and he was very weak," but he would remain at his post.[85]

While Ruiz struggled to recover, the work at Tenoxtitlán became tedious for his men as well, and the number of desertions increased significantly. The same desperation evident in Ruiz's writings and his application for retirement expressed itself in the urge to desert among the enlisted men. The soldiers must have known of Ruiz's illness and his lack of faith in the ultimate success of the project. During the nine months between March and December of 1831, no less than fourteen soldiers deserted the post. Every desertion required Ruiz to perform an investigation and report. Many of these men were serial deserters, who had been given frontier duty as punishment. All of those who deserted under Ruiz were eventually caught or surrendered themselves.[86]

Indian affairs also remained a constant concern at Tenoxtitlán. On August 8, 1831, Ruiz reported that immigrant Indians had visited, including "Cados, Aonais, Nadacos, Couchates, Kicapus, Chatas, Chicasas, and others." They met with Ruiz in the "Indian style" and maintained they would not be friends with the Wacos, Tawakonis, and Taovayas. Ruiz offered these Indians six pesos for each Tawakoni scalp they brought him, and he offered to pay the sum himself if need be.[87] He had apparently run out of patience with the lack of support for his detachment, and so he took matters into his own hands. Ruiz also noted that forty militiamen from Austin's colony passed through en route to fight the Wichitas.[88]

Despite the efforts of Ruiz and others, the Indian situation was worsening for the Anglo and Tejano settlers in Texas. Tawakonis continued to raid Béxar and San Felipe. Comanche bands raided Goliad, Béxar, and along the Medina River. Ruiz's Tenewah ally, Incoroy, attempted to keep the peace, but to no avail. Elosúa believed any peace talks were disingenuous. On August 23, 1831, Mier y Terán declared war on the Comanches.[89]

In a devastating turn of events, Ruiz's longtime Tenewah friend and ally, Paruakevitsi, and his son were killed by Mexican soldiers during a campaign against the Tawakonis on November 13, 1831. Paruakevitsi and other Comanches had camped with Tawakonis to engage in peace talks on behalf of the Mexicans. When soldiers charged the camp in a surprise attack, they killed indiscriminately. In an awkward diplomatic moment, the Mexicans allowed the Comanches to mourn their loss and shared the Tawakoni booty with them.[90] Ruiz commented upon the irony of Paruakevitsi's death, "It is regrettable that, due to the fact that [Paruakev-itsi's] people had joined the [Tawakonis], it was not possible to achieve a complete victory over the latter."[91]

Even as the Indian situation deteriorated across Texas, the lack of provisions continued to strain Ruiz's outpost. On May 23, 1832, Elosúa reported to José Mariano Guerra, the commandant general of Coahuila y Texas, that Tenoxtitlán might be abandoned because "it is impossible for it to last much longer without receiving some kind of assistance."[92] Ruiz made a similar point in a June 4 letter in which he requested additional provisions and reported having "reached bottom" and that not even the "miserable American merchants" would extend him much-needed credit to buy supplies.[93] While such pleading certainly must have moved Ruiz's superiors, there was little they could do about his situation.

Despite the problems at the post, Ruiz attempted to continue carrying out his duties. The day after sending his long letter of complaint, Ruiz sent eighteen soldiers to the Kichai's village to meet with Uña de Oso (Bear Claw) and discuss peace with the Lipans and Tonkawas at their request.[94] The report turned out to be false; Uña de Oso simply wanted gifts and to "have a good time."[95] While these troops were still away, Ruiz got a letter from Colonel Piedras of Nacogdoches, asking him to march on Anáhuac to assist in putting down an uprising of Americans. Ruiz responded that he was alone at Tenoxtitlán, having issued leave to other troops to forage.[96]

In fact, Ruiz's response had more to do with his political opinions than the condition of his garrison. General Antonio López de Santa Anna had rebelled that summer against President Anastacio Bustamante, whom the general had previously supported. Santa Anna's rebels issued the Plan de Veracruz, whereby they endorsed the Constitution of 1824 but called for the removal of Bustamante and the appointment of Santa Anna to lead the army.[97] Ruiz received a series of letters from Mier y Terán instructing him and his troops to remain loyal to the government.[98] But Ruiz's sympathies lay with Santa Anna and the federalist cause. He wrote to Austin, "you have known me for a long time and are well aware of how much I have always labored for my Country and the welfare of my fellow man . . . consequently you may rest assured that I am ready to follow and second anything that is not opposed to the Constitution and my Country. I do not do so at the moment because I am without officers and even without troops . . . I promise to do it any minute, and in addition I shall endeavor to gain ground for the cause among my friends in Béxar."[99]

An official order from Elosúa arrived for Ruiz on June 28, ordering twenty-five men to be sent from Tenoxtitlán to Anáhuac. Ruiz, having no privates at his disposal, sent a reply to Elosúa by civilian courier that no troops were available at Tenoxtitlán.[100] Then, several Indian groups seeking advice on which side to take in the uprising visited. Ruiz admitted to Austin in a letter that he advised them to "not get mixed up in anything with the White Men" and asked them to spread this notice in their villages. The Indians remained neutral in the affair.[101] Ruiz allowed two prisoners, Lieutenant Colonel Ignacio Villasana and Lieutenant Manuel Palacios, "to travel without guard" to San Felipe to buy food. Ruiz validated his actions by securing their word of honor as officers that they would return, but they took the opportunity to flee and joined the rebel forces.[102]

Ruiz later received news that an armistice had been signed between Santa Anna and the Mexican army, and that same day learned of the suicide of Mier y Terán, who impaled himself on his own sword at the execution site of Emperor Agustín Iturbide in Padilla, Tamaulipas.[103]

Ruiz decided to utilize the chaos of the uprising and Mier y Terán's death to return to Béxar. He first wrote to Elosúa about his fear that Austin's colony had pronounced for Santa Anna. He noted the poor condition of Tenoxtitlán and declared that he would be unable to defend it against an attack from San Felipe. For these reasons, he told Elosúa, he intended to abandon the outpost and march to Béxar on August 15, 1832, unless supplies arrived.[104] Ruiz received a stern reply: "you should remain there until you receive new orders from me, and be very careful, as you should, and as I urge you to do . . . to see that your troops maintain the best order and discipline." Ruiz was not being truthful with Elosúa; he had already written to Austin that his failure to openly support Santa Anna and his federalist uprising was only due to the insignificance of his garrison. He believed that doing so at home in Béxar would be much more effective. He explained to Austin his plans to abandon Tenoxtitlán and march to Béxar, but he declined Austin's request to surrender fifty swords to the rebel cause. Ruiz argued that to reveal his allegiance for such a minor gain was a wasted opportunity and instead proposed that Austin buy them. He closed with the plea, "don't say anything about my eagerness to arrive in Béxar so as not to spoil my plans."[105]

Ruiz and the Mexican inhabitants of Tenoxtitlán marched for Béxar on the morning of August 22, 1832. Ruiz, too sick to write, instructed Francis Smith, a nearby settler, to inform Austin of his leaving, "All of the Spanish inhabitants left here this morning for Béxar. I met Col. Ruiz two miles from this place quite sick, he requested me to write you about his situation, of being sick and not having help enough to move on conveniently, that it was out of his power to go to Béxar in haste as you requested."[106] Vicente Filisola wrote in his memoirs that Ruiz went to Béxar to support Santa Anna's revolution and that most of the troops under his command left the march to join with those that had left Nacogdoches for Matamoros.[107] Ruiz arrived in Béxar after an arduous twenty-six day journey home and boldly pronounced for the Plan de Veracruz on September 14, 1832.[108]

Within months of his return to Béxar, he was immersed once more in family affairs; he and María Josefa served as godparents for the baptism of José de los Ángeles Navarro, son of José Ángel Navarro, at San Fernando Church.[109] Ruiz also got an unexpected reply to his retirement request; the junta assigned to review his service granted him half credit for his time in exile, giving him credit for four years, eight months, and nine days. This left him six months short of being eligible for retirement.[110] His thoughts, then, must have focused on plans for a future beyond the army.

CHAPTER XI

Retirement

I can move my family and what few possessions I have . . . for I
am ready to abandon Béxar.

—José Francisco Ruiz, 1832[1]

J osé Francisco Ruiz returned to Béxar in the summer of 1832, but he did
not settle in his old house on the Plaza de Armas. Instead, he resided
for three years near the mouth of Elm Creek and the Medina River
on the ranch of José Ignacio Pérez, a nephew who was just three years his
junior.[2] José Ignacio Pérez was the son of Juan Ignacio Pérez and Clemencia Hernández, the sister of Ruiz's wife, María Josefa Hernández. Ruiz
and the elder Pérez were politically far apart, but family ties had endured
the turmoil of the struggle for Mexican independence and its aftermath.[3]

José Ignacio Pérez, unlike his father, chose not to engage in politics or
serve in the army. Instead, he focused on his ranch, which allowed him to
develop a close relationship with Ruiz.[4] In 1829, six years after he inherited
the family ranch, the younger Pérez signed a power of attorney granting
Ruiz the ability to collect debts owed to him, essentially naming him as
the agent for his goods.[5] Pérez most likely issued this document for the
trading expedition that Ruiz led to Presidio San Juan Bautista del Río
Grande in April 1829.[6]

Back in Béxar, Ruiz's extended family stirred with activity as the Veramendi family prepared to move to Saltillo, where Juan Martín de Veramendi would serve as governor. The two compadres, Ruiz and Veramendi,
had been close, even spending time together in exile. The governor's party,
which left in December 1832, included Jim Bowie and his young wife, Doña
Ursula de Veramendi, with Sterling Robertson coming along to secure confirmation of his empresario contract.[7] Ruiz meanwhile prepared for a significant change in his own life: retirement. In January 1833, he completed an
audit of his accounts with Commissary Erasmo Seguín. Seguín concluded

that the army owed Ruiz 2,375 pesos, three reales, and ten granos, a large sum, for his time in the wilderness from January 1, 1830, to the end of December 1832.[8] Official retirement was still a few months away, and he did not receive his commission to retire until September 24, 1833.

The discovery that the army owed him money must have been a great comfort to Ruiz. During his time at Tenoxtitlán, he had suffered not only physically and mentally, but also financially. He served without pay. The situation became so dire that during May 1831, the commissary of Saltillo acknowledged that it did not have enough cash to pay Ruiz his reimbursements and salary.[9] There were forms of compensation other than cash, and Ruiz understood as well as anyone that Tenoxtitlán could become the capital of Texas, a development that would benefit landowners in the area. On September 25, 1830, he applied for a grant of nine leagues of land near Tenoxtitlán.[10] He wrote to Austin asking for help, "I can move my family and what few possessions I have to this post, for I am ready to abandon Béxar, and for that purpose in the last mail I requested that the Supreme Government discharge me from Military Service."[11] Ruiz sought two leagues directly opposite Tenoxtitlán, four leagues upstream on the same side of the Brazos facing the mouth of the Little River, two leagues on the west bank of the Brazos below the mouth of the Little River, and a final league on Nuncio Creek at the crossing of the road from Béxar to Nacogdoches.[12]

Ruiz had reason to seek Austin's assistance, because American John Teal had already applied for a league of land directly across from Tenoxtitlán and occupied it. Ruiz claimed superior right under the National Colonization Law of 1824, which gave preference to Mexican citizens and applicants with military service and merit. Jefe político Múzquiz rejected Teal's application under the Law of April 6, 1830, because he was from the United States.[13] Ruiz's surveys were completed in January 1833. Two leagues sat on the east bank of the Brazos at the present site of Hearne, Texas. Ruiz received title to these lands on August 31, 1833, and paid 1,028 pesos for 39,855.6 acres, or roughly 2.5 centavos per acre.[14]

It was not long before Ruiz had his grant of six leagues challenged by squatters. Sterling C. Robertson sought to dispossess Mexican grantees in favor of Anglo squatters. The dispute was first addressed in the final days of the federalist state legislature at Monclova during the 1835 crisis in government. In a hastily passed bill, Ruiz's claims were upheld, but the controversial nature of the session and resulting war for independence provided Robertson another venue in which to advance his interests. In

1836, the issue was revived in the Texas Senate, in which both Robertson and Ruiz served. Austin interceded on behalf of Ruiz and the other "eleven leaguers" who had gained title through Austin's colony, and he wrote to President Sam Houston that Ruiz's prior title was clear and unambiguous. Robertson argued that eleven leagues was too much for any one person, although he himself sought that amount as an empresario. After the Texas Senate failed to resolve the matter, Ruiz sent his son, Francisco Antonio Ruiz, to New Orleans to sell some of his property on the Brazos River. He sold four leagues to Edwin Morehouse and John R. Cunningham for $70,000, nearly double what his father paid for all nine leagues.[15]

It was during this time following his return from Tenoxtitlan that Ruiz first became acquainted with Sam Houston. Houston arrived in Texas with two objects: to purchase land and to visit with Comanches and other tribes on behalf of the United States federal government.[16] Ruiz first dined with Houston before traveling with him to meet the Comanches. The two Indian agents discussed the Comanche threat and the legends of silver and gold at San Sabá, the site of an abandoned mission northwest of San Antonio.[17] This meeting certainly made a good impression on Houston, who grew to greatly respect Ruiz for his abilities as an Indian agent. Houston wrote in 1837, "The great influence of Colonel Ruis, with the Indians and his perfect knowledge of their character, entitle him to be consulted in everything important."[18] Houston reported to U.S. president Andrew Jackson, "having been as far as Béxar in the Province of Texas, where I had an interview with the Comanche Indians. I am now in possession of some information, that will doubtless be interesting to you; and maybe calculated to forward your view if you should entertain any; touching the acquisition of Texas by the Government of the United States."[19] After the Comanche meetings with Ruiz, Houston returned to the United States, arriving in Natchitoches in February 1833.

Numerous tragedies befell the Ruiz, Veramendi, and Navarro families in 1833. The year began with promise when Ruiz's brother-in-law, Veramendi, was serving as governor of Coahuila y Texas and his nephew, José Antonio Navarro, was elected an alternate deputy to the federal congress. Then suddenly, only a few months into his term as governor, Veramendi died in a cholera epidemic that claimed his entire family along with more than 450 other Monclova residents. The first to die was María Josefa Navarro de Veramendi, Ruiz's niece. Her husband, the governor, died the next morning. A few days later young Ursula de Veramendi, their daughter and Bowie's wife, also died. The Veramendis were buried in Monclova in a mass grave. This singular event resulted in the death of a third of the Ruiz-Veramendi-Navarro extended family, whose bonds had survived exile in the swamps of the Neutral Ground years before.[20]

Disease and disaster also ravaged Texas. In September 1833, while cholera struck Monclova, the ayuntamiento of Béxar canceled public activities for the month of October in order to combat a whooping cough epidemic that afflicted the local schoolchildren.[21] All schools remained closed until November 1, and both Ruiz and Erasmo Seguín were called upon "to supply mutton to the public throughout the coming month, as the meat is very helpful in guarding oneself against the epidemic that is expected." Ruiz, the former schoolmaster, complied with the request to help the children of Béxar, and José María Cárdenas was appointed to oversee the distribution.[22] In December, floods inundated Texas and Béxar became overrun with Tawakoni refugees fleeing the horror of the cholera epidemic that was ravaging their villages. The Comanches, no longer led by the amicable Paruakevitsi, raided on the Medina River, killed one of Ruiz's servants, and stole cattle.[23] Ruiz wrote to his friend, Samuel May Williams, in February 1834 that he might abandon the Medina ranch: "As a last resort I plan to leave here, travel until I cross the Colorado, and remain at some safe point before I reach the Brazos, if it should be possible for me to do so."[24]

The cholera epidemic that killed the Veramendis reached Béxar in the spring of 1834.[25] Ruiz's mother, Manuela de la Peña, suddenly became ill. Ruiz and his sister, María Josefa Ruiz de Navarro, tended to their mother during her illness. But realizing the inevitable, Alcalde Domingo Bustillos and three witnesses were summoned for Manuela to dictate her last will and testament.[26] Noting particularly her gratitude to her children for their care and attention, Manuela left her estate to José Francisco, his sister María, and her grandchildren by daughters María Antonia and María Rosalia, which consisted solely of the "the little country estate which my son José, who died intestate in the jurisdiction of Natchitoches, left at his death."[27] Ruiz's sister María Josefa Ruiz de Navarro, his sole surviving sibling, was the next to succumb to the epidemic. She survived her mother by only a few days.

Ruiz's wife, María Josefa Hernández, also disappeared from the public record at this time. Her last public act was selling her interest in the San Bartolo Ranch to José Cassiano on February 4, 1834.[28] No record of her burial is found in the incomplete records of the time, however, oral reports indicate that she was buried in San Fernando Church.[29] As a note in the San Fernando burial records for 1834 explains, "The reason for such a short list is because of the conditions of [the] time in San Antonio. There was too much unrest whereas the priest was having a difficult time keeping the records straight. Some of the burials were held at other places, such as private cemeteries or at other missions."[30] Ruiz was listed as a widower at his death in 1840.[31]

In May of 1834, the Ruiz and Navarro families gathered to bury their matriarchs. Manuela de la Peña was buried on May 18, 1834, at the camposanto in Béxar. Her brief burial record reads, "Peña, Manuela, widow, left no will and died at 84 of dysentery."[32] She requested that her funeral be held in the San Antonio de Valero church.[33] María Josefa Ruiz de Navarro's burial is not listed in the burial records. Perhaps in the confusion of the epidemic her name was omitted, or she may have died and was buried at the Navarro's Atascosa County Ranch.[34] The population of the city had dwindled as some residents had started to move out of the city to ranches or other small towns.[35]

As José Antonio Navarro withdrew from the town to his ranch on the Atascosa River to grieve the loss of his mother and grandmother and wait for the epidemic to end, Ruiz also decided to leave. He volunteered to transport a prisoner, José Mireles, to the city of Guerrero on the Río Grande, affording himself a means to get away from the epidemic and time to grieve alone.[36] Both men, nephew and uncle, in self-exile to grieve their losses and escape the raging cholera epidemic, would soon be drawn back to Béxar to face a political challenge as large as Texas: independence from Mexico.

CHAPTER XII

Texas Independence

The die is cast, and in a few months will begin the revolution that
will forever separate Texas from the Republic of Mexico.

—José Francisco Ruiz, 1835[1]

General Antonio López de Santa Anna was elected president of
Mexico as a federalist in 1833, winning all but two states. Typical
of his style of governing, he deferred to his vice president, Valentín Gómez Farías, to govern the daily operations of the country. Santa
Anna was not even present for his investiture as president, allowing Gómez Farías to step in as acting president. When the general did arrive
in Mexico City more than a month later, he stayed only briefly and not
long enough to set an agenda for the nation.[2] His popularity stemmed
from a patriotic personality cult, and remaining distant from the political
battles and ugliness of governance provided him with the political distance
to maintain the public posture of a patriotic paternal guardian.[3] In times
of disorder or conflict he would reinsert himself into government affairs,
ironically overthrowing his own government at times. Unfortunately for
him, and Mexico, that tactic led to an angry backlash in Texas in the mid-
1830s that resulted in the creation of the Republic of Texas.

The 1833 Mexican Congress was far more liberal than the moderate
acting president, Gómez Farías. The liberal Congress pursued a staunchly
secular and anticlerical agenda. They proposed taxing church property and
barring the Catholic Church, the only legal denomination in the country, from participation in public affairs. Reforms of the army included a
reduction in troop strength, which was initially endorsed by Santa Anna.
Congress also passed the controversial Ley del Caso, whereby fifty-one
politicians were accused of being unpatriotic and expelled from Mexico. A
conservative backlash emerged following the passage of these radical proposals. The press fueled the crisis by proposing even more radical propos-

als, particularly the end of church and military *fueros* (special privileges), which provided those institutions with great power in Mexican politics and society.[4]

In the summer of 1833, a series of military commanders called on Santa Anna to reverse the liberal agenda of the Congress and restore military and church privileges.[5] He returned to Mexico City, assumed the presidency for one short month, then again retired to his hacienda at Veracruz.[6] It was during his short return to the presidency that Santa Anna met with Stephen F. Austin in Mexico City. Austin had traveled to the capital city with a request from a convention at San Felipe for Texas statehood and independence from Coahuila. Austin first met with Gómez Farías and several cabinet members. That meeting did not go well. Austin recalled in a letter, "I told the vice president the other day that Texas must be made a state by the Government or she would make herself one . . . This he took as a threat and became much enraged."[7] Austin continued to pressure the Mexican government. He met with Santa Anna and other officials, including Lorenzo de Zavala, on November 5, 1833.[8] While the general did not grant Austin's request for independent statehood for Texas, he did authorize a repeal of Article 11 of the Law of April 6, 1830, which had prohibited immigration from the United States, promised more support for Austin's colonization efforts, and pledged some reforms of the state legal system.[9] These concessions were not enough for Austin; he left Mexico City for Texas greatly disappointed.[10]

Austin wrote a series of letters during his trip that reveal his frustration. In a letter to John Austin he wrote, "I have had a long trip so far and more difficulties to work through here than you can well form an idea of. But I hope to get along and that Texas will be a State of this, or the U.S., republic before another year, for I am so weary that life is hardly worth having, situated as we are now." Mexican officials acquired a letter Austin sent to the ayuntamiento of Béxar, then led by centralist alcalde José Ángel Navarro, urging the members to join other Texas ayuntamientos for a unilateral move toward statehood.[11] Orders were sent to arrest Austin for treason and he was intercepted in Saltillo on January 3, 1834, and taken prisoner. A few days later at Monterrey, Austin wrote to Ruiz and others regarding his situation.[12] Austin's letter to Ruiz did not survive, but he noted in his prison diary that he sent similar letters to other recipients including the ayuntamiento of San Felipe de Austin. This missive, which survived, asked Texas leaders to "keep quiet" and "discountenance all revolutionary measures and men."[13] This shift toward a cautious tone likely reflects Austin's knowledge that Mexican officials might be intercepting and reading his letters. Austin was transferred from prison to prison until Christmas Day of 1834, when he was released on bond but told to remain in Mexico City. He was included in a general amnesty in July 1835 and at the end of August finally returned to Texas by way of New Orleans.[14]

While Austin was in Mexico City, Congress continued its anticlerical agenda, raising tensions among the traditional elites and the staunchly Catholic popular classes. On December 2, 1833, General Nicolás Bravo issued his own pronouncement calling for the defense of the church and military and a new Congress. This time Santa Anna stayed in Veracruz, opting only to write Bravo and ask him to lay down his arms. He also wrote to Gómez Farías, criticizing him for not restraining Congress, which led to a series of openly hostile letters between the president and the acting president. On April 16, 1834, these were read aloud in Congress, providing the nation with proof that the president and vice president were no longer in accord. Santa Anna then decided to resume the presidency and close Congress, ostensibly to maintain moderate control of the country.[15]

Santa Anna appeared to generally support liberal reforms, but repeatedly he and members of his cabinet called for Congress to moderate its positions and allow time for reforms to gain gradual acceptance. Santa Anna also feared the ultra-conservative reactionary factions positioning themselves for a politically timed take over. Many vendettas and unresolved aspirations continued to swirl in Mexican politics. Santa Anna himself, a liberal reformer in past times, had many personal and political enemies in the ranks of the traditionalists.[16]

Santa Anna returned to Mexico City and issued a manifesto on April 29, 1834. In it he declared that he did not support the disorganized plans of the "demagogues." He asserted his popular mandate as president to "contain or moderate precipitated decisions or excessive passions," he promised to defend religion, liberty, security, and all rights guaranteed by the Constitution; and he expressed concern for the "immature introduction of [certain] reforms." Santa Anna called for Congress to meet on May 21, and, when they refused to do so, he orchestrated a takeover of the national government. He called upon the governor of the Federal District, José María Tornel, to issue the Plan de Cuernavaca on May 28, 1834. It contained five articles: (1) all decrees issued against individuals and the Church, and in favor of the Masonic sects, were abolished; (2) all laws violating the constitution and the general will were reversed; (3) Santa Anna was given the authority to execute these demands; (4) all deputies who favored these deeply unpopular reforms were removed from office and replaced following the procedure of the Constitution of 1824; and (5) Santa Anna would have those forces who defended the plan at his service to ensure that it was executed accordingly.[17] Over three dozen municipalities passed resolutions in favor of the plan, many centered near Mexico City, giving Santa Anna the justification he needed to close Congress and repeal unpopular reforms.

On June 12, Santa Anna threw off his mask, dissolved the Congress and announced his decision to adopt the Plan de Cuernavaca for the nation. Church bells pealed and signs were posted reading "'Religión y Fueros."[18] Throughout that long summer, Santa Anna systematically implemented the objectives of the plan. He reversed the Ley del Caso, restored the fueros of the church and army, oversaw the election of a centralist Congress, dismissed several state legislatures and governors who opposed him, and ultimately discarded the Constitution of 1824.[19]

Texans were thrown into a panic. The sudden public shift in allegiances by Santa Anna confused many leaders and provided the centralist movement with additional time to undercut state and local power.[20] The Governor of Coahuila y Texas, Juan José de Vidaurri y Villaseñor, and a small group of legislators who served on a committee that was responsible for overseeing governmental matters between their regular sessions, declared themselves against the Plan de Cuernavaca.[21] Centralists in Saltillo responded by declaring the Monclova legislature unconstitutional, appointing their own centralist military governor (José María Goribar), and establishing a state legislature in Saltillo. In turn, the federalist ayuntamiento at Monclova declared that Juan José Elguézabal was the governor ad interim. Asked to intervene, Santa Anna authorized an election in September 1834, which was won by Agustín Viesca, a federalist who opposed the centralization of power in the national capital. When Viesca took office in early 1835, he clashed with General Martín Perfecto de Cos, who was serving as commander of the Eastern Interior Provinces and supported the centralists in Saltillo.[22]

On October 7, 1834, Ruiz and other Bexareños met to discuss the deteriorating and confusing situation in the state and national governments.[23] José Antonio Navarro noted at that time that the circumstances represented "the most miserable conditions of the Mexican states since their independence."[24] In an interesting twist of fate, the centralist state legislature in Saltillo nominated José Antonio Navarro to be a senator in the centralist-dominated Congress in Mexico City. Navarro quickly sought the advice of his uncle, José Francisco Ruiz, who replied in April 1835:

> I will give you my advice in a few words, remembering the favorite expression of your worthy father, Bread is Bread, Wine is Wine. The die is cast, and in a few months will begin the revolution that will forever separate Texas from the Republic of Mexico. I feel a lump in my throat when I say this. I spent the flower of my life and freely shed my blood for the Independence of Mexico, and I would willingly do so again, though I am now old, could I see any evidence that unfortunate Mexico was capable of governing herself, or upholding the honor of her flag and her nationality; but I have lost all hope of remedy, and see nothing in the future but her inevitable ruin and degradation. I have military honors (you know it well), and receive a pension from the Government of Mexico. I will lose it all rather than go to Mexico and unite myself to the ranks of that oppressive army. Do not go to the Senate of Mexico, for you will only go to assist in quenching the dying embers of Mexican liberty; let us rather stay in Texas, and throw in our lot with our native State, which can never be worse than now. This is all I have to say.[25]

Navarro heeded his uncle's advice and remained in Texas. Less than one year later, he and Ruiz would be the only native-born Texans who signed the Texas Declaration of Independence and the Constitution of the Republic of Texas.

The Tejanos found themselves in an unfortunate situation where they were likely to be politically dominated by either their Anglo neighbors or Mexican centralists. Most strongly supported the federalists because that political perspective provided for local autonomy. They, therefore, signed a petition declaring that "Mexico and the Federal System is Our Motto." It denounced the centralist leaders in Saltillo for being unconcerned about the strife and loss of life that could result because so many communities remained loyal to the federalist legislature at Monclova. In addressing the threat of possible anarchy, the Bexareños made it clear that they would defend themselves and their interests.[26] Their petition asked representatives from ayuntamientos in Texas to meet in Béxar and decide how to best protect themselves. Ruiz was among forty-nine Bexareños who signed this document.[27] This was Ruiz's first public act in opposition to Santa Anna and the centralist takeover of the Mexican nation. The proposed Béxar convention never materialized, possibly because some feared a contentious reaction from Anglo colonists. Nonetheless, the petition demonstrated Bexareño unity in their support of the federalist legislature in Monclova and opposition to the centralism of Santa Anna.

The federalists in Monclova desperately attempted to hold onto power. Their impending collapse in the face of centralist military action resulted in a hasty and panic-ridden final session of the Monclova legislature in early 1835. During these meetings, the legislators passed a series of bills that drew public criticism, even among federalist sympathizers, including the award of large grants to anyone who raised troops in support of the state and a failed attempt to grant Texas statehood. The public perception of a corrupt federalist state government that favored established elites resulted in a cold response by Anglo Texans to Monclova's pleas for support.[28] In May 1835, the first call to arms had come from Texas's representatives in the Monclova legislature. Samuel M. Williams and Francis W. Johnson reported that Santa Anna's supporters intended a "complete destruction of the existing political and social order in Texas."[29] Though both called for armed Texans to assist their government, only Juan Seguín answered the call.[30] A company of one hundred militia from Béxar under the command of Seguín, who had stepped down as interim jefe político of Béxar to focus on military matters, set out for Monclova on May 16.[31]

Centralist Domingo de Ugartechea, commandant of the Mexican army in Texas and post commander at the presidio in Béxar, ordered the new jefe político of Béxar, José Ángel Navarro, to recall Seguín. Navarro initially refused and called a meeting of the ayuntamiento. Passions ran high at the meeting but ultimately the ayuntamiento decided to order the militia to return via a route that would avoid the troops Ugartachea had sent to stop them. A citizens meeting, attended by Ruiz, was also held with over seventy people in attendance. Though no record remains of the proceeding, Navarro wrote that the crowd initially favored attacking the soldiers posted at Béxar but agreed to support the ayuntamiento's decision after older members advised peace and patience.[32] All but twenty-five of Seguín's militiamen returned upon receiving orders. The remainder, including Seguín, arrived at Monclova to discover that Governor Viesca had capitulated to the centralists, ordered the dissolution of all militias, and fled Monclova in advance of Ugartechea's troops. Seguín later recalled being "disgusted with the weakness of the Executive, who had given up the struggle."[33]

The Tejanos were not alone in their resistance; skirmishes erupted in California and Zacatecas. In order to suppress local resistance, the centralist Congress dramatically reduced the state militias. Santa Anna led an army to Zacatecas and brutally suppressed the uprising there. A month later, Congress revoked the Constitution of 1824. General Martín Perfecto de Cos in Saltillo began planning to fortify Texas, preparing six hundred troops to occupy Béxar, with plans for more to be stationed at Goliad and Nacogdoches. Cos publicly cited the need for Indian defense, but privately wrote of his concern with the "strangers" (Anglo Americans) plotting to wrestle the frontier territories from Mexico on behalf of the United States.[34]

The march of centralism and the repeal of the federalist Constitution of 1824 divided both Anglos and Tejanos. The political climate was one of bewilderment and confusion because the ultimate political ends of the centralists remained unclear. A "war party" gradually developed among Anglos that fostered revolutionary attitudes and a political break from Mexico. It also strongly opposed the land policies of the Coahuila y Texas state government. Such sentiments resulted in citizen skirmishes with Mexican soldiers. In contrast, a "peace party" emerged under the leadership of Austin that sought to find accord with Mexico.

Tejanos were divided as well. On the eve of Texas independence, most of the four thousand Tejanos lived in four communities. Nacogdoches had approximately six hundred Tejanos, who did not engage in the conflict within their region. The Tejanos in Martin de León's colony of Victoria, who numbered approximately four hundred and fifty, remained largely neutral during the fight for independence. The 1,350 Tejanos of the Goliad/La Bahía region and 1,600 Tejanos in Béxar suffered greatly by living in the war zone. Most Tejanos were federalists and politically aligned with the peace party. Yet Béxar, with its large garrison, became the center of centralist power in Texas. This muted much of the federalist sympathy there. Tejanos understood that they were in a particularly difficult situation. If a war began, it would be waged in their homeland. Any action that they took, even declaring neutrality, would appear as traitorous to one side or the other.[35]

Local reactions against centralist policies were mixed. Some commu-

nities, such as San Felipe, Liberty, and Brazoria, formed Committees of
Public Safety that claimed the right to rule in the absence of legitimate
government, in the spirit of earlier Spanish and Mexican juntas. These
committees were largely concentrated in Austin's colony and the areas
leading to the Gulf Coast that held large numbers of war party sympathizers. Episodes at Anáhuac, San Felipe, and Brazoria drew the ire of other
communities, who complained that the rashness of these violent actions
was drawing them into unwanted conflict with Mexican authorities. The
ayuntamientos of Mina, Liberty, and Gonzáles formally complained to
San Felipe that its residents were drawing them into a fight they did not
wish to fight. The ayuntamiento of Columbia went as far as asserting that
"the citizens of this Jurisdiction hold themselves to be true, faithful, loyal,
and unoffending Mexican citizens" who sought a restoration of "peace,
quiet harmony," and they criticized the rebellious "uncautious and unre-
flecting" minority. Historian Paul D. Lack attributed this mixed response
to the fact that "the would-be leaders of Texas operated in ignorance and
confusion regarding the nature and meaning of events outside the province; in contrast, Mexican policy makers had an abundance of accurate
information."[36]

General Cos in July 1835 warned the people of Texas that he was prepared to use his "strong arm" to demand "subjugation to the laws." Blam-
ing the situation on land speculators and impoverished adventurers from
the United States who had nothing to lose, he warned of the destruction
that would occur if war came. The response in Texas was again mixed, but
a stronger thread of unity and rebellion also emerged. Several communities declared loyalty to Cos. José Antonio Menchaca, the procurador of
Nacogdoches, warned Cos about an impending Anglo plot to overthrow
local authorities. Still other communities called for a convention or "Consultation" to meet on October 15, 1835, at San Felipe to discuss a unified
response. This call was initially made by the peace faction, who sought to
temper war agitators. Though Santa Anna freed Austin to go home that
summer, he also ordered the arrests of several outspoken Texans. A growing number of Anglos rallied against such actions, emboldened by similar
resistance in other Mexican states, such as Zacatecas. In the months leading up to the Consultation, Texas patriotism, military preparedness, and
support for the war party all strengthened.[37]

Before the Consultation at San Felipe, the first shots of the Texas Revolution were fired. Concerned with growing tensions, Ugartechea ordered

the alcalde of Gonzáles to return a cannon loaned to Green DeWitt's colony for defense against the Indians several years earlier. When the official did not comply, Ugartechea sent Captain Francisco de Castañeda, whom Ruiz had previously investigated for payroll improprieties. He arrived at Gonzáles with his dragoons on September 29, 1835. The federalist colonists refused to surrender their cannon to a centralist officer and defiantly flew a banner stating, "Come and Take It." Settlers from nearby communities hurried to defend Gonzáles, and on the morning of October 2, Texas colonists attacked Mexican soldiers encamped on the west bank of the Guadalupe River. The war for Texan independence had begun.[38]

The unexpected confrontation precipitated a quick scramble for leadership and coordination among the colonists. A war council organized and authorized the election of a commander. Austin arrived a few days later so feeble from his imprisonment that a servant had to help him mount his horse. He reported to the San Felipe Committee of Public Safety, "War is declared—public opinion has proclaimed it against a Military despotism—The campaign has commenced . . . One spirit and one purpose animates the people of this party of the country, and that is to take Béxar, and drive the military out of Texas." He added, "A combined effort of all Texas would soon free our soil of Military despots." Despite his weakened condition, Austin was elected commander-in-chief and prepared for a march to Béxar, the center of centralist authority in Texas. He held elections of officers, gathered supplies, and attempted to impose order and discipline on his men, few of whom had any formal military training.[39]

In response to the unrest in Texas, Santa Anna sent General Cos to Béxar. He reached Goliad by October 1, and arrived in Béxar two days after the skirmish at Gonzáles. His 400 troopers reinforced the 247 men already stationed at Béxar. Cos ordered the infantry to fortify the Plaza de Armas, where the Ruiz home was located, with a few artillery pieces, while the majority of his soldiers garrisoned the Alamo.[40]

Understanding that any forthcoming battle might well occur in the immediate vicinity of his home on the Plaza de Armas, Ruiz remained at the ranch owned by José Ignacio Pérez during what became known as the Siege of Béxar. Other prominent Tejanos, including José Antonio Navarro, also evacuated the town to wait out the campaign.[41] Again, the Tejanos of Béxar found themselves in an awkward situation. Most shared the concerns of their Anglo neighbors regarding centralization, Texas statehood, and Santa Anna's dismissal of the Constitution of 1824. But they worried about the talk of national independence among the Anglos not only because a civil war would be fought in their homeland, but because their place in an Anglo-led Texas was uncertain.[42]

Austin marched his militia to the outskirts of Béxar and set up camp on Salado Creek on October 20, 1835, to await reinforcements. Tejano federalists joined Austin there. Eventually numbering more than 135, they proclaimed themselves defenders of the Constitution of 1824, which at that time was the official position of Austin and the Consultation, and apparently most of the Anglo troops. Juan N. Seguín brought thirty-seven men, the remnant of the militia that had been disbanded by Ugartechea after their ride to defend the Monclova legislature.[43]

Austin sent Seguín and fifty men to identify friendly Tejanos in the area and bring back food for the camp.[44] Ruiz was among the sympathetic Tejanos that Seguín visited. Ruiz did not hesitate to assist the Texan army led by his longtime friend Austin. He provided $1,274.87 worth of food to the cause, which was a significant sum—over four times the annual salary of a Mexican soldier.[45] He also provided Seguín with five horses and two mules, valued at $180.00, and various supplies, such as soap, pecans, and candy, valued at an additional $767.37.[46]

On October 28, 1835, the Texans clashed with the troops of General Cos near Mission Concepción. In the resulting skirmish, the Texans held their ground during three charges by the Mexican army. The rebels managed to defeat the larger force, although they sustained one fatality, Georgian Richard Andrews. Having lost at Concepcíon, Cos decided to refrain from further offensives and dug more defensive works.[47]

The rebels' victory at Mission Concepción emboldened the Texans to take more aggressive measures. In mid-November 1835, the Consultation established a provisional Texas state government, with Henry Smith as governor and a council. The latter promptly created a regular army to be commanded by Sam Houston.[48] Because Austin had been selected by the Consultation at San Felipe to represent the Texan cause in the United States, he called for an election to select a new commander, which was won by Edward Burleson.[49]

Burleson ordered an assault on Béxar at dawn on December 4, 1835. The men gathered at midnight to organize for the assault. Reports of a mysterious figure headed to Béxar from the Texan camp spread through the troops. Burleson, fearing that Cos would have notice of the attack, canceled the operation to the great frustration of his men. A war council met in which Burleson offered to resign and suggested they retreat to Goliad. Benjamin R. Milam, who had just rejoined the army, then stepped forward and famously asked: "Who will go with old Ben Milam into San Antonio?" Two hundred troops volunteered, and Milam was elected to lead the advance column. Burleson agreed to supervise the operation of the reserves, which totaled nearly 500 men.[50]

The first column of Texans entered Béxar on December 5 and took over some abandoned buildings, from which they began inching toward the Plaza de Armas and the Plaza Principal. As the Texans inched towards the plazas, Milam was killed on the third day of fighting. Despite this setback, the Texans advanced again and took a long, interconnected group of buildings known as Zambrano Row. Mexican soldiers fought for each room, but the Texans won by tunneling through walls, breaking through windows, and engaging in close combat. Cos responded with a heavy bombardment of the structure, leaving its walls in ruins. Cos found himself in an unexpectedly desperate situation by December 9. Some of his officers raised a flag of truce and met with the Texans in the Plaza de Armas. On the morning of December 11, the terms of the treaty were presented to the Texan troops. The Mexican army prepared to leave and surrender their arms to the Texans. Because the victorious rebels did not have supplies to feed so many prisoners, Cos was allowed to march his defeated troops south into Mexico after they all signed pledges not to fight against the Texans again.[51]

The Texans turned their military sights elsewhere, in particular Matamoros. Reassignments quickly depleted the number of Texan soldiers left at Béxar, and Ruiz again contributed to their support. He helped to gather supplies for the rebel soldiers who were to stay behind while the others marched on to other places.[52] Captain Juan N. Seguín's company, comprised mostly of Tejanos from Béxar, was among the units that stayed. Ordered to pursue a Mexican force and take from them a *cavallado* (herd of horses), the Tejanos succeeded in capturing one hundred horses. Seguín was then "detailed to the ranches on the San Antonio River, to see if I could find more horses."[53] Ruiz again contributed to the defense of Béxar, this time by donating five horses valued at $130 on January 1, 1836, presumably to Seguín's foragers.[54]

The battle at Béxar had greatly depleted the supplies and arms of the Texans, and the departure of so many weakened the town defenses. Jim Bowie arrived at the Alamo on January 18 with reinforcements and orders from Houston to remove the artillery and blow up the fortifications if necessary. On January 26, one of the newly arrived reinforcements, James Bonham, organized a rally which passed a resolution in favor of holding the Alamo, and so the men decided to stay. William B. Travis and David Crockett arrived on February 10 with thirty Tennesseans.[55] But the growing garrison of the Alamo made it imperative that someone find supplies.

An expedition of twenty Tejanos, each with a team and cart, was organized under Ruiz's command. José Antonio Menchaca, Ignacio Espinosa, and Juan Ximénes later recalled in an affidavit for a pension claim, "Cols. Travis and Bowie asked for volunteers who would go to Port Lavaca with their own teams to fetch us arms and stores sent from New Orleans. Several good citizens that were very much in favor of the Cause of Independence offered their services and a train of 20 ox carts were sent down and placed under the order of Don Francisco Ruiz." As to why all the members of the expedition were Tejanos, Menchaca explained, "Mexicans alone could be employed for said service since the others was all strangers to that section of the Country."[56] Seguín recalled how *carreteros* (cart drivers) hauled supplies to the Texan army commanded by General Thomas J. Rusk at Camp Preston, "a train of over 20 carts was organized and sent under the command of Don Francisco Ruiz. On the arrival of said train at Fort Preston near La Vaca means of transportation being very much needed, Gen. T. Rusk who was in command detained the train for about two months and used it for the exclusive service of the Camp."[57] The teams arrived at a critical time. Menchaca confessed, "but for the said teams arriving in time the camp would have been obliged to disband for they were in great need."[58] The carreteros hauled supplies for the Texan army until mid-February 1836, when they at last returned to Béxar with supplies for the besieged Alamo. There these unpaid volunteers were discharged from military service and allowed to return to their families.[59]

In addition to his work commanding the carreteros, Ruiz's involvement in the rebellion was about to become even stronger as Texas began reorganizing its political future. The provisional government of Texas on December 13, 1835, called for the election of delegates from each settlement to meet at Washington-on-the-Brazos for a convention to draft a constitution. On February 1, 1836, the citizens of Béxar met at the Alamo and voted for delegates to this convention. They decided to allow the residents of Béxar to elect two delegates to represent the residents of the municipio and to let the soldiers elect two delegates to represent them. Out of 278 votes cast in the municipal election at the Alamo, Ruiz received sixty-one, a total that was surpassed only by his nephew, José Antonio Navarro, who had sixty-five.[60] Elder statesman Erasmo Seguín and Gaspar Flores de Abrego, a federalist born in Béxar who had served several terms as alcalde, received sixty and fifty-nine votes respectively. The mostly Anglo volunteers at the Alamo chose Samuel A. Maverick and Jesse Badgett as their representatives. Juan N. Seguín, who was also serving as alcalde of Béxar at that time, wrote to Ruiz on February 10, 1836, informing him that he won the election to represent his district at Washington-on-the Brazos.[61] (The full election results are shown in Appendix 2.)

As Ruiz prepared for his journey to Washington-on-the-Brazos, news arrived of the unexpectedly rapid approach of the Mexican army, this time under the personal command of Santa Anna. The Tejano scout who brought the news to Béxar was Ruiz's son-in-law, Blas María Herrera. On February 18, 1836, Travis, now in command at the Alamo, wrote that "our spies have just returned from Rio Grande—The enemy is there one thousand strong & is making every preparation to invade us."[62] He summoned his council to deliberate the accuracy of the report. John Sutherland recalled in his memoirs, "The council adjourned without coming to any conclusion as to whether it was necessary to give any heed to the warning or not."[63] Sutherland included a defense of the Anglos' disbelief of Herrera, based primarily on the intrepid scout's race: "so many false alarms had been given by a degraded class of 'greasers' continuously passing to and fro. . . the little excitement which was created passed off as fast as the report which produced it became more and more discredited." Although the newly arrived Anglos may have ignored Herrera because of his race, his fellow Béxareños gave his report the utmost respect. Sutherland noted that "the inhabitants were observed to be in quite an unusual stir. The citizens of every class were hurrying to and fro, through the streets, with obvious signs of excitement. Houses were emptied, and their contents put into carts, and hauled off. Such of the poorer class, who had no better mode of conveyance, were shouldering their effects, and leaving on foot." Alarmed, Travis investigated the cause of the commotion, but "no satisfactory answer could be obtained." He ordered that no one would be allowed to leave Béxar, but this only increased the departures and hostilities. Travis continued to interrogate the Tejanos leaving Béxar, but none would disclose their reasons for leaving. Finally, "a friendly Mexican" informed Travis that the enemy's cavalry had reached León Creek and that Béxar would be attacked the next day (February 20), reminding him that "a messenger [Herrera] had arrived, a day or two before." Heavy rains delayed the arrival of the Mexican cavalry, giving Travis time to ponder the trustworthiness of yet another report, and also giving Herrera time to leave Béxar.[64]

Herrera left Béxar on February 21, 1836, and escorted his father-in-law Ruiz and cousin José Antonio Navarro to Washington-on-the-Brazos.[65] Strong winds and a bitter cold drizzle gripped Béxar as the Ruiz party prepared to depart. A "blue norther" blew into Texas in the final days of February of that year, slowing down Santa Anna's main column as it marched toward the Texan rebels, just as it impeded Ruiz and Navarro.[66]

When Ruiz and Navarro arrived for the convention, they found that the new town of Washington-on-the-Brazos was crude and had a population of only about one hundred people. It consisted mostly of log cabins and storehouses, which relied on goods brought up the Brazos River. The delegates crammed into a few hotels and boarding houses, as well as businesses and private homes. Ruiz, Navarro, and Lorenzo de Zavala, who arrived the day after they did, joined fellow Béxar delegate Jesse Badgett in bunking in a carpenter shop with William F. Gray, who was an observer and not a delegate. Gray wrote in his diary that the benefits of their quarters included "a good floor" where they could be "comparatively comfortable."[67]

The Convention at Washington-on-the-Brazos opened on March 1, in the only building in town capable of accommodating the forty-four delegates, a roughly finished wooden structure with cloth coverings tacked over its few windows, which did little to stop the chilly wind. News of the pending confrontation in Béxar had already arrived. William B. Travis's famous "I shall never surrender or retreat" letter, dated February 24, had arrived the previous day and the Convention considered reinforcing the Texans at the Alamo.[68] Travis's correspondence placed Ruiz and Navarro in a peculiar situation. Travis repeatedly berated the Bexareños for disloyalty and demanded that the Convention adopt a policy of forced contributions from Mexican Texans, whom he considered "public enemies."[69] No action was taken on this appeal at the Convention, but Ruiz would later face the same issue during his term in the Texas Senate.

The first order of business for the Convention was certifying the credentials of the delegates. Having done that, the body elected Richard Ellis of Pecan Point as president. Ellis quickly appointed a committee of five to draft a declaration of independence, which settled the long debate between that status and statehood for Texas with hardly a murmur of dissent. All proceedings were conducted in English, a language which Ruiz and Navarro did not fully command. However, there were enough bilingual delegates present (including their roommate, Zavala) for them to actively participate.[70] The second day, March 2, the committee chair, George C. Childress, presented the Texas Declaration of Independence to the delegates. It followed the model of the United States Declaration of Independence by including a statement about natural law and government, a list of grievances with the Mexican government, and a pronouncement of independence. In particular, it charged the government under Santa Anna with transforming from a federal republic to despotic centralist military rule. It was adopted without change by unanimous vote. However, when written drafts were received, it contained so many errors that it was returned to the committee for correction.[71]

That night Ruiz carefully reviewed the Texas Declaration of Independence with Navarro and the bilingual delegates.[72] The following day, March 3, 1836, all of the delegates present signed five large copies of the document. Ruiz was the second delegate to endorse the declaration, while Navarro was third. Several accounts, including Jacob de Cordova's, recount Navarro's hesitation to sign when the gravity of the situation briefly overcame him. According to Cordova, the reassuring guidance of his uncle, Ruiz, rallied him.[73] However, other historians, such as Navarro scholar David McDonald, have raised some serious doubts about this account of what transpired.[74] Nevertheless, the only two-native born Texans who served as delegates, Ruiz and Navarro, both signed the Texas Declaration of Independence at a time when the success of their venture was far from assured.

On March 7, the Convention resumed its work on a constitution for the Republic of Texas. Navarro was selected to serve on the drafting committee. The main issue of contention was a proposal that threatened the status of large land grants. The proposal read "no claim of eleven leagues of land or more shall be valid; and all titles . . . for more than one league and one labor of land shall be null and void and of no effect." This was a direct attack on the landed elites of Texas who had received eleven-league grants, especially during the years 1834 and 1835, when the centralist state government of Coahuila y Texas was attempting to re-Mexicanize Texas. These grants were comparatively large and only available to Mexican citizens, although many had been transferred into the hands of American speculators. The proposal affected several members of the Ruiz-Navarro family, and Navarro strongly objected to it. He argued that many of these grants had already been subdivided and sold. The nullification provision failed, but the issue would resurface in the First Congress of the Republic of Texas.[75]

The Convention received the stunning news of the fall of the Alamo on March 13. Three different letters arrived. Among the first letters to arrive was one from Juan N. Seguín to Ruiz and Navarro. Written in Spanish, it reported the fall of the Alamo and warned of Santa Anna's movement eastward. This letter was later lost, but Gray in his diary recalled its arrival, "In half an hour after an express was received from General Sam Houston, bringing the sad intelligence of the fall of the Alamo, on the morning of March 6. His letters were dated on 11 and 13, and a letter from John [Juan] Seguín, at Gonzales, to Ruiz and Navarro, brought the same account. Still others did, or affected to, disbelieve it."[76] Other letters arrived later that day. The Convention adjourned early, no doubt to allow the delegates to reflect on the sobering implication of that fateful event.

For Ruiz, the news was even more troubling than it was for those who did not live in Béxar. When Santa Anna secured the town on February 29, 1836, he found that it had no government because the municipal elections scheduled for December 1835 had not taken place, except for the one for procurador.[77] Santa Anna appointed Ruiz's son, Francisco Antonio Ruiz, as alcalde ad interim until an election could be held.[78] This put Francisco Antonio in the precarious position of working with Santa Anna and the invading army while his father was in open rebellion against them.

The Convention resumed its work with a sense of urgency. It crafted a document in just three days that was primarily modeled on that of the United States, except that it unambiguously established the legality of slavery. It also stripped citizenship and land from any person "who shall leave the country for the purpose of evading participation in the present struggle, shall refuse to participate in it, or shall give aid or assistance to the present enemy." Borrowing from Anglo American legal traditions, the new constitution adopted the common law but eliminated the old English distinction between courts of law and courts of equity so that claims could be remedied in a single court. Borrowing from the Spanish-Mexican tradition, it granted married women separate rights of property and an equal share of all marital property. Drawing also from their common experience, the delegates invented legal exemptions that protected debtors' homes and means of support from creditors.[79] This document was quickly adopted by the delegates at midnight on March 16, 1836.

That night's session continued into the early morning hours of March 17. The delegates had to vote for interim officials for the new republic. The election for an interim president resulted in the election of David G. Burnet, an empresario and lawyer from northeastern Texas. Burnet was not a delegate to the convention. He arrived at Washington-on-the-Brazos seeking an opportunity to win clemency for two clients who had been convicted of murder, although some later claimed he was en route to offer his assistance to Travis at the Alamo. After hearing of the fall of the Alamo, the chair of the Convention, Richard Ellis, wanted to adjourn and begin again in Nacogdoches. Burnet leapt onto a bench and made a speech asking delegates to stay and finish their business. They did so, and the new constitution was adopted that evening. The frontrunners for the presidency—Austin, Houston, and William H. Wharton—were absent, so Burnet and Samuel Price Carson were nominated. Burnet won, on a vote of 29–23, in the early hours of March 17. Ruiz, together with Navarro and Zavala, supported the enthusiastic Burnet.[80] Several of the other races were uncontested, such as vice president, which went to Zavala.[81] The new officers were sworn in at 4:00 a.m., and the Convention recessed. The next morning, after only a few hours of sleep, the delegates approved a $1,000,000 loan to finance the government and adjourned sine die.[82] They were in a near panic, fearing the approach of Santa Anna. Navarro wrote that many delegates left Washington-on-the-Brazos "before the ink had dried from the signatures," and some did not sign at all before departing.[83]

Ruiz, Navarro, and Zavala were eager to leave. Gray noted in his diary, "My Mexican friends are packing up, with the intention of crossing the Brazos to-night."[84] They left Washington-on-the-Brazos on March 18, at ten o'clock in the morning, with their attendants, mules, and packhorses. They were not alone. Gray wrote, "Many persons, moving eastward to escape the anticipated storm of war, came along with their families, some in wagons, some in carts, and some on foot, with mules and horses, packed with their movables." The weather that day was cloudy and drizzly. The Ruiz party traveled down the Brazos to the ferry crossing located on the plantation of Jared E. Groce, arriving on March 20. There they settled for the night and learned more of the fall of the Alamo from Joe, Travis's slave, who had survived the battle and escaped. Joe told them about the fighting and its grim aftermath.[85]

Ruiz learned that night that his son, Francisco Antonio Ruiz, as alcalde of Béxar, had been ordered by Santa Anna to gather the bodies of the Alamo defenders and burn them.[86] Santa Anna had the bodies of the Mexicans separated from those of the Anglos before ordering the latter to be burned. The younger Ruiz led a company of his dragoons to gather wood, and by late afternoon on March 6, a funeral pyre had been assembled, with alternating layers of wood and bodies. Kindling was distributed throughout, and at about 5:00 the entire pile was set ablaze. As for the Mexican dead, Francisco Antonio was instructed to bury them in San Antonio's camposanto, but he confessed later that, "not having sufficient room for them, I ordered some of them to be thrown in the river, which was done on the same day."[87]

On March 21, Zavala and the other members of the new Texas government crossed the Brazos and rode for Harrisburg. Ruiz and Navarro departed for San Felipe, intending to continue to Brazoria or Velasco, where they hoped to catch a ship bound for New Orleans. Their plans were dashed when they learned that Houston had abandoned San Felipe and was marching for Groce's Plantation. They followed the retreating Texas army under Houston and returned to Groce's Plantation. Several historians have written that Ruiz's son-in-law, Blas María Herrera, at this point left Ruiz and joined Houston's army, for which he continued to serve as a scout through the Battle of San Jacinto.[88] However, Herrera himself recounted his service during the war in a pension application on November 11, 1874, and made no mention of serving under Houston.[89] Ruiz and Navarro joined others bound for Nacogdoches and continued on to Natchitoches, Louisiana, where Ruiz had friends with whom they could stay.[90] During this second exodus from Texas, Ruiz certainly must have recalled his 1813 flight from Texas to nearly the same place.

As Ruiz and Navarro arrived in Natchitoches, the Mexican and Texan armies continued the cat-and-mouse chase that would end on the San Jacinto River near Buffalo Bayou. Unlike 1813, when Ruiz and many others failed to secure independence and became exiles, the Texans prevailed at the Battle of San Jacinto on April 21, 1836. Ruiz remained in Natchitoches for the duration of this fateful campaign, while Navarro continued to New Orleans, where he reunited with fellow convention candidates Erasmo Seguín and Gaspar Flores de Abrego.[91] Among Ruiz's concerns in Natchitoches was finding a buyer for his late brother José Antonio Ruiz's nearby ranch, where Ruiz, Vicente Tarín, and other Tejano exiles had fled

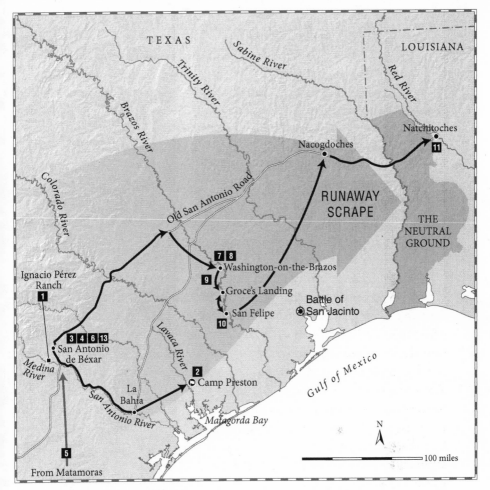

1 **Oct. 12, 1835–Dec. 11, 1835** During Seige of Béxar, Ruiz is at Ignacio Pérez Ranch on Medina River where he donates cattle, horses, and supplies.

2 **December 1835** Ruiz leads ox cart expedition from Béxar to Camp Preston to bring supplies to the Alamo Defenders.

3 **Feb. 1, 1836** Election is held at Alamo for delegates to convention at Washington-on-the-Brazos. Ruiz is elected as a delegate.

4 **February 1836** Ruiz returns with 20 ox carts to resupply Alamo.

5 **Feb. 18, 1836** Blas Herrera (Ruiz's son-in-law) arrives at Alamo from Matamoros with news of Santa Anna's approach.

6 **Feb. 21, 1836** Ruiz, Navarro, Herrera, and Coy leave San Antonio de Béxar for Washington-on-the-Brazos.

7 **March 3, 1836** Ruiz signs Texas Declaration of Independence at Washington-on-the-Brazos.

8 **March 18, 1836** Ruiz, Navarro, and Herrera leave Washington-on-the-Brazos.

9 **March 20, 1836** Ruiz party arrives at the ferry crossing at Groce's Plantation, where they meet Travis' slave, Joe.

10 **March 21,1836** Ruiz's party departs for San Felipe intending to continue to Brazoria or Velasco. Enroute they learn of Houston's retreat and they return to Groce's Plantation.

11 **April 1836** Ruiz joins the Runaway Scrape to Nacogdoches and continues on to Natchitoches.

12 **Summer 1836** Ruiz returns to Béxar.

Carol Zuber-Mallison / ZMGraphics.com

Ruiz and the Texas Revolution, 1835–36.

following the Battle of Medina in 1813.[92] He entrusted this to a longtime friend and attorney, Ambrosio Sompayrac of Natchitoches.[93] Ruiz left a power of attorney granting Sompayrac the authority to sell the land and divide it among the heirs as determined by the laws of Louisiana. It noted that the whereabouts of José Antonio Ruiz's wife were unknown and that Manuela de la Peña, their late mother, had inherited half of the estate because José Antonio did not have any children. The land apparently never found a buyer. It was later sold by the sheriff of Sabine Parish in 1847 for unpaid taxes.[94]

José Francisco Ruiz remained in Louisiana for four months tending to personal affairs and business. He was among the many that flooded back into Texas following the victory at San Jacinto in April 1836. When he returned to Béxar, he was again called back into public service. But this time it would be for the Republic of Texas, the third national government under which he had held public office. The frontier federalist had finally achieved his greatest dream: the borderland in which he was born and raised, and on whose behalf he fought several times in different uniforms, was now independent. But he did have to share power with newcomers, Anglos who did not have his values and attachments to the region and its people. The new immigrants also mistrusted him, and this would further complicate Ruiz's last efforts as a public servant.

Texas Senate

The labors of the first Congress demanded the highest exercise
of wisdom and prudence. They were herculean in magnitude,
involving the enactment of primary laws embracing within their
scope the entire machinery of civil government under a written
constitution.

—John Henry Brown, 1892[1]

For Anglos, the Battle of San Jacinto ended the war for Texas independence and ushered in a new era of the Republic of Texas. Most
Anglos perceived Tejanos as "Mexican," which served to describe
both a national identity and an ethnic description. Tejanos were thus a
suspect category of people, whose loyalty to the new Republic was questioned. Many Texan leaders feared that most Tejanos wanted Texas to remain part of Mexico.[2] The greatest threat of a loyalist uprising appeared
to be in Tejano-dominated urban centers, of which Béxar was the largest. Following the provisions of the Texas Constitution of 1836, Thomas J.
Rusk, the commander of the Texas army, tasked José Francisco Ruiz with
determining which residents of Béxar were "friends of Texas" and empow-
ered him to confiscate the possessions of non-loyal residents.[3]

The constitutional provision that stripped citizenship and property
from all who aided the Mexicans in the war posed a real threat to Mexican
loyalists at Béxar. Two prominent loyalists appealed to Ruiz for protection of their properties, Ramón Múzquiz and José Ignacio Pérez. Ramón
Múzquiz had long served as jefe político of Béxar.[4] He remained loyal to
Mexico, and General Martin Perfecto de Cos used him to negotiate with
the Texans during the Siege of Béxar. Múzquiz was appointed jefe político
ad interim by Santa Anna and helped Francisco Antonio Ruiz to bury
the dead after the Battle of the Alamo.[5] After the Mexican defeat at San

Jacinto, his fortune soured. Múzquiz fled to Monclova with his family and never returned. Before he departed, he issued a power of attorney granting José Francisco Ruiz authority over his property in Texas.[6] Ruiz, however, was unable to prevent the confiscation of the Músquiz home on Main Plaza, which was awarded to Erastus "Deaf" Smith.[7]

Ruiz's nephew, José Ignacio Pérez, left Texas after being harassed by Anglos for his loyalties to Mexico. He too left Ruiz in control of his property, hoping that his influence would be able to secure his land from confiscation.[8] Ruiz proved to be a faithful steward of his nephew's property. During the years leading up to the independence of Texas, José Ignacio Pérez became increasingly isolated from Anglo neighbors who were federalists. That isolation soon turned to harassment. A bounty was placed on Pérez's head for being a centralist. Erastus "Deaf" Smith and his brothers-in-law, José María Ruiz de Castañeda, Esmergildo Ruiz de Castañeda, and Bernardino Ruiz de Castañeda, expedited his departure in December 1835.[9] Pérez notified the alcaldes, Erasmo Seguín and Francisco Antonio Ruiz, that he was leaving for Tamaulipas.[10] His preparations included naming agents to handle his affairs while he was in self-imposed exile. A power of attorney filed by Pérez asked José Francisco Ruiz to "manage, care for, and attend to and defend all his properties."[11] Among the business Ruiz completed for Pérez was payment of 413 pesos owed to him for thirty head of cattle given to William B. Travis for use by the Alamo garrison on February 24, 1836.[12] Smith later boasted to fellow Anglos at Béxar that he "chased Pérez and some other Mexicans" out of Béxar County.[13]

Pérez settled on the Río Grande near Guerrero and did not return to Texas until 1847. He then found his land claimed by squatters, including Esmergildo Ruiz, Stephen Jett, and Samuel McCulloch Jr. Two cases concerning the title to his Medina River ranch reached the Supreme Court of Texas.[14] Among the questions raised by the Court was whether occupation by Ruiz and others constituted continuous presence by the titleholder. The judges noted that the constitution of the Republic of Texas stated that "all persons who shall leave the country, for the 'purpose of evading a participation in the present struggle' or shall refuse to participate in it, or shall give aid or 'assistance to the present enemy, shall forfeit all rights of citizenship' and such lands as they may hold in the Republic." The Court found that Ruiz's residence at the Pérez ranch while simultaneously serving as Pérez's legal agent did not constitute lawful presence. They ruled plainly, "He could not adhere to the enemy and be represented here by proxy."[15] Due to this ruling, Pérez lost title to two *sitios* of land consisting of 16,000 acres, despite Ruiz's best efforts to help his nephew.[16]

While Ruiz was carrying out his duties in Béxar, the Republic of Texas prepared for its first election, to be held on September 5, 1836.[17] Stephen F. Austin and Henry Smith announced their candidacies for president. Houston remained quiet in New Orleans but ultimately was swayed by public support to join the race. Looking back, George B. Erath remembered the political climate of that summer, "We here in Texas had nothing to do with parties in the United States. We were Sam Houston or anti-Sam Houston; Eastern Texas was largely for and Western Texas against him."[18] Houston entered the race with only two weeks remaining before the balloting, and he won handily.[19] He named Austin as his secretary of state and Smith as his secretary of the treasury in an effort to promote unity. Meanwhile, the residents of the Béxar District elected Ruiz as their senator and Thomas J. Green to represent them in the House of Representatives.[20]

The First Congress of the Republic of Texas convened on October 3, 1836, in the town of Columbia. The building in which it met was "meager in every respect."[21] Of the fourteen senators, Ruiz was the only native-born Texan. He was one of six senators who had signed the Texas Declaration of Independence earlier that year, while four had fought at the Battle of San Jacinto.[22]

The Senate of the First Congress took up many practical matters of organizing a nation. The large municipios were replaced with smaller counties with defined borders. Mail routes and roads were established. The Army Reorganization Act in the fall of 1836, which Ruiz supported, created a permanent structure for the military. President Houston's nominations of Thomas J. Rusk, Felix Huston, and Albert Sidney Johnston to command the Texas army were endorsed by Ruiz. A navy was also established. The Supreme Court and lower courts were organized, and two of Ruiz's fellow senators, James Collinsworth and Shelby Corzine, were among those appointed as judges. The offices of sheriff, constable, and coroner were defined. The General Land Office was organized. Through it all, Ruiz was an engaged and supportive member of the first Texas Senate, advocating for all Texans, especially his fellow Tejanos.[23]

On its first day, the first Texas Senate adopted the rules of the constitutional convention as its own and elected Richard Ellis to be the president pro tempore replacing Vice President Lorenzo de Zavala, who was gravely ill.[24] Before the senators could address more important issues, they had to resolve four disputed senatorial elections, which took about two weeks to untangle. An election that likely drew Ruiz's attention was the one between Robert A. Irion and Isaac W. Burton. Irion had defeated Burton by a vote of 270 to 252, but Burton asserted that Irion owed his victory to votes from Mexicans in Nacogdoches who were "opposed to the Government and consequently not entitled to citizenship." A Senate committee decided in favor of Irion, declaring that the challenged voters were citizens under the Texas Constitution and could not be disenfranchised except by "due course of law." The Texas Constitution also called for senators to have three-year terms and for them to be divided "by lot into three classes" to stagger their terms "as nearly equal as practicable."[25] In keeping with this requirement, a lottery was held on November 11. Ruiz drew a three-year term along with fellow senators Shelby Corzine (San Augustine), Stephen H. Everitt (Jasper, Jefferson), and Robert Wilson (Harrisburg, Liberty).[26]

To complete its organization, the First Senate established eleven committees: Claims and Accounts; County Boundaries; Indian Affairs; Judiciary; Military Affairs; Naval Affairs; Post Offices and Post Roads; Public Lands; Roads, Bridges, and Ferries; State of the Republic; and Ways and Means. Ruiz served on the Committee on Indian Affairs, a fitting assignment given his career among the Indians. Frontier security had always been of utmost concern for the residents of Texas as a Spanish and Mexican province, and the Republic of Texas era was no different. Interim president David G. Burnet sent a message concerning the problems facing the new nation to both houses of the Texas Congress. Of highest importance, he declared, was "the defense of our country and the achievement of our independence."[27]

The first bill introduced into the Senate originated in the Committee on Indian Affairs. Entitled "A bill for the further protection of the Indian frontier," it was drafted by Sterling C. Robertson and filed on October 21, 1836. It authorized the raising "with as little delay as possible" of a battalion of mounted riflemen and authorized Houston as president to raise more troops and to negotiate peace treaties with the Indian tribes. It was approved in early December 1836, though of course the meager financial resources of the Republic hindered its implementation.[28] Ruiz and his fellow senators also approved the appointments of Kelsey H. Douglass and Henry Millard as Indian commissioners.[29]

Debate in November focused on the annexation of Texas by the United

States. The first Senate voted to send one of its own members, William H. Wharton, as minister plenipotentiary to Washington, D.C., to pursue that goal. Letters from Washington indicated President Andrew Jackson of the United States would approve annexation.[30] The fate of General Antonio López de Santa Anna, a prisoner of the Texans since his defeat at San Jacinto, was also a topic of debate in the Senate. President Sam Houston, installed in September 1836, wanted to send the Mexican leader to Washington, where he pledged to assist in negotiating a treaty of annexation with President Jackson.[31] As Austin wrote on November 7, "Probably Mexico will not refuse to treat with the U.S. for a quit claim, or a final adjustment of limits, and thus give to Texas what she wants, without compromising her pride and prejudices by treating direct with Texas or the same results may be attained by means of the mediation of the U.S. which Santa Anna has solicited from Gen. Jackson—Could not Santa Anna be used in that matter? And if he can, why not use him?" Ruiz voted against this proposal, preferring to keep Santa Anna imprisoned.[32] The Texas Congress, however, passed a joint resolution that authorized the general's release but made Houston solely responsible for him. Houston freed Santa Anna and Colonel Juan N. Almonte, who served as Santa Anna's aide, and then appointed three Texans to escort Santa Anna and Almonte to Washington, where they arrived on January 17, 1837.[33] Unfortunately for Texas, Jackson did not agree to annexation, but he did officially recognize the Republic as a nation before leaving office.[34]

The Texan Congress reorganized the Mexican municipio of Béxar as the County of Bexar on December 22, 1836; its urban center was incorporated into an American-style municipality named the City of San Antonio on June 5, 1837.[35] The newly minted city swelled with American and German immigrants, fundamentally changing its demographic character. Harassment of Tejanos escalated as more Anglos settled in Béxar. A shifting balance of power away from Tejanos and into the hands of Anglos was evident in the immediate aftermath of San Jacinto. Suspicion of Tejano loyalties was coupled with negative perceptions of "Mexican" ethnic traits.[36]

Ruiz witnessed hostility toward Tejanos personally and pleas for help reached him while he was serving in the Texas Senate. In response, he wrote a resolution, introduced by Senator Irion on November 26, 1836, calling upon Congress to abandon any plans to punish Tejanos who had been forced by circumstances to accept a pardon from Santa Anna when he occupied Béxar. After all, "if that tyrant in the midst of his cruelty wished to be humane, will the descendants of the immortal Washington and the imitators of his virtue show less generosity?" The Texans had a great opportunity to be merciful so that "future generations will remember with gratitude and exultation that the Texians knew how at the same time to triumph, to punish, and to pardon." Waxing almost poetic in his appeal on behalf of his fellow Tejanos, Ruiz continued:

> Your petitioner would therefore respectfully [direct] the attention of your Hon. Body to the situation of those unhappy families who in the midst of confusion, terror, and affright have been scattered throughout the country – compelled to abandon their home with the loss of all or the most of their property, but who will entertain the pleasing hope that they will be permitted once more to occupy their humble cottages, and who are only restrained from doing so at this time by the fear that from doing so they may be again driven away and despoiled of their little remaining all. Your petition prays that your Hon. Body will adopt some measure which will give them the assurance that they may return without the fear of harm or molestation. Let it not be recorded Gentlemen, in the bright page of the history of Texas that the property of these unfortunate families was confiscated—many of them it is true through their ignorance and through fear have committed errors but not from any disaffection to the most righteous cause of Texas. Then arrest the guilty, punish the delinquent, or rather try and condemn him who is really the enemy of Texas, but let the innocent go free.[37]

Ruiz argued eloquently for simple forgiveness, but his resolution was referred to the Committee on Claims and Accounts and failed to pass out of committee.[38] It was a sad fate for the sole statement in defense of Tejanos in the First Congress.

On November 30, 1836, a joint session of the House and Senate met in order to establish the capital of the Republic of Texas. Béxar was nominated for consideration by Ruiz.[39] This was a logical suggestion, as Béxar had long served as the capital of Texas, but the fortunes of the town had changed dramatically since independence. In addition to persistent Indian hostilities, it now lay near a hostile frontier with Mexico. Reinvasion of Texas from the south seemed imminent, and Béxar was a likely first target. Mexican General Rafael Vásquez would in fact occupy the town in March

1842, followed in September of that same year by General Adrián Woll, who captured one hundred and fifty prisoners before retreating to the Río Grande. Béxar was also still mostly populated by Tejanos, whose loyalties were still suspect in the eyes of Anglos. Other nominated towns included Brazoria, Columbia, Fort Bend, Hidalgo, Houston, Matagorda, Nacogdoches, Orozimbo, San Patricio, and Washington-on-the-Brazos.[40]

On the first ballot for a capital in 1836, Béxar received three votes, far from a winning total. John Kirby Allen, the representative from Nacogdoches County, lobbied his colleagues to have the new community of Houston declared to be the capital of the Republic. Less than two months before the opening of the first Congress, on August 26, 1836, Allen and his brother, Augustus Chapman Allen, had purchased 6,600 acres on Buffalo Bayou for $5,000, intending to build a city. They promised Congress that they would build at their own expense a new capital, including government buildings and lodgings. The other towns in contention were unable to match this offer. Béxar received just one vote on the second ballot, and Houston won the fourth vote.[41] Ruiz did not appear on the Senate rolls again until December 10, 1836. His week-long absence was likely due to illness, but perhaps he was unhappy over the spurning of his native community.[42]

In the final weeks of the session, the Senate took up the difficult issue of funding the Republic. The new nation had a debt of about $1,250,000 but no apparent means to pay it.[43] Furthermore, an international financial crisis known in the United States as the Panic of 1837 made the prospect of securing loans there or in Europe very unlikely. The Texas Congress passed a bill authorizing the government to agree to a five-million-dollar bank loan secured by public lands, but this effort failed. Taxes, the most common means for any national government to raise funds, were also problematic for the fledgling country. To finance the war for independence, the provisional government of Texas had issued land scrip and warrants with the promise that they would be redeemed at full face value by the Republic. This paper had greatly devalued due to the financial, political, and military uncertainty of the Republic. Had the Texas Congress in 1836 relied on internal taxation as the primary means of raising funds, these taxes would have been paid in the almost worthless scrip and warrants issued by the provisional government.[44] Congress did pass the Customs Act, which established import duties to be paid in specie. These duties ultimately provided most of the hard currency held by the Texas treasury during the life of the Republic.[45]

Since Texas lacked both credit and hard currency, the Senate turned to land. The Republic claimed 237,906,080 acres, of which only 26,280,080 had been granted to landowners by Spain or Mexico. Land was the chief marketable asset of the Republic. The Congress voted to allow the president to establish agents in New Orleans for the purpose of selling up to 700,000 acres of the public domain at no less than fifty cents per acre. The results were disappointing and did not produce the expected revenue. The Congress also passed a bill establishing a General Land Office for the purpose of assigning grants and selling public land, but President Houston, believing the nation too unstable to protect against frauds, vetoed it.[46]

In December 1836, the Texas Senate took up the issue of overlapping grants within Robertson's colony.[47] Two central figures in the controversy, Sterling C. Robertson and Ruiz, were members of the Senate, and Robertson had been deported from Texas by Ruiz in 1831 under the Law of April 6, 1830. At issue was an empresario contract issued by the state of Coahuila y Texas to Robertson. His contract had been voided by the Law of April 6, 1830, so he was denied not only entry but the ability to grant land under the agreement. After Robertson's deportation, Stephen F. Austin had taken the grant with the approval of Governor José María Viesca of Coahuila y Texas. This expansion of Austin's colony came to be known as the upper colony. In 1834, Robertson got a new empresario contract from the legislature of Coahuila y Texas and resumed control of the upper colony. It then became known as Robertson's colony. As a member of the legislature in 1834, Austin understood that Robertson would soon get a new empresario contact for the upper colony. Austin's partner, Samuel M. Williams, rushed to complete grants totaling 850,250 acres in the area, but the resulting paperwork was sloppy and riddled with errors. Robertson rejected these claims as invalid and overlapping land claims resulted. Robertson then attempted to use anti-Mexican sentiment to discredit Austin's grants, declaring they were "under color of pretended grants from the Government of Mexico, and of Coahuila and Texas."[48]

Ruiz was among those granted four leagues of land in the upper colony by Austin, and his claim became the example used by Austin to legitimize his grants over those issued by Robertson.[49] The Texas Senate failed to resolve the issue, and the result was litigation that delayed the development of Central Texas by nearly forty years.[50] Ruiz prudently sold his grants in Robertson's colony to his fellow senator, Edwin Morehouse, and his partner John R. Cunningham in 1838 for $70,000, a tidy sum. But the ensuing litigation, *Republic of Texas v. Francisco Ruiz et al.*, retained his name.[51]

The Texas Congress adjourned for Christmas on December 22, 1836, with its second session scheduled to open in the new capital city of Houston on May 1, 1837. A strong wind blew in from the north as the congressmen prepared to depart, dropping the temperature and making travel uncomfortable.[52] Perhaps the bad weather convinced Ruiz to spend that Christmas in Columbia, where the Texas Congress had met, but most likely it was friendship. His longtime friend and confidant, Stephen F. Austin, had also resided in Columbia during the fall of 1836 and remained there after Congress adjourned. Over the years, Ruiz's personal letters to Austin show the growth of a close friendship. In one letter, in which Ruiz entrusted Austin with helping his son Francisco Antonio, he told Austin that he is among his best friends.[53] During the first congressional session, Ruiz had ample opportunity to visit with him to discuss politics and old acquaintances.[54] But Austin had been in poor health since his return to Texas, and he took a turn for the worse on December 22. By Christmas Day he was bedridden, and he died on December 27, 1836.[55]

On the day that Austin died, Ruiz wrote a letter to his son-in-law, Blas María Herrera. Ruiz's somber mood at the loss of his close friend was evident in the many personal messages to his family contained in this letter. He wrote, "Tell my daughter, who I constantly dream and suffer to see with her children, that I have hopes of seeing you relatively soon." And he continued, "Give my greetings to everyone and you receive the affection of one who cares and wishes you happiness."[56] Ruiz then turned his attention to his family's political situation. He begged them to remain faithful to the cause of independence but, knowing well that the Mexican army might return to Béxar, he offered Herrera some advice based on his own experiences:

> Even though it might mean leaving your family, I would like for you to come if the Mexican troops should approach and you feel endangered. Anyway, you could be of no service to your family if you were killed or taken prisoner. If for any reason you should remain, then by no means should you take arms against the Texans. Give the same advice to your friends for only God could possibly return the territory of Texas to the Mexican Government. Texas has the arms and money for her defense

and shall remain forever free. Tell the same to Francisco and also tell him not to be misled by the snake [Santa Anna] for I, as your father, wish you no harm. However, both you and he are free to follow your decisions whatsoever they may be. The most important thing is for you to unite and take care of each other.[57]

Two days later, on December 29, 1836, a procession for Austin's remains was held at Columbia. Officials of the Republic of Texas, including friends like Ruiz, watched as Austin's casket was loaded onto a steamboat bound for Peach Point, the plantation of Austin's sister, Emily Austin Bryan Perry, and her husband, James F. Perry.[58] There his body would remain until it was relocated to the Texas State Cemetery in 1910.

Ruiz then returned to Béxar for the remainder of the congressional interim, intending to focus his attention on his Medina River ranch. The postscripts to his Christmas letter were instructions regarding cattle operations and concluded, "I hope no delay is taken with the cattle."[59] The economic situation in Béxar was grim. In addition to the ravages of war, the United States economy was in a deep recession. Ranching once again proved to be a safe haven from collapsing markets. Even the Navarro brothers closed their mercantile business and moved to their ranches.[60] As a consequence of many residents moving into the countryside, Ruiz also found that Béxar's greatest vulnerability, frontier security, once again dominated its local politics.

Such issues may have been on Ruiz's intended agenda when he traveled to Houston for the second session of Congress, which was set to open on May 1, 1837, but he did nothing because he fell "dangerously sick."[61] The Senate record does not include any reference to him, and it was likely that he never attended a single meeting of the second session. On May 22, 1837, he resigned because of ill health.[62] Blas María Herrera, then stationed at Camp Preston near Lavaca, was tasked by General Felix Huston to attend to his uncle and escort him back to Béxar.[63]

Ruiz's departure from the Texas Senate was not unusual. Many of the members of the first Senate did not finish their terms. William H. Wharton resigned on November 16, 1836, after being appointed by President Houston as minister plenipotentiary for Texas to the United States. Edwin Morehouse resigned December 22, 1836, upon his confirmation to be the adjutant general of the Texas army. James Collinsworth and Shelby Corzine did not return for the second session because they had been appointed as judges by the Texas Congress. While the seats held by Wharton and Morehouse apparently remained empty, William G. Hill was elected in place of Collinsworth for the second session of the First Senate, although he resigned in August 1837, while Henry W. Augustine was elected to replace Corzine. Thomas J. Green, who served Béxar in the House of Representatives, won the special election to replace Ruiz in the second session of the Senate, but this was voided. Juan Seguín was elected in August 1837 to succeed Ruiz in the Senate, and he served until 1840.[64]

Upon his return home to Béxar, Ruiz set about planning for his retirement. With the limitations of his illness, which seemed to be the lingering effects of the malady that had struck him at Tenoxtitlán, he understood that he would spend the remainder of his life in the vicinity of Béxar. He purchased the remaining share of his parent's house from his sister-in-law, Micaela Flores. His son, Francisco Antonio Ruiz, traveled to New Orleans and sold his remaining four leagues of land on the east bank of the Brazos near Tenoxchitlán for $70,000.[65] This sum allowed the elder Ruiz to settle his outstanding debts and provided a comfortable retirement. Ruiz had become one of the largest landowners in Texas, totaling 39,852 acres in 1837.[66] Ruiz's daughter, María Antonia recalled later that during this time he often spoke to her "of land grants and far away forests . . . all the places he had seen and the ideals of freedom he had assimilated."[67] Continuing his established habit, Ruiz retired on the Medina River. It was unclear from the records whether he returned to the Pérez Ranch or that of Herrera. José Ignacio Pérez testified years later in an affidavit that Ruiz lived on his ranch during this period, possibly on the 1808 grant near Garza's Crossing (present-day Von Ormy). The September 3, 1838, presidential election returns indicated that Ruiz lived in the ranch precinct and voted at the ranch of Bernardino Ruiz, a distant cousin, on the Medina River.[68]

Although Ruiz retired to the countryside, Béxar politics continued to be ever-present issues in his life. Ruiz's immediate family continued to hold many leadership positions in the local government during his lifetime. Ruiz served as a Bexar County election official during the 1838 Texas presidential and congressional election and subsequently testified in an investigation regarding irregularities.[69] His son, Francisco Antonio Ruiz, served as alcalde, regidor, city councilman (three times) and justice of the peace between 1836 and 1841.[70] José Antonio Navarro, his nephew, also served as an associate justice for Bexar County and as a congressman. Without expressing any desire for the position, José Francisco Ruiz finished second in the election for city tax collector in San Antonio held June 5, 1837. This family political legacy continued on even after the Civil War. When Ruiz's grandson Alejandro Modesto Ruiz was elected to the San Antonio City Council in 1867, it marked the fourth generation of Ruizes to serve in that capacity.[71]

CHAPTER XIV

Final Years

In the event that Colonel Ruis, is able to cooperate with you, in
making a treaty with the Comanche, I have to suggest that you
will abide by his judgment in the mode of conducting it.
                                        —President Sam Houston, 1837[1]

Frontier security at San Antonio became dire in the winters of 1836
and 1837.[2] In addition to the ever-persistent Indian threat, residents
prepared for the inevitable return of Mexican troops. A crisis in
leadership resulted in the temporary disbandment of the Texas army.[3] After independence, the ranks of the voluntary militia dwindled and funding
for the army was slow to come from the new Republic. Lieutenant Colonel
Juan N. Seguín, commander at San Antonio, recalled in his memoir, "As
I had received neither funds nor stores for the subsistence of my command, I was compelled to make requisitions upon the citizens for corn
and beeves."[4] On February 22, 1837, José Francisco Ruiz donated $426 to
Seguín for the support of the officers and soldiers of his garrison. He provided an additional $131.31 to Erastus "Deaf" Smith's ranger company for
"frontier support" on June 15, 1837.[5] He also slaughtered seven of the cattle
at his ranch to feed hungry troopers.[6] Ruiz even revived his contraband
connections, buying horses stolen in northern Mexico by Comanche raiders and selling them to provision the army of the Republic of Texas.[7]

The security situation at San Antonio worsened with the appointment
of Colonel Henry W. Karnes rather than Lieutenant Colonel Seguín to
command the troops there. Seguín had the respect of local Tejanos, and
their resentment over his replacement resulted in two dozen Tejanos being
dishonorably discharged from the army by Karnes, as well as a lingering
resentment among the Tejanos of San Antonio. By the end of 1837, only

forty-seven enlisted cavalrymen remained, most of them without horses and ill-prepared to protect San Antonio in case of a crisis.[8] At the same time, Tejanos reaffirmed their confidence in Seguín's leadership by electing him to succeed Ruiz as their senator in the Texan Congress.[9]

Under Karnes's leadership, Comanche gifts intended to ensure the security of San Antonio were misappropriated. Perhaps this was to be expected, considering the lack of provisions provided to the military, but it was exacerbated by entrusting these goods to Deaf Smith, who vocally disagreed with President Sam Houston's policy of securing the frontier by signing peace treaties with various Indian groups. Asserting his presidential authority, Houston wrote to Karnes and insisted that he consult with Ruiz on the matter and follow his advice on securing a new treaty with the Comanches:

> In the event that Colonel Ruis, is able to cooperate with you, in making a treaty with the Comanche, I have to suggest that you will abide by his judgment in the mode of Conducting it, and also, in regard to the Manner of distributing presents, among them, as it is important that the greatest discretion should be used in that respect. The great influence of Colonel Ruis, with the Indians and his perfect knowledge of their character, entitle him to be consulted in every thing important . . . you will therefore in all cases where you can, take advantage of his advice particularly in the matter of distributing presents, taking care that none shall be made without your or his *express permission*.[10]

President Houston's peace policy with the Comanches ended in 1838 with the election of Mirabeau B. Lamar as president. Lamar favored the removal of all Cherokees and Comanches from Texas, even if that meant extermination.[11] Lamar was successful in removing the Cherokees, but the Comanches proved to be resilient against the Texans. Hostilities and raiding increased in and around Béxar.[12]

The Comanches maintained their tactics of raiding remote outposts and isolated parties with quick assaults. While the Texas Rangers adapted and were eventually able to combat this style of warfare, the Comanches initially held a tactical advantage. One such raid occurred in October 1838 on a party of land surveyors camped on Leon Creek upstream from the Ruiz-Herrera Ranch and about four miles from San Antonio. Five men were killed during the raid. Their scalped corpses were found the next day, some with arrows protruding from them. A few escaped the raiders and fled to San Antonio on foot. Francisco Antonio Ruiz and Nicolás Flores were captured, taken to the war party's camp, and tied up. Ruiz, who spoke Comanche like his father, was soon recognized by the Comanche leader and untied, given a gun, and allowed to return to San Antonio, but Flores was never seen again.[13]

A Texas Ranger group pursued the Comanche war party. It consisted of fourteen men from Deaf Smith's company led by Benjamin F. Cage. The Rangers encountered nearly one hundred Comanche warriors on Leon Creek. Three Texans were killed in the initial skirmish before, in a flanking maneuver, the Comanches opened their lines, allowing a retreat to San Antonio. The Texans took the opportunity and a wild, disorganized retreat ensued. The Comanches chased the Texans all the way to San Antonio and easily killed another eight men and wounded the others, including Joseph Hood, then a district judge and soon to be the sheriff. A mounted party of Tejanos under Captain Mauricio Carrasco returned to the battle site to retrieve the bodies of the survey crew and the Rangers. Due to a scarcity of lumber, they were buried in a single grave in the "American" cemetery next to the camposanto in San Antonio.[14]

The lessons of Leon Creek were plainly evident to the Ruiz family. Lamar's policy of war with the Comanches would result in a period of bloodshed and insecurity on the frontier. While they narrowly escaped personal tragedy at Leon Creek, they might not be so lucky in their next engagement. During the first days of June 1839 a Comanche trading party arrived on the Ruiz-Herrera Ranch southwest of San Antonio. The party's leader was the son of a Comanche leader well known to José Francisco Ruiz. The son insisted that their sole intention was to trade and asked that Ruiz ride with them to San Antonio in order to avoid alarming the residents by their approach: Ruiz declined due to his poor heath but sent his twenty-five-year-old nephew, Fernando Ruiz, in his place.[15] Fernando never arrived in San Antonio. His body was found the following day, mutilated and scalped. He had been robbed of his horse and rifle.[16]

The Ruiz family was not the only one to suffer grievous losses at San Antonio during the spring of 1839. On May 14 another survey crew was ambushed on the outskirts of town, with four fatalities, and the local court clerk was killed and scalped at Mission Concepción on May 28. Texas

Ranger Miles Bennett recalled in his memoir:

> The appeals from the ranches for help and by influential Mexicans
> was so urgent that the Americans, though few in number, could
> not withhold their sympathy and aid. Such men as Don Erasmo Seguín,
> the brothers Flores, Senor Arroche, Don José Antonio Navarro, sec-
> onded by Major V. Bennet, Captain William H. Patton (who was after-
> wards killed at his ranch down on the river), Captain Henry W. Karnes,
> Hendrick Arnold, Samuel A. Maverick, and others urged an offen-
> sive campaign against the common enemy, which was resolved upon
> the measures taken to secure such a demonstration against the hos-
> tiles as would tend to keep them at a more respectful distance from the
> settlements.[17]

President Lamar ordered Colonel Karnes to organize companies of
Rangers to "fight the hostile Comanche Indians then committing depre-
dations on the frontier."[18] Two companies were raised: one Anglo and the
other Tejano. Captain Louis Franks, a veteran of San Jacinto and the owner of the surveying company whose employees had been killed a few weeks
prior, organized the Anglo company of fifty-four men. Juan Seguín organized the Tejano company, also of fifty-four men, including men of the
Ruiz-Navarro-Veramendi family: José Francisco Ruiz, Francisco Antonio
Ruiz, Antonio Ruiz, Antonio G. Navarro, Luciano Navarro, and Marcos
A. Veramendi.[19] (See Appendix III: Captain Juan N. Seguín's Mounted
Volunteers, June 6–23, 1839.)

The expedition camped at San Pedro Springs while "supplies of such
provisions as could be obtained were collected; dried beef, cooking tallow
incased in skins and bladders, corn meal (ground at Mr. Small's mill down
at the mission), small stores of salt, coffee, rice, and such other delica-
cies as were obtainable were prepared."[20] The party spotted Indian scouts,
so Karnes divided his men into three groups, each scouting up a fork of
the upper Medina River. On June 18, Private Pedro Flores Morales, of
Seguín's unit, was accidently shot and mortally wounded. The next morning, Karnes left several guards at camp to look after Morales and continued his quest, where they located more Indians and concluded they were
being spied upon.[21]

This short campaign marked the end of the military career of José

Francisco Ruiz. He served as a private, alongside his brother, Antonio, and son, Francisco Antonio, which was his only military experience in which he did not serve as an officer. His common rank was likely due to his ill health. By enlisting in the Comanche expedition in 1839, although it was brief, Ruiz earned the distinction of serving as a Texas Ranger.

Epilogue

Ruiz was a man of large mind, given to political speculation.
                                        —Reuben M. Potter, 1878[1]

Six months after the completion of the Comanche expedition, on Sunday, January 19, 1840, José Francisco Ruiz died at his home on the Plaza de Armas, after enduring bad health for years. His burial record stated the cause of his death was "hydropsy."[2] This term has been replaced in modern medical terminology with "edema." This debilitating condition was symptomatic of organ damage from the unknown illness Ruiz contracted while he served at Tenoxtitlán.[3] That night his relatives gathered at Ruiz's house to remember and plan for the funeral. According to family tradition, the only painting of José Francisco Ruiz was hurriedly completed during his wake.[4] He was buried in an elaborate funeral the next day in San Fernando Church.[5] He was interred in the main chapel, possibly with his wife, inside the rotunda of the church, on the right side of the altar, just inside the large thick wall of the church. A plaque engraved with "J. F. Ruiz" marked the grave until it was removed around 1921 following restorations of the church.[6]

José Francisco Ruiz died without a will. This required his son, Francisco Antonio Ruiz, to petition the probate court in Bexar County to serve as administrator of his estate. His petition was granted by Probate Judge John S. Simpson on July 28, 1840. The elder Ruiz, a widower at the time of his death, left only two heirs: his son, Francisco Antonio, and his daughter, María Antonia. Francisco Antonio filed an inventory and appraisal with the court, valuing his father's estate at 14,207 pesos. Of this sum, about 40 percent was from real estate holdings, including the Ruiz home, which was described as "a stone house situated on the south side of the Plaza de Armas made fifteen varas from the front, and two and five eighth varas without buildings on Nueva Street, valued at six hundred pesos." Additional real estate included a *chamacuero* (house in ruins) of eleven varas, one third of the front and the back on Nueva Street, next to the stone house, valued at three hundred pesos; two leagues of land along the San Antonio River, at San Simón de Capote, valued at one thousand pesos each; one league of land on Nuncio Creek on the old road to Nacogdoches, valued at one thousand pesos; and two leagues of land at the junction of the Brazos and San Andrés Rivers valued at one thousand pesos each. The estate also held unredeemed land scrip worth 1,002 pesos.[7]

Ruiz's personal property tells much about his life as a member of the Bexareño elite. He had three calving cows, worth ten pesos each; an ox, valued at fifteen pesos; sixty-six head of small livestock or sheep, worth one peso each; twelve yellow bench chairs, valued at two pesos each; three wooden benches or couches, two of them valued at four pesos each and the other worth two pesos; a large mirror with a gilded frame, valued at twenty pesos; a large iron pot, worth fifteen pesos; a saddle with silver trim, valued at twenty pesos; and 361 pesos in gold and silver. Two indentured servants were still working to pay their debts to Ruiz when he died. Anselmo Prú, *peón sirviente*, owed fifty-three pesos, three and a half reales, while Ricarda Sánchez, *criada de casa*, owed ninety pesos, five reales, nine granos. The estate was owed a debt of five thousand eight hundred pesos by "Mr. Mojares and Company" and another eight hundred pesos by Francisco Antonio Ruiz.[8]

The estate was evenly divided between Francisco Antonio and María Antonia with a few exceptions.[9] Francisco Antonio received the chamacuero, the remaining indenture of Anselmo Prú, the housewares, and cash, while María Antonia received the stone house, the remaining indenture of Ricarda Sánchez, and every animal. The lands on the Brazos and Nuncio Creek were sold by the estate in 1847 and 1859, and the proceeds were divided among the siblings.[10]

Ruiz's true legacy did not lie in the trappings of his estate, but in the leadership he exhibited during his lifetime and the model he became for other Tejanos in Texas. He was a product of the Texas frontier. He lived his entire life in a physical and cultural borderland, operating within Tejano, Mexican, Spanish, American, and Native American cultures and ever-changing political boundaries. His political worldview was shaped by Iberian jurisprudence, the Jesuit Enlightenment, Mexican liberalism, Native American traditions, and the American experiment with democracy.

His unique cultural experience growing up in Béxar ingrained in him the value of physical security, a distrust of distant governments, and the ability to see beyond cultural divisions.

Ruiz's life and importance in Texas history cannot be understood fully unless examined from within the Tejano experience. His support of Texas's independence had more in common with Mexican federalists than his American counterparts. His support for the Texas uprising in 1836 was not the political or intellectual child of American political thought or aspirations, but instead was deeply rooted in the traditions of Hispanic provincialism, Spanish-Mexican liberalism, his revolutionary experience, and the frontier influence in Texas. He did not think in terms of manifest destiny, white supremacy, or American political thought. In the decades prior to Texas's independence, Tejanos engaged in a fiery struggle to define their place on the far northern frontier of the Mexican republic in light of the numerous questions left unresolved when independence from Spain was achieved in 1821. Within this early Mexican dialectic on national identity, Ruiz's political views diverged from the strong tendency towards metropolitanism and the dominance of Mexico City over the nation. His political and revolutionary careers revealed a distinctively provincial outlook rooted in the culture and experiences of early Tejanos. Ultimately, this divergent view of national politics resulted in his support of independence from Mexico and participation in the establishment of the Republic of Texas.

Ruiz's regionalism also had deep personal roots. Born the son of a migrant family, he married into one of the longest established families of Béxar. His family and compadrazgo networks helped him rise to the highest ranks of Tejano society. Between 1803 and 1808, he engaged in commerce and practiced law in Béxar under the tutelage of his brother-in-law and father figure, Ángel Navarro, through whose influence he secured various positions, including regidor, inspector of butchers, and assistant procurador. In 1811 Ruiz was elected procurador in his own right. If not for Father Miguel Hidalgo's revolution, Ruiz would have likely continued advancing in his public careers as a successful Tejano within a system defined by Spain.

That world of comfort and privilege disappeared in 1812 as Ruiz was thrust into a confusing period of revolutions and counter-revolutions. His initial royalist sympathies were influenced by the impulse of all elites to maintain the social and political order that supported their elevated status.

Ruiz's political leanings underwent a dramatic shift in 1812, as the social and political institutions in which he had participated during his entire adult life dissolved around him. As the Spanish army demonstrated its arbitrary power over the Béxareños, Ruiz began to embrace the political philosophy of Mexican liberals and their distaste for "bad government." Being a member of the extended Ruiz-Veramendi-Navarro family of merchants, his economic prospects were dependent on a stability that disappeared rapidly as events unfolded, which not only eroded the colonial order but threatened his relatives.

Out of this chaos, Ruiz emerged as a new man. By 1813, he was a military and political leader of the rebellion in Béxar and an ardent supporter of a new political system. His contemporaries universally remembered him among the staunchest liberals of his era, with the resolve and willingness to take great risks for his principles. The term "liberal" is highly contextual, and the political liberalism espoused by Ruiz was based on principles of provincial autonomy, municipalism, secular politics, the divine authority of the Catholic Church, rule by consent, and a distinct frontier identity. Ruiz's father first introduced him to these liberal principles, but over time he engaged in the liberal debate in Béxar, starting with the polemical writings of Hidalgo and Bernardo Gutiérrez de Lara. This inspired his revolutionary activities and participation in the first experiments with Hispanic forms of republican government. Becoming an Indian agent and military leader placed him in contact with Anglo colonists, immigrant Indians, and what his contemporaries termed "indios bárbaros"— Comanches, Wichitas, and Lipan Apaches. Working with these diverse cultures contributed to the development of a distinct Tejano identity that differed from those of Mexicans elsewhere.

This divergent development was reinforced by the political struggle for independent statehood and separation from Coahuila, as well as the perceived need for immigration to ensure a necessary defense against indios bárbaros and build a strong local economy. By 1835, Ruiz's political views were distinctly provincial, characterized by loyalty to Texas. As he did several times before, when distant regimes failed to live up to promises of good government, Ruiz acted in a manner he felt was best for Texas and specifically Béxar.

The difficulty that many historians have in placing Ruiz's political actions within the context of the Anglo narrative of Texas history has resulted in his misinterpretation, diminution, or outright omission. When examined against the backdrop of Ruiz's experience within the Spanish and Mexican legal systems and political structures, his decisions make much more sense. Like his Iberian antecedents, Ruiz viewed government as a judicial structure whose purpose was to ensure *equidad* (equity) in society. He believed this mandate for social justice was divine in origin, written into the natural law, and, when vacated by the sovereign, passed to the local community represented by an elected ayuntamiento or junta. His philosophical basis for belief in a secular state was based on his understanding of the Catholic Church as the sole divine institution. Early in his career he suppressed both Protestantism and freemasonry as threats to that divine institution. This was a very different political foundation than American revolutionary thinkers, who championed the theories of John Locke as justification for rebellion. The Americans found authority in a "deified" or "elevated" natural law, arguing certain inalienable rights were granted by natural law, while Mexican liberals justified their revolts on the secular nature of the state and the divine mandate to govern justly.

Properly considered, Ruiz emerges as a thoughtful leader who well represents the perspectives and interests of his fellow Bexareños. While his worldview was different from that of his Anglo contemporaries, with whom he shared Texas during the last two decades of his life, he was just as dedicated as they were to individual liberty, responsible government, and the security and prosperity of his community. Few who met him could doubt that, and many, including Stephen F. Austin, found him to be a valuable partner because they shared common goals. Ruiz's contributions to Béxar and Texas during the Spanish, Mexican, and Republic periods have been obscured by those who did not quite understand him, but his story belongs within modern scholarship, which seeks to provide a more comprehensive and accurate perspective on the development of Texas. Ruiz, a frontier federalist who often found himself embroiled in political and social change, is essential to understanding the foundation of modern Texas.

Appendix 1

Álamo de Parras Company, May 16, 1830.[+]

José Francisco Ruiz, Captain

Sergeants
Timoteo Núñez
Francisco Meza

Corporals
José Chacón
Francisco de León
José María de la Garza
José María Román
Eligio Albarado
Antonio Soto

Carbineers
Juan José Reyes
Monico Gonsales
Antonio Palacios

Cadet
D. Ángel de Castañeda

Armorer
Antonio Salazar

Bugler
Justo Reyes

Privates
Antonio de León
Rafael Canales
Nicolás Morales
Trinidad Guerra
Tomás Román
Santos Mansolo
Miguel Gortaris
Rumaldo Quintanilla
Ildefonso Rodrígues
Antonio Herrera
Sesario de la Serda
Cosme Arredondo
Jesús Castañeda
Nicanor Maldonado
Francisco de León
Leocadio Ramíres
Guadalupe Durán
Anastasio Guerrero
Juan José Reyes
Tomás Martines
Crisanto Pedrasa
Pedro Herrera
Faustino Calanche
Teodoro Bargas
Cayetano Lerma
Seferino Villa
Elogio García
Nicolás Mendes

Torbio Losoya
Anastasio de la Hoya
Félix Losoya
Tomás Laso
Pedro Ximénez
Juan José Lopes
Manuel Aldrete
José María Vasques
Pedro Guana
Francisco Gonsales
Agapito Hernandes

Leandro Rodrigues
Manuel Tarín
Juan José Arocha
Eduardo Treviño
José María Vidales
Bernavé Gamboa
Leonardo Ramires
Vicente Ansures
Antonio Rodrigues
Juan Antonio de la Garsa
Felipe Hernandes

Appendix II

Béxar Election for Delegates to Convention at
Washington-on-the-Brazos, 1836

José Antonio Navarro, 65
José Francisco Ruiz, 61
Erasmo Seguín, 60
Gaspar Flores de Abrego, 59
José María Salinas, 8
Miguel Arciniega, 6
Ignacio Herrera, 3
J. B. Badgett, 3
Collard, 2

José Luciano Navarro, 2
Samuel A. Maverick, 2
James B. Bonham, 1
Green B. Jameson, 1
Antonio de León, 1
Antonio de la Garza, 1
José María Flores, 1
Juan Ángel Seguín, 1
Ramón Alusguaro, 1

Appendix III
Captain Juan N. Seguín's Mounted Volunteers, June 6–23, 1839

Captain
Juan N. Seguín

First Lieutenant
Salvador Flores

Second Lieutenant
Leandro Arriola

Privates
Eusebio Almaguez
Miguel Arciniega Jr.
Antonio Benites
Pedro Camarillo
José Luis Carbajal
Ignacio Castillo
Nemecio de la Cerda
Augustin Chávez
Trinidad Coy
Nicolás Delgado
Polinio Dias
Ignacio Espinosa
Antonio Estrada
Manuel Estrada
Nepomuceno Flores
Francisco Flores Morales
Pedro Flores Morales
Damacio Galbán

Leandro Garza
Vicente Garza
Antonio Hernández
Manuel Hernández
Felipe Jaimes
Xavier Lazo
Manuel Leal
Cayetano Lerema
Manuel López
Gabriel Martínez
Manuel Martínez
Manuel Montalvo
Antonio G. Navarro
[José] Luciano Navarro
José María Rios
Cayetano Rives
Ambrosio Rodríguez
Juan Rodríguez
Francisco Rodríguez
Mariano Romano
Cristobal Rubio
Antonio Ruiz
[José] Francisco Ruiz
Francisco Antonio Ruiz
Nicolás de los Santos
Agapito Servantes
Antonio Sombraña
Juan Sombraña

Gregorio Soto
Ramón Treviño
José María Valdez

Marcos A. Veramendi
Jesús Zavala

Notes

INTRODUCTION

[1] "Díos y Libertad" (God and Liberty) was the standard valediction used on official correspondence during the Mexican era of Texas. Ruiz himself signed dozens if not hundreds of pieces of correspondence with these words.

[2] The full text of the Ruiz exhibit read, "Before the movement for Texas independence, San Antonio-born José Francisco Ruiz served as an officer in the Mexican Army, commanding detachments at Nacogdoches and Tenoxtitlán. Since he did not speak English, Ruiz did not take an active part in the convention." Shawn B. Carlson to Art Martínez de Vara, Jul. 25, 2014, email correspondence in the possession of the author.

[3] Thomas W. Kavanagh, *The Comanches: A History, 1706–1875* (Lincoln: University of Nebraska Press, 1996), 26; Brian DeLay, *War of a Thousand Deserts: Indian Raids and the U.S.–Mexican War* (New Haven, Conn.: Yale University Press, 2008), 17. For the Spanish text of the 1828 report and an English translation, see José Francisco Ruiz, *Report on the Indian Tribes of Texas in 1828*, ed. John C. Ewers (New Haven, Conn.: Yale University Press, 1972).

[4] The term "Tejano" is Spanish for "Texan." Its meaning has evolved over time and it is important to understand its context when used. During the Spanish and Mexican eras the term was applied to all residents of Texas, except the unincorporated Indians. In the late twentieth century, the term evolved to refer to Texans of Mexican heritage. This usage falls under the latter.

[5] For an English translation of the 1850 publication, see Jean Louis Berlandier, *Journey to Mexico During the Years 1826 to 1834*, trans. Sheila M. Ohlendorf, Josette M. Bigelow, and Mary M. Standifer (2 vols.; Austin: Texas State Historical Association, 1980).

[6] The first half of José Antonio Navarro's memoir can be found in Charles A. Gulick Jr. (vols. 1–4), Katherine Elliott (vols 1–3), Winnie Allen (vol. 4), and Harriet Smither (vols. 5–6) (eds.), *The Papers of Mirabeau Buonaparte Lamar* (6 vols.; Austin: Von Boeckmann-Jones, 1973) IV, 5–12. The remainder has not been reprinted and can be found in the editions of the *San Antonio Ledger* for Dec. 12 and 19, 1857, and Jan. 2, 1858.

[7] Jacob de Cordova, *Texas: Her Resources and Her Public Men* (Philadelphia: J. B. Lippincott, 1858).

[8] Francisco Antonio Ruiz's account of the fall of the Alamo has been reprinted in Todd Hansen (ed.), *The Alamo Reader: A Study in History* (Mechanicsburg, Penn.: Stackpole Books, 2003), 500–501.

[9] *Biography of Jose Antonio Navarro by an Old Texan* (Houston: Telegraph Steam Printing House, 1876).

[10] Reuben M. Potter, "The Texas Revolution: Distinguished Mexicans Who Took

Part in the Revolution of Texas, with Glances at Its Early Events," *The Magazine of American History* 2 (October 1878): 577–603.

    [11] Raúl A. Ramos, *Beyond the Alamo: Forging Mexican Ethnicity in San Antonio, 1821–1861* (Chapel Hill: University of North Carolina Press, 2008), 4.

    [12] See, for example, John H. Brown, *History of Texas from 1685 to 1892* (2 vols.; St. Louis: L. E. Daniell, 1892), I, 558–559, and II, 102; Hubert H. Bancroft, *History of the North Mexican States and Texas, 1531–1889* (2 vols.; San Francisco: A. L. Bancroft & Company, 1883, 1889), II, 216. Ruiz is not mentioned in Henderson K. Yoakum, *History of Texas from Its First Settlement in 1685 to Its Annexation to the United States in 1846* (2 vols.; New York: Redfield, 1856), and he is also absent from Dudley G. Wooten (ed.), *A Comprehensive History of Texas and Texans, 1865 to 1897* (2 vols.; Dallas: William G. Scarff, 1898), because the first volume is simply a reprint of Yoakum's earlier tome.

    [13] Sam Houston Dixon, *The Men Who Made Texas Free* (Houston: Texas Historical Publishing, 1924), 315.

    [14] The term *Herrenvolk* democracy was coined by sociologist Pierre van den Berghe in *Race and Racism: A Comparative Perspective* (New York: Wiley, 1967), 29, as a "regime in which the exercise of power and suffrage is restricted, *de facto* and often *de jure*, to the dominant group." The dominant and subordinate groups are usually defined along racial and ethnic lines. A prominent example is Apartheid-era South Africa.

    [15] See, for example, Dixon, *The Men Who Made Texas Free*; Frederick C. Chabot, *With the Makers of San Antonio: Genealogies of the Early Latin, Anglo American, and German Families with Occasional Biographies, Each Group Being Prefaced with a Brief Historical Sketch and Illustrations* (San Antonio: Artes Graficas, 1937); Walter G. Struck, *José Francisco Ruiz: Texas Patriot* (San Antonio: Witte Memorial Museum, 1943); and Ewers's introduction to Ruiz, *Report on the Indian Tribes of Texas in 1828*.

    [16] Arnoldo de León, *They Called Them Greasers: Anglo Attitudes toward Mexicans in Texas, 1821–1900* (Austin: University of Texas Press, 1983), 49.

    [16] Ibid., 316.

    [18] Ruben Rendón Lozano, *Viva Texas: The Story of the Mexican-born Patriots of the Texas Revolution* (San Antonio: Alamo Press, 1936), 40. Lozano also includes some factual errors about Ruiz, such as declaring that he was the mayor of Bexar during the siege of the Alamo.

    [19] Chabot, *With the Makers of San Antonio*, 198; Struck, *José Francisco Ruiz*, 1.

    [20] Louis W. Kemp, *The Signers of the Texas Declaration of Independence* (Houston: Anson Jones Press, 1944); Carlos E. Castañeda, *Our Catholic Heritage in Texas, 1519–1936* (7 vols.; Austin: Von Boeckmann-Jones, 1936–1958); in Malcolm D. McLean (ed.), *Papers Concerning Robertson's Colony in Texas* (19 vols.; Arlington: University of Texas at Arlington, 1974–1993).

    [21] Al J. McGraw and V. Kay Hindes, *Chipped Stone and Adobe: A Cultural Resources Assessment of the Proposed Applewhite Reservoir, Bexar County, Texas* (San Antonio: Center for Archaeological Research, University of Texas at San Antonio, 1987); V. Kay Hindes, *The Herrera Gate: An Archival, Architectural and Conservation Study*, Studies in Archeology, Number 28 (Austin: Texas Archeological Research Laboratory, The University of Texas at Austin, 1998); David R. McDonald, *José Antonio Navarro: In Search of the American Dream in Nineteenth-Century Texas* (Denton: Texas State Historical Association, 2010).

    [22] Pekka Hämäläinen, *The Comanche Empire* (New Haven, Conn.: Yale University Press, 2008); Gary Clayton Anderson, *The Conquest of Texas: Ethnic Cleansing in the*

Promised Land, 1820–1875 (Norman: University of Oklahoma Press, 2005); Kavanagh, *Comanches;* Ramos, *Beyond the Alamo;* Jack Jackson, *Indian Agent: Peter Ellis Bean in Mexican Texas* (College Station: Texas A&M University Press, 2005).

[23] Patsy M. Spaw, *The Texas Senate, Volume I: Republic to Civil War, 1836–1861* (College Station: Texas A&M University Press, 1990).

[24] The term *gente de razón* has its origin in Roman law, which categorized people into those able to use reason (some adult males) and those unable to use reason, either by natural causes or by social minority status (women, children, and adult males still subject to their father as paterfamilias). In colonial America, the term came to be used to describe indigenous people who had been baptized, adopted Spanish names and lived within the Spanish cultural milieu, see Marvyn Helen Bacigalupo, *A Changing Perspective: Attitudes Toward Creole Society in New Spain (1521–1620)* (London: Tamesis Books Limited, 1981), 12–13.

[25] For a fine study of the fluidity of social classes in Béxar, and the importance of family ties and other such bonds, see Jesús F. de la Teja, *San Antonio de Béxar: A Community on New Spain's Northern Frontier* (Albuquerque: University of New Mexico Press, 1995).

[26] See Timothy M. Matovina, *Guadalupe and Her Faithful: Latino Catholics in San Antonio, from Colonial Origins to the Present* (Baltimore: The Johns Hopkins University Press, 2005), 55; De la Teja, *San Antonio de Béxar,* 152.

[27] A comprehensive overview is available in Paul D. Lack, *The Texas Revolutionary Experience: A Political and Social History, 1835–1836* (College Station: Texas A&M University Press, 1992), 183–207.

CHAPTER 1: ORIGINS

[1] De la Teja, *San Antonio de Béxar,* 17.

[2] Gerald E. Poyo, "The Canary Islands Immigrants of San Antonio: From Ethnic Exclusivity to Community in Eighteenth-Century Béxar," in *Tejano Origins in Eighteenth-Century San Antonio,* ed. Gerald E. Poyo and Gilberto M. Hinojosa (Austin: University of Texas Press, 1997), 47–49.

[3] Thomas H. Naylor and Charles W. Polzer, *The Presidio and Militia on the Northern Frontier of New Spain, Volume 1, 1570–1700* (Tucson: University of Arizona Press, 1986), 102. As early as 1716, the part of Texas that lay north of the Medina River was called variously Nuevo Reino de las Filipinas, Nuevas Filipinas, and Provincia de Tejas y las Nuevas Filipinas. By the end of the eighteenth century, the term "Nuevas Filipinas" was only used in certain formal legal documents, such as land grants.

[4] Naylor and Polzer, *The Presidio and Militia on the Northern Frontier of New Spain, Volume 1,* 34–50. San Luis de la Paz was the northernmost settlement in the jurisdiction of San Pedro Tolimán, Querétaro. It was also located in the Diocese of Santiago de Querétaro. Historians have incorrectly listed the birthplace of José Francisco Ruiz's father and grandfather as "Spain" and sometimes "Querétaro, Spain." However, there is no city of Querétaro in Spain, and the word "Querétaro" is derived from either the Otomí word meaning "place of the ball game" or from the Purhépecha word "Créttaro," meaning place of crags.

[5] Naylor and Polzer, *The Presidio and Militia on the Northern Frontier of New Spain, Volume 1,* 38.

[6] James D. Riley, "The Wealth of the Jesuits in Mexico, 1670–1767," *The Americas* 33 (October 1976): 226–266; Gerardo Decorme, "Catholic Education in Mexico, 1525–1912,"

Catholic Historical Review 2 (July 1916): 168–181; M. Ramírez Monte (ed.), *Querétaro en 1743: Informe Presentado al Rey por el Corregidor Esteban Gómez de Acosta* (Querétaro: Gobierno del Estado de Querétaro, 1997).

[7] Phillip W. Powell, *La Guerra Chichimeca, 1550–1600* (Mexico City: Fondo de Cultura Económica, 1975), 33, 206.

[8] Joseph Ruiz De Mora, son of Manuel Ruiz and Augustina Servín de Mora, February 1695, Baptismal Records (Archivo de la Parroquia de Santiago en Queretaro, Santiago de Querétaro, Querétaro; hereafter cited as SQ Baptisms). The family name appears as both "Ruis" and "Ruiz" in official records; for consistency, the latter spelling will be used in the text of this work.

[9] Agustín Ruis, son of Manuel Ruis and Augustina Servín, June 23, 1708, SQ Baptisms. Augustin married Anna Maria Cumplido. José Felix Ruis, born May 20, 1740, Santiago, Querétaro, son of Agustin Ruiz and Ana Maria Cumplido, May 20, 1740, SQ Baptisms. Francisca Manuela Ruis, daughter of Agustin Ruis and Ana Maria Cumplido, July 27, 1745, SQ Baptisms.

[10] Montes (ed.), *Querétaro en 1743*, 217.

[11] Juan Manuel Ruiz is recorded as testifying that he was thirty-three years old in Ángel de Martos y Navarrete to Juan Galván, Aug. 19, 1762, which would make his birth year as 1729 or 1730. See Bexar Archives, 10:81 (Dolph Briscoe Center for American History, The University of Texas at Austin, hereafter cited as BA); In Sumaria of Luis Mariano Menchaca, Nov. 8, 1785, BA, 17:660–692, Ruiz testified that he was fifty-four years old, which would make his birth year as 1730 or 1731.

[12] Oakah L. Jones Jr., *Los Paisanos: Spanish Settlers on the Northern Frontier of New Spain*, (Norman: University of Oklahoma Press, 1979), 66–67.

[13] Gilbert R. Cruz, *Let There Be Towns: Spanish Municipal Origins in the American Southwest, 1610–1810* (College Station: Texas A&M University Press, 1988), 56–57.

[14] Diana Hadley, Thomas H. Naylor and Mardith K. Schuetz-Miller (eds.), *The Presidio and Militia on the Northern Frontier of New Spain, Volume Two, Part Two: The Central Corridor and the Texas Corridor, 1700–1765* (Tucson: University of Arizona Press, 1997), 362.

[15] Félix D. Almaráz Jr., *The San Antonio Missions and Their System of Land Tenure* (Austin: University of Texas Press, 1989), 2–3; De la Teja, *San Antonio de Béxar*, 144.

[16] John O. Leal, *San Fernando Church Burials, 1761–1808* (San Antonio: privately published, 1976), 42. When María Gertrudis married in Béxar in 1774, her father, Agustín Ruiz, was already deceased. Ana María was buried at San Fernando Church on July 26, 1783.

[17] De la Teja, *San Antonio de Béxar*, 18.

[18] David J. Weber, *The Mexican Frontier 1821–1845: The American Southwest Under Mexico* (Albuquerque: University of New Mexico Press, 1982), 1.

[19] Charles R. Porter Jr., *Spanish Water, Anglo Water: Early Development in San Antonio* (College Station: Texas A&M University Press, 2009), 73–74, 76, 79–80. The first non-mission *acequia*, known as the San Pedro Ditch, was dug by the soldiers of the presidio in 1719. King Felipe V bestowed the title of *hijo dalgo de solar conocido*, more commonly known by its shortened version, *hidalgo*, to male Isleños coming to Béxar. Incidents such as the 1819 flood of the San Antonio River exacerbated issues related to water access. See Charles R. Cutter, *The Legal Culture of Northern New Spain, 1700–1810* (Albuquerque: University of New Mexico Press, 1995), 99–100, and De la Teja, *San Antonio de Béxar*, 77–79.

[20] Gerald E. Poyo, "Immigrants and Integration in Late Eighteenth-Century Béxar," in Poyo and Hinojosa, *Tejano Origins*, 94.

[21] Herbert G. Uecker, Frances K. Meskill, and I. Wayne Cox, *Archaeological Investigations at The Ruiz Family Property (41 BX 795), San Antonio, Texas* (San Antonio: Center for Archaeological Research, University of Texas at San Antonio, 1991), 3.

[22] A different Juan Manuel Ruiz was stationed at Presidio Los Adaes in the 1740s. This Ruiz was appointed to serve as constable in 1745 and witnessed several letters of the governor in 1741. There is no known relation between this Juan Manuel Ruiz and Juan Manuel Ruiz de Pesia. See translation of certified copy of proceedings concerning Sandoval's petition that he be given certified copy of dispatch and proceedings concerning investigations on removal of French presidio of Natchitoches, September 25, 1741, BA, and translation of certified copy of the residencia proceedings of Justo Boneo y Morales, deceased, conducted by García Larios, November 4, 1744, BA.

[23] Ángel de Martos y Navarrete to Comandancia General, Aug. 26, 1760, BA, 34:1–14. Poyo, in "Immigrants and Integration in Late Eighteenth-Century Béxar," stated that "Despite his economic success and social ties, [Juan Manuel Ruiz] apparently never served in the cabildo" (94). This is contradicted by Martos y Navarrete, who reported that upon his arrival in San Fernando "the following were councilmen at the time: Don Joseph Padrón, Don Alberto López, Don Juan Manuel Ruiz, Don Ignacio Lorenzo, and Don Juan Granades." See also Land Grant Request of Joséf Curbelo, Mar. 5, 1761, Land Grants, Spanish Archives, Béxar County Clerk's Office (Bexar County Courthouse, San Antonio, Texas; hereafter cited as BCSA). Juan Manuel Ruiz signed Curbelo's request as a *regidor*. The terms *cabildo* and *ayuntamiento* both referred to the Spanish version of a town council. Béxar switched the terms in the late 1700s. Henceforth the author will use ayuntamiento for consistency.

[24] Poyo, "Immigrants and Integration in Late Eighteenth-Century Béxar," 91, 92, 94. Ángel Navarro arrived in Béxar in the 1770s. He married María Josefa Ruiz, the sister of José Francisco Ruiz, entered into commerce, and served on the ayuntamiento at various times from the 1770s to the 1790s. See Frederick C. Chabot, *San Antonio and Its Beginnings, 1691–1731* (San Antonio: Naylor Printing Company, 1931), 243. Fernando de Veramendi was born in Pamplona; he founded a merchant house in Béxar. See Poyo, Immigrants and Integration in Late Eighteenth-Century Béxar," 97. Antonio Gil Y'Barbo was the leader of the Spanish capital of Los Adaes. In 1774, the Crown ordered the removal of its inhabitants to Béxar. Most residents returned to East Texas led by Gil Y'Barbo, re-founding Nacogdoches. Marcos Gil Y'Barbo, the son of Antonio, married María Antonia Ruiz, another sister of José Francisco. See María Ester Domínguez, *San Antonio en la Epoca Colonial, 1718–1821* (Madrid: Instituto de Cooperación Iberoamericana, 1989), 146–147. Bartolomé Seguín was born in Aguascalientes and moved to Béxar; he was the great grandfather of Juan Seguín. See Chabot, *With the Makers of San Antonio*, 118.

[25] Robert S. Weddle and Robert H. Thonhoff, *Drama & Conflict: The Texas Saga of 1776* (Austin: Madrona Press, 1976), 70.

[26] Auto of Governor Barón de Ripperdá, Aug. 13, 1770, BA; Petition of Juan Manuel Ruiz, July 14, 1782, BA.

[27] Cabildo to Governor Domingo Cabello y Robles, Feb. 28, 1783, BA, quoted in Jesús F. de la Teja, "Buena Gana de Ir a Jugar: The Recreational World of Early San Antonio, Texas, 1718–1845," *International Journal of the History of Sport* 26 (2009): 889–906.

[28] De León, *They Called Them Greasers*, 9.

[29] James Donovan, *The Blood of Heroes: The 13-Day Struggle for the Alamo–and the Sacrifice That Forged a Nation* (New York: Little, Brown & Company, 2012), 219.

[30] McGraw and Hindes, *Chipped Stone and Adobe*, 130; Poyo, "Immigrants and Integration in Late Eighteenth-Century Béxar," 94.

[31] Weddle and Thonhoff, *Drama & Conflict*, 152, 154.

[32] Translation of record of roundup licenses issued to Texas citizens and missions, Feb. 10, 1778, BA. *Añeja* derives from añejar, to grow old or mature, and refers to two adult cows.

[33] McGraw and Hindes, *Chipped Stone and Adobe*, 71.

[34] Petition to Extend Payment Deadline on Fine for Gathering Wild Game, July 14, 1782, BA.

[35] In July 1827 the Legislature of Coahuila y Texas approved the sale of the Alamo walls and buildings. José Francisco Ruiz was given the order to undertake the sale. This was the possible origin of the Herrera Gates, found on the Herrera Ranch in the 1980s and have been identified as having belonged to one of the San Antonio Missions. Order to Sell Buildings and Walls at Mission San Antonio de Valero, July 16, 1827, BCSA, 105:418–20. See also McGraw and Hindes, *Chipped Stone and Adobe*, 23–24.

[36] Jesús F. de la Teja, "The Saltillo Fair and Its San Antonio Connections," in *Tejano Epic: Essays in Honor of Félix D. Almaráz Jr.*, ed. Arnoldo De León (Austin: Texas State Historical Association, 2005), 16.

[37] Leslie S. Offutt, *Saltillo, 1770–1810: Town and Region in the Mexican North* (Tucson: University of Arizona Press, 2001), 13.

[38] David R. McDonald, "Juan Martín de Veramendi: Tejano Political and Business Leader," in *Tejano Leadership in Mexican and Revolutionary Texas*, ed. Jesús F. de la Teja (College Station: Texas A&M University Press, 2010), 30–31.

[39] Translation of Proceedings Concerning the Cabildo's Order to Citizens to Aid in the Repair of Government Buildings, Feb. 15, 1779, BA, 78:102–131.

[40] *Baptismal Records of the Parish of Santiago de Saltillo, Volume 7* (Saltillo, Coahuila: Parish of Santiago de Saltillo, n.d.), 200. The notation reads as follows: "24 June 1748 Juana Ma. Antonia Josefa Manuela, espanola, h[ij]a.l[egitim]a. En la iglesia parro[quia] l de el Saltillo en bie[n]te y cuatro de junio de [mil] siete cie[n]tos cua[ren]ta y ocho baptise solemente a Juana Ma. Antonia Josefa Manuela de la Peña hija lexiti[m]a de D[o]n Martín de la Peña y de D[on]a Petra Baldes. Padrinos: D[o]n Antonio Gonsales, Ysabel Ma. Baldes."

[41] As was not unusual for the time, their son, Ildefonso de la Peña (born 1603), adopted his mother's maternal name. Raúl Guerra Jr., Nadine M. Vásquez, and Baldomero Vela Jr., *Index to the Marriage Investigations of the Diocese of Guadalajara Pertaining to the Former Provinces of Coahuila, Nuevo León, Nuevo Santander, and Texas, Volume 1* (n.p.: R. J. Guerra, 1989), 285. Ildefonso de la Peña's son, Capitán Juan Esteban de la Peña, served as *alcalde ordinario* of Saltillo during 1702. The captain's son surpassed him: Lieutenant General Martín de la Peña (1687–1745) was at various times *alcalde ordinario, alcalde mayor, procurador*, and *capitán de guerra* of Saltillo. Ana María del Refugio G. de González and Práxedis Francke Ramírez de la Peña, *Nuestras Raices: Un Recorrido a Traves del Tiempo* (Saltillo, Coahuila: Privately published, 1998), 45; Martha Durón Jiménez and Ignacio Narro Etchegaray, *Diccionario Biográfico de Saltillo* (Saltillo, Coahuila: Archivo Municipal de Saltillo, 1995), 137. José Martín de la Peña left a will dated July 29, 1745, which can be found in the Saltillo Municipal Archives. Archivo Municipal de Saltillo,

Catalogo del Fondo Testamentos, Volume I: 1607–1743 (Saltillo, Coahuila: Archivo Municipal de Saltillo, 1988), 452.

⁴² Guillermo Garmendia Leal, *Diego de Montemayor, Sus Descendientes* (Monterrey,
Nuevo León: privately published, 1993), 49.

⁴³ Election Results, Jan. 1, 1768, BA, 45:36. Martín de la Peña lost to Marcos de Castro
in a race for *alcalde de segundo voto.*

⁴⁴ Ayuntamiento's Report on the Number of Ranches in Béxar as Requested by Manuel María de Salcedo on Oct. 3 and Nov. 8, 1791, BA, 21:872.

⁴⁵ Robert H. Thonhoff, *The Texas Connection with the American Revolution* (Austin:
Eakin Publications, 2000), 15.

⁴⁶ John O. Leal, *San Fernando Church Marriages, 1798–1856* (San Antonio: privately
published, 1976), 7. They married on Jan. 15, 1759. San Fernando Church records were
missing from this era; see the marriage record of their son, José Ignacio de la Peña.

⁴⁷ Translation of Proceedings Concerning Election of Cabildo Officers, Jan. 1, 1776,
BA, 62:1–6; Translation of Ygnasio [Ignacio] de la Peña to the Governor, n.d. [July
1774], BA.

⁴⁸ Of the eight children who died in infancy, the first two were daughters, born in
1769 and 1770, both of whom were named for Manuela's mother, Ana Petra Valdés. Leal,
San Fernando Baptisms, 1761–1793, 20, 24. Four other children were born and died in the
same year as their birth: José Antonio in 1774, María Ygnacia in 1779, María Gertrudis
in 1786, and Juan Francisco in 1789. Leal, *San Fernando Baptisms, 1761–1793*, 40, 59, 88,
101. Twins were born on March 8, 1789, Juan Francisco and José Francisco, of which
only José Francisco survived into early childhood. Oddly, Manuela named two of her
sons José Francisco, without a middle name to distinguish them. Leal, *San Fernando
Baptisms, 1761–1793*, 75, 101. All church and civil records clearly showed the presence of
two brothers named José Francisco in the household. The younger José Francisco disappeared from the historic record and it is likely that he died in childhood. He has been
the source of confusion over the birth date of José Francisco Ruiz, who was born in 1783.

⁴⁹ Navarro to Muñoz, May 12, 1792, BA 22:370. The San Fernando Church marriage
records are incomplete and missing for this year. The marriage, however, is referred to
by Navarro in the aforementioned letter.

⁵⁰ Will of María Manuela de la Peña, 1834, Wills and Estates 92, BCSA.

⁵¹ José Antonio Navarro sadly recalled this period in his memoirs, noting "behold
here a family scattered and persecuted by so many disasters." McDonald, *José Antonio
Navarro*, 30.

⁵² Will of María Manuela de la Peña, 1834, Wills and Estates 92, BCSA. The only
asset listed was an interest in the ranch near Natchitoches, Louisiana, previously owned
by her son José Antonio Francisco Victoriano Ruiz.

⁵³ John O. Leal, *San Fernando Church Baptismals, 1731–1793, Book I, Part 1* (San An-
tonio: privately published, 1976), 27. The notation reads, as translated: "Ruis, María
Antonia, Spanish, 8 days old, legitimate child of Juan Manuel Ruis and Manuela de la
Peña. Godparents: José Macario Zambrano and Juana Oconitrillo."

⁵⁴ Leal, *San Fernando Church Marriages*, 34.

⁵⁵ Ibid., 6. The record reads, in translation: "20 Mar 1803. Rodrigues, Don Francisco,
Spanish, of this city, legitimate son of the late Don Francisco Rodrigues and the late
Catarina Leal and widower of Doña Juana Travieso; to Doña Antonia Ruis, Spanish,
of this city, legitimate daughter of the late Juan Manuel Ruis and Doña Manuela de
la Peña, of this city, widow of her second marriage to Francisco Calvillo. Godparents:

Manuel Mora and Gertrudes Ximenes. Witnesses: José Cortinas and Manuel Cano, all of this city. Father Bernardino Vallejo performed the marriage."

⁵⁶ Elizabeth S. Mills, *Natchitoches: Translated Abstracts of Register Number Five of the Catholic Church Parish of St. Francois des Natchitoches in Louisiana: 1800–1826* (Westminster, Md.: Heritage Books, 2007), 143. The record reads, in translation: "Francisco Rodríguez, 22 March 1814, burial in cemetery of this parish of a Spaniard, aged 62 years, widower by first nuptials with _____na Travieso, by whom he left 2 daughters, and who was now married with María Ruiz by whom he left 2 sons and 1 daughter. Deceased did not confess and received only the sacrament of extreme unction since he died suddenly of pain. Priest: F. Magnes."

⁵⁷ Leal, *San Fernando Church Baptismals, 1731–1793*, 44. The notation reads, in translation: "Mar. 21 (1775) Ruis, José Antonio Pablo Longino, Spanish, 8 days old, legitimate son of Juan Manuel Ruis and Manuel de la Peña. Godparents: Ignacio Lucero and María Antonia Ruis."

⁵⁸ Ibid., 51. The notation reads, in translation: "May 20 (1777) Ruis, María Rosalía, Spanish, 8 days old, legitimate child of Juan Manuel Ruis and Doña Manuela de la Peña. Godparents: Don José de Antonio Bustillos and Doña Margarita Salinas (his wife)."

⁵⁹ Institute of Texan Cultures, *Residents of Texas, 1782–1836* (3 vols.; San Antonio: Institute of Texan Cultures, 1984), I: 395. The entry reads: "Dn. Franco. Ruiz, Spaniard, 23 yrs. Old; married to Da. Josefa Hernández, Spaniard, 26 yrs. Old; had a child 9 mos. Old; and Franco. de la Zerda, widow, 62 yrs. old lived with them."

⁶⁰ Leal, *San Fernando Church Baptismals, 1731–1793*, 63. The record reads, in translation: "Sept. 8 (1780) Ruis, José Antonio Francisco Victoriano, Spanish, 8 days old, legitimate son of Juan Manuel Ruis and Manuela de la Peña. Godparents: Bartolomé Seguín and Cathalina Seguín." José Antonio Francisco Victoriano Ruiz was married at the time of his death. Unfortunately, his wife's name has not been found. An 1847 tax sale of his ranch listed "Honetto Ruice." This was possibly an Anglicization of her name, because in some records José is written as "Hosea." See Power of Attorney, Francisco Ruiz to Ambrosio Sompayrac, July 10, 1836, Nacogdoches Archives (Daughters of the Republic of Texas Library, San Antonio; hereafter cited as DRT), 2:199–200; Tax Sale to S.S. Eason, Land Conveyances, Sabine Parish, Book C, Page 28 (Clerk of Court Office, Many, Louisiana). José Francisco Ruiz in official correspondence was often recorded as "Francisco Ruiz," indicating that he signed his name in this manner; however, hereafter he will be cited as JFR.

⁶¹ U.S. Department of the Treasury, *Claims to Land Between the Rio Hondo and Sabine Rivers in Louisiana*, 18th Cong., 2nd sess., 1825, Senate Report 445, 95, 14. In this report his name was spelled as José Ruez.

⁶² Power of Attorney, JFR to Sompayrac, July 10, 1836, Nacogdoches Archives, DRT, 2:199–200.

⁶³ Institute of Texan Cultures, *Residents of Texas*, II, 228.

⁶⁴ Institute of Texan Cultures, *Residents of Texas*, I, 351; Census Report of the Presidial Company of San Antonio de Béxar, Dec. 31, 1803, BA. The record, in translation, reads: "José Antonio Ruiz, of __ yrs; single; his mother Manuela de la Peña, widow of 50 years; Spaniard; his brother Francisco, of 13 yrs; had one niece, María Ybarvo, of 12."

⁶⁵ Will of Juan Manuel Ruiz, 1797, Wills 94, BCSA. The Spanish practice of dividing property with one's wife eventually led to community property laws in American states that once were part of New Spain, including Texas. See Jean A. Stuntz, *Hers, His,*

And Theirs: Community Property Law in Spain and Early Texas (Lubbock: Texas Tech University Press, 2005). Excluded from the division of Juan Manuel's land was a *solar* or town lot of six *varas* (16.66 feet) frontage by ten *varas* (27.78 feet) depth. This was part of the Ruiz family lot on the corner of Calle Real and Calle de los Flores, and Juan Manuel stated that it had been sold to his son-in-law, Ángel Navarro, who subsequently gave it to José Francisco Ruiz.

⁶⁶ Will of Juan Manuel Ruiz, 1797, Wills and Estates 94, BCSA.

⁶⁷ Leal, *San Fernando Church Baptismals, 1731–1793*, 75. José Francisco Ruiz was baptized eight days after he was born on January 28, 1873. The walls of the old church today form the sanctuary of San Fernando Cathedral.

⁶⁸ Leal, *San Fernando Baptisms 1793–1812*, 88. The record reads, in translation, "Rodríguez, María de Jésus, Spanish, 5 days old, legitimate daughter of José Antonio Rodríguez and María Farias. Grandparents, paternal: Prudencio Rodríguez and Polonia Curbelo. Grandparents, maternal: Francisco Farias and Encarnación Rosales. Godparents: Don Francisco Ruiz and Doña Ysabel Hernandes."

⁶⁹ Leal, *San Fernando Church Baptismals, 1731–1793*, 6. The record reads, in translation: "Aug 30 [1763]. Caemusquis, José Viterbo, Indian coyote, born legitimate son of Javier Caemusquis and Clara de Sandoval. Godparents: Juan Manuel Ruiz and Juana Jiménez." *Coyote* had various meanings in the various locations where it was used. In Béxar, it typically meant a person of mixed Spanish and Indian heritage, typically half or "mestizo" or of more salient Indian ancestry or physical characteristics. See De la Teja, *San Antonio de Béxar*, 25–26.

⁷⁰ Leal, *San Fernando Church Baptismals, 1731–1793*, 6. The record reads, in translation: "Nov. 3 [1763] Manuel, José, Apache Indian, natural child of Infieles, Apache Indian, Godfather: Juan Manuel Ruiz."

⁷¹ Castañeda, *Our Catholic Heritage in Texas*, IV:18, 159–161.

⁷² Leal, *San Fernando Church Baptismals, 1731–1793*, 5–6.

⁷³ Ibid., 51; Leal, *San Fernando Church Baptismals, 1731–1793*, 44; Leal, *San Fernando Church Baptismals, 1731–1793*; Leal, *San Fernando Church Marriages*, 6.

⁷⁴ Leal, *San Fernando Church Baptismals, 1731–1793*, 51. The record reads, in translation: "May 20 [1777] Ruis, María Rosalía, Spanish, 8 days old, legitimate child of Juan Manuel Ruis and Doña Manuela de la Peña. Godparents: Don José de Antonio Bustillos and Doña Margarita Salinas (his wife)."

⁷⁵ The lot on which the home stood was granted to Joseph Antonio Rodríguez on October 11, 1736. It was fifty square varas (a colonial vara is 33 inches, so fifty square varas would be about 50 square yards) and located south of the presidio. Rodríguez had arrived in Béxar from Los Adaes before the arrival of Canary Islanders in 1731. He initially built a jacal on his tract, and then in 1749 built the limestone house that faced the Plaza de Armas. Juan Manuel Ruiz purchased the home and a sliver of land, slightly under one-half an acre in area, which was approximately forty feet wide (east to west) and four hundred feet long (north to south) between Dolorosa and Nueva Streets (streets that still exist in downtown San Antonio). Over the years he added to the property, building a privy, well house, kitchen, and several utility sheds. Archaeological excavations of the old home site uncovered material associated with sites of higher social status, such as majolicas, lead glazed wares, Tonalá pottery, and indigenous pottery. The study concluded that these relics suggest "a continuation of Indian presence, activity, and traditions alongside European and Mexican cultures." These findings

match the historic record, which clearly indicated the presence of Indians who lived in the Ruiz home. Uecker, Meskill, and Cox, *Archaeological Investigations,* 29.

⁷⁶ McDonald, *José Antonio Navarro,* 15. This early Navarro home was different from the Casa Navarro State Historic Site, which José Antonio Navarro built around 1850.

⁷⁷ Petition of priest of San Fernando to build a two-story home on Plaza de las Armas, June 23, 1780, BA. The *procurador general* (city attorney), at the request of the priest, personally notified the neighbors, including Placido Hernández and Juan Manuel Ruiz.

⁷⁸ Leal, *San Fernando Church Baptismals, 1731–1793,* 75. José Francisco Ruiz's padrinos were José Hernández and Luisa Guerrero.

⁷⁹ Inventory and Appraisal of the Estate of José Francisco Ruiz, 1840, Wills and Estates 101, BCSA. The text of Texas Historical Commission marker number 4386 contains several common errors, including that Ruiz was educated in Spain.

CHAPTER 2: EARLY YEARS

¹ I. J. Cox, "Educational Efforts in San Fernando de Béxar," *Southwestern Historical Quarterly* [hereafter cited as *SHQ*] 6 (July 1902): 28.

² Weddle and Thonhoff, *Drama & Conflict,* 70.

³ "The Priest Francisco Maynes signed at my request, because I do not know how to write." Will of María Manuela de la Peña, May 12, 1834, Wills and Estates 92, BCSA.

⁴ Among the historians claiming a Spanish education for José Francisco Ruiz were Sam Houston Dixon, Frederick C. Chabot, Walter G. Struck, and John C. Ewers, all cited previously in this work. Dixon, who also wrote that José Antonio Navarro attended school in Spain, appears to be the source for the other three, while his assertion that Ruiz had a Spanish education also appears on Texas Historical Commission marker number 4386, which was placed in 1973 at the original site of the Ruiz home on the Military Plaza (Plaza de las Armas).

⁵ Adrian J. Pearce, *British Trade with Spanish America, 1763–1808* (Liverpool: Liverpool University Press, 2007), 120. Spain initially fought a war against Revolutionary France and was defeated. In 1796, Spanish Prime Minister Manuel de Godoy allied with the French, hoping for a better result for Spain. The British responded by declaring war and imposing a blockade in 1797, impairing Spain's communications with its American colonies. These events are known as the Anglo Spanish War of 1796–1808.

⁶ Pablo M. Cuellar Valdés, *Historia de la Ciudad de Saltillo* (Saltillo: Biblioteca de la Universidad de Coahuila, 1982), 27.

⁷ McDonald, *José Antonio Navarro,* 16. Navarro was a student of his uncle José Francisco Ruiz while he served as the schoolmaster of Béxar. Only after Ruiz resigned was Navarro sent to Saltillo, where he remained until 1808, the year that his father died.

⁸ Minutes of the Cabildo of San Fernando Discussing the Founding of a School and Naming of a Teacher, Jan. 20, 1803, BA, 115:34. The cabildo designated the Ruiz home to serve as a school house, but they noted its poor condition, probably due to a lack of habitation during the previous five years.

⁹ Weddle and Thonhoff, *Drama & Conflict,* 70.

¹⁰ Bertrand M. Roehner, "Jesuits and the State: A Comparative Study of their Expulsions (1590–1990)," *Religion* 27 (April 1997): 165–182.

¹¹ Proceedings concerning José Francisco de la Mata's petition to the Cabildo of San Fernando that his school be made an official institution, May 1, 1789, BA, 19:768–770.

[12] Cox, "Educational Efforts in San Fernando de Béxar," 28.

[13] Municipal ordinances concerning public order and good government, Jan. 10, 1802, BA. See Article 15 concerning school children.

[14] Weddle and Thonhoff, *Drama & Conflict,* 70.

[15] Cox, "Educational Efforts in San Fernando de Béxar," 28.

[16] Minutes discussed the founding of a school and the naming of a teacher, Jan. 20, 1803, BA, 1:115. Those who signed the minutes were Governor Juan Bautista Elguezábal; *alcaldes* Ángel Navarro and José Félix Menchaca; Antonio Baca, Manuel Delgado, Tomás de Arocha, José Ignacio de la Peña, Joseph María Zambrano, José Luis Gallardo, and Joseph Salvador Días.

[17] McDonald, *José Antonio Navarro,* 16.

[18] Captain Joaquín de Ugarte to Juan Bautista Elguézabal, Feb. 4, 1804, BA, 32:132.

[19] Ruiz's legacy as San Antonio's first public school teacher was honored with the naming of Francisco Ruiz Elementary on San Antonio's west side; in 2002 it was merged with Barkley Elementary to form Barkley-Ruiz Elementary, a school of the San Antonio Independent School District.

[20] Governor Juan Bautista Elguézabal to Nemesio Salcedo, Oct. 12, 1803, BA 31:390–391.

[21] Cox, "Educational Efforts in San Fernando de Béxar," 30.

[22] Leal, *San Fernando Church Marriages,* 10. The record reads, in translation: "Ruis, Don Francisco, Spanish, of this city, legitimate son of the late Don Juan Manuel Ruis and Doña Manuela de la Peña; to Doña Josefa Hernandes, Spanish, of this city, legitimate daughter of the late Plácido Hernandes and Doña Rosalía Montes. Godparents: Don Ygnacio Peres and Doña Clemencia Hernandes. Witness: José Labom and Pedro Acosta, all of this city. Father José María Dalgadillon performed the marriage and signed the book. Married at Mission Concepción." Leal omits from his transcription the report of the canonical investigation and marriage banns.

[23] The Canon law of the Catholic Church required marriage banns be read three times before the wedding, and certification that the couple were not related by blood or affinity. The handwritten marriage record gives the dates of these events, but they are not logical. The record states that marriage bans were read on March 7, 11 and 18, but gives the date of marriage as March 8, 1804. It also states that on April 11, the priest cleared the couple from canonical impediments. "En la Yglecia de la Misión de la Purísima Concepción de ocho dias del mes de Marzo de 1804 el R.P.F. José María de Jesús Delgadillo, Supernuncio de estas misciones con mi licencia, leidas las primeras amonentación *inter misarium solemnia,* en siete de dicho Marzo, no habiendo resultado canonico impedimiento amas del parentesco, en segundo grado de afinidad por copulo ilintas disponsado como consta por el despacho superior, que se hallara en el legajo de diligencias matrionios de esta año, por convenir, asi a la seguridad del matrimonio y honor de las pretenas caso, solemente, y yo vele en esta iglesia de mi cargo el dia once de abril del presente ano, no haviendo remitado otro impedimiento de las otras dos amonentaciones corridas en los dias once y diez ocho de dicho marzo, a D. Fran^{co} Ruiz, español, origino de este Presidio h.l. de D. Juan Manuel Ruiz, ya difunto, y de D. Manuela dela Peña, con Da. Josefa Hernández, Española, del mismo origen, h.l. de D. Plasido Hernandes, ya difunto, y de Da. Rosalia Montes, fueron sus Padrinos D. Ygnacio Peres, y D. Clemencia Hernández, y testigos averlos casar, y velar, D. José Labom y Pedro Acorta todos de esta vecinidad para que conste lo firme con dicho Padre. Br. Gavino Valdez (rubric), Fr. José María Delgadillo (rubric)." Copy of Marriage Record

of Fran^co Ruiz with Josefa Hernandez, José Francisco Ruiz Vertical File, DRT Library.

²⁴ Jack Jackson, *Los Mesteños: Spanish Ranching in Texas, 1721–1821* (College Station: Texas A&M University Press, 2006), 178n8, 330, 408n36; Proceeding Concerning Pedro Flores's Petition to have Ranch Owners Brand their Cattle, Jan. 8, 1794, BA, 24:424–427.

²⁵ In 1834, the San Bartolo Ranch was sold by the heirs of Plácido Hernández, which included María Josefa Hernández, Ignacio Pérez, Antonia Arocha, Antonia Hernández and Fernando Ruiz. See Pérez et al to José Cassiano, February 4, 1834, Cassiano-Pérez Family Papers, Col 880, Texas A&M–San Antonio Special Collections Library.

²⁶ Jackson, *Los Mesteños*, 186–187.

²⁷ Sale of lot by Miguel de la Garza to Plácido Hernández, July 11, 1791, Land Grants 324, BCSA.

²⁸ Institute of Texan Cultures, *Residents of Texas*, I, 351, 375. See 1804 Census of the Villa of San Fernando and Presidio of Béxar, BA. "Jose Antonio Ruiz, of __ yrs; single; his mother Manuela de la Peña, widow of 50 years; Spaniard; his brother Francisco, of 13 yrs; has one niece, Maria Ybarvo, of 12." The Gil Y'Barbo family was among the first in Nacogdoches, suggesting that the Ruiz family may have spent the years immediately following the death of Juan Manuel Ruiz in or near Nacogdoches.

²⁹ Institute of Texan Cultures, *Residents of Texas*, I, 395. The record reads, in translation: "Benito Errera, Spaniard, laborer, 38 yrs. old; married to María Facova de las Fuentes, Spaniard, 25 yrs. old; had two children, a son and daughter, the first a yr. old, the 2nd 6 months."

³⁹ Leal, *San Fernando Church Baptismals, 1731–1793*, 65. The record reads, in translation: "June 21, 1804, Ruiz, María Lugarda de Jesús, Spanish, 6 days old, legitimate daughter of Don Francisco Ruiz and Doña Josefa Hernández. Godparents: Antonio de Castro and María Guadalupe de Levia, all of this city." See also Leal, *San Fernando Church Burials*, 86. The record reads, in translation: "June 21, 1804. Ruiz, María Lugarda, Spanish, 7 days old, legitimate child of Francisco Ruiz and Josefa Hernández, all from here."

³¹ Leal, *San Fernando Church Baptismals, 1731–1793*, 92. The record reads, in translation: "June 20, 1809. Ruiz, María Antonia Paula de la Concepción, Spanish, 6 days old, legitimate daughter of Don Francisco Ruiz and Doña Josefa Hernández. Grandparents, paternal: Don Juan Manuel Ruiz and Doña Manuela de la Peña. Grandparents, maternal: Don Plasido Hernández and Doña Rosalía Montes de Oca. Godparents: Don Ygnacio Peres and Doña Gertrudis Peres. Father Arocha baptized the child, but he did not sign the book."

³² Ruiz lived on Alamos Creek in a jacal on the ranch in 1828 and from 1832 to 1835. The Ruiz occupation was identified by at least one witness at the Paso de Los Carretas near the mouth of Cottonwood Creek and was opposite the Pérez Ranch headquarters. This would rest near present-day Elm Creek. Between 1837 and 1841, Ruiz lived within approximately four miles of the Pérez Ranch. Kristi M. Ulrich, Jennifer L. Thompson, Kay Hindes, Bruce K. Moses, Jon J. Dowling, Lynn K. Wack, and Barbara A. Meissner, *Testing and Data Recovery at the Pérez Ranch (41BX274), San Antonio, Bexar County, Texas* (San Antonio: Center for Archaeological Research, University of Texas at San Antonio, 2010), 17.

³³ Proceedings relevant to the municipal elections, Dec. 20, 1804, BA, 4:232. A *regidor* was the community representative (commissioner) to the municipal government.

³⁴ De la Teja, *San Antonio de Béxar*, 141–142.

³⁵ Juan Cortés petition to be Indian trader at Bayou Pierre, June 14, 1808, BA, 38:249;

Marcelo Soto's petition to establish a trade post at Bayou Pierre to permit trade with Americans at Natchitoches, Aug. 25, 1808, BA, 38:591.

³⁶ Presidial Company of Béxar, Sept. 31, 1805, BA, 8:432–435. José Antonio Ruiz served at the rank of *soldado*.

³⁷ *"United States v. Davenport's Heirs*, 56 U.S. 1 (1853)," U.S. Supreme Court, Justia, https://supreme.justia.com/cases/federal/us/56/1/case.html [Accessed Oct. 29, 2017]. La Nana Post was on the Nacogdoches to Natchitoches Road at the point where La Nana Bayou crossed the road in modern Sabine Parish; Patrol of the Río Hondo, Dec. 19, 1805, BA, 10:148.

³⁸ Land Conveyance of United States to José Ruez, July 23, 1832, Land Conveyances, Sabine Parish, M:241.

³⁹ Order on Illegal Immigration, BA, 33:695.

⁴⁰ De la Teja, *San Antonio de Béxar*, 108–110.

⁴¹ Jackson, *Los Mesteños*, 157–158, 298, 482–483.

⁴² Provision of a Butcher Shop, or Slaughterhouse, BA, 114:64–67.

⁴³ Receipt of Slaughterhouse Accounts, Jan. 3, 1803, BA, 11:56–57.

⁴⁴ McDonald, "Juan Martín de Veramendi," in De la Teja, *Tejano Leadership*, 38.

⁴⁵ Cutter, *The Legal Culture of Northern New Spain*, 99–100.

⁴⁶ Cruz, *Let There Be Towns*, 152.

⁴⁷ Proceedings against Juan Joseph Flores for illegal sale of alcohol, BA, 12:136–138, 287–288. Numerous examples exist in the Bexar Archives of legal proceedings which reference the lack of *notarios* and *escríbanos*. One such example was as follows: "Thus have I decreed, ordered, and signed, acting as Delegate Judge with my Attendant Witnesses, because there is no Notary Public or Royal Scribe in the Province, and on this common paper since there is none with a seal."

⁴⁸ Sentence of Exile of Bernardo Contreras for theft, Dec. 13, 1806, BA, 29:191. Ángel Navarro presiding as alcalde. José Francisco Ruiz and Juan Lira as testigos de asistencia.

⁴⁹ Auto of Pérez v. Baca, BA, 26:68–69; "This be declared and signed with me, said judge [Luis Galán], and my attendant witnesses, with whom I am acting as delegate judge, in lieu of a notary public, as provided by law."

⁵⁰ Report of the Death of María Josefa Carrio, Feb. 22, 1808, BA 23:200–201.

⁵¹ Bill of Sale for Negro, July 7, 1808, BA, 37:21.

⁵² Manuel María de Salcedo to Luis Galán, Tómas de Arocha, and [José] Francisco Ruiz, Dec. 23, 1809, BA, 43:607.

⁵³ Almaráz, *Tragic Cavalier*, 16.

⁵⁴ Cruz, *Let There Be Towns*, 149.

⁵⁵ Ibid., 151.

⁵⁶ Case against José Rodríguez (alias Jocito), accused of horse theft, Apr. 12, 1810, BA, 44:737–739; Case against Máximo Mejía for assault and battery, contempt, and concubinage, Feb. 16, 1810, BA, 44:243–257.

⁵⁷ Proceedings in case against José Andrés Patiño, charged with resisting arrest, Feb. 19, 1810, BA 44:294.

⁵⁸ Luis Galán to Mariano Varela, on transmittal of sumaria against Gil Guillermo de la Barr for treason, June 6, 1810, BA, 45: 588. A sumaria was the report resulting from the investigation of charges.

⁵⁹ J. Villasana Haggard, "The House of Barr and Davenport," *SHQ* 49 (July 1945): 66–88.

⁶⁰ Bernardo Bonavía to Nemesio de Salcedo, on the case against José Megue for

smuggling, May 30, 1810, BA, 45:465–486. See also Mariano Varela to Bernardo Bonavía, on the cases against Francisco Álvarez and companions, Julían Lartigue, and Juan de la Forcade, June 13, 1810, BA, 45:678; and Luis de Galán to Manuel de Salcado, on the case against smugglers arrested in La Bahía and the auction of their contraband goods, Feb. 10, 1810, BA, 44:197.

⁶¹ Mariano Rodríguez's petition to investigate the legitimacy of the birth of Francisco Javier Bustillos, Feb. 16, 1810, BA, 44:252.

⁶² An edict naming three persons to perform the office of *procurador* or *notario public*, BA, 16:234–235.

⁶³ Jaime E. Rodriguez O., *Political Culture in Spanish America, 1500–1830* (Lincoln: University of Nebraska Press, 2017), 140.

⁶⁴ Timothy E. Anna, *Forging Mexico, 1821–1835* (Lincoln: University of Nebraska Press, 1998), 42–43, 48–49. The juntas formed in Spain and Spanish America during the Napoleonic Wars and the Wars for Independence were not the same as modern military dictatorships, which also use the word "junta."

⁶⁵ Nettie Lee Benson, "Texas's Failure to Send a Deputy to the Spanish Cortes, 1810–1812," *SHQ* 64 (July 1960): 34–35.

CHAPTER 3: ROYALIST

¹ Military Service Record of [José] Francisco Ruiz, Oct. 25, 1831, in McLean (ed.), *Papers Concerning Robertson's Colony*, VI, 494.

² Hubert J. Miller, *Padre Miguel Hidalgo: Father of Mexican Independence* (Edinburg, Tex.: Pan American University Press, 1986), 13–15.

³ Nemesio de Salcedo to the People of the Interior Provinces, Oct. 24, 1810, BA, 15:110–117.

⁴ Governor Manuel Antonio Cordero y Bustamante had familial ties to Béxar and José Francisco Ruiz. In 1813, he requested permission from the viceroy to marry María Gertrudis Pérez, daughter of Juan Ignacio Pérez and Clemencia Hernández, and therefore by marriage the niece of Ruiz. The request was granted on January 1, 1814. With her marriage to Cordero, María became known as La Brigaviella ("the Brigadier General") and was permitted to carry out her husband's duties, including reviewing the troops, in his absence. Her apparent ease in handling his duties may have come from the fact that she was considered an equal to men in some business dealings, such as the inheritance, administration, buying, and selling of property. Upon her father's death, María inherited the Pérez homestead on Plaza de Armas, known today as the "Governor's Palace." After Cordero's death in 1823, she married the wealthy Italian-born merchant and businessman, José Cassiano, on April 12, 1826. With him she had a son. Cassiano had been Ruiz's New Orleans supplier when he was engaged in illicit trade with the Comanches during his time in exile. María died of dropsy or edema and was buried in San Fernando Church on September 29, 1832.

⁵ Castañeda, *Our Catholic Heritage in Texas*, VI, 3.

⁶ The Spanish word *filibustero*, derives originally from the Dutch *vrijbuiter*, "privateer, pirate, robber." The Spanish word entered the English language in the 1850s, as applied to military adventurerers in Spanish America. In this context it means a land pirate/robber. Rodríguez O, *Political Culture in Spanish America*, 203n3.

⁷ Castañeda, *Our Catholic Heritage in Texas*, VI, 4, citing José María Guadiana to the Junta, Apr. 19, 1811, BA, 48:619–622.

[8] Almaráz, *Tragic Cavalier,* 108.

[9] Ibid., 111-113.

[10] Ibid., 115.

[11] J. Villasana Haggard, "The Counter-Revolution of Béxar," *SHQ* 43 (October 1939): 222-235.

[12] Benson, "Texas Failure to Send a Deputy to the Spanish Cortes," 35. Eligibility for the Cortes included the requirement of being born in the province the member represented. Manuel María de Salcedo was not born in Texas and therefore ineligible.

[13] Manuel María de Salcedo to Manuel Royuela, Jan. 13, 1811, BA, 47:842.

[14] Military Service Record of [José] Francisco Ruiz, Oct. 25, 1831, in McLean (ed.), *Papers Concerning Robertson's Colony,* VI, 494.

[15] Record of the election of political and military chiefs of Texas for 1811 which resulted in the election of Manuel María de Salcedo, Jan. 19, 1811, BA, 47:852-868. All votes supported the Royalist leaders. Those voting were: Mariano Rodríguez, Juan Ignacio Pérez, Thomas de Arocha, José Ramírez, Ricardo Contreras, Pedro de la Garza Falcon, Luis Galán, Fernando de Veramendi, Gaspar Flores de Abrego, Isidro de la Garza, José Martínez Cantú, Juan Manuel Escavarria, Juan Antonio de la Ibarra, Andrés de Saldaña, Joseph Miguel de Arcos, Joseph María Muñoz, José Nicolás Benites, José Antonio de la Garza, Manuel Barrera, José María Sánchez, Cayatano Cantú, Bisente Lozano, Gregorio Amador, José Clemente Arocha, José Cipriano de la Garza, José Ángel Cabasos, Geronimo Herrera, Vicente Travieso, Erasmo Seguín, José Flores, and Simón de Herrera.

[16] Haggard, "Counter-Revolution of Béxar," 222-235.

[17] Donald E. Chipman and Harriett Denise Joseph, *Spanish Texas, 1519-1821* (Austin: University of Texas Press, 2010), 246. On Pérez's ownership of the Governor's Palace, see Tim Draves, "Spanish Governor's Palace (*Comandancia*)" *The Handbook of Texas Online,* <https://tshaonline.org/handbook/online/articles/ccs03> [Accessed Sept. 5, 2019].

[18] Castañeda, *Our Catholic Heritage in Texas,* VI, 10.

[19] Ibid., VI, 10-11. Castañeda listed the conspirators as Sergeant Miguel de Reyna, Sergeant Blas José Perales, Sergeant Patricio Rodríguez, Sergeant Trinidad Pérez, Corporal Tómas Pinedo of Nuevo Santander Company, Capitán Pedro de la Garza Falcon, Capitán Vicente Tarín, Lieutenant Vicente Flores, Alcalde Francisco Travieso, and Regidor Gabino Delgado. Governor Manuel María de Salcedo, Lieutenant Colonel Simón de Herrera, Captain Geronimo de Herrera, Captain Juan Martín Echevarria, Captain José Goseasochea, Captain Miguel de Arcos, Captain Joaquín de Ugarte, Captain Francisco Pereira of Saltillo, Lieutenant Juan de Castañeda of Lampasos, Lieutenant Gregorio Amador, Lieutenant José Montero, Ensign Miguel Serrano of Lampazos, Captain Juan Ignacio Arrampidez of Parras, Lieutenant Juan José Elguézabal, and all the European-born civilians in Béxar were singled out for arrest.

[20] Robert S. Weddle, *San Juan Bautista: Gateway to Spanish Texas* (Austin: University of Texas Press, 1968), 27-28. Presidio San Juan Bautista del Río Grande was located on the south bank of the Río Grande in present day Guerrero Viejo, Tamaulipas. Ignacio Elizondo, the military commander there, was originally from Béxar.

[21] Haggard, "Counter-Revolution of Béxar," 227.

[22] Ibid., 228

[23] Ibid., 229n20. Others elected were Antonio Sáenz, Juan Ignacio Pérez, Miguel Eca y Múzquiz, Luciano García, Erasmo Seguín, Luis Galán, Manuel Barrera, Juan José

Zambrano, Gavino Delgado, and Vizente Gortari. José Antonio Saucedo was chosen to serve as secretary.

[24] Julia Kathryn Garrett, *Green Flag Over Texas* (New York: Cordova Press, 1939), 55–57.

[25] Frederick C. Chabot, "Proclamation Relating to the Revolution Which Took Place at Béxar on January 22nd," in *Texas in 1811: The Las Casas and Sambrano Revolutions,* ed. Frederick C. Chabot (San Antonio: Yanaguana Society Publications, 1941), 106.

[26] Chabot, "Proclamation," 106. The list included Juan Manuel Zambrano, José Dario Zambrano, José María Zambrano, Ignacio Pérez, Erasmo Seguín, Juan Martín de Veramendi, José Francisco Ruiz, Miguel Múzquiz, Luis Galán, José Muñoz, Miguel Navarro, Antonio Sáenz, Gavino Delgado, Manuel Barrera, Miguel Díaz de Luna, José Antonio Saucedo, Francisco Flores, Francisco Montes, Pedro Fuentes, Patricio Rodríguez, José Abal, Francisco Vasquez, José Castro, Juan Caso, Santiago Tixerina, Luciano García, and Vicente Gortari.

[27] Haggard, "Counter-Revolution of Béxar," 235.

[28] Junta to Manuel Royuela on the Appointments of Cavalry and Infantry Officers Appointed by Nemesio de Salcedo, June 13, 1811, BA, 48:710. Other royalist appointments included Tómas de Arocha (Second Cavalry of Texas), José Ángel Navarro (Infantry of Béxar), and Ignacio Pérez (First Cavalry of Texas).

[29] All counter-revolutionary junta members were rewarded with military promotion or cash remuneration. Almaráz, *Tragic Cavalier,* 124.

[30] JFR to Juan Manuel Zambrano, Mar. 9, 1811, BA, 48:188; Report of the Second Militia Cavalry Company of Texas of Mariano Rodríguez, Nov. 13, 1811, BA, 49:463. The only *teniente* of the company was José Francisco Ruiz, who is described as *"abilitado,"* or "one who provisions."

[31] Request for clothing needed by militia troops, Mar. 9, 1811, BA, 48:188; [José] Francisco Ruiz's list of supplies needed to equip the militia of Texas, Sept. 3, 1812, BA, 52:412–413; [Juan] Ignacio Pérez to Cristobal Domínguez, Sept. 25, 1813, BA, 52:231.

[32] [José] Francisco Ruiz's request for clothing needed by militia troops, Mar. 9, 1811, BA, 48:188.

[33] Muster Roll of Captain Mariano Rodríguez Company of the Militia of the Presidio of Texas, June 16, 1811, BA, 48:719–720 [signed by Ruiz]; [José] Francisco Ruiz's list of supplies needed to equip the militia of Texas, Sept. 3, 1812, BA, 52:412–413.

[34] Ibid.

[35] Bravery of certain soldiers of the Mariano Rodríguez Company during Indian attack on Béxar, Jan. 24, 1812, BA, 50:115.

[36] Junta's Orders to Increase Defenses of Béxar, Feb. 6, 1812, BA, 50:308; Junta to Manuel María de Salcedo, Apr. 28, 1812, BA, 51:9.

[37] Bernardino Montero to Manuel María de Salcedo, Mar. 12, 1812, BA, 50:710.

[38] José Antonio López, *The Last Knight: Don Bernardo Gutiérrez de Lara Uribe, A Texas Hero* (Bloomington, Ind.: privately published, 2008), 17, 19–20.

[39] Garrett. *Green Flag Over Texas,* 85, 94–95.

[40] Ibid., 140–142.

[41] Bradley Folsom, *Arredondo: Last Spanish Ruler of Texas and Northeastern New Spain* (Norman: University of Oklahoma Press, 2017), 72.

[42] Montero to Manuel María de Salcedo, June 8, 1812, BA, 51:482, on the transmittal of Gutiérrez de Lara's papers, captured by Ermegildo Guillen; Juan Martín Echevarria

to Manuel María de Salcedo, Nov. 17, 1812, BA, 52:3, on remarks concerning seditious proclamations introduced into Béxar, see Patria Espanola Americana's letter on Rafael Trevino's departure for Monterrey to deliver proclamations of Gutiérrez de Lara, June 27, 1812, BA, 51:698.

[43] Orders to stop circulation of seditious papers to be distributed by Juan Galván and Félix Arispe, June 8, 1812, BA, 51:486.

[44] J. C. A. Stagg, *Borderlines in Borderlands: James Madison and the Spanish-American Frontier, 1776–1821* (New Haven, Conn.: Yale University Press, 2009), 147. Shaler advanced Gutiérrez de Lara $100.00 to distribute pamphlets in Mexico.

[45] Garrett, *Green Flag Over Texas*, 126–127; Ban on Enlightenment Authors Including Rousseau, BA, 32:132. The banned literature contained messages from Bernardo Gutiérrez de Lara and Bernardo Martin Despallier, a Frenchman from Louisiana, calling on the soldiers of Nacogdoches to declare independence and follow Gutiérrez de Lara.

[46] Proceedings concerning the questioning of José María Valdez in connection with seditious conversation he had with Miguel Lienda, Nov. 28, 1812, BA, 51:35.

[47] [Juan] Ignacio Pérez to Manuel María de Salcedo, June 9, 1812, BA, 51:518, on the recording of information in military service records of merits attained by Andrés Cadena, Joaquín Muñoz, Manuel Lombrana, and others in skirmish with Indians.

[48] Folsom, *Arredondo*, 72.

[49] W. D. C. Hall, "The First Republic of Texas, April-August 1813: Bernardo Gutiérrez de Lara and José Álvarez de Toledo," *Sons of the DeWitt Colony of Texas,* http://www. tamu.edu/faculty/ccbn/ dewitt/Spain2.htm [accessed Jan. 30, 2011].

[50] John O. Leal, *Camposanto: An Ancient Burial Ground of San Antonio, Texas, 1808–1860* (San Antonio: privately published, 1975), 14. The record reads, in translation: "Feb. 13, 1812, Ruiz, José Antonio, adult, single, legitimate son of Juan Manuel Ruis and Manuela Peña."

[51] U.S. Treasury, *Claims to Land Between the Río Hondo and Sabine Rivers in Louisiana,* 18th Cong., 2nd sess., 1825, Senate Report 445, 95.

[52] Accounts of the Béxar Company, Dec. 3, 1805, BA, 10:93; Military Report of Detachment at Nana and Vayupier, Dec. 1, 1805, BA, 10:81–83.

[53] Art Martínez de Vara and Marina Dávalos, *History and Records of Santisima Trinidad Church at Paso de las Garzas, Texas* (Von Ormy, Tex.: Santa Helena Publishing, 2009), 210. The entry in this volume reads: "10/19/1876, Ruiz, Francisco Antonio, died last night at 9:30 at 64 years old."

[54] Leal, *San Fernando Church Marriages,* 22.

CHAPTER 4: REVOLUTIONARY

[1] *Biography of Jose Antonio Navarro by an Old Texan,* 15–16.

[2] Jose Antonio Aguilar Rivera, *Liberty in Mexico: Writings on Liberalism from the Early Republican Period to the Second Half of the Twentieth Century* (Indianapolis: Liberty Fund, 2012), ix–xxix.

[3] Weddle and Thonhoff, *Drama & Conflict,* 70.

[4] Raúl Coronado, *A World Not to Come: A History of Latino Writing and Print Culture* (Cambridge, Mass.: Harvard University Press), 59.

[5] See Francisco Suárez, *Selections from Three Works of Francisco Suárez, Volume II: An English Version of the Texts,* ed. Gladys L. Williams, Ammi Brown, John Waldron, and Henry Davis (Oxford, UK, 1944; reprint, Buffalo, N.Y.: William S. Heins, 1995), es-

pecially "Defensio Fidei Catholicae, et Apostolicae Adversus Anglicanae Sectae Errores," originally written in 1613. The Jesuits were expelled from Hispanic realms due to their use of Scholasticism to reject the political philosophy of the divine right of kings and their belief that sovereignty was based upon the will of society. Francisco Suárez and the Salamanca University school were seen as the most dangerous of these Scholastic political philosophers and they were suppressed in 1767. Coronado, *A World Not to Come*, 56.

[6] Suárez, *Selections*, 417–429.

[7] Coronado, *A World Not to Come*, 52–59.

[8] Ibid., 52–63.

[9] The Spanish municipio was the local unit of Spanish government. It consisted of an urban center and its rural hinterlands with generally undefined boundaries. It was governed by an elected town council headed by an alcalde (judge) and several regidores (council members). Each municipo, alternatively called an ayuntamiento, also had other public officials such as a city attorney, law enforcement officers, town secretary and various commissioners. Béxar was organized as a municipio under both Spanish and Mexican governments. Upon independence in 1836, Texas had 23 municipios. The congress of the Republic of Texas reorganized these into American-style counties. The municipio of Béxar became the county of Bexar on December 22, 1836. This area was vast, including nearly all of West Texas, and was eventually divided into 128 counties. The urban center of Béxar was incorporated as an American-style municipality named the City of San Antonio on June 5, 1837. San Antonio and the other Texas municipalities governed only the urban centers within its defined city limits and were governed by a mayor and town council. The municipio was judicial in structure, reflecting the Spanish government's organization as a hierarchy of courts. The municipality was administrative in structure, reflecting the Anglo American political tradition.

[10] Chipman and Joseph, *Spanish Texas*, 238–239. The settlement of Santísima Trinidad de Salcedo, or Trinidad for short, was a small Spanish villa on the east bank of the Trinity River located near present-day Madisonville, Texas. It was founded in 1806 and destroyed in 1813. It is not the same town as modern-day Trinidad, Texas.

[11] Almaráz, *Tragic Cavalier*, 164–165.

[12] Garrett, *Green Flag Over Texas*, 173. See also Almaráz, *Tragic Cavalier*, 167. According to Gutiérrez de Lara's account of the battle, found in the Mirabeau B. Lamar Papers, Magee was poisoned by his own men, many of whom he had previously mistreated at his former post. Gutierrez de Lara to the Mexican Congress, Aug. 1, 1815, in Gulick and Elliott (eds.), *Lamar Papers*, I, 4-29.

[13] Almaráz, *Tragic Cavalier*, 168. Samuel Kemper had been involved in the 1804 rebellion against Spanish authorities in West Florida.

[14] [Juan] Ignacio Pérez to Cristobol Domínguez, on [José] Francisco Ruiz's report of individuals financially indebted to the Béxar Company, Sept. 25, 1813, BA, 53:231. Pérez was submitting the report because Ruiz was an exile by September 1812.

[15] Military Service Record of [José] Francisco Ruiz, Oct. 23, 1831, in McLean (ed.), *Papers Concerning Robertson's Colony*, VI, 494.

[16] Kevin Brady, "Unspoken Words: James Monroe's Involvement in the Magee-Gutierrez Filibuster," *East Texas Historical Journal* 45 (March 2007): 64.

[17] Jack Jackson, "Menchaca, Miguel," *The Handbook of Texas Online*, <http://www.tshaonline.org/handbook/online/articles/fme15> [Accessed May 1, 2019]. Miguel Menchaca is often confused with his cousin José Antonio Menchaca. Miguel deserted

his post at Nacogdoches and joined the Gutiérrez de Lara expedition. He was accused of smuggling propaganda into Béxar. He was promoted to Colonel and led the Tejano forces under Gutiérrez de Lara at Alazán Creek and Medina.

[18] Jarratt Rie, *Gutiérrez de Lara, Mexican Texan: The Story of a Creole Hero* (Austin: Creole Texana, 1949), 29.

[19] JFR to Miguel Menchaca, Mar. 22, 1813, Bernardo Gutiérrez de Lara Papers, 2-22/923 (Texas State Library and Archives Commission, Austin, Texas; hereafter cited as TSLAC).

[20] Rodríguez O., *Political Culture*, 133. The term *patria* was used in the Americas to refer to the locality, Texas in this case.

[21] JFR to Miguel Menchaca, Mar. 22, 1813, Gutiérrez de Lara Papers, 2-22/923, TSLAC. The original text of the letter reads: "yo hablo con la maior ingenuidad pues jamas he sido lisongero, y si amo atodos los de mi Paiz."

[22] JFR to Miguel Menchaca, Mar. 22, 1813, Gutiérrez de Lara Papers, 2-22/923, TSLAC. This letter began with a reference to a prior letter "en dias pasados," or "days before." Ruiz's retirement application also claimed that he was corresponding with Gutiérrez de Lara since February 1813 about independence. Ruiz asked that the time he served in the royalist army be omitted from the calculation of his retirement pension. The motive for this request appeared to be genuine patriotism.

[23] James C. Milligan, "José Bernardo Gutiérrez de Lara: Mexican Frontiersman, 1811–1841" (Ph.D. diss., Texas Tech University, 1975), 74.

[24] Castañeda, *Our Catholic Heritage in Texas*, VI, 96.

[25] Almaráz, *Tragic Cavalier*, 171.

[26] Ted Schwarz, *Forgotten Battlefield of the First Texas Revolution: The Battle of Medina, August 18, 1813* (Austin: Eakin Press, 1986), 33.

[27] Stagg, *Borderlines in Borderlands*, 159.

[28] Gutierrez de Lara to the Mexican Congress, Aug. 1, 1815, in Gulick and Elliott (eds.), *Lamar Papers*, I, 4-29.

[29] Castañeda, *Our Catholic Heritage in Texas*, VI, 100.

[30] Schwarz, *Forgotten Battlefield*, 33.

[31] Ibid., 34.

[32] Henry P. Walker (ed.), "William McLane's Narrative of the Magee-Gutiérrez Expedition, 1812–1813," *SHQ* 66 (January 1963): 465.

[33] JFR to Miguel Menchaca, Mar. 22, 1813, Gutiérrez de Lara Papers, 2-22/923, TSLA.

[34] Garrett, *Green Flag Over Texas*, 182–183. Gutiérrez de Lara's declaration of independence predated that of José María Morelos, which is celebrated in Mexico as the first Mexican declaration of independence.

[35] Castañeda, *Our Catholic Heritage in Texas*, VI, 102.

[36] López, *Last Knight*, 74.

[37] Francisco Arocha and Mariano Rodríguez to the Farmers of Natchitoches, Aug. 5, 1813, Gutiérrez de Lara Papers, 2-23/923, TSLAC.

[38] Schwarz, *Forgotten Battlefield*, 34.

[39] Folsom, *Arredondo*, 73.

[40] Ibid., 73.

[41] Arredondo also enlisted the help of the Bishop of Monterrey, who issued an indulgence for military service and warned of 1,000 years in purgatory for each month a man avoided enlistment. Ibid., 74.

[42] Arredondo warned that Spanish citizens would become "vile slaves" to these

"stranger dogs, without religion, and with customs very different than our own." Ibid., 73. See also Castañeda, *Our Catholic Heritage in Texas,* IV, 106.

[43] Folsom, *Arredondo*, 73–74.

[44] Ignacio Elizondo to Gutiérrez de Lara, Apr. 19, 1813, BA, 17:116–117.

[45] Folsom, *Arredondo*, 73–74.

[46] Castañeda, *Our Catholic Heritage in Texas,* VI, 108.

[47] Garrett, *Green Flag Over Texas,* 214–215.

[48] Folsom, *Arredondo*, 84.

[49] José Antonio Navarro, *Memoirs,* 36.

[50] Folsom, *Arredondo*, 84.

[51] Castañeda, *Our Catholic Heritage in Texas,* VI, 108.

[52] Military Service Record of [José] Francisco Ruiz, Oct. 23, 1831, in McLean (ed.), *Papers Concerning Robertson's Colony,* VI, 494.

[53] Folsom, *Arredondo*, 84.

[54] Ibid., 86. Many of these troops were recently arrived veterans of the Napoleonic Wars.

[55] Schwarz, *Forgotten Battlefield,* 46.

[56] Garrett, *Green Flag Over Texas,* 217–219.

[57] Schwarz, *Forgotten Battlefield,* 59–60.

[58] Garrett, *Green Flag Over Texas,* 218–219.

[59] Ibid., 61.

[60] Ibid., 61–62.

[61] Ibid., 64.

[62] Folsom, *Arredondo,* 87. Archaeologist Bruce Moses locates Rancherías at La Loma de San Cristobal which lies between the cities of Pleasanton and Poteet in Atascosa County, Texas. See Bruce Moses, *Roads to the Battle of Medina* (Von Ormy, Tex.: Alamo Press, 2020), forthcoming.

[63] Schwarz, *Forgotten Battlefield,* 75–76.

[64] Ibid., 79–82.

[65] Folsom, *Arredondo,* 88.

[66] Walker, "McLane's Narrative," 474–475.

[67] Bruce Moses has identified the campsite on the north bank of the current crossing of the Medina River at FM 1937. See Moses, *Roads to the Battle of Medina,* forthcoming.

[68] Schwarz, *Forgotten Battlefield,* 82.

[69] Folsom, *Arredondo,* 88.

[70] Ibid.

[71] Walker, "McLane's Narrative," 475–476.

[72] Folsom, *Arredondo,* 90.

[73] Ibid,.

[74] Ibid., 91.

[75] Ibid., 93.

[76] Walker, "McLane's Narrative," 477–478.

[77] Folsom, *Arredondo,* 93.

[78] Menchaca, *Memiors,* 17–18; Schwarz, *Forgotten Battlefield,* 108–109.

[79] Navarro, *Memiors,* 40.

[80] Folsom, *Arredondo,* 96.

[81] José Antonio Navarro to Mirabeau B. Lamar, May 18, 1841, in Gulick and Elliott (eds.), *Lamar Papers,* III, 597.

[82] Castañeda, *Our Catholic Heritage in Texas*, VI, 119.

[83] Gregorio Carrizo to Feliciano Ramírez, Oct. 18, 1814, BA, 54:322–331.

[84] José Antonio Navarro to Lamar, May 18, 1841, in Gulick and Elliott (eds.), *Lamar Papers*, III, 598.

[85] Ibid., III, 597–598.

[86] Elizondo released the Americans, even giving them horses to aid their exit from Texas. The Tejanos did not receive the same treatment: 71 men were executed on the Trinity, while the women were forced to bathe nude in the river for the amusement of the soldiers. Folsom, *Arredondo*, 99.

[87] Ibid., 98.

[88] Ibid., 104.

[89] Joe W. Hipp, *The Oldest Ranch in Texas: Rancho de la Purísima Concepción, A Ranch on the Road to History* (Austin: Eakin Press, 2000), 30. "From the above mentioned regulations there shall be excepted as not worthy of obtaining any consideration whatsoever, the accursed leaders, Bernardo Gutiérrez, Jose Alvarez Toledo, Francisco Arocha, Francisco Ruiz, Juan Beramendi, Vicente Travieso and the infamous blood-thirsty Pedro Prado."

[90] Arredondo, General Amnesty Order, Oct. 10, 1813 in Ericson, *Nacogdoches*, 204–205.

[91] José Antonio Navarro to Lamar, May 18, 1841, in Gulick and Elliott (eds.), *Lamar Papers*, III, 597.

[92] Institute of Texan Cultures, *Residents of Texas*, I, 169, II, 108.

[93] Report of [Juan] Ignacio Pérez, Nov. 11, 1816, BA, 57:402.

CHAPTER 5: EXILE

[1] José Antonio Navarro to Lamar, May 18, 1841, in Gulick and Elliott (eds.), *Lamar Papers*, III, 597.

[2] Military Service Record of [José] Francisco Ruiz, Oct. 23, 1831, in McLean (ed.), *Papers Concerning Robertson's Colony*, VI, 494.

[3] McDonald, "Juan Martín de Veramendi," in De la Teja, *Tejano Leadership*, 33. Veramendi did not participate in the Battle of Medina. He and Juan Manuel Zambrano were traveling to Louisiana with large shipments of wool when they encountered the Republican Army of the North. The goods were confiscated and Veramendi continued to Natchitoches where he waited the outcome of the expedition.

[4] Leal (ed.), *Camposanto*, no. 409. The entry reads, in translation: "Burial. José Antonio Ruiz, single, legitimate son of Juan Manuel Ruiz and Manuela de la Peña, 2-13-1812."

[5] Proceedings concerning the conduct of Vicente Farin, Mariano Rodríguez, [José] Francisco Ruiz, Félix Estrada, Juan de la Cruz, Miguel Castro, and Ignacio Góngora, with reference to rebels and enemy Indians, October 15, 1814–October 18, 1814, BA, 54:321-331.

[6] Ashbury Dickens and James C. Allen (eds.), *American State Papers – Documents of the Congress of the United States, in Relation to the Public Lands, From the First Session of the Eighteenth to the Second Session of the Nineteenth Congress, Inclusive: Comencing December 1, 1823, and Ending March 2, 1827* (Washington: Gales & Seaton, 1859), 95, 193. "Jose Rues, of the Parish of Natchitoches, filed his notice by virtue of occupation and habitation, and cultivation, a tract of land lying within the neutral territory, situated on the Bayou Santa Barbara, bounded on all sides by vacant land, and containing 640

acres." Ruiz's associates Juan Cortés, Bernardo Gutiérrez de Lara, José María Mora, and Samuel Davenport testified that the land titles in the area had been "removed and carried off by Don José Montero in 1812, then commanding at Nacogdoches, when he abandoned that place with his troops at the approach of Gutiérrez de Lara and Magee, who were attempting to revolutionize the country...the most part of them were destroyed at San Antonio, where said Montero carried them to."

[7] Elizabeth Shown Mills (ed.), *Natchitoches: Translated Abstracts of Register Number Five of the Catholic Church Parish of St. Francois des Natchitoches in Louisiana, 1800–1826* (Westminster, Md.: Heritage Books, 2007), 140–141. The entry for Ignacio Peña reads: "Ignacio Peña, 23 October 1813, burial in [the] cemetery of this church of a 40 year old native of Béxar in the province of Texas, who died leaving a widow María de la Luz Navarrete, a resident of Béxar, and one son. Deceased did not receive the sacraments nor make a confession since he was unconscious with putrid fever. Priest: F. Magnes." Ignacio de la Peña was the son of Ignacio de la Peña, the uncle of Ruiz through his mother, Manuela de la Peña. Francisco Rodríguez was married to María Rosalía Ruiz.

[8] Mills, *Natchitoches: Translated Abstracts*, 143. The entry for Francisco Rodríguez reads: "Francisco Rodríguez, 22 March 1814, burial in cemetery of this parish of a Spaniard, aged 62 years, widower by first nuptials with [Jua]na Travieso, by whom he left 2 daughters, and who was now married with María Ruiz by whom he leaves 2 sons and 1 daughter. Deceased did not confess and received only the sacrament of extreme unction since he died suddenly of a pain. Priest F. Magnes." Francisco Rodríguez was married to Ruiz's sister, María Antonia Ruiz, in 1803.

[9] Mills, *Natchitoches: Translated Abstracts*, 140, 142–144, Other Béxar refugees who died in the epidemic included Pedro Jiménez, José Estevan Borrego, Juan Morales, José Luis Durán, María Teresa Sánchez, María Sierra, Joaquin Musquiz, María Gertrudis Soto, Joaquín Múzquiz, and José Pablo Montoya. The burial record book of the parish for this period is damaged, other exiles may have been buried whose records were lost. At least two partial records of exiles exist: "___ [San]chez, age 35, native of Besar, left a widow named __a Rodríguez and 2 sons." and "Jose ___ underneath is a partial name "__rcelo Bor__".

[10] McDonald, *Jose Antonio Navarro*, 31.

[11] Carolyn Reeves Ericson, *Nacogdoches, Gateway to Texas: A Biographical Directory, 1773–1849* (Fort Worth: Arrow/Curtis, 1974), 204–205.

[12]Among the more infamous of Ruiz's neighbors were Peter Parker and his four brothers, who had built a large tavern in 1813 on the old Camino Real one mile east of Fort Jessup. This place became a notorious hangout for the shady characters of the Neutral Ground, who were infamous for robbing its patrons. In 1822, Stephen F. Austin passed through the Neutral Ground on his way to Texas and persuaded the Parker brothers to abandon their tavern, find wives, and come with him to Texas. They did so by hastily going to Bayou Pierre and marrying local girls. They became part of Austin's Old Three Hundred. John Doe, a successful counterfeiter, "minted" fake silver eight real coins. A flaw in his press made the fakes obvious to locals, but not to outsiders. His coins became the de facto currency in the Neutral Ground. Frank and Jim Copland and their cousin, William Jennings, were seen as the dominant Neutral Ground outlaws. They mostly rustled cattle and horses, but they were tied closely to Doe's counterfeiting scheme. Raymond Delay, Latney Parrott, and John Ayres, were involved in the slave trade with Pierre Lafitte. They served on his ships and assisted the Texas Revolution by

maintaining supply lines to Louisiana. All three married daughters of Edmund Quirk, who participated in the Gutiérrez-Magee expedition and was imprisoned by the Spanish. Jackson (ed.), *Texas by Terán*, 272.

[13] Proceedings concerning the conduct of Vicente Farin, Mariano Rodríguez, [José] Francisco Ruiz, Félix Estrada, Juan de la Cruz, Miguel Castro, and Ignacio Góngora, with reference to rebels and enemy Indians, October 15–18, 1814, BA, 54:321–331.

[14] Juan Antonio Padilla, "Texas in 1820," trans. Mattie Austin Hatcher, *SHQ* 23 (July 1919): 62.

[15] Anderson, *Conquest of Texas*, 30.

[16] Kavanagh, *Comanches*, 26.

[17] F. Todd Smith, *From Dominance to Disappearance: The Indians of Texas and the Near Southwest, 1789–1859* (Lincoln: University of Nebraska Press, 2005), 9.

[18] José Francisco Ruiz, Texas Comanche Customs and Characteristics, 184?, in Gulick and Elliott (eds.), *Lamar Papers*, IV, 221.

[19] Ibid., 4:221–222.

[20] Ruiz described the Eastern-Western division among the Comanche in his report to Mirabeau B. Lamar. "[The Comanche] is the most numerous tribe of Indians known in the territory of Texas. It is comprised of various small tribes, such as the Orientals or Eastern Commanches who are generally friendly, and frequently visit Bexar and other parts of Texas for the purpose of trading. Yaparicuts, who occupy the western parts of Texas, and frequently visit N. Mexico." José Francisco Ruiz, Texas Comanche Customs and Characteristics, 184?, in Gulick and Elliott, *Lamar Papers*, 4:221.

[21] The Tenewah gained prominence because of the Red River horse trade in which Ruiz and other Tejano exiles participated. This association continued even after Mexico achieved its independence in 1821, when the refugees re-established their political power in Béxar. Their close relations with the Tenewahs allowed for the establishment of peaceful relations between Mexico and the Comanches led by Paruakevitsi of the Tenewahs. Kavanagh, *Comanches*, 484.

[22] Kavanagh, *Comanches*, 157. In the summer of 1810, El Sordo broke away from his prior allegiances and formed his own band comprised of Comanches, Wichitas, and Tawakonis, who raided Texas. In 1811 Parauaquita, a prominent leader from New Mexico, arrived in Texas seeking to establish peace and trade relations. Cordero gave his daughter in marriage to Parauquita to cement their relationship as principal leaders. Both men were pro-Spanish and attempted to control all of the Comanches.

[23] Hämäläinen, *Comanche Empire*,149–150; Antonio Martínez to Joaquín de Arredondo, May 13, 1818, in Virginia H. Taylor (ed.), *The Letters of Antonio Martínez, The Last Spanish Governor of Texas, 1817–1821* (Austin: Texas State Library, 1957), 136.

[24] Hämäläinen, *Comanche Empire*,150.

[25] Folsom, *Arredondo*, 104.

[26] Prior to 1830, the Red River had a large log jam, known as the "Great Raft", which forced the river to redirect its flow into an elbow that passed through colonial Natchitoches. In 1830, the jam burst and the river changed its course, converting its former elbow into an oxbow lake and severely damaging the city's economy. The name of the elbow was changed to "Cane River" to reflect this dramatic change. Jacques D. Bagur, *A History of Navigation on Cypress Bayou and the Lakes* (Denton: University of North Texas Press, 2001), 60–67.

[27] Inventorie General au Magarin ve Natchitoches fout le 10-febrier 1819, 18 Feb 1819, Natchitoches Genealogy and Historical Library, in Carol Wells, "Inventory of the

Natchitoches Warehouse," *The Natchitoches Genealogist* 14 (October 1989): 11–14. Other exiles with accounts include Bernardo Gutiérrez [de Lara], Mariano Rodríguez and Joseph Arocha.

[28] Jackson, *Indian Agent*, 23. Bean had served under José María Morelos and had come to the Neutral Ground to attempt to raise a campaign against Texas.

[29] Anderson, *Conquest of Texas*, 30.

[30] In order to combat illicit trade, Arredondo established an annual trade fair at La Bahia for Indians and Spanish tradesmen. He also granted the residents of La Bahia use of a port, duty free, for five years. However, nearby Matagorda Bay lacked a port and there were no funds to construct one. The plan failed. Folsom, *Arredondo*, 105.

[31] José Francisco Ruiz, Texas Comanche Customs and Characteristics, 184?, in Gulick and Allen (eds.), *Lamar Papers*, IV, 221.

[32] Padilla, "Texas in 1820," 55. The villages to which Padilla refers are likely the five Río Grande settlements of Laredo, Revilla, Reynosa, Mier, and Camargo.

[33] Folsom, *Arredondo*, 141.

[34] Kavanagh, *Comanches*, 157.

[35] Ruiz, *Report on the Indian Tribes of Texas in 1828*, 7.

[36] Hämäläinen, *Comanche Empire*, 186–187

[37] José Antonio Navarro, *Autobiography of José Antonio Navarro* (San Antonio: privately published, 1841), 4. "The King of Spain has already as early as the year 1815 issued a Proclamation granting Pardon to all the Insurgents of Texas. Among others my Brother-in-law Veramundi and myself have returned to Bexar pardoned by the King of Spain or by Arredondo in his Royal Name." See also José Antonio Cordero to Governor of Texas, Notice of the insurgents pardoned, March 8, 1814, BA. Among those listed as having received pardons by March 8, 1814 was Ruiz's sister, María Josepha Ruiz, the notation reads "Juan Beramendi and consequently that of his mother-in-law." The 1815 list of pardons also names "Uncle Ruiz, his teacher and his family, citizen of Concepcíon." This mention is often confused with José Francisco Ruiz. However, this "Uncle Ruiz" refers to another Francisco Ruiz who resided at Mission Concepción. The 1815 Census of Mission Concepción lists this other Francisco Ruiz as "Francisco Ruiz, native of Parras, age 50, widower; his children; María Navora, age 25, widow; José Francisco, age 15; José Polito, age 7 and José Alba, age 9." Institute of Texan Cultures, *Residents of Texas*, II, 90.

[38] McDonald, "Juan Martín de Veramendi," in De la Teja, *Tejano Leadership*, 33.

[39] Navarro, *Autobiography*, 4.

[40] Folsom, *Arredondo*, 114.

[41] McDonald, "Juan Martín de Veramendi," in De la Teja, *Tejano Leadership*, 33.

[42] Ibid., 32.

[43] Ibid., 33–34.

[44] Anderson, *Conquest of Texas*, 30.

[45] Kavanagh, *Comanches*, 180.

[46] Andrés Reséndez, *Changing National Identities at the Frontier: Texas and New Mexico, 1800–1850* (New York: Cambridge University Press, 2004), 99.

[47] Barbara Jo Coleman Dove, *The Life and Legacy of Luciano Nepomuceno Navarro, 1800–1869* (San Antonio: privately published, 2001), 11–12.

[48] Reséndez, *Changing National Identities*, 99, citing Naomi Fritz, "José Antonio Navarro," (master's thesis, St. Mary's University, San Antonio, Tex., 1941).

[49] Uecker, Meskill, and Cox, *Archaeological Investigations*, 5.

⁵⁰ Jésus F. de la Teja and John Wheat, "Béxar: Profile of a Tejano Community, 1820–1832," in Poyo and Hinojosa, *Tejano Origins*, 4.

⁵¹ Institute of Texan Cultures, *Residents of Texas*, I, 169.

⁵² John O. Leal, *San Fernando Church Baptismals, 1812–1825* (San Antonio: privately published, 1976), Entry 505. See also Wallace L. McKeehan, "Hispanic Texian Patriots in the Struggle for Independence," *Sons of the DeWitt Colony of Texas*, <http://www.tamu.edu/faculty/ccbn/dewitt/ tejanopatriots.html> [Accessed May 28, 2011]. Juan José Arocha fought in the Texas Revolution at the Siege of Béxar.

⁵³ Confiscated Property of Nepumuceno San Miguel, n.d., Rebel Property 2, BCSA.

⁵⁴ Institute of Texan Cultures, *Residents of Texas*, I, 169. Ignacia Almanze, a Spaniard, was listed in the 1817 Census of Béxar (BA) as a resident of the Barrio del Sur, where she resided with her family: Josefa Franca, 47, Rafael Almanze, 18, and Ignacia Almanze, 16. In the 1831 Census of Béxar (BA), she was married and lived in the household of José Ángel Navarro with numerous other servants. Trinidad Santa Cruz, an Indian, was not listed in any other census contained in *Residents of Texas.*

CHAPTER 6: INDIAN AGENT

¹ "[José] Francisco Ruiz in the Mexican Army," in McLean (ed.), *Papers Concerning Robertson's Colony*, IV, 35.

² Padilla, "Texas in 1820," 62.

³ De la Teja, *San Antonio*, 14, 15. De la Teja described a situation in which "notwithstanding formal peace treaties with the Comanches and other Norteño tribes . . . total peace remained elusive."

⁴ Kavanagh, *Comanches*, 194–195. Cortés recognized the already peaceful nature of the local Caddos and suggested a trade agreement be negotiated with them immediately, while preparations were made for an expedition into Texas. A treaty was made with the Caddos near Natchitoches and a delegation of Caddos led by Pierre Roubleau traveled to Saltillo, where they signed the document.

⁵ Kavanagh, *Comanches*, 195.

⁶ Folsom, *Arredondo*, 121.

⁷ López to Martínez, Oct. 10, 1821, BA, 68:56–61.

⁸ Félix Almaráz, *Governor Antonio Martínez and Mexican Independence in Texas: An Orderly Transition* (San Antonio: Bexar County Historical Commission, 1979), 5–7; José Antonio Navarro to Captain [José] Menchaca, n.d., BA, 168:426–427.

⁹ Almaráz, *Governor Antonio Martínez*, 9–11. José Ángel Navarro was the elder brother of José Antonio Navarro and thus a nephew of José Francisco Ruiz.

¹⁰ Folsom, *Arredondo*, 215. The treaty was signed at Córdoba in the province of Veracruz.

¹¹ Juan Cortés to López, June 30, 1821, BA, 68:585.

¹² López to Trespalacios, July 9, 1822, BA, 22:234.

¹³ Juan Cortés to Antonio Martínez, Oct. 16, 1821, BA 68:591–592; Antonio Martínez to *Diputado Provincal*, Aug. 5, 1821, BA 68:35–37.

¹⁴ Kavanagh, *Comanches*, 168–169, 184. *Piloncillos* are pure, unrefined cane sugar pressed into a cone shape.

¹⁵ López to Martínez, Oct. 10, 1821, BA 68:58–59.

¹⁶ López to JFR, Aug. 10, 1821, BA, 68:60–64. Translation by author.

[17] Kavanagh, *Comanches*, 195; JFR to Martínez, Oct. 15, 1821, BA, 68:587–588. See also JFR to Martínez, Oct. 15, 1821, José Francisco Ruiz Papers (Dolph Briscoe Center for American History, University of Texas at Austin).

[18] JFR to Martínez, Oct. 15, 1821, BA, 68:587–588; Cortés to Martínez, Dec. 30, 1821, BA, 68:689–690.

[19] Cortés to Martínez, Oct. 16, 1821, BA, 68:591–594.

[20] Military Service Record of [José] Francisco Ruiz, Oct. 23, 1831, in McLean (ed.), *Papers Concerning Robertson's Colony*, VI, 494; JFR to Ayuntamiento of Béxar, Jan. 25, 1822, BA, 70:674–676.

[21] F. Todd Smith, *The Wichita Indians: Traders of Texas and the Southern Plains, 1540–1845* (College Station: Texas A&M University Press, 2000), 112.

[22] Ibid., 3, 112.

[23] López to Trespalacios, July 9, 1822, BA, 22:234. "it appears that the *[Lipans]* on their first interview with Ruiz . . . have ceased to be friendly with the Comanches and wish to be so toward us."

[24] Thomas A. Britten, *The Lipan Apaches: People of Wind and Lightning* (Albuquerque: University of New Mexico Press, 2009), 177–178. In July 1822, Cuelgas de Castro and Yolcha Poca Ropa traveled to Monclova, Coahuila, and signed a temporary peace treaty. They promised to wait for the Comanches to sign their treaty so that the two groups could go to Mexico City together for ratification. After waiting a month, the Lipan leaders became impatient and departed for the Mexican capital, arriving shortly after the coronation of Emperor Agustín Iturbide. The Lipans signed a formal peace treaty on August 17, 1822, with the new regime at Mexico City. See Britten, *Lipan Apache*, 178; Treaty with the Lipan Indians, Aug. 17, 1822, in Thomas W. Streeter, *Bibliography of Texas, 1795–1845* (5 vols. Cambridge, Mass.: Harvard University Press, 1955–1960), II, No. 690.

[25] See JFR to Ayuntamiento of Béxar, Feb. 12, 1822, BA, 70:674–676; Ayuntamiento of Béxar to López, Feb. 20, 1822, BA, 70:792; López to Ayuntamiento of Béxar, Mar. 11, 1822, BA, 71:8–13; López to Ayuntamiento of Béxar, Mar. 13, 1822, BA, 71:47–50.

[26] Kavanagh, *Comanches*, 196.

[27] JFR to Ayuntamiento of Béxar, Apr. 3, 1822, BA, 71:283–285. Ruiz described the open ceremony of Comanche councils: "A fire is built in the center of the Chief's tent . . . the Chief takes the principal seat and sends the crier to give notice to all the warriors to come and to the council of the pipe. He goes out and cries [through] the town 'Come to the pipe, the pipe is ready.' A [sentinel] is placed at the door and they come to the door one at a time and say 'here am I, what seat shall I occupy?' The answer is given by the Chief, on the right or left, as the case may be, and he enters and seats himself accordingly, each one as he enters depositing them in the enclosure in the back part of the tent. All the men having entered and seated themselves in this matter (no woman is allowed to attend) a profound silence reigns in the meeting, while the preparation is made for commencing the ceremony. The Chief then fills his pipe from a pouch in which he carries tobacco mixed with leaves of another quality, everyone holding his nose to prevent inhaling the smoke before the ceremony commences. The Chief then lights the pipe and draws a mouthful of smoke which ascends to the top of the tent. This is intended as an offering to the sun. He again fills his mouth and turning his face towards the earth blows the smoke downward and then blows smoke first to the right then to the left. After this he draws from the pipe four times and swallows the smoke,

then passes the pipe to the next person asking at the same whence he will receive it. If he answers from below, he takes hold near the bowl. If from above, he takes hold of the end of the stem. In this way the pipe is passed all around and smoked by everyone in the same manner as by the Chief. Each one after smoking rubbing himself all over. This is continued until three pipes of tobacco are consumed, the Chief carefully preserving the ashes. Consultation then commences. José Francisco Ruiz, Texas Comanche Customs and Characteristics, 184?, in Gulick and Elliott, *Lamar Papers*, 4:221–223.

[28] Carlos Justo Sierra, "Los Comanches en México," *Boletín Bibliográfico de la Secretaría de Hacienda y Crédito Público* (México, D.F., 1968), 14–15, cited in McLean (ed.), *Papers Concerning Robertson's Colony*, IV, 432.

[29] Bustamante's Instructions for Indian Commissioner [José] Francisco Ruiz, Sept. 7, 1822, BA, 72:789–810. Ruiz's formal title was "comisionado para tratar las paces con los indios comanches."

[30] Agreement between Antonio Martínez, the Ayuntamiento of Béxar, and Pichinampa, July 11, 1822, BA, 72:165–166; Kavanagh, *Comanches*, 196.

[31] In an interview in the *San Antonio Light*, dated November 10, 1901, Enrique Esparza reported that his father, Gregorio Esparza, was captured by Comanche Indians as a child and after he had grown was ransomed by Col. Ruiz. No date for the ransoming was given in the article, but the 1822 Comanche Treaty negotiations dealt with captives like Esparza and may have included him. Gregorio Esparza would later die at the Battle of the Alamo. Hansen (ed.), "Another Child of the Alamo," in *Alamo Reader*, 95.

[32] On [José] Francisco Ruiz's Military Appointment, July 12, 1822, BA, 72:169–170; On Receipt of [José] Francisco Ruiz's Appointment to the Mounted Militia of Texas, July 18, 1822, BA, 72:259–260. In addition to resuming his military duties, Ruiz resumed his social responsibilities by serving as padrino at the baptism of Juan Ancelmo Losoya. See Leal, *San Fernando Church Baptismals, 1812–1825*, 79. The record reads, in translation: "Losoya, Juan Anselmo, Spanish, 6 months old, legitimate son of Don Ventura Losoya and Doña Concepción Charle. Godparents: Don Francisco Ruis and Doña Josefa Hernández."

[33] Kavanagh, *Comanches*, 198. *The Gaceta del Gobierno Imperial de Mexico* recorded the arrival of Ruiz and the Comanche delegation: "The chief named Guonique, a subject who deserves the general applause of the Comanches because he is enterprising, truthful, observant, prudent, and resolute and with the plenipotentiary power conferred upon him by his nation . . . presented himself to this Court, where he was liberally entertained with his retinue." Kavanagh, *Comanches*, 197. Lucas Alamán, the Imperial Minister of Foreign Affairs, described the same meeting in a more officious manner: "There came to Mexico, sent by the *Comandante of the Provincias Internas*, a captain of the Comanche Nation named Guonique to treat for peace with the government. Guonique, among whose qualities is counted voraciousness . . . was received as an envoy of a civilized nation . . . They celebrated a treaty in which they established the rules which must be observed between the two nations."

[34] Passport Issued to [José] Francisco Ruiz to travel with Comanche party to Mexico, Sept. 7, 1822, BA, 72:806–807. Part of this reads, in translation, "I grant free and secure passage to the Court of the Mexican Empire to Lieutenant Don Francisco Ruiz, to the five individuals listed in the margin and three soldier escorts who conduct a chief captain, eight braves, and four women of the Comanches delegated by their nation to ratify with the Supreme Government the peace that with friendship and good will has been proposed."

³⁵ Trespalacios to López, Sept. 18, 1822, BA, 72:897; Trespalacios to López, Oct. 1, 1822, BA, 73:6–30. McLean, *Papers Concerning Robertson's Colony*, 4:428n.
³⁶ Treaty Between the Mexican Empire and the Comanche, Dec. 14, 1822, in McLean (ed.), *Papers Concerning Robertson's Colony*, IV, 433.
³⁷ Kavanagh, *Comanches*, 198.
³⁸ Anna, *Forging Mexico*, 94–95.
³⁹ Kavanagh, *Comanches*, 198.
⁴⁰ McLean (ed.), *Papers Concerning Robertson's Colony*, IV, 433.

CHAPTER 7: RESTORATION

¹ JFR to Stephen F. Austin, Nov. 26, 1830, in McLean (ed.), *Papers Concerning Robertson's Colony*, III, 27–28.
² Almaráz, *Governor Antonio Martínez*, 6.
³ McDonald, *José Antonio Navarro*, 56.
⁴ Ibid., 55.
⁵ Will Fowler, *Santa Anna of Mexico* (Lincoln: University of Nebraska Press, 2007), 65–66.
⁶ *Biography of Jose Antonio Navarro by an Old Texan*, 9.
⁷ Leal, *San Fernando Marriages*, 148; Dove, *Luciano Nepomuceno Navarro*, 14.
⁸ Leal, *San Fernando Baptisms 1821–1825*, 84. "April 19, 1823, Veramendi, Juan Martin Bacilio, 4 days old, legitimate son of Don Juan Martin de Veramendi and Doña Josefa Navarro. Godparents: Lt. Col. Don Francisco Ruiz and Doña Maria Antonia Navarro."
⁹ Andrés Tijerina, *Tejanos and Texas Under the Mexican Flag, 1821–1836* (College Station: Texas A&M University Press, 1994), 95–96; McDonald, *José Antonio Navarro*, 64.
¹⁰ Béxar Junta Gubernativa to Béxar Ayuntamiento, Mar. 24, 1823, BA, 74:434–435.
¹¹ La Bahía Ayuntamiento Minutes, May 25, 1823, BA, 74:848.
¹² Fowler, *Santa Anna of Mexico*, 65–66.
¹³ Santa Anna to Trespalacios, May 6, 1823, BA, 297:190.
¹⁴ McDonald, *José Antonio Navarro*, 66–67.
¹⁵ Juan Martín de Veramendi to Luciano García, July 8, 1823, BA, 75:169.
¹⁶ Benson, *The Provincial Deputation*, 151–152. Texas was awarded a provincial deputation by the Congress of Mexico on August 18, 1823. Its initial deputies were José Antonio Saucedo, José María Zambrano, Ramón Múzquiz, Juan José Hernández, Miguel Arciniega, Baron de Bastrop, and Mariano Rodríguez. See García to Béxar Ayuntamiento, Sept. 25, 1823, BA, 75:591–592.
¹⁷ Tijerina, *Tejanos and Texas*, 96–97.
¹⁸ Margaret Swett Henson, *Lorenzo de Zavala: The Pragmatic Idealist* (Fort Worth: Texas Christian University Press, 1996), 27.
¹⁹ Béxar Political Deputation to Béxar Ayuntamiento, Jan. 12, 1824, BA.
²⁰ Vito Alessio Robles, *Coahuila y Texas Desde la consumación de la Independencia hasta el Tratado de Paz de Guadalupe Hidalgo* (Mexico City: Editorial Porrua, S.A., 1979), 328.
²¹ Tijerina, *Tejanos and Texas*, 98–99. The office of jefe político was the highest civil governmental officer of a province.
²² Ibid., 100–101, 105.
²³ Ibid. 101.
²⁴ Ramos, *Beyond the Alamo*, 123–128.
²⁵ Tijerina, *Tejanos and Texas*, 113–114.

²⁶ Military Service Record of [José] Francisco Ruiz, Oct. 23, 1831, in McLean (ed.), *Papers Concerning Robertson's Colony,* VI, 494.

²⁷ Trespalacios to JFR, Apr. 8, 1823, BA, 74:523–524.

²⁸ McDonald, *José Antonio Navarro,* 55.

²⁹ JFR to Luciano García, Aug. 10, 1823, BA, 75:411. Paruakevitsi was Hispanicized as "Barbaquista" and this latter name appeared throughout the Spanish and Mexican records. In order to provide consistency, the Comanche spelling is used in this work.

³⁰ JFR to Superior Governor of the Capital of Texas, Aug. 10, 1823, BA, 75:411.

³¹ Juan Guzmán to Antonio Saucedo, Feb. 26, 1823, BA, 76:436–437.

³² Alamán to Saucedo, June 1, 1824, BA, 77:295–296.

³³ JFR to Gaspar Flores, Oct. 18, 1824, BA, 78:131–132. The sole act recorded of this short term as Indian agent was providing an interpreter for Chief Hoyoso who was travelling to Saltillo. JFR to Gaspar Flores, Oct 19, 1824, BA, 78:137–141.

³⁴ Milligan, "Gutiérrez de Lara," 173. JFR to Ayuntamiento of Béxar, Nov. 27, 1824, BA, 78:350–351. Ruiz also submitted receipts for 270 pesos in presents "that were given to the Indians that have presented themselves to me up to this day."

³⁵ Rafael Gonzales to Veramendi, Mar. 3, 1825, BA, 80:105–108.

³⁶ Antonio Elosúa to Commandant of Béxar Garrison, Mar. 26, 1827, BA, 101:737–738.

³⁷ Daniel Walker Howe, *What Hath God Wrought: The Transformation of America, 1815–1848* (New York: Oxford University Press, 2007), 348–352. Among those voting against the Indian Removal Act of 1830 was Representative David Crockett of Tennessee.

³⁸ Anderson, *Conquest of Texas,* 51.

³⁹ Kavanagh, *Comanches,* 202.

⁴⁰ Anderson, *Conquest of Texas,* 52.

⁴¹ Dianna Everett, *The Texas Cherokees: A People Between Two Fires, 1819–1840* (Norman: University of Oklahoma Press, 1990), 36–37.

⁴² H. W. Brands, *Lone Star Nation: The Epic Story of the Battle for Texas Independence* (New York: Anchor Books, 2004), 56–66.

⁴³ Jesús F. de la Teja, *A Revolution Remembered: The Memoirs and Selected Correspondence of Juan N. Seguín* (Austin: Texas State Historical Association, 2002), 6.

⁴⁴ Gregg Cantrell, *Stephen F. Austin, Empresario of Texas* (New Haven: Yale University Press, 1999), 89–90.

⁴⁵ Tijerina, *Tejanos and Texas,* 107. The Baron de Bastrop had personal experience in American colonization, having recently served as the land commissioner for Austin's colony. An example of his pro-colonization efforts on the committee was his success in changing the proposed requirement that the religion of colonists be "Catholicism" to the less specific "Christianity."

⁴⁶ Ibid. *Texas,* 113.

⁴⁷ JFR to Stephen F. Austin, Nov. 26, 1830, in McLean (ed.), *Papers Concerning Robertson's Colony,* III, 27–28.

⁴⁸ Tijerina, *Tejanos and Texas,* 115.

⁴⁸ Joseph E. Chance, *José María de Jesús Carbajal: The Life and Times of a Mexican Revolutionary* (San Antonio: Trinity University Press, 2006), 87.

⁵⁰ McDonald, *José Antonio Navarro,* 72.

⁵¹ Tijerina, *Tejanos and Texas,* 107.

⁵² McDonald, "Juan Martín de Veramendi," in De la Teja, *Tejano Leadership,* 35. Juan

Martín de Veramendi was named alternate representative, to serve in the absence of either Navarro or Arciniega.

⁵³ Tijerina, *Tejanos and Texas*, 116; McDonald, *José Antonio Navarro*, 79–82.

⁵⁴ Inventory and Appraisal of the Estate of José Francisco Ruiz, 1840, Wills and Estates 101, BCSA. It reads: "Anselmo Prú deve seguir su cuenta que como peón sirviente se le girava cincuenta y tres pesos, tres y medio reales." Anselmo Prú was clearly not a slave. In 1836 he fought with the Texans at the Siege of Béxar and received land grants for his military service to the Texas Republic. As can be understood from the quotation, Prú still owed money to Ruiz under their contract, but he was no longer bound to service as a peon.

⁵⁵ Stuntz, *Hers, His, and Theirs*, 74–75; McDonald, *José Antonio Navarro*, 251.

⁵⁶ J. Villasana. Haggard, "The Counter-Revolution of Béxar, 1811," *SHQ* 43 (July 1939): 227n17.

⁵⁷ JFR to Samuel M. Williams, Sept. 13, 1831, in McLean (ed.), *Papers Concerning Robertson's Colony*, VI, 414; 1804 Census of the Villa of San Fernando and Presidio of Béxar, BA; 1811 Census of Bexar, BA; McDonald, *José Antonio Navarro*, 72, 82.

⁵⁸ Tijerina, *Tejanos and Texas*, 120.

⁵⁹ Mateo Ahumada to JFR, Nov. 9, 1825, BA, 85:728–730.

⁶⁰ Ibid.

⁶¹ Ibid.; JFR to Ahumada, Apr. 16, 1826, BA, 91:785–786.

⁶² JFR to Ahumada, Dec. 1, 1825, BA, 86:392–393; Bernardo Gutiérrez de Lara to Ahumada, Dec. 8, 1825, BA, 86:556–557; Ahumada to JFR, Dec. 29, 1825, BA, 87:238–239.

⁶³ Ahumada to Gutiérrez de Lara, Nov. 10, 1825, BA, 85:792–793.

⁶⁴ Erasmo Seguín Certification that [José] Francisco Ruiz and José Vicente Flores were present at Commissary Review in Béxar, Jan. 3, 1826, BA, 87:695–696.

⁶⁵ Ahumada to JFR and Francisco Roxo, Feb. 9, 1826, BA, 89:468.

⁶⁶ JFR to Ahumada, Mar. 3, 1826, BA, 90:215–216.

⁶⁷ JFR to Ahumada, Mar. 20, 1826, BA, 90:649–650; Tomás Mungia to Erasmo Seguín, Mar. 20, 1826, BA, 90:651–654; JFR to Erasmo Seguín, Mar. 20, 1826, BA, 90:655–658.

⁶⁸ JFR to Ahumada, Feb. 25, 1826, BA, 89:896–897; Roxo to Ahumada, Feb. 25, 1826, BA, 89:894–895.

⁶⁹ JFR to Ahumada, Apr. 16, 1826, BA, 91:785–786. Ruiz reported that *soldado* Guillermo Rivera deserted at Pueblo Viejo, but apparently Tomas Múngia remained with him. Sergeant José María Sánchez of the Álamo de Parras Company told them about the recent attack in Tampico.

⁷⁰ Milligan, "Gutiérrez de Lara," 167.

⁷¹ JFR to Ahumada, Apr. 21, 1826, BA, 91:958-959; Gutiérrez de Lara to Ahumada, Apr. 21, 1826, BA, 91:960–961; Gutiérrez de Lara to Ahumada, Apr. 24, 1836, BA, 92:53–54.

⁷² Erasmo Seguín Certification that [José] Francisco Ruiz, Mateo Ahumada, and José Vicente Flores were present at Commissary Review, May 3, 1826, BA, 92:432–436; JFR to Ahumada, June 4, 1824, BA, 93:629. [José] Francisco Ruiz's statement concerning the sumaria of Pedro Martínez, June 17, 1826, BA 94:122–123.

⁷³ [José] Francisco Ruiz's petition for military promotion, June 22, 1826, BA, 94:259–260; Estado Mayor General Del Ejercito José Moran to Ahumada, Aug. 14, 1826, BA, 96:43–47.

CHAPTER 8: REDEMPTION

[1] Anderson, *Conquest of Texas*, 65.

[2] Edmund Parsons, *The Fredonian Rebellion* (privately published, n.d), 2.

[3] Anderson, *Conquest of Texas*, 60.

[4] Parsons, *Fredonian Rebellion*, 3.

[5] Cantrell, *Austin, Empresario of Texas*, 181–182.

[6] Parsons, *Fredonian Rebellion*, 4–6.

[7] Anderson, *Conquest of Texas*, 63–64.

[8] Parsons, *Fredonian Rebellion*, 18–19, 24.

[9] Cantrell, *Austin, Empresario of Texas*, 181–182.

[10] Parsons, *Fredonian Rebellion*, 18–19, 24.

[11] Saucedo to Austin, Dec. 10, 1826, BA.

[12] Jackson, *Indian Agent*, 86.

[13] Parsons, *Fredonian Rebellion*, 24.

[14] Ibid., 33–34.

[15] Jackson, *Indian Agent*, 86.

[16] Anastascio Bustamante to Comisario Particular of Béxar, Apr. 5, 1827, BA, 102:111–112.

[17] José Vicente Flores to JFR, May 9, 1827, BA.

[18] Parsons, *Fredonian Rebellion*, 41; JFR to Ahumada, May 14, 1827, BA, 103:368–373.

[19] Ruiz was fluent in Cherokee. Jackson, *Indian Agent*, 96.

[20] Jackson, *Indian Agent*, 96.

[21] Ibid., 96.

[22] Ibid., 91.

[23] "Tenoxtitlán, Dream Capital of Texas," in McLean (eds.), *Papers Concerning Robertson's Colony*, III, 45.

[24] Parsons, *Fredonian Rebellion*, 40; Ahumada to Bustamante, Apr. 18, 1827, BA. Benjamin R. Milam had participated in the Mexican Revolution and earned a commission as a colonel. He received a colonization contract along the Colorado River in 1825.

[25] JFR to Ahumada, Apr. 14, 1827, BA, 102:398–401. The Kichai were the southernmost of the five Wichita tribes. Over the course of the eighteenth century, the Wichita tribes engaged in a southward migration. Smith, *From Dominance to Disappearance*, 7.

[26] Smith, *Wichita Indians*, 121.

[27] JFR to Austin, May 28, 1827, in McLean (ed.), *Papers Concerning Robertson's Colony*, III, 250–251.

[28] Anderson, *Conquest of Texas*, 65.

[29] Ahumada to JFR, Apr. 19, 1827, BA, 102:536–537; JFR to Commandant of Texas, May 1, 1827, BA, 102:1024–1025.

[30] JFR to Austin, May 28, 1827, in McLean (ed.), *Papers Concerning Robertson's Colony*, III, 251.

[31] JFR to Austin, June 2, 1827, in McLean (ed.), *Papers Concerning Robertson's Colony*, III, 253–254.

[32] Bean's mood was certainly not improved by his personal situation. When he arrived in San Felipe in December 1826 during the march to Nacogdoches to confront the Fredonians, he learned that his wife, believing him to be dead, had married Martin Parmer, one of the prominent leaders of the rebellion. She had also trans-

ferred title of Bean's property to Parmer, who allegedly resided in Bean's house while serving as president of the short-lived Republic of Fredonia. See Jackson, *Indian Agent*, 69–71.

[33] Peter Ellis Bean to Austin, June 3, 1827, in McLean (ed.), *Papers Concerning Robertson's Colony*, III, 255.

[34] Jackson, *Indian Agent*, 94.

[35] Anderson, *Conquest of Texas*, 62, 65.

[36] Kavanagh, *Comanches*, 200.

[37] Smith, *Wichita Indians*, 122.

[38] José Antonio Saucedo to the Governor of Coahuila y Texas, August 1827, Archivo General del Estado de Coahuila (cited hereafter as AGEC), Fondo Jefatura Política de Bejar, caja 4, expediente 89.

[39] Ibid.

[40] Anderson, *Conquest of Texas*, 65–66. This author refers to Incoroy and Quellunes as leaders of the Penateka Comanche.

[41] Kavanagh, *Comanches*, 226. Tanemues translates as "Those Who Stay Downstream."

[42] Ibid., 293.

[43] Anderson, *Conquest of Texas*, 66.

[44] DeLay, *War of a Thousand Deserts*, 20.

[45] Kavanagh, *Comanches*, 204. The Gallinas River is a short tributary of the Pecos River. Its headwaters are northwest of Las Vegas, New Mexico, and it merges with the Pecos River just north of Santa Rosa, New Mexico.

[46] Ibid., 204.

[47] Ibid., 200. The treaty included an oath to the sun and Earth that the Comanche would do no more harm to Mexicans. Ruiz later wrote to President Mirabeau Lamar on the importance of invoking the sun and Earth in an oath to the Comanches: "The sun is their god and father and the creator of all things, the earth the Mother, and the most solemn oaths they can make is to swear by them." José Francisco Ruiz, Texas Comanche Customs and Characteristics, 184?, in Gulick and Elliott, *Lamar Papers*, 4:221. In his 1823 report to Mier y Teran he noted the same practice, "If a Comanche wants to be believed by his peers, he calls the sun and the Earth as witness in an oath. In the oath he will state he should fall dead if he is not telling the truth. Such an oath is believed by all who were in fear of punishment from the supreme powers." Ruiz, *Report on the Indian Tribes of Texas in 1828*, 15. A promise to the sun and Earth therefore was a sacred promise of the highest order in Comanche culture.

[48] Smith, *Wichita Indians*, 122–123.

[49] Kavanagh, *Comanches*, 293.

[50] Victor Blanco to the Chief of the Department of Béxar, Sept. 7, 1827, BCSA, 107:4–35. Ruiz's requested for payment of 328 pesos for his services in auctioning the secularized missions was denied in this correspondence.

[51] Almaráz, *San Antonio Missions*, 19–20, 57.

[52] Porter, *Spanish Water, Anglo Water*, 54, 71. A *dula* was an allotment to use a communal water source, in this case the San José Acequia Madre. Dulas were usually measured in 24-hour periods, during which the possessor had use of the water from the acequia. All acequia systems had an "acequia madre," which refers to the main channel of the system.

[53] Land Grant to [José] Francisco Ruiz, 1824, Land Grants, MR89, BCSA; This land was eventually sold to the Diocese of San Antonio and given to the Sisters of Charity of the Incarnate Word, who established an orphanage there. See Claudius María Dubuis to Sister St. Pierre of the Sisters of Charity of the Order of the Incarnate Word, Mar. 16, 1874, Deed Records, Bexar County (County Clerk's Office, Bexar County Courthouse, San Antonio, Texas), 1:561–572.

[54] Ramos Arispe to the Chief of the Department of Texas, July 16, 1827, BCSA, 105:418-420.

[55] Blanco to the Chief of the Department of Béxar, Sept. 7, 1827, BCSA, 107:4–35.

[56] Hindes, *Herrera Gate*, 2.

CHAPTER 9: BOUNDARY COMMISSION

[1] Kavanagh, *Comanches*, 26.

[2] Anderson, *Conquest of Texas*, 68.

[3] Jackson (ed.), *Texas by Terán*, 1.

[4] Ibid., 2–3.

[5] Ibid., 4.

[6] Berlandier serialized his diary, starting on January 26, 1831, in the Mexico City newspaper *Registro Oficial*, under the title "Diario del viage de Luis Berlandier." In 1832, a pamphlet that focused solely on his botanical observations was published under the title of *Memorias de la Comisión de Límites*. In 1850 a lengthy volume entitled *Diario de viage de la Comisión de Límites que puso el gobierno de la república, bajo la dirección del exmo. sr. general de division d. Manuel de Mier y Terán* authored by Berlandier and Chovell was published. Multiple editions of Berlandier's diary were subsequently published over the years in French and usually entitled *Voyage au Mexicque*. The most recent and comprehensive English edition of Berlandier's work on Texas is Jean Louis Berlandier, *Journey to Mexico During the Years 1826 to 1834*, trans. Sheila M. Ohlendorf, Josette M. Bigelow, and Mary M. Standifer (2 vols.; Austin: Texas State Historical Association, 1980).

[7] Anderson, *Conquest of Texas*, 71; Elosúa to Casimiro Leal, Oct. 11, 1830, in McLean (ed.), *Papers Concerning Robertson's Colony*, V, 65–66n3. McLean in footnote 3 reports that Elosúa was a native of Havana, Cuba, and served with the Spanish forces at the Battle of Medina opposite José Francisco Ruiz.

[8] Anderson, *Conquest of Texas*, 71; Ruiz, *Report on the Indian Tribes of Texas in 1828*, 3.

[9] Jackson (ed.), *Texas by Terán*, 8.

[10] Anderson, *Conquest of Texas*, 72.

[11] JFR to Austin, July 23, 1829, in McLean (ed.), *Papers Concerning Robertson's Colony*, III, 422–424.

[12] Ruiz, *Report on the Indian Tribes of Texas in 1828*, 2.

[13] Kavanagh, *Comanches*, 231.

[14] Art Martínez de Vara, *The Jose Francisco Ruiz Papers, Vol. 1 Report on the Indian Tribes of Texas* (Von Ormy, Tex.: Alamo Press, 2014), 10–11.

[15] Ibid., 95.

[16] Ramos, *Beyond the Alamo*, 55.

[17] Ruiz, *Report on the Indian Tribes of Texas in 1828*, 11.

[18] Martínez de Vara, *The Jose Francisco Ruiz Papers, Vol. 1*, 108.

[19] Ruiz, *Report on the Indian Tribes of Texas in 1828*, 15.

20 José Francisco Ruiz, Texas Comanche Customs and Characteristics, 184?, in Gulick and Elliott (eds.), *Lamar Papers*, IV, 221.

21 Earlier that year, on February 3, 1828, Ruiz's daughter María Antonia married Blas María Herrera of Béxar. Blas was the son of Benito Herrera, who had resided two doors down from the Ruiz home on the Plaza de las Armas, and certainly met María Antonia early in his life. Adolph Casias Herrera, "Herrera, Blas Maria," *The Handbook of Texas Online*, <https://tshaonline.org/handbook/online/articles/fhe73> [Accessed Jan. 16, 2020].

22 Berlandier, *Journey to Mexico*, 363.

23 Ibid.

24 Inventory of goods carried by [José] Francisco Ruiz to be sold in Coahuila, BA, 121:338.

25 Anastacio Bustamante to Austin, Mar. 23, 1829, in Barker (ed.), *Austin Papers*, II, 194–195. Bustamante enclosed a copy of his letter to Elosúa, outlining a plan whereby the civil militia of San Felipe and Nacogdoches would join forces with troops from Béxar to destroy the village of the Tahuayases.

26 Bustamante's Plan for Destroying the Tahuayases, n.d., in McLean (ed.), *Papers Concerning Robertson's Colony*, III, 54.

27 Anderson, *The Conquest of Texas*, 73.

28 Ramón Múzquiz to Austin, May 28, 1829, in McLean (ed.), *Papers Concerning Robertson's Colony*, III, 394–395.

29 Anderson, *Conquest of Texas*, 74.

30 Smith, *Wichita Indians*, 123.

31 Report of Money Paid to [José] Francisco Ruiz, Oct. 30, 1829, BA, 126:541.

32 JFR to Erasmo Seguín, Sept. 9, 1829, Land Grants, 31:205, BCSA. The grant was near present-day Seguin in Guadalupe County, Texas.

33 Inventory and Appraisal of the Estate of [José] Franciso Ruiz, 1840, Wills and Estates 101, BCSA.

34 Elosúa to Manuel de Mier y Terán, Nov. 11, 1829, BA, 126:788.

35 Mier y Terán to Elosúa, Dec. 12, 1829, BA, 127:202.

36 JFR to Miguel Arciniega, Feb. 1830, in Archivo Municipal de Saltillo, *Catálogo del Fondo Testamentos, Volume I*, 156. See also JFR to Arciniega, Mar. 1830, in Archivo Municipal de Saltillo, *Catálogo del Fondo Testamentos, Volume I*, 157.

37 JFR to Austin, Apr. 11, 1830, in Barker (ed.), *Austin Papers*, II, 367–368.

CHAPTER 10: TENOXTITLÁN

1 Mier y Terán to Elosúa, Apr. 24, 1830, in McLean (ed.), *Papers Concerning Robertson's Colony*, III, 511–516.

2 For the Law of April 6, 1830, see McLean (ed.), *Papers Concerning the Robertson's Colony*, III, 494–500.

3 Mier y Terán to Elosúa, Apr. 24, 1830, in McLean (ed.), *Papers Concerning Robertson's Colony*, III, 511–516. The general enclosed a copy of the Law of April 6, 1830, and detailed instructions for Ruiz. A presidio, or fort, was not necessarily enclosed by walls or fortified, but it did serve as quarters for troops posted there. Rather than palisades or enclosures, some had a blockhouse or strong point. Ultimately, due to a lack of funding and personnel, Ruiz's outpost apparently had quarters for troops and little else.

[4] Mier y Terán to Minister of Internal and External Relations, Jul. 31, 1830, in "Tenoxtitlán, Dream Capital of Texas," *SHQ* 70 (July 1966): 25. "I have had the name of Tenoxtitlán given to the central point on the Brazos River . . . In my opinion this point, if it is developed, will in time become the capital of all Texas."

[5] Stephen L. Hardin, "Efficient in the Cause," in *Tejano Journey, 1770–1850*, ed. Gerald E. Poyo (Austin: University of Texas Press, 1996), 56.

[6] JFR to Elosúa, May 10, 1830, BA, 130:376–377; McLean (ed.), *Papers Concerning Robertson's Colony*, IV, 92.

[7] "The Buffalo and Bear Hunt," in McLean (ed.), *Papers Concerning Robertson's Colony*, IV, 36.

[8] Múzquiz to Austin, May 13, 1830, in McLean (ed.), *Papers Concerning Robertson's Colony*, IV, 109–111.

[9] Presidial Company from Álamo de Parras, May 16, 1830, BA, 130:541–542; McLean (ed.), *Papers Concerning Robertson's Colony*, IV, 127–128. Report showed the articles of armament, munitions, clothing, saddles, equipment, horses, and mules on hand in the Álamo de Parras Company.

[10] Elosúa to JFR, June 2, 1830, BA, 131:257–258; McLean (ed.), *Papers Concerning Robertson's Colony*, IV, 176–177.

[11] Budget for Álamo de Parras Company, Aug. 1, 1830, BA, 132:76; McLean (ed.), *Papers Concerning Robertson's Colony*, IV, 329. Ruiz's base salary for 1831, the year that he took charge of the case against Castañeda and Ruiz, was 1,130 pesos and four reales, plus a campaign gratification of 615 pesos, seven reales, and six granos. See Béxar Commissariat to Subordinate to the General Commissariat in San Luis Potosí, Oct. 23, 1831, BA, 145:529; McLean (ed.), *Papers Concerning Robertson's Colony*, VI, 491.

[12] Elosúa to JFR, June 2, 1830, BA, 131:257–258; McLean (ed.), *Papers Concerning Robertson's Colony*, IV, 176–177.

[13] Elosúa to JFR, June 2, 1830, BA, 131:257–258; McLean (ed.), *Papers Concerning Robertson's Colony*, IV, 176–177.

[14] Elosúa to JFR, June 23, 1830, BA, 132:819; McLean (ed.), *Papers Concerning Robertson's Colony*, IV, 218.

[15] John O. Leal, "San Fernando Church Baptismals, Book I, Part 2, 1826–1842," typescript (n.d.), Texana Collection (San Antonio Public Library, San Antonio, Texas), 21. The record reads, in translation: "1830 Jun 26. Beramendi, Teresa de los Ángeles, 8 days old, legitimate daughter of Don Juan de Beramendi and Doña Josefa Navarro. Godparents: Don Francisco Ruiz and Doña Josefa Hernández. Father de la Garza baptized the child and signed the book."

[16] Elosúa to Mier y Terán, June 28, 1830, BA, 132:12; McLean (ed.), *Papers Concerning Robertson's Colony*, IV, 227.

[17] Budget for the Álamo de Parras Company, Aug. 1, 1830, BA, 131:964–965; McLean (ed.), *Papers Concerning Robertson's Colony*, IV, 219–220.

[18] "A Shortage of Funds," in McLean (ed.), *Papers Concerning Robertson's Colony*, IV, 38–39.

[19] Commandant of Coahuila y Tejas to Commandant of the Álamo de Parras Company, July 15, 1830, BA, 132:628; McLean (ed.), *Papers Concerning Robertson's Colony*, IV, 269. This soldier was most likely Guillermo Rivera, who was charged with desertion "for the second time" the day after the company arrived on the Brazos.

[20] Diary of the Marches Made by the Álamo de Parras Company to the Brazos River, Under the Orders of Lieutenant Colonel [José] Francisco Ruiz, With Mention of In-

cidents Along the Way, July 13, 1830, BA, 132:557–558; McLean (ed.), *Papers Concerning Robertson's Colony*, IV, 262–264.

²¹ JFR to Elosúa, June 19, 1830, BA, 132:712–714; McLean (ed.), *Papers Concerning Robertson's Colony*, IV, 275–279.

²² JFR to Elosúa, Aug. 2, 1830, BA, 133:53–55.

²³ JFR to Elosúa, June 19, 1830, BA, 132:712–714; McLean (ed.), *Papers Concerning Robertson's Colony*, IV, 277.

²⁴ Austin to Mier y Terán, July 20, 1830, in McLean (ed.), *Papers Concerning Robertson's Colony*, IV, 283. Austin also mentioned that he was leaving the next day to help Ruiz choose a site for Tenoxtitlán. *The Gazette* was published in San Felipe de Austin.

²⁵ JFR to Elosúa, July 23, 1830, BA, 132:821–822; McLean (ed.), *Papers Concerning Robertson's Colony*, IV, 290. Ruiz wrote that with this letter he established the official mail route from his department via San Felipe to Béxar.

²⁶ JFR to Elosúa, Aug. 1, 1830, BA, 133:30–32; McLean (ed.), *Papers Concerning Robertson's Colony*, IV, 335–336. Ruiz also acknowledged his receipt of a copy of a letter Elosúa wrote to Bean on June 20, 1830, relative to the war between friendly frontier tribes and the Tahuacanos, Hecos (Huecos?), and Tahuayases, and added that he believed Mexicans should work through the Comanches to subdue the hostile tribes.

²⁷ JFR to Elosúa, Aug. 2, 1830, BA, 133:53–55; McLean (ed.), *Papers Concerning Robertson's Colony*, IV, 339–342. Ruiz notes that the price for the homes could probably be negotiated down. The footnotes to the document found in McLean's compilation include an English translation of the grant of one league of land to William Mathis, in Austin's colony, on July 19, 1824. See also "Excerpt from General Land Office map showed location of the William Mathis league, which served as the temporary site for Fort Tenoxtitlán," in McLean, *Papers Concerning Robertson's Colony*, IV, 349. Ruiz thought so highly of this land that he applied for and later received a land grant in this location.

²⁸ JFR to Williams, July 23, 1830, in McLean (ed.), *Papers Concerning Robertson's Colony*, IV, 293; JFR to Williams, Aug. 7, 1830, in McLean (ed.), *Papers Concerning Robertson's Colony*, IV, 362–363.

²⁹ JFR to Williams, Aug. 21, 1830, in McLean (ed.), *Papers Concerning Robertson's Colony*, IV, 407. Ruiz also asked Williams to use his influence to have Ramón Múzquiz reelected as the "Chief of the Department." One *arroba* was about 25 pounds.

³⁰ JFR to Williams, Oct. 16, 1830, in McLean (ed.), *Papers Concerning Robertson's Colony*, V, 88.

³¹ JFR to Elosúa, Sept. 9, 1830, BA, 134:239–240; McLean (ed.), *Papers Concerning Robertson's Colony*, IV, 457.

³² Severo Ruiz to the Commandant of Coahuila y Texas, Sept. 10, 1830, BA, 134:287–288; McLean (ed.), *Papers Concerning Robertson's Colony*, IV, 461. Ruiz asked him for time to permit nine more families to join the troops at Tenoxtitlán.

³³ Mier y Terán to Elosúa, July 16, 1830, in McLean (ed.), *Papers Concerning Robertson's Colony*, IV, 270.

³⁴ Stanley C. Green, *The Mexican Republic: The First Decade, 1823–1832* (Pittsburgh: University of Pittsburgh Press, 1987), 62.

³⁵ JFR to Elosúa, Aug. 7, 1830, BA, 133:257–258; McLean (ed.), *Papers Concerning Robertson's Colony*, IV, 360.

³⁶ JFR to Elosúa, Aug. 7, 1830, BA, 133:259–260; McLean (ed.), *Papers Concerning Robertson's Colony*, IV, 361.

[37] Commandant of Coahuila y Texas to JFR, Aug. 16, 1830, BA, 133:589; Commandant of Coahuila y Texas to Nicasio Sánchez, Aug. 17, 1830, BA, 133:598–599; McLean (ed.), *Papers Concerning Robertson's Colony,* IV, 387–388, 393–394.

[38] Severo Ruiz to Elosúa, Sept. 3, 1830, BA, 134:99–100; McLean (ed.), *Papers Concerning Robertson's Colony,* IV, 444.

[39] JFR to Elosúa, Sept. 3, 1830, BA, 134:101–102; McLean (ed.), *Papers Concerning Robertson's Colony,* IV, 445–446. Ruiz also reported that Private Remijio Garza, a deserter from the Second Permanent Company of Tamaulipas, had appeared in Tenoxtitlán on August 21, 1830, and would be sent to Béxar as soon as possible.

[40] JFR to Elosúa, Oct. 9, 1830, BA, 135:144–145; JFR to Elosúa, Oct. 30, 1830, BA, 135:865–866; McLean (ed.), *Papers Concerning Robertson's Colony,* IV, 579, V, 132.

[41] Diary of Sánchez, Sept. 22, 1830, BA, 134:596–599; Diary of Gaspar Flores de Abrego, Sept. 22, 1830, BA, 134:600–603; McLean (ed.), *Papers Concerning Robertson's Colony,* IV, 489–527.

[42] Mier y Terán to Elosúa, Sept. 20, 1830, BA, 134:532–534; McLean (ed.), *Papers Concerning Robertson's Colony,* IV, 486–487.

[43] Santiago Navayra to JFR, Oct. 10, 1830, BA, 135:180–181; McLean (ed.), *Papers Concerning Robertson's Colony,* IV, 586–587.

[44] JFR to Elosúa, Oct. 9, 1830, in McLean (ed.), *Papers Concerning Robertson's Colony,* IV, 573–574; JFR to Elosúa, Oct. 29, 1830, in McLean (ed.), *Papers Concerning Robertson's Colony,* V, 125.

[45] JFR to Elosúa, Oct. 26, 1830, in McLean (ed.), *Papers Concerning Robertson's Colony,* V, 117; Elosúa to JFR, Nov. 10, 1830, in McLean (ed.), *Papers Concerning Robertson's Colony,* V, 168.

[46] Mier y Terán to Elosúa, Oct. 30, 1830, in McLean (ed.), *Papers Concerning Robertson's Colony,* V, 131.

[47] Juan Nepomuceno de Ayala to Elosúa, Nov. 19, 1830, in McLean (ed.), *Papers Concerning Robertson's Colony,* V, 224.

[48] Álamo de Parras Company, Dec. 1, 1830, BA, 136:672; McLean (ed.), *Papers Concerning Robertson's Colony,* V, 278. Father Ayala requested the following items needed to perform the Mass: 1 white chasuble, one fresh-colored, and one berry colored; 1 black cape; 1 alb; 1 altar cloth; 1 missal; 1 altar; 1 hand bell; 1 very small vial for the holy oil for the sick; 2 more vials for the catechumens and to hold chrism. See Nepomuceno de Ayala to Elosúa, Dec. 3, 1830, BA, 136:830–840.

[49] "The Plans for the Fort," in McLean (ed.), *Papers Concerning Robertson's Colony,* V, 38.

[50] Ibid.

[51] JFR to Elosúa, Apr. 29, 1830, BA, 140:449–451; McLean (ed.), *Papers Concerning Robertson's Colony,* VI, 211.

[52] JFR to Williams, June 11, 1831, in McLean (ed.), *Papers Concerning Robertson's Colony,* VI, 269.

[53] JFR to Elosúa, Mar. 30, 1831, BA, 132:235–237; McLean (ed.), *Papers Concerning Robertson's Colony,* VI, 159–161.

[54] JFR to Elosúa, May 14, 1831, BA, 141:180–182; McLean (ed.), *Papers Concerning Robertson's Colony,* VI, 233–234.

[55] JFR to Elosúa, June 11, 1831, BA, 141:871–873; McLean (ed.), *Papers Concerning Robertson's Colony,* VI, 268.

[56] JFR to Elosúa, Oct. 30, 1830, in McLean (ed.), *Papers Concerning Robertson's Colony*, V, 133–134.

[57] JFR to Elosúa, Nov. 13, 1830, in McLean (ed.), *Papers Concerning Robertson's Colony*, V, 189–190.

[58] JFR to Williams, Nov. 13, 1830, in McLean (ed.), *Papers Concerning Robertson's Colony*, V, 191–192.

[59] "Robertson and Thomson Visit Tenoxtitlán," in McLean (ed.), *Papers Concerning Robertson's Colony*, V, 44.

[60] Ibid.

[61] Mier y Terán to Elosúa, Dec. 20, 1830, in McLean (ed.), *Papers Concerning Robertson's Colony*, V, 342–343.

[62] "The Law of April 6, 1830," in McLean (ed.), *Papers Concerning Robertson's Colony*, V, 47.

[63] Ramos, *Beyond the Alamo*, 122, 140.

[64] JFR to Elosúa, May 14, 1831, BA, 141:180–182; McLean (ed.), *Papers Concerning Robertson's Colony*, VI, 233–234.

[65] JFR to Elosúa, June 11, 1831, BA, 141:871–873; McLean (ed.), *Papers Concerning Robertson's Colony*, VI, 268.

[66] JFR to Williams, Oct. 30, 1830, in McLean (ed.), *Papers Concerning Robertson's Colony*, V, 135.

[67] Elosúa to JFR, Dec. 6, 1830, BA, 136:722–773; JFR to Elosúa, Dec. 9, 1830, BA, 136:966; Severo Ruiz to Elosúa, Dec. 9, 1830, BA, 136:970; JFR to Elosúa, Jan. 7, 1831, BA, 137:708–709; McLean (ed.), *Papers Concerning Robertson's Colony*, V, 300–301, 310–312.

[68] JFR to Williams, Feb. 15, 1831, in McLean (ed.), *Papers Concerning Robertson's Colony*, V, 513–514. Ruiz wrote that by the last mail he received an order not to permit any North American families to settle at Tenoxtitlán; consequently, Sterling C. Robertson's enterprise had been suspended.

[69] JFR to Williams, Jan. 7, 1831, in McLean (ed.), *Papers Concerning Robertson's Colony*, V, 394.

[70] Elosúa to JFR, Jan. 19, 1831, BA 138:52; McLean (ed.), *Papers Concerning Robertson's Colony*, V, 446.

[71] Continuation of the Case Against Severo Ruiz and Francisco de Castañeda, Jan. 19, 1831, BA, 131:1–248.

[72] Ibid.; McLean (ed.), *Papers Concerning Robertson's Colony*, V, 448.

[73] JFR to Williams, Feb. 19, 1831, in McLean (ed.), *Papers Concerning Robertson's Colony*, V, 539–540.

[74] Nicolás Flores to Elosúa, June 19, 1831, BA, 142:81–83; McLean (ed.), *Papers Concerning Robertson's Colony*, VI, 270.

[75] JFR to Jesús García, Jun 8, 1831, in 2008 June Signature Texana Auction, Heritage Auctions Catalogue, 6003.

[76] Vicente Arreola to Elosúa, Mar. 3, 1832, BA, 148:380.

[77] Elosúa to JFR, June 29, 1831, BA, 142:370–371; McLean (ed.), *Papers Concerning Robertson's Colony*, VI, 287.

[78] JFR to Elosúa, June 9, 1831, BA, 142:710–712; McLean (ed.), *Papers Concerning Robertson's Colony*, VI, 302–303.

[79] JFR to Austin, Aug. 20, 1831, in McLean (ed.), *Papers Concerning Robertson's Colony*,

VI, 376. Ruiz also wrote that the Waco Village would be the best place on the Brazos River to establish the Cherokees.

[80] JFR to Elosúa, Aug. 21, 1831, BA, 143:935–936; McLean (ed.), *Papers Concerning Robertson's Colony*, VI, 377.

[81] Dr. Cesar Sostre is a professor at the University of Texas Health Science Center in San Antonio. He reviewed the limited information and personal accounts of the illness of Francisco Ruiz at the request of the author in November of 2012. In addition to the comments above, he further noted, "Streptococcus, commonly known as 'Rheumatic fever' can cause heart damage to the valves and heart failure. Strep can also cause kidney damage with a condition called glomerulonephritis. There are other possibilities in the differential diagnosis such as some of the tick-borne diseases such as rickettsia (Rocky Mountain spotted fever and related diseases) and Lyme disease which is a multi-organ disease as well." Dr. Cesar Sostre to Art Martínez de Vara, email, November 24, 2012 (correspondence in author's possession).

[82] JFR to Elosúa, Oct. 13, 1831, BA, 145:329–330; McLean (ed.), *Papers Concerning Robertson's Colony*, VI, 463–464.

[83] JFR to Elosúa, Oct. 16, 1831, BA, 145:377–378; McLean (ed.), *Papers Concerning Robertson's Colony*, VI, 474.

[84] JFR to Anastacio Bustamante, Oct. 16, 1831, BA, 145:380–381; McLean (ed.), *Papers Concerning Robertson's Colony*, VI, 475.

[85] JFR to Elosúa, Nov. 13, 1831, BA, 145:942–944; McLean (ed.), *Papers Concerning Robertson's Colony*, VI, 518–519.

[86] McLean (ed.), *Papers Concerning Robertson's Colony*, VI, 49. Known deserters from Tenoxtitlán during this time period were Hombono Carbajal, Tómas Lazo, Joaquín Marroquin, Francisco Mendiola, Nepomuceno Navarro (who later served under Juan N. Seguín at San Jacinto), Guadalupe Núñez, Rumaldo Quintanilla, Guillermo Rivera, Manuel Tarín, Eduardo Treviño, Magdaleno Treviño, Antonio Vergara, José María Vidal, and Fermín Villa.

[87] "Ruiz Applies for Land," in McLean (ed.), *Papers Concerning Robertson's Colony*, VI, 51.

[88] JFR to Elosúa, Aug. 6, 1831, BA, 143:528–529; McLean (ed.), *Papers Concerning Robertson's Colony*, VI, 334–335.

[89] McLean (ed.), *Papers Concerning Robertson's Colony*, VI, 64.

[90] Ibid., 71.

[91] JFR to Elosúa, n.d., BA, 146:865–866; McLean (ed.), *Papers Concerning Robertson's Colony*, VII, 72.

[92] Elosúa to José Mariano Guerra, May 23, 1832, BA, 150:209–210; McLean (ed.), *Papers Concerning Robertson's Colony*, VII, 211–212.

[93] JFR to Elosúa, June 9, 1832, BA, 150:686–688; McLean (ed.), *Papers Concerning Robertson's Colony*, VII, 237–238.

[94] JFR to Elosúa, June 10, 1832, BA, 150:692–693; McLean (ed.), *Papers Concerning Robertson's Colony*, VII, 239.

[95] JFR to Elosúa, June 28, 1832, BA, 151:95; McLean (ed.), *Papers Concerning Robertson's Colony*, VII, 253–254.

[96] JFR to Elosúa, June 23, 1832, BA, 63:103–104; McLean (ed.), *Papers Concerning Robertson's Colony*, VII, 249–250.

[97] The Plan de Veracruz of 1832 was different than the similarly named Plan de Ve-

racruz of 1822, in which Santa Anna repudiated Emperor Agustín Iturbide and the Mexican monarchy in favor of a Republican form of government.

⁹⁸ JFR to Elosúa, n.d., BA, 148:694–695; JFR to Elosúa, n.d., BA, 148:696–697; JFR to Elosúa, n.d., BA, 148:698–699; JFR to Elosúa, n.d., BA, 148:700–701; McLean (ed.), *Papers Concerning Robertson's Colony*, VII, 145.

⁹⁹ JFR to Austin, July 20, 1832, in McLean (ed.), *Papers Concerning Robertson's Colony*, VII, 270.

¹⁰⁰ JFR to Elosúa, June 28, 1832, BA, 151:98–99; McLean (ed.), *Papers Concerning Robertson's Colony*, VII, 254. See also Guerra to Elosúa, June 20, 1832, BA, 150:929–930; McLean (ed.), *Papers Concerning Robertson's Colony*, VII, 245.

¹⁰¹ JFR to Austin, Aug. 15, 1832, in McLean (ed.), *Papers Concerning Robertson's Colony*, VII, 312–314.

¹⁰² JFR to Elosúa, July 22, 1832, BA, 151:807–809; McLean (ed.), *Papers Concerning Robertson's Colony*, VII, 274–275.

¹⁰³ JFR to Elosúa, Aug. 4, 1830, BA, 152:279–280; McLean (ed.), *Papers Concerning Robertson's Colony*, VII, 288. See also Elosúa to JFR, July 23, 1832, BA, 151:825–827; McLean (ed.), *Papers Concerning Robertson's Colony*, VII, 278–279.

¹⁰⁴ JFR to Elosúa, Aug. 1, 1832, BA, 152:207–209; McLean (ed.), *Papers Concerning Robertson's Colony*, VII, 282–283; Castañeda, *Our Catholic Heritage*, V, 249.

¹⁰⁵ Elosúa to JFR, Aug. 6, 1832, BA, 152:386–387; McLean (ed.), *Papers Concerning Robertson's Colony*, VII, 295.

¹⁰⁶ Francis Smith to Austin, Aug. 22, 1832, in McLean (ed.), *Papers Concerning Robertson's Colony*, VII, 319.

¹⁰⁷ Vicente Filisola, *Memorias para la Historia de la Guerra de Tejas* (2 vols.; Mexico City: Tipografica de R. Rafael, 1849), I, 271–272; McLean (ed.), *Papers Concerning Robertson's Colony*, VII, 319n2.

¹⁰⁸ JFR to Elosúa, Sept. 20, 1832, BA, 153:256–257; McLean (ed.), *Papers Concerning Robertson's Colony*, VII, 327. Ruiz's 26-day journey home, was twice as long as his "prolonged" 13-day initial journey from Béxar.

¹⁰⁹ John O. Leal, *San Fernando Church Baptismals, 1826–1858* (San Antonio: privately published, 1977), 33.

¹¹⁰ Guerra to Elosúa, July 20, 1832, BA, 151:737:740; McLean (ed.), *Papers Concerning Robertson's Colony*, VII, 268–269.

CHAPTER 11: RETIREMENT

¹ JFR to Austin, Oct. 30, 1831, in McLean (ed.), *Papers Concerning Robertson's Colony*, VI, 500–501.

² Oliver C. Hartley (comp.), *Reports of Cases Argued and Decided in the Supreme Court of the State of Texas, Volume VII: Austin Term, 1851, and a Part of Galveston Term, 1852* (Houston: E. H. Cushing, 1883), 170 [*Paul v. Pérez*, 7 Tex. 338; 1851 Tex. (1851)]. See also McGraw and Hindes, *Chipped Stone and Adobe*, 135.

³ Hipp, *Oldest Ranch in Texas*, 30.

⁴ Ibid., 36.

⁵ Power of Attorney Granted by [José] Ignacio Pérez to JFR, 1829, Powers of Attorney 54, BCSA. Other possible refuges for María Josefa Hernández were the ranch of her brother, Ignacio de la Peña, on the San Antonio River or with her daughter on the ranch of her husband, Blas Herrera, on the Medina River. María did not appear in the

Béxar census for 1828, and others who also were not listed were known to reside on their ranches or those of family members at that time.

[6] [José] Francisco Ruiz's Inventory of Goods Taken to Coahuila for Sale, Apr. 6, 1829, BA, 121:538.

[7] McDonald, "Juan Martín de Veramendi," in De la Teja, *Tejano Leadership*, 37. Juan Martín had been elected vice-governor in 1831 and was called to serve as governor following the death of Governor José María Letona in September of 1832.

[8] Erasmo Seguín to JFR, Jan. 12, 1832, BA, 154:622; McLean (ed.), *Papers Concerning Robertson's Colony*, VII, 391.

[9] José de Irala to JFR, May 11, 1831, BA, 141:6; McLean (ed.), *Papers Concerning Robertson's Colony*, VI, 223.

[10] Múzquiz to the Governor of Coahuila y Texas, Sept. 25, 1830, BA, 134:734; McLean (ed.), *Papers Concerning Robertson's Colony*, IV, 550. Ramón Musquíz to Governor of Coahuila y Texas, September 1830, AGEC, Fondo Jefatura Política de Béjar, caja 17, expediente 18.

[11] JFR to Austin, Oct. 30, 1831, in McLean (ed.), *Papers Concerning Robertson's Colony*, VI, 500–501.

[12] Grant to [José] Francisco Ruiz for Nine Leagues of Land: Two in present Brazos County, Four in Robertson County, Two in Milam County, and One in Burleson County, in McLean (ed.), *Papers Concerning Robertson's Colony*, VII, 519–526.

[13] McLean (ed.), introduction to *Papers Concerning Robertson's Colony*, VI, 52.

[14] Grant to [José] Francisco Ruiz for Nine Leagues of Land: Two in present Brazos County, Four in Robertson County, Two in Milam County, and One in Burleson County, in McLean (ed.), *Papers Concerning Robertson's Colony*, VII, 519–526.

[15] Power of Attorney, Apr. 14, 1838, in McLean (ed.), *Papers Concerning Robertson's Colony*, VII, 522. In a case entitled *Republic of Texas v. Francisco Ruiz et. al.*, in the district court of Robertson County, the judge heard suits brought by squatters seeking to gain lands against sixteen Tejanos and one Anglo, all of whom had gotten grants from the Republic of Mexico. Ruiz was named in the lawsuit because he was the original grantee, but by the time the case was disposed of his interest had been sold to Morehouse and Cunningham.

[16] McLean (ed.), *Papers Concerning Robertson's Colony*, VII, 31, 32.

[17] Excerpt from Yoakum's *History of Texas* in McLean (ed.), *Papers Concerning Robertson's Colony*, VII, 375.

[18] Houston to Karnes, Mar. 31, 1837, in *The Writings of Sam Houston, 1813–1863*, ed. Amelia W. Williams and Eugene C. Barker (8 vols.; Austin: University of Texas Press), II, 77.

[19] McLean (ed.), *Papers Concerning Robertson's Colony*, VII, 33.

[20] McDonald, *José Antonio Navarro*, 115.

[21] Minutes of the Special Session of Sept. 28, 1833, in City of San Antonio, Minutes of the City Council from 1830 to 1835 (City Clerk's Office, San Antonio, Texas), 305.

[22] Ibid.

[23] Arciniega to Governor, Dec. 1833, in Archivo Municipal de Saltillo, *Catálogo del Fondo Testamentos, Volume I*, 284.

[24] Ruiz to Williams, Feb. 1834, in McLean (ed.), *Papers Concerning Robertson's Colony*, VIII, 280–281.

[25] Porter, *Spanish Water, Anglo Water*, 83. The cholera epidemic of 1833–34 caused so

many inhabitants to flee Béxar for the countryside that the annual census could not be performed.

[26] The witnesses to Manuela's will were Victoriano Zepeda, Bruno Huizar, and Alejo Perez, citizens of Bexár, and Domingo Bustillo, alcalde. The document is signed by the priest, Francisco Maynes, because Manuela did "not know how to write." Will of María Manuela de la Peña, May 12, 1834, Wills and Estates 92, BCSA.

[27] "Maria, Antonia and Rosalia are dead; Josefa and Francisco are living. The latter and the children of the former I declare to be my sole heirs of the little country estate which my son José, who died intestate in the jurisdiction of Natchitoches, left at his death, although he had been married, he left no children." Will of María Manuela de la Peña, May 12, 1834, Wills and Estates 92, BCSA.

[28] María Josefa inherited a portion of the San Bartolo Ranch from her father Plácido Hernández. See Heirs of Plácido Hernández to José Cassiano, February 4, 1834, José Francisco Ruiz Vertical File, DRT Library.

[29] Elizabeth LeNoir Jennet, *Biographical Directory of the Texan Conventions and Congresses, 1832–1845* (Austin: Book Exchange, 1941), 164.

[30] María Josefa Hernandez is often misreported to have died on October 6, 1814, and buried at Mission San José de Aguayo. That burial is actually for María Pascuala Hernandes, wife of Francisco Ruiz, of Mission Concepción. The record reads "Hernandes, María Pascuala, wife of Francisco Ruiz, a neighbor from mission Concepción." John O. Leal, *Mission San Jose Burials* (San Antonio: privately published, 1977), 22. The 1815 Census of Mission Concepción lists this other Francisco Ruiz "Francisco Ruiz, native of Parras, age 50, widower; his children; María Navora, age 25, widow; José Francisco, age 15; José Polito, age 7 and José Alba, age 9." Institute of Texan Cultures, *Residents of Texas*, II, 90.

[31] Leal, *Camposanto Burials*, 68.

[32] This entry erroneously states that Manuela left no will. The *camposanto*, sometimes spelled *campo santo*, literally "holy ground" was the early cemetery for San Fernando Church. It is located at present-day Milam Park and Santa Rosa Hospital. The church started using the cemetery on November 1, 1808. Leal, *Camposanto Burials*, 68.

[33] "I declare that my funeral shall be in the San Antonio de Valero church, if the civil authorities permit it, and in the case it shall be as my children Josefa and Francisco direct." Will of María Manuela de la Peña, May 12, 1834, Wills and Estates 92, BCSA.

[34] McDonald, *José Antonio Navarro*, 117.

[35] Leal, *Camposanto Burials*, 68.

[36] Archivo Municipal de Saltillo, *Catálogo del Fondo Testamentos*, *Volume I*, 290. María Josefa Ruiz de Navarro was the widow of Ángel Navarro, who had died in 1808.

CHAPTER 12: TEXAS INDEPENDENCE

[1] *Biography of Jose Antonio Navarro by an Old Texan*, 15–16.

[2] Fowler, *Santa Anna*, 143. Gómez Farías was sworn in as vice president on April 1, 1833. Santa Anna arrived on May 15 of the same year.

[3] Santa Anna to Gómez Farías, Feb. 16, 1833, Valentín Gómez Farías Family Papers, Benson Latin American Collection, University of Texas at Austin. Santa Anna demurred to Gómez Farías in this letter written just before the latter took office as interim president, stating that it was preferable for the "reins of government not to be in the

hands of a poor soldier like me, but in those of a citizen like you, known for his virtues and enlightenment."

[4] Fowler, S*anta Anna*, 145. Other radical proposals included trying ex-President Anastasio Bustamante's cabinet for the execution of Vicente Guerrero and decreeing that the Mexican government could appoint all Catholic clergy and officials.

[5] Ibid., 146–147. General Mariano Arista's plan was issued in the town of Huejotozingo.

[6] Ibid., *Santa Anna*, 148–149.

[7] Brands, *Lone Star Nation*, 221.

[8] Cantrell, *Austin, Empresario of Texas*, 274. At the meeting were Senator Victor Blanco of Coahuila y Texas, two other *Coahuiltejano* congressmen, three generals, and four cabinet ministers. Blanco reported, "[Austin] was fought by my colleagues and even more by me."

[9] Fowler, *Santa Anna*, 145.

[10] Cantrell, *Austin, Empresario of Texas*, 275.

[11] Brands, *Lone Star Nation*, 222.

[12] Stephen F. Austin, "The 'Prison Journal' of Stephen F. Austin," *Quarterly of the Texas State Historical Association* 2 (January 1899): 194–195.

[13] Cantrell, *Austin, Empresario of Texas*, 279.

[14] Ibid., 296–307.

[15] Fowler, *Santa Anna of Mexico*, 154.

[16] Ibid., 155–156.

[17] Fowler, *Santa Anna*, 154. Tornel was a Santa Anna ally and his former Minister of War.

[18] De la Teja, *Revolution Remembered*, 21.

[19] McDonald, *José Antonio Navarro*, 119.

[20] Lack, *Texas Revolutionary Experience*, 17–18.

[21] De la Teja, *Revolution Remembered*, 21.

[22] Ramos, *Beyond the Alamo*, 139.

[23] McDonald, *José Antonio Navarro*, 119.

[24] José Antonio Navarro to Williams, Oct. 8, 1834, Samuel May Williams Collection, Rosenberg Library, Galveston, Texas.

[25] McDonald, *José Antonio Navarro*, 123; *Biography of Jose Antonio Navarro by an Old Texan*, 15–16.

[26] McDonald, *José Antonio Navarro*, 119–120.

[27] The signers were a virtual who's who of the leadership at Béxar. Among the list were José Antonio Navarro, José Luciano Navarro, Juan N. Seguín, and Erasmo Seguín.

[28] Lack, *Texas Revolutionary Experience*, 18.

[29] Williams to Wyly Martin, May 3, 1835, in John H. Jenkins (ed.), *The Papers of the Texas Revolution, 1835–1836* (10 vols.; Austin: Presidial Press, 1973), I, 88–89.

[30] Francis W. Johnson to Martin, May 3, 1835, in Jenkins (ed.), *Papers of the Texas Revolution*, I, 100; McDonald, *José Antonio Navarro*, 121.

[31] McDonald, *José Antonio Navarro*, 121.

[32] Jose Ángel Navarro to Secretary of State, May 18, 1835, BA.

[33] Lack, *Texas Revolutionary Experience*, 22; McDonald, *José Antonio Navarro*, 123. This same company of Tejano volunteers later served in the Siege of Béxar and the Battle of San Jacinto during the war for Texas independence.

34 Lack, *Texas Revolutionary Experience,* 20.

35 Ibid., 15, 183.

36 Ibid., 26–27.

37 Alwyn Barr, *Texans in Revolt: The Battle for San Antonio, 1835* (Austin: University of Texas Press, 1990), 4, 28-29. This José Antonio Menchaca, born in 1795 and a resident of the Neutral Ground who was relocating to Nacogdoches, is not the same Tejano who later served in the Texas military and wrote a memoir. See Roderick B. Patten, "Menchaca, Jose Antonio [1795–?]," *Handbook of Texas Online,* <http://www. tshaonline. org/handbook/online/articles/fme13> [Accessed Oct. 25, 2017].

38 Barr, *Texans in Revolt,* 4.

39 Ibid., 4, 6–7; Stephen L. Hardin, *Texian Iliad: A Military History of the Texas Revolution* (Austin: University of Texas Press, 1994), 7–13.

40 Barr, *Texans in Revolt,* 13.

41 McDonald, *José Antonio Navarro,* 126–127. José Antonio Navarro also packed up and took his family to their ranch in present day Atascosa County. General Cos passed the Navarro ranch on his march to Béxar and later testified that although Navarro was known to hold federalist sympathies, he remained at his ranch during the Siege of Béxar.

42 Barr, *Texans in Revolt,* 12.

43 Ibid., 18.

44 De la Teja, *Revolution Remembered,* 78.

45 By comparison, a soldado of the Álamo de Parras Company earned 300 pesos per year in 1831 and its captain 1,404 pesos per year. Budget for Álamo de Parras Company, Aug. 1, 1830, BA, 132:76; McLean (ed.), *Papers Concerning Robertson's Colony,* IV, 329.

46 Claim of Don [José] Francisco Ruiz, Dec. 13, 1836, Republic of Texas Claims, 91:42–51, TSLAC. Anselmo Prú, an indentured servant of Ruiz and a member of the Ruiz household in 1840, joined the Federalist forces.

47 Scott Huddleston, "Remember Battle of Concepción," *San Antonio Express-News,* Oct. 29, 2010.

48 Richard Bruce Winders, *Sacrificed at the Alamo: Tragedy and Triumph in the Texas Revolution* (Abilene, Tex.: State House Press, 2004), 71.

49 Barr, *Texans in Revolt,* 31.

50 Ibid., 42, 44; Hardin, *Texian Iliad,* 77–78.

51 Hardin, *Texian Iliad,* 89–90.

52 Claim of Don [José] Francisco Ruiz, Dec. 13, 1836, Republic of Texas Claims, 91:43–46, TSLAC.

53 Hansen (ed.), *Alamo Reader,* 193.

54 Claim of Don [José] Francisco Ruiz, Dec. 13, 1836, Republic of Texas Claims, 91:46, TSLAC.

55 Ron J. Jackson and Lee Spencer White, *Joe: The Slave Who Became an Alamo Legend,* (Norman: University of Oklahoma Press, 2015), 143.

56 Pension Application of Miguel Benites, Republic of Texas Claims, 202:565–566, TSLAC.

57 Pension Application of Francisco Flores, Republic of Texas Claims, 215:259–260, TSLAC.

58 Pension Application of Benites, Republic of Texas Claims, 202:565–566, TSLAC.

59 See Pension Application of Miguel Benites, Republic of Texas Claims, 202:565–566,

TSLAC; Pension Application of Francisco Flores, Republic of Texas Claims, 215:259–260, TSLAC; Pension Application of Benites, Republic of Texas Claims, 202:565–566, TSLAC.

[60] Béxar Election Results, Feb. 1, 1836, BA, 167:484–500.

[61] De la Teja, *Revolution Remembered*, 135–136; Juan N. Seguín to JFR, Feb. 10, 1836, BA.

[62] William B. Travis to Henry Smith, Feb. 13, 1836, in Hansen (ed.), *Alamo Reader*, 22–23. Santa Anna decided to cross the Río Grande at Guerrero in the hope of finding military supplies at the Presidio San Juan Bautista del Río Grande that he could use. No such provisions were available. See Robert S. Weddle, *San Juan Bautista: Gateway to Spanish Texas* (Austin: University of Texas Press, 1968), 384.

[63] John Sutherland, "The Alamo," ca. 1860, in Hansen (ed.), *Alamo Reader*, 140.

[64] Ibid. Accounts of whether Travis had advanced warning of Santa Anna's approach differ greatly. Some commentators, such as Juan N. Seguín, contradict themselves on this matter. But it is important to note that when Blas María Herrera's warning is mentioned, it is always accompanied by the fact that Travis did not believe him. Those who recalled years later the surprise of Travis and the Texians may have simply omitted the Herrera message, or forgotten it. Though warned, Travis was surprised.

[65] McDonald, *José Antonio Navarro*, 129, 136.

[66] Gray, *From Virginia to Texas*, 120.

[67] Ibid., 121, 127.

[68] Ibid., 129. The letter arrived on February 29, 1836.

[69] Lack, *Texas Revolutionary Experience*, 94.

[70] McDonald, *José Antonio Navarro*, 130.

[71] Gray, *From Virginia to Texas*, 123.

[72] McDonald, *José Antonio Navarro*, 130.

[73] Jacob de Cordova, *Texas: Her Resources and her Public Men* (Philadelphia: J.B. Lippincott & Co., 1858), 150.

[74] McDonald, *José Antonio Navarro*, 131.

[75] Ibid., 132–133.

[76] Hansen (ed.), *Alamo Reader*, 192.

[77] Richard G. Santos, *Santa Anna's Campaign Against Texas 1835–1836* (Waco: Texian Press, 1986), 83.

[78] Antonio López de Santa Anna to Rafael Hernández, Feb. 29, 1836, BA, 40:126-128. Santa Anna also appointed Ramón Múzquiz as jefe político ad interim in February 1836. The official election was held on April 3 and 4, 1836. José María Salinas was elected as alcalde and Francisco A. Ruiz was elected regidor. This was the final election held under Mexican law. The Battle of San Jacinto occurred less than three weeks later. See Results of Elections of Béxar, Apr. 3, 1836, BA, 136:443–453.

[79] For the text of the Texas Constitution of 1836, see "Constitution of the Republic of Texas (1836)," *Texas Constitutions 1824–1876*, <https://tarltonapps.law.utexas.edu/constitutions/texas1836> [Accessed Oct. 28, 2017].

[80] Vote for president ad interim, Mar. 16, 1836, in McLean (ed.), *Papers Concerning Robertson's Colony*, XIII, 683; Richard B. McCaslin, *Washington on the Brazos: Cradle of the Texas Republic* (Austin: Texas State Historical Association, 2016), 15–16.

[81] Ruiz's other recorded votes for interim officials at the Convention of 1836 were Robert Potter for treasurer and David Thomas for attorney general, both of whom won their positions. See vote for treasurer ad interim, Mar. 16, 1836, and vote for attorney

general ad interim, Mar. 16, 1836, in McLean (ed.), *Papers Concerning Robertson's Colony,* XIII, 684–685.

⁸² Gray, *From Virginia to Texas,* 134. *Sine die* meant literally "without day." A legislative body adjourns sine die when it adjourns without appointing a day on which to appear or assemble again.

⁸³ McDonald, *José Antonio Navarro,* 134.

⁸⁴ Gray, *From Virginia to Texas,* 134.

⁸⁵ Ibid.; Jackson and White, *Joe,* 210–211.

⁸⁶ Gray, *From Virginia to Texas,* 138.

⁸⁷ Francisco Antonio Ruiz, "Fall of the Alamo, and Massacre of Travis and his Brave Associates," in Hansen (ed.), *Alamo Reader,* 500–501.

⁸⁸ See, for example, Roy F. Sullivan, *The Texas Revolution: Tejano Heroes* (Bloomington, Ind.: AuthorHouse, 2011), 121; and Adolph Casias Herrera, "Herrera, Blas Maria," *The Handbook of Texas Online,* <http://www.tshaonline.org/handbook/online/articles/fhe73> [Accessed Oct. 28, 2017].

⁸⁹ Blas María Herrera voted in the April 4, 1836, municipal elections in Béxar. See Record of election of alcalde and regidor of Béxar, Apr. 3, 1836, BA, 167:534–444. Antonio Menchaca later recalled in an affidavit attached to Herrera's pension application that Herrera was among the volunteers who joined Seguín in the summer of 1836 and was dispatched to General Houston to argue against an order by General Felix Huston to abandon and burn Béxar. Herrera was detained by General Huston at Camp Preston and used for "sensitive" matters, until sent to assist his father-in-law in his return from his duties as senator to Béxar. The family tradition that Herrera served Sam Houston presumably originated from his service under General Felix Huston. See Pension Application of Blas Herrera, Nov. 11, 1874, Republic of Texas Land Claims, 220:246–250, BCSA.

⁹⁰ McDonald, *José Antonio Navarro,* 135.

⁹¹ Ibid. Years later, during José Antonio Navarro's trial for treason in Mexico, he recalled these events in his testimony.

⁹² Ibid., 136–137. José Ruiz Land Certificate, Land Conveyances, Sabine Parish, Book M, 241. The ranch is located in present-day Sabine Parish, Lousisiana, "on the west half of Section No. 28, Township No. 8, North Range No. 11, west half of Section No. 33, Township No. 8, North Range No.11."

⁹³ Power of Attorney of JFR to Ambrosio Sompayrac, July 10, 1836, Nacogdoches Archives, DRT, 75:141–142.

⁹⁴ Tax Sale to S.S. Eason, Land Conveyances, Sabine Parish, Book C, 28. The Sheriff sold 640 acres "not described" assessed in the name of "Honetto Ruice" [José Ruiz] to S. S. Eason. In Tax Sale to Wm. B. Stille, Land Conveyances, Sabine Parish, Book C, 102, the same tract was sold in another tax sale to Stille in 1849, when it was described as "property confirmed in the name of Hosea Ruiz [José Ruiz]", 640 acres as the property of S S Eason deceased." In 2014, the ranch remained undeveloped and covered by dense pine trees. A dirt road skirted along the northern boundary with several timber trails leading from it. An unnamed bayou flowed into Lewis Creek, creating a near perfect "Y" and dividing the ranch almost evenly. Either one of these waterways may have been "Bayou Santa Bárbara," a name which no longer exists on modern Sabine Parish maps; Map of Sabine Parish, Section No. 28, Township No. 8, North Range No. 11, Tax Assessor Office, Many, Louisiana. The northern half of the ranch was owned in 2014 by Handcock Timberland X, Inc. Sabine Reality, Inc. et. al., owned the southern half.

CHAPTER 13: TEXAS SENATE

[1] Brown, *History of Texas*, II, 110.

[2] Ramos, *Beyond the Alamo*, 167–168.

[3] Rusk to JFR, Aug. 29, 1836, in William C. Brinkley (ed.). *Official Correspondence of the Texan Revolution, 1835–1836* (New York: D. Appleton-Century Company, 1936), 346–347.

[4] L. Lloyd MacDonald, *Tejanos in the 1835 Texas Revolution* (Gretna, La.: Pelican Publishing Company, 2009), 50.

[5] Santa Anna to Rafael Hernández, Feb. 29, 1836, BA, 40:126–128; Deposition of Francisco Antonio Ruiz, Apr. 16, 1861, in Timothy M. Matovina (ed.), *The Alamo Remembered: Tejano Accounts and Perspectives* (Austin: University of Texas Press, 1995), 37. Ruiz's deposition reads, in part, "That after the fall of the Alamo, General Santa Anna sent for affiant, Don Ramón Múzquiz and others to identify the bodies of Travis, Bowie, and Crockett which was done; that affiant was commanded by General Santa Anna to procure carts and men and proceed to make a funeral pile of the Texans, which order he carried out with much difficulty as there were but few male citizens remaining in the town."

[6] Power of Attorney Granted by Múzquiz to JFR, May 29, 1836, Powers of Attorney 40, BCSA. Power of Attorney Granted by Múzquiz to JFR, Oct. 14, 1836, Powers of Attorney 40, BCSA. Ramon Múzquiz was *jefe político* of Texas, 1828–1834.

[7] Andrés Reséndez, "Ramón Músquiz: The Ultimate Insider," in De la Teja, *Tejano Leadership in Mexican and Revolutionary Texas*, 140. The Congress of the Republic of Texas passed an act in November of 1836 allowing Smith to select any house and lot of his choosing for the services he rendered to Texas.

[8] Power of Attorney Granted by [José] Ignacio Pérez to JFR, Oct. 14, 1836, Powers of Attorney 55, BCSA.

[9] These Ruiz brothers were distant cousins of José Francisco Ruiz through their father, Salvador Ruiz de Castañeda of Querétaro. Their mother was María Ignacia Robleau, the sister of Pierre Robleau, who resided at Bayou Pierre in the Neutral Ground and helped Ruiz with the Caddo Peace Treaty of 1821.

[10] Hipp, *Oldest Ranch in Texas*, 39.

[11] Power of Attorney Granted by [José] Ignacio Pérez to JFR, May 29, 1836, Powers of Attorney 55, BCSA.

[12] William Barret Travis signed receipt from the Alamo, Feb. 24, 1836, 2007 December Signature Texana Auction, Heritage Auctions Catalogue, #661.

[13] Hipp, *Oldest Ranch in Texas*, 39.

[14] The two cases were *Paul v. Pérez*, 7 Tex. 338, 1851 Tex. (1851) and *Pascal v. Pérez*, 7 Tex. 348, 1851 Tex. (1851). See Hartley, *Reports of Cases in the Texas Supreme Court, Volume VII*, 169–186. Esmergildo Ruiz continued to serve in the army of the Republic of Texas following the battle of San Jacinto. He received a land grant from the Republic of Texas in South Bexar County and was killed during a Comanche raid while serving in the army.

[15] Hartley, *Reports of Cases in the Texas Supreme Court, Volume VII*, 169 [*Paul v. Pérez*, 7 Tex. 338, 1851 Tex. (1851)].

[16] Hipp, *Oldest Ranch in Texas*, 43; McGraw and Hindes, *Chipped Stone and Adobe*, 113.

[17] Siegel, *Political History of the Texas Republic*, 48. The Texas Constitution of 1836 required that elections would be held on the first Monday in September.

[18] Lucy A. Erath (ed.), "Memoirs of George Bernard Erath," *SHQ* 27 (July 1923), 140.

[19] Siegel, *Political History of the Texas Republic*, 54. Texas had fewer than 6,000 people eligible to vote in 1836. Sam Houston received 4,374 votes for president. Henry Smith received 743 votes. Stephen F. Austin received only 578 due to the unpopularity of his involvement in the eleven league land grants while serving in the Monclova legislature. Cantrell, *Austin, Empresario of Texas*, 355. Austin felt betrayed by Houston's entry into the presidential race, claiming that Houston promised to never oppose him in a public election.

[20] Juan N. Seguín polled a close second to Ruiz in the 1836 senatorial race in Béxar.

[21] Spaw, *The Texas Senate, Volume I*, 3.

[22] Senators in the First Congress of the Republic of Texas who signed the Texas Declaration of Independence were José Francisco Ruiz (Béxar), Richard Ellis (Red River), Steven H. Everitt (Jasper, Jefferson), Sterling C. Robertson (Milam), Jesse Grimes (Washington), and James Collinsworth (Brazoria).

[23] Spaw, *The Texas Senate, Volume I*, 3–30.

[24] Ibid., 5. Zavala died on November 15, 1836.

[25] "Constitution of the Republic of Texas (1836)," Article 1, Sections 8 and 9.

[26] Spaw, *The Texas Senate, Volume I*, 7. Two-year terms were drawn by Senators Albert C. Horton (Matagorda, Jackson, Victoria), James S. Lester (Mina, Gonzales), Sterling C. Robertson (Milam), Alexander Somervell (Austin, Colorado), and William H. Wharton (Brazoria). One-year terms were drawn by Senators Richard Ellis (Red River), Jesse Grimes (Washington), Robert A. Irion (Nacogdoches), Willis H. Landrum (Shelby, Sabine), and Edwin Morehouse (San Patricio, Refugio, Goliad).

[27] Ibid., 5.

[28] Ibid.; Robert A. Irion (comp.), *The Constitution and Laws of the Republic of Texas* (Ingleside, Tex.: Copano Bay Press, 2007), 16.

[29] Ernest William Winkler (ed.), *Secret Journals of the Senate of the Republic of Texas, 1836–1845* (Austin, Tex.: Austin Printing Company, 1911), 22.

[30] *Telegraph and Texas Register*, Nov. 23, 1836.

[31] Siegel, *Political History of the Texas Republic*, 58–59.

[32] Spaw, *The Texas Senate, Volume I*, 14.

[33] Siegel, *Political History of the Texas Republic*, 60. The three Texans who accompanied Santa Anna to Washington were Barnard E. Bee, George Hockley, and William H. Patton. They sailed for New Orleans on November 25, 1836, and arrived in Washington on January 17, 1837.

[34] Carrie Gibson, *El Norte: The Epic and Forgotten Story of Hispanic North America* (New York: Atlantic Monthly Press, 2019), 204–205.

[35] Spaw, *The Texas Senate, Volume I*, 33.

[36] De León, *They Called Them Greasers*, 14–23.

[37] Petition of [José] Francisco Ruiz to the Congress of the Republic of Texas, Nov. 26, 1836, Memorial and Petitions File, 100-456, TSLAC.

38 *Telegraph and Texas Register*, Nov. 30, 1836.

[39] *Journals of the Senate of the Republic of Texas, First Congress, First Session* (Columbia, Tex.: Gail & Thomas H. Borden, 1836), 68.

[40] Orozimbo Plantation was located nine miles northwest of Angleton in west central Brazoria County. Santa Anna was held as a prisoner of war at Orozimbo Plantation from July until November 1836.

[41] Spaw, *The Texas Senate, Volume I*, 11.

[42] See *Journals of the Senate of the Republic of Texas, First Congress, First Session*, 84.

[43] Siegel, *Political History of the Texas Republic*, 61.

[44] Ibid., 63. Some taxes were created, including a poll tax, various license taxes, and property taxes, but tariffs continued to be the main means of raising revenue.

[45] Spaw, *The Texas Senate. Volume I*, 15–17. The law established ad valorem duties ranging from 1 percent on bread stuffs to 50 percent on silks, with an average of about 25 percent on total imports. The act also placed a duty of twenty-five cents per ton on all foreign vessels with a carrying capacity of ten tons or more arriving in Texas ports.

[46] Siegel, *Political History of the Texas Republic*, 61–62.

[47] *Journals of the Senate of the Republic of Texas, First Congress, First Session*, 93.

[48] *Republic of Texas v. Francisco Ruiz et al.*, in McLean (ed.), *Papers Concerning Robertson's Colony*, XVII, 50.

[49] Austin to Lamar, Dec. 5, 1839, in McLean (ed.), *Papers Concerning Robertson's Colony*, XV, 348–353.

[50] McLean (ed.), *Papers Concerning Robertson's Colony*, VII, 51.

[51] The grant of Tomás de la Vega was litigated until 1872. John Lapsley, as the owner of the property, filed suit against Elihas Spencer and eleven other squatters and won in 1856, a decision upheld by the Texas Supreme Court. However, in 1857 original owner Tomás de la Vega filed suit against Lapsley by claiming that the power of attorney by which he sold the land to Samuel M. Williams was forged. Lapsley won the suit in 1858, and in 1872 he employed Waco attorney William W. Kendall to rid the land of all squatters and uphold Lapsley's clear legal title to the land. See Roger N. Conger, "The Tomás de la Vega Eleven-League Grant on the Brazos," *SHQ* 61 (January 1958): 371–382.

[52] Cantrell, *Austin, Empresario of Texas*, 363.

[53] JFR to Austin, Apr. 11, 1830 in Barker (ed.), *Austin Papers*, II, 367–368.

[54] McDonald, *José Antonio Navarro*, 138.

[55] Cantrell, *Austin, Empresario of Texas*, 363–364.

[56] Richard G. Santos, *Letter from Columbia, Texas, December 27, 1836, Addressed to Blas Herrera* (San Antonio: James W. Knight Publisher, 1966), 14. The original is in the Dolph Briscoe Center for American History at the University of Texas in Austin.

[57] Ibid., 14. Ruiz used the world *culebra*, meaning "rattlesnake," here in reference to Antonio López de Santa Anna.

[58] Cantrell, *Austin, Empresario of Texas*, 363.

[59] Santos, *Letter from Columbia*, 16.

[60] Dove, *Luciano Nepomuceno Navarro*, 26.

[61] Claim of Blas Herrera, Nov. 11, 1874, Republic of Texas Claims, 43:246–251, TSLAC.

[62] Claim of Don [José] Francisco Ruiz, Mar. 27, 1837, Republic of Texas Claims, 91:38–40, TSLAC. Ruiz claimed a salary of $1000.31.1/2 for his service in the Texas Senate from September 8, 1836, to March 30, 1837. The claim was attested to by President Sam Houston and payment was delivered to Eugenio Navarro on Ruiz's behalf.

[63] Claim of Blas Herrera, Nov. 11, 1874, Republic of Texas Claims, 43:246–251, TSLAC.

[64] Spaw, *The Texas Senate, Volume I*, 327.

[65] Power of Attorney, Apr. 14, 1838, in McLean (ed.), *Papers Concerning Robertson's Colony*, VII, 522. Francisco Antonio Ruiz, as agent for José Francisco Ruiz, sold four leagues of land on the east bank of the Brazos to Edwin Morehouse and John R. Cunningham, for $70,000.00. The transaction took place in New Orleans, Louisiana.

[66] Bexar County Tax Rolls, 1837, TSLAC .

[67] Amelia Patiño Ramirez, *Col. Francisco Antonio Ruiz* (privately published: 1992), 4.

⁶⁸ Election Returns for Béxar County in 1838, Texas Secretary of State, Election Returns, Béxar County, 2-9/44, TSLAC. José Francisco Ruiz was the *escritador* (tallier) for the 2nd precinct of Béxar County along with Gabriel Areola and Bernardino Ruiz, at whose ranch the election took place. The *secretarios* were Francisco Antonio Ruiz and Manuel Pérez. Erasmo Seguín was the presiding officer. José Francisco Ruiz and Francisco Antonio Ruiz voted in precinct 2, indicating they lived on the Pérez or Herrera Ranch. Voters in this precinct largely supported Mirabeau B. Lamar for president and José Antonio Navarro for Congress.

⁶⁹ Ruiz gave a written deposition given before Erasmo Sequin, attesting that in the election for president and Congress at La Villita, that Vincent Micheli was appointed president of the board of election, and that he was not sworn in prior to or during that election. Francisco Ruiz's Sworn Deposition Regarding Irregularities in the 1838 Election, Sep. 12, 1838, Historical 2018 March 17 Western Americana & Texana Grand Format Auction, Heritage Auctions Catalogue, 6190. Ruiz had prior service as an election official. On December 24, 1825, Ruiz, along with Fernando Rodríguez, served as escritadores of the ayuntamiento election of Béxar. Ayuntamiento Elections for 1825, Dec. 24. 1824, BA, 73:775-777.

⁷⁰ Francisco Antonio Ruiz was appointed interim alcalde on Feb. 29, 1836. San Antonio was incorporated that summer and Francisco Antonio was elected three times to the City Council of San Antonio, serving from Sep. 19, 1837–Mar. 9, 1838, Jan. 8, 1839–Jan. 8, 1840, and Jan. 8, 1840–Jan. 9, 1841. He was elected Justice of the Peace, Bexar County, Precinct 4 on Aug. 15, 1839, defeating Francisco Bustillo. 1839 – Bexar Co., Aug. 23, 1839, Election Returns, 307:1-2, TSLAC.

⁷¹ Alejandro Modesto Ruiz was the son of Francisco Antonio Ruiz. He served one term on the San Antonio City Council in 1867. Office of the City Clerk, "Elected Officials of San Antonio," *Municipal Archives & Records*, <https://www.sanantonio.gov/Municipal-Archives-Records/About-Archives-Records/Officials#13098665-1900-1850> [Accessed Apr. 29, 2019].

CHAPTER 14: FINAL YEARS

¹ Houston to Karnes, Mar. 31, 1837, Andrew Jackson Houston Collection, 2–22/159, TSLAC.

² Brands, *Lone Star Nation*, 491–492.

³ Siegel, *Political History of the Texas Republic*, 65–67.

⁴ De la Teja, *Revolution Remembered*, 112.

⁵ Claim of Don [José] Francisco Ruiz, Mar. 27, 1837, Republic of Texas Claims, 91:35–40, TSLAC.

⁶ Claim of Don [José] Francisco Ruiz, Aug. 23, 1837, Republic of Texas Claims, 91:54–55, TSLAC. Ruiz claimed a value of $12.00 per head for a total of $82.00.

⁷ DeLay, *War of a Thousand Deserts*, 110. Mexican military officers officially complained about this practice by Ruiz, noting his Comanche trade connections.

⁸ Stephen L. Moore, *Savage Frontier, Vol. II, 1838–1839: Rangers, Riflemen, and Indian Wars in Texas* (Denton: University of North Texas Press, 2006), 1.

⁹ De la Teja, *Revolution Remembered*, 112. Thomas J. Green held the seat for twenty-five days between the resignation of Ruiz and the election of Seguín.

¹⁰ Houston to Karnes, Mar. 31, 1837, Houston Collection, 2-22/159, TSLAC. Houston also complained about the misuse of Indian gifts by Deaf Smith, and directed that they

would be entrusted to Karnes and Ruiz. He instructed Karnes to deliver the letter to Ruiz.

[11] Siegel, *Political History of the Texas Republic,* 104. President Lamar asserted that the Indians had never received patents for their land from the Mexican government and that they had no rights under the treaties negotiated by the Provisional Government of Texas because the Republic of Texas had never ratified them. He recommended to Congress the establishment of a line of frontier military posts to afford protection against Cherokee raids. The sale of lands occupied by the Cherokees by the Republic of Texas sparked a military conflict known as the Cherokee War of 1839.

[12] Moore, *Savage Frontier, Vol. II,* 355.

[13] Ibid., 83; Homer S. Thrall, *A Pictorial History of Texas: From the Earliest Visits of European Adventurers, to A.D. 1879* (St. Louis: N. D. Thompson, 1879), 457. Both of these sources give the name of the unfortunate captive as Nicolás Flores Ruiz, but in fact there was a Nicolás Flores serving as justice of the peace for the first district of Bexar County in 1837.

[14] Moore, *Savage Frontier, Vol. II,* 83–85; Thrall, *Pictorial History of Texas,* 457–458. This cemetery is modern-day Milam Park.

[15] Census records show that Fernando Ruiz was a member of José Francisco Ruiz's household at the age of two. Census of San Fernando de Béxar, Jul. 21, 1817 in Institute of Texan Cultures, *Residents of Texas,* I, 108. "Doña Josefa Hernandez, 30; Antonia Ruiz, 8; Francisco Ruiz, 6; Fernando Ruiz, 2; Igina Castro, 34; Nasario Martinez, 16." It has been suggested by some that Fernando Ruiz was the son of José Francisco Ruiz, however, Fernando Ruiz was listed as an heir of Plácido Hernández, along with Ruiz's wife Josefa Hernández and Ignacio Perez, Antonia Arocha and Antonia Hernández in a land transaction dated Feb. 4, 1834. If he was the son of Josefa Hernández and José Francisco Ruiz, he would not be listed as an heir alongside his mother, or his siblings would also be named. Heirs of Placido Hernández to José Cassiano, Feb. 4. 1834, José Francisco Ruiz Vertical File, DRT Library.

[16] Fernando Ruiz's sole heir was his wife Micaela Flores, who sold his first-class headright land grant Wilson J Riddle. First Class Headright to Fernando Ruiz, deceased, 27 Aug 1847, Bexar-1-001063, Texas Land Grant Records, Archives and Records Program (Texas General Land Office, Austin, Texas).

[17] Miles S. Bennett, "Experiences on the Western Frontier, Republic of Texas, 1838–1842," (1898), 1, in Valentine Bennett Scrapbook (Dolph Briscoe Center for American History, the University of Texas at Austin).

[18] Moore, *Savage Frontier, Vol. II,* 228.

[19] Ibid., 230.

[20] Bennett, "Experiences on the Western Frontier," 1.

[21] Moore, *Savage Frontier, Vol. II,* 231–232.

EPILOGUE

[1] Potter, "The Texas Revolution," 585.

[2] D. Fran.co Ruiz, Jan. 20, 1840, San Fernando Burial Records, 250. "recivio los Santos Sacramentos y murio de Ydropccia a las 61 anos de su edad" (He received the Holy Sacraments and died of Hydropsy at the age of 61 years).

[3] JFR to Antonio Elosúa, Aug. 21, 1831, BA, 143:935–936; McLean (ed.), *Papers Concerning Robertson's Colony,* VI, 377. Ruiz described his condition in the first few days following the development of symptoms: "for several days I have been pretty sick, and,

although it is not serious, it makes me too uncomfortable to sit down or lie down, due to a multitude of pimples and blisters that have broken out all over my body . . . but it looks like I am getting better now."

[4] See note on family oral tradition placed by descendent Vee Gómez in the José Francisco Ruiz File, General Photograph Collection (Institute of Texan Cultures, San Antonio, Texas).

[5] The funeral cost 141 pesos and one real, a substantial sum approximately ten times the cost of a calving cow or oxen at that time. See Inventory and Appraisal of the Estate of José Francisco Ruiz, 1840, Wills and Estates 101, BCSA. The burial entry for José Francisco Ruiz in the records of San Fernando Church reads "En la ciudad de San Fernando de Bejar a 20 de Enero de 1840. Yo el Presbit.° D. Refugio dela Garza cura propio de esta ciudad sepulte en esta Parroquia en rotura de dies pesos al cuerpo del Ten.ᵗᵉ Coronel D. Franc.ᶜᵒ Ruiz, vuido, hizo testam·ᵗᵒ, no dejo obra pia alguna, recivio los Santos Sacramentos y murio de Ydropccia alas 61 anos de su edad. Yp.ᵃ que conste lo firme. Refugio dela Garza" (In the city of San Fernando de Bejar on January 29, 1840. I, the Priest Don Refugio de la Garza, parish priest of this city, buried in this Parish, in a tomb of 10 pesos, the body of Lt. Colonel Don Francisco Ruiz, widower, he made a will, but did not leave any pious works, he received the Holy Sacraments and died of Hydropsy at 61 years of age. And to attest to this, I sign. Refugio de la Garza. See D. Fran.ᶜᵒ Ruiz, Jan. 20, 1840, San Fernando Burial Records, 250. The priest states that Ruiz made a last will and testament because none was ever produced. Ruiz's tomb cost 10 pesos, which is comparatively high. No other burial on the page cost more than 2.5 pesos.

[6] Adolph Casias Herrera, great-great-grandson of José Francisco Ruiz stated in an Affidavit that beginning in 1917 and for many years thereafter he and his grandfather, José María Herrera, would "lay flowers at the grave site of Colonel José Francisco Ruiz, inside the Cathedral of San Fernando . . . the grave site is located inside the rotunda of the church, on the right side of the Altar, just inside the large thick wall of the church. There used to be a small plaque on the wall, just above the floor of the rotunda . . . It had the name of J.F. Ruiz on the plaque . . . In 1921, after the big flood . . . I came to San Antonio again . . . it was at this time I noticed that the small plaque was missing." Adolph Casias Herrera (Affidavit), Sep. 23, 1985, Jose Francisco Ruiz Vertical File, DRT Library. The government of Texas placed a centennial grave marker at San Fernando Cemetery No. 1 in 1936. It reads, "Col. José Francisco Ruiz, officer in the Mexican Army, 1831; signer of the Texas Declaration of Independence, 1836; senator of the first Congress of the Republic, 1836–37. Born in San Antonio January 29, 1783; died January 20, 1840."

[7] "*Chamacuero*" can alternatively refer to a jacal with a door or windows covered by animal hides.

[8] Inventory and Appraisal of the Estate of José Francisco Ruiz, 1840, Wills and Estates 101, BCSA.

[9] A military sword was given to Ruiz's grandson Manuel Herrera and was passed down through the family and is presently in the University of Texas at Austin's Texas Memorial Museum (TNSC) collection, as accession #2642-969.

[10] Inventory and Appraisal of the Estate of José Francisco Ruiz, 1840, Wills and Estates 101, BCSA.

Bibliography

PRIMARY SOURCES

Archives and Libraries
Archivo General del Estado de Coahuila. Ramos Arizpe, Coahuila.
Fondo Jefatura Política de Béjar.

Archivo de la Parroquia de Santiago en Queretaro. Santiago de Querétaro, Querétaro.
Bautismos de Españoles.

Bexar County Courthouse. San Antonio, Texas.
Bexar County Deed Records.
Bexar County Spanish Archives.

Daughters of the Republic of Texas Library. Texas A&M University-San Antonio. San Antonio, Texas.
Nacogdoches Archives.

Dolph Briscoe Center for American History. The University of Texas at Austin. Austin, Texas.
Valentine Bennett Scrapbook.
Bexar Archives.
José Francisco Ruiz Papers.

Institute of Texan Cultures. University of Texas at San Antonio. San Antonio, Texas.
General Photograph Collection.

Nettie Lee Benson Latin American Collection. The University of Texas at Austin. Austin, Texas.
Valentín Gómez Farías Papers.

Rosenberg Library. Galveston, Texas.
Samuel May Williams Collection.

Sabine Parish Clerk of Court Office. Many, Louisiana.
Land Conveyances.

Sabine Parish Tax Assessor Office. Many, Louisiana.
Maps.

San Antonio City Clerk's Office. San Antonio, Texas.
Minutes of the City Council from 1830 to 1835.

Texas State Library and Archives. Austin, Texas.
Bernardo Gutiérrez de Lara Papers.
Houston, Andrew Jackson Houston Collection.
Memorial and Petitions File.
Secretary of State, Republic of Texas (RG 307), Communications Received.

Published
Austin, Stephen F. "The 'Prison Journal' of Stephen F. Austin." *Quarterly of the
Texas State Historical Association* 2 (January 1899).
Baptismal Records of the Parish of Santiago de Saltillo, Book 7. Saltillo, Coahuila:
Parish of Santiago de Saltillo, n.d.
Barker, Eugene C., editor. *The Austin Papers*. 3 volumes. Washington, D.C.:
Government Printing Office, 1924–1928.
Berlandier, Jean Louis. *The Indians of Texas in 1830*. Edited John C. Ewers.
Washington, D.C.: Smithsonian Institute Press, 1969.
Berlandier, Jean Louis. *Journey to Mexico During the Years 1826 to 1834*. Trans-
lated by Sheila M. Ohlendorf, Josette M. Bigelow, and Mary M. Standifer.
2 volumes. Austin: Texas State Historical Association, 1980.
Biography of José Antonio Navarro by an Old Texan. Houston: Telegraph Steam
Printing House, 1876.
Brinkley, William C., editor. *Official Correspondence of the Texan Revolution,
1835–1836*. New York: D. Appleton-Century Company, 1936.
Chabot, Frederick C., editor. *Texas in 1811: The Las Casas and Sambrano Revolu-
tions*. San Antonio: Yanaguana Society Publications, 1941.
De la Teja, Jesús F., editor. *A Revolution Remembered: The Memoirs and Selected
Correspondence of Juan N. Seguín*. Austin: Texas State Historical Association,
2002.
Dickens, Ashbury and James C. Allen, editors. *American State Papers – Documents of the Congress of the United States, in Relation to the Public Lands, From*

the First Session of the Eighteenth to the Second Session of the Ninteenth Congress, Inclusive: Comencing December 1, 1823, and Ending March 2, 1827. Washington, D.C.: Gales & Seaton, 1859.

Erath, Lucy A., editor. "Memoirs of George Bernard Erath." Part III. *Southwestern Historical Quarterly* 26 (July 1923): 27–51.

Filisola, Vicente. *Memorias para la Historia de la Guerra de Tejas.* 2 volumes. Mexico City: Tipográfica de R. Rafael, 1849.

Gray, William F., *From Virginia to Texas, 1835: Diary of Colonel Wm. F. Gray Giving Details of His Journey to Texas and Return in 1835–1836 and Second Journey to Texas in 1837.* Houston: Gray, Dillaye & Co., 1900.

Guerra, Raúl Jr., Nadine M. Vasquez, and Baldomero Vela Jr. *Index to the Marriage Investigations of the Diocese of Guadalajara Pertaining to the Former Provinces of Coahuila, Nuevo León, Nuevo Santander, and Texas, Volume 1.* n.p.: R. J. Guerra, 1989.

Gulick, Charles Adams Jr., and Katherine Elliott, editors. *The Papers of Mirabeau Buonaparte Lamar.* 6 volumes. Austin: Von Boeckmann-Jones, 1973.

Hansen, Todd, editor. *The Alamo Reader: A Study in History.* Mechanicsburg, Pa.: Stackpole Books, 2003.

Hartley, Oliver C., compiler. *Reports of Cases Argued and Decided in the Supreme Court of the State of Texas, Volume VII: Austin Term, 1851, and a Part of Galveston Term, 1852.* Houston: E. H. Cushing, 1883.

Institute of Texan Cultures. *Residents of Texas, 1782–1836.* 3 volumes. San Antonio: Institute of Texan Cultures, 1984.

Irion, Robert A., compiler. *The Constitution and Laws of the Republic of Texas.* Ingleside, Tex.: Copano Bay Press, 2007.

Jackson, Jack, editor. *Texas by Terán.* Austin: University of Texas Press, 2000.

Jenkins, John H., editor. *The Papers of the Texas Revolution 1835–1836.* 10 volumes. Austin: Presidial Press, 1973.

Journals of the Senate of the Republic of Texas, First Congress, First Session. Columbia, Tex.: Gail & Thomas H. Borden, 1836.

Leal, Guillermo Garmendia, editor. *Diego de Montemayor, Sus Decendientes.* Monterrey, Nuevo León: Privately published, 1993.

Leal, John O., editor. *Camposanto: An Ancient Burial Ground of San Antonio, Texas, 1808–1860.* San Antonio: Privately published, 1975.

_____. *Mission San Jose Burials, 1781–1824.* San Antonio: Privately published, 1977.

_____, editor. *Mission San José Records.* San Antonio: Privately published, 1974.

_____, editor. *San Fernando Church Baptismals, 1731–1793, Book I, Part 1.* San Antonio: Privately published, 1976.

_____, editor. *San Fernando Church Baptismals, 1812–1825.* San Antonio: Privately published, 1976.

_____, editor. *San Fernando Church Baptismals, 1826–1843.* San Antonio: Privately published, 1977.

_____, editor. *San Fernando Church Burials, 1761–1808.* San Antonio: Privately published, 1976.

_____, editor. *San Fernando Church Marriages, 1798–1856.* San Antonio: Privately published, 1976.

Martínez de Vara, Art, and Marina Dávalos, editors. *History and Records of Santisima Trinidad Church at Paso de las Garzas, Texas.* Von Ormy, Tex.: Santa Helena Publishing, 2009.

Martínez de Vara, Art. *The Jose Francisco Ruiz Papers, Vol. 1 Report on the Indian Tribes of Texas.* Von Ormy: Alamo Press, 2014.

_____, *El Carmen –The Chapel of the Battle of Medina.* Von Ormy, Tex.: Alamo Press, 2017.

Matovina, Timothy M., editor. *The Alamo Remembered: Tejano Accounts and Perspectives.* Austin: University of Texas Press, 1995.

McLean, Malcolm D., editor. *Papers Concerning Robertson's Colony in Texas.* 19 volumes. Arlington: University of Texas at Arlington Press, 1974–1993.

Menchaca, Antonio. *Memoirs: by Antonio Menchaca.* San Antonio: Yanaguana Society, 1937.

Mills, Elizabeth S. *Natchitoches: Translated Abstracts of Register Number Five of the Catholic Church Parish of St. Francois des Natchitoches in Louisiana: 1800–1826.* Westminster, Md.: Heritage Books, 2007.

Montes, M. Ramírez, editor. *Querétaro en 1743: Informe Presentado al Rey por el Corregidor Esteban Gómez de Acosta.* Querétaro: Gobierno del Estado de Querétaro, 1997.

Padilla, Juan Antonio. "Texas in 1820." Translated by Mattie Austin Hatcher. *Southwestern Historical Quarterly* 23 (July 1919): 47–68.

Ruiz, José Francisco. *Report on the Indian Tribes of Texas in 1828.* Edited John C. Ewers. New Haven, Conn.: Yale University Library, 1972.

Saltillo, Archivo Municipal de. *Catálogo del Fondo Testamentos, Volume I: 1607–1743.* Saltillo, Coahuila: Archivo Municipal de Saltillo, 1988.

Santos, Richard G. *Letter from Columbia, Texas, December 27, 1836, Addressed to Blas Herrera.* San Antonio: James W. Knight, 1966.

Streeter, Thomas W. *Bibliography of Texas, 1795–1845.* 5 volumes. Cambridge, Mass.: Harvard University Press, 1955–1960.

Suárez, Francisco. *Selections from Three Works of Francisco Suárez, Volume II: An English Version of the Texts.* Edited Gladys L. Williams, Ammi Brown, John

Waldron, and Henry Davis. Oxford, UK, 1944; reprint, Buffalo, N.Y.: William S. Heins, 1995.

Taylor, Virginia H., editor. *The Letters of Antonio Martínez, The Last Spanish Governor of Texas, 1817–1821.* Austin: Texas State Library, 1957.

United States Department of the Treasury. *Claims to Land Between the Rio Hondo and Sabine Rivers in Louisiana.* 18th Congress, 2nd session, 1825. Senate Report 445.

Walker, Henry P., editor. "William McLane's Narrative of the Magee-Gutiérrez Expedition, 1812–1813." *Southwestern Historical Quarterly* 66 (January 1963).

Williams, Amelia W., and Eugene C. Barker, editors. *The Writings of Sam Houston, 1813–1863.* 8 volumes. Austin: University of Texas Press, 1938–1943.

Winkler, Ernest William, editor, *Secret Journals of the Senate of the Republic of Texas, 1836–1845.* Austin: Austin Printing Company, 1911.

NEWSPAPERS

San Antonio Ledger
San Antonio Express-News
Telegraph and Texas Register (Houston, Tex.)

SECONDARY SOURCES

Articles and Chapters

Benson, Nettie Lee. "Texas Failure to Send a Deputy to the Spanish Cortes, 1810–1812." *Southwestern Historical Quarterly* 64 (July 1960): 14–35.

Brady, Kevin. "Unspoken Words: James Monroe's Involvement in the Magee-Gutiérrez Filibuster." *East Texas Historical Journal* 45 (March 2007): 58–68.

Cox, I. J. "Educational Efforts in San Fernando de Bexar." *Quarterly of the Texas State Historical Association* 6 (July 1902): 27–63.

Conger, Roger N. "The Tomás de la Vega Eleven-League Grant on the Brazos." *Southwestern Historical Quarterly* 61 (Jan 1958): 371–382.

Decorme, Gerardo. "Catholic Education in Mexico, 1525–1912." *The Catholic Historical Review* 2 (July 1916): 168–181.

De la Teja, Jesús F. "Buena Gana de Ir a Jugar: The Recreational World of Early San Antonio, Texas, 1718–1845." *International Journal of the History of Sport* 26 (2009): 889–905.

———. "The Saltillo Fair and Its San Antonio Connections." *Tejano Epic: Essays in Honor of Félix D. Almaráz Jr.*, 15–28. Edited by Arnoldo De León. Austin: Texas State Historical Association, 2005.

Haggard, J. Villasana. "The Counter-Revolution of Béxar." *Southwestern Historical Quarterly* 43 (October 1939): 222–235.

McDonald, David R. "Juan Martín de Veramendi: Tejano Political and Business Leader." *Tejano Leadership in Mexican and Revolutionary Texas*, 28–41. Edited by Jesús F. de la Teja. College Station: Texas A&M University Press, 2010.

Potter, Reuben M. "The Texas Revolution: Distinguished Mexicans Who Took Part in the Revolution of Texas, With Glances At Its Early Years." *The Magazine of American History* 2 (October 1878): 577–608.

Riley, James D. "The Wealth of the Jesuits in Mexico, 1670–1767." *The Americas* 33 (October 1976): 226–266.

Roehner, Bertrand M. "Jesuits and the State: A Comparative Study of Their Expulsions, 1590–1990." *Religion* 27 (April 1997): 165–182.

Wells, Carol. "Inventory of the Natchitoches Warehouse." *The Natchitoches Genealogist* 14 (October 1989), 11–13.

Books

Aguilar Rivera, José Antonio, *Liberty in Mexico: Writings on Liberalism from the Early Republican Period to the Second Half of the Twentieth Century.* Indianapolis: Liberty Fund, 2012.

Almaráz, Félix D. *Governor Antonio Martínez and Mexican Independence in Texas: An Orderly Transition.* San Antonio: Bexar County Historical Commission, 1979.

_____. *The San Antonio Missions and Their System of Land Tenure.* Austin: University of Texas Press, 1989.

_____. *Tragic Cavalier: Governor Manuel Salcedo of Texas, 1808–1813.* Austin: University of Texas Press, 1971.

Anderson, Gary Clayton. *The Conquest of Texas: Ethnic Cleansing in the Promised Land, 1820–1875.* Norman: University of Oklahoma Press, 2005.

Anna, Timothy E. *Forging Mexico, 1821–1835.* Lincoln: University of Nebraska Press, 1998.

Arellano, Dan. *Tejano Roots.* Austin: Privately published, 2005.

Bacigalupo, Marvyn Helen. *A Changing Perspective: Attitudes Toward Creole Society in New Spain (1521–1620).* London: Tamesis Books Limited, 1981.

Bagur, Jacques D. *A History of Navigation on Cypress Bayou and the Lakes.* Denton: University of North Texas Press, 2001.

Bancroft, Hubert H. *History of the North Mexican States and Texas, 1531–1889.* 2 volumes. San Francisco: A. L. Bancroft & Company, 1883, 1889.

Barr, Alwyn. *Texans in Revolt: The Battle for San Antonio, 1835.* Austin: University of Texas Press, 1990.

Benson, Nettie Lee. *The Provincial Deputations in Mexico: Harbinger of Provincial Autonomy, Independence, and Federalism.* Austin: University of Texas Press, 1992.

Brands, H. W. *Lone Star Nation: The Epic Story of the Battle for Texas Independence.* New York: Anchor Books, 2004.

Britten, Thomas A. *The Lipan Apaches: People of Wind and Lightning.* Albuquerque: University of New Mexico Press, 2009.

Brown, John H. *History of Texas from 1685 to 1892.* 2 volumes. St. Louis, Mo.: L. E. Daniell, 1892.

Cantrell, Gregg. *Stephen F. Austin: Empresario of Texas.* New Haven, Conn.: Yale University Press, 1999.

Castañeda, Carlos E. *Our Catholic Heritage in Texas, 1519–1936.* 7 volumes. Austin: Von Boeckmann-Jones, 1936–1958.

Chabot, Frederick C. *San Antonio and Its Beginnings, 1691–1731.* San Antonio: Naylor Printing Company, 1931.

_____. *With the Makers of San Antonio: Genealogies of the Early Latin, Anglo-American and German Families with Occasional Biographies.* San Antonio: Artes Graficas, 1937.

Chance, Joseph E. *José María de Jesús Carbajal: The Life and Times of a Mexican Revolutionary.* San Antonio: Trinity University Press, 2006.

Chipman, Donald E. and Harriett Denise Joseph, *Spanish Texas 1519–1821.* Austin: University of Texas Press, 2010.

Coronado, Raúl, *A World Not to Come: A History of Latino Writing and Print Culture.* Cambridge: Harvard University Press, 2013.

Cruz, Gilbert R. *Let There Be Towns: Spanish Municipal Origins in the American Southwest, 1610–1810.* College Station: Texas A&M University Press, 1988.

Cutter, Charles R. *The Legal Culture of Northern New Spain, 1700–1810.* Albuquerque: University of New Mexico Press, 1995.

De Cordova, Jacob. *Texas: Her Resources and Her Public Men.* Philadelphia: J. B. Lippincott & Company, 1858.

De González, Ana María del Refugio G., and Práxedis Francke Ramírez de la Peña. *Nuestras Raices: Un Recorrido a Traves del Tiempo.* Saltillo, Coahuila: Privately published, 1998.

De la Teja, Jesús F. *San Antonio de Béxar: A Community on New Spain's Northern Frontier.* Albuquerque: University of New Mexico Press, 1996.

De León, Arnoldo. *They Called Them Greasers: Anglo Attitudes Towards Mexicans in Texas, 1821–1900.* Austin: University of Texas Press, 1983.

De Olavarría y Ferrari, Enrique, and Vicente Riva Palacio, editors. *México a Través de los Siglos.* Octava Edicion. Mexico City: Editorial Cumbre, S.A., 1970.

DeLay, Brian. *War of a Thousand Deserts: Indian Raids and the U.S.–Mexican War*. New Haven, Conn.: Yale University Press, 2008.

Dixon, Sam Houston. *The Men Who Made Texas Free*. Houston: Texas Historical Publishing, 1924.

Domínguez, María Ester. *San Antonio en la Epoca Colonial, 1718–1821*. Madrid: Instituto de Cooperación Iberoamericana, 1989.

Donovan, James. *The Blood of Heroes: The 13-Day Struggle for the Alamo – and the Sacrifice That Forged a Nation*. New York: Little, Brown & Company, 2012.

Dove, Barbara Jo Coleman. *The Life and Legacy of Luciano Nepomuceno Navarro, 1800–1869*. San Antonio: Privately published, 2001.

Edmondson, J. R. *The Alamo Story: From History to Current Conflicts*. Plano: Republic of Texas Press, 2000.

Ericson, Carolyn Reeves. *Nacogdoches, Gateway to Texas: A Biographical Directory, 1773–1849*. Fort Worth: Arrow/Curtis, 1974.

Everett, Dianna. *The Texas Cherokees: A People Between Two Fires, 1819–1840*. Norman: University of Oklahoma Press, 1990.

Folsom, Bradley, *Arredondo: Last Spanish Ruler of Texas and Northeastern New Spain*. Norman. University of Oklahoma Press, 2017.

Fowler, Will. *Santa Anna of Mexico*. Lincoln: University of Nebraska Press, 2007.

Garrett, Julia Kathryn. *Green Flag Over Texas*. New York: Cordova Press, 1939.

Green, Stanley C. *The Mexican Republic: The First Decade, 1823-1832*. Pittsburgh: University of Pittsburgh Press, 1987.

Hadley, Diana, Thomas H. Naylor, and Mardith K. Shuetz-Miller, editors. *The Presidio And Militia on the Northern Frontier of New Spain, Volume 2, Part Two: The Central Corridor and the Texas Corridor, 1700–1765*. Tucson: University of Arizona Press, 1997.

Hämäläinen, Pekka. *The Comanche Empire*. New Haven, Conn.: Yale University Press, 2008.

Hardin, Stephen L. *Texian Iliad: A Military History of the Texas Revolution*. Austin: University of Texas Press, 1994.

Henson, Margaret Swett. *Lorenzo de Zavala: The Pragmatic Idealist*. Fort Worth: Texas Christian University Press, 1996.

Hindes, V. Kay. *The Herrera Gate: An Archival, Architectural and Conservation Study*. Studies in Archeology Number 28, Texas Archeological Research Laboratory, The University of Texas at Austin, 1998.

Hipp, Joe W. *The Oldest Ranch in Texas: Rancho de la Purísima Concepción, A Ranch on the Road to History*. Austin: Eakin Press, 2000.

Howe, Daniel Walker. *What Hath God Wrought: The Transformation of America, 1815–1848*. New York: Oxford University Press, 2007.

Jackson, Jack. *Los Mesteños: Spanish Ranching in Texas, 1721–1821.* College Station: Texas A&M University Press, 2006.

_____. *Indian Agent: Peter Ellis Bean in Mexican Texas.* College Station: Texas A&M University Press, 2005.

Jackson, Ron J. and Lee Spencer White. *Joe: The Slave Who Became an Alamo Legend.* Norman: University of Oklahoma Press, 2015.

Jennet, Elizabeth LeNoir. *Biographical Directory of the Texan Conventions and Congresses, 1832–1845.* Austin: Book Exchange, 1941.

Jiménez, Martha Durón, and Ignacio Narro Etchegaray. *Diccionario Biográfico de Saltillo.* Saltillo, Coahuila: Archivo Municipal de Saltillo, 1995.

Jones, Jr., Oakah L. *Los Paisanos: Spanish Settlers on the Northern Frontier of New Spain.* Norman: University of Oklahoma Press, 1979.

Kavanagh, Thomas W. *The Comanche: A History, 1706–1875.* Lincoln: University of Nebraska Press, 1996.

Kemp, Louis W. *The Signers of the Texas Declaration of Independence.* Houston: Anson Jones Press, 1944.

Lack, Paul D. *The Texas Revolutionary Experience: A Political and Social History, 1835–1836.* College Station: Texas A&M University Press, 1992.

López, José Antonio. *The Last Knight: Don Bernardo Gutiérrez de Lara Uribe, A Texas Hero.* Bloomington, Ind.: Privately published, 2008.

Lozano, Ruben Rendón. *Viva Texas: The Story of the Tejanos, the Mexican-born Patriots of the Texas Revolution.* San Antonio: Alamo Press, 1936.

MacDonald, L. Lloyd. *Tejanos in the 1835 Texas Revolution.* Gretna, La.: Pelican Publishing Company, 2009.

Matovina, Timothy M. *Guadalupe and Her Faithful: Latino Catholics in San Antonio, from Colonial Origins to the Present.* Baltimore: The Johns Hopkins University Press, 2005.

McDonald, David R. *José Antonio Navarro: In Search of the American Dream in Nineteenth-Century Texas.* Denton: Texas State Historical Association, 2010.

McGraw, A. Joachim, and V. Kay Hindes. *Chipped Stone and Adobe: A Cultural Resources Assessment of the Proposed Applewhite Reservoir, Bexar County, Texas.* San Antonio: Center for Archaeological Research, University of Texas at San Antonio, 1987.

Miller, Hubert J. *Padre Miguel Hidalgo: Father of Mexican Independence.* Edinburg, Tex.: Pan American University Press, 1986.

McCaslin, Richard B. *Washington on the Brazos: Cradle of the Texas Republic.* Austin: Texas State Historical Association, 2016.

Moore, Stephen L. *Savage Frontier, Volume II, 1838–1839: Rangers, Riflemen, and Indian Wars in Texas.* Denton: University of North Texas Press, 2006.

Naylor, Thomas H., and Charles W. Polzer, editors. *The Presidio and Militia on the Northern Frontier of New Spain, Volume 1, 1570–1700*. Tucson: University of Arizona Press, 1986.

Navarro, José Antonio, *Autobiography of José Antonio Navarro*. San Antonio, 1841.

Offutt, Leslie S. *Saltillo, 1770–1810: Town and Region in the Mexican North*. Tucson: University of Arizona Press, 2001.

Parsons, Edmund Morris. *The Fredonian Rebellion*. Privately published, n.d.

Patiño Ramirez, Amelia. *Col. Francisco Antonio Ruiz*. Privately published, 1992.

Pearce, Adrian J. *British Trade with Spanish America, 1763–1808*. Liverpool: Liverpool University Press, 2007.

Porter, Charles R. Jr. *Spanish Water, Anglo Water: Early Development in San Antonio*. College Station: Texas A&M University Press, 2009.

Powell, Phillip W. *La Guerra Chichimeca, 1550–1600*. Mexico City: Fondo de Cultura Economica, 1975.

Poyo, Gerald E., and Gilberto M. Hinojosa, editors. *Tejano Origins in Eighteenth-Century San Antonio*. Austin: University of Texas Press, 1997.

Ramos, Raúl A. *Beyond the Alamo, Forging Mexican Ethnicity in San Antonio, 1821–1861*. Chapel Hill: University of North Carolina Press, 2008.

Reséndez, Andrés. *Changing National Identities at the Frontier: Texas and New Mexico, 1800–1850*. New York: Cambridge University Press, 2004.

Rie, Jarratt, Gutiérrez de Lara, *Mexican Texan: The Story of a Creole Hero*. Austin: Creole Texana, 1949.

Robles, Vito Alessio. *Coahuila y Texas Desde la Consumación de la Independencia Hasta el Tratado de Paz de Guadalupe Hidalgo*. Mexico City: Editorial Porrua, S.A., 1979.

Rodríguez O., Jaime E., editor, *The Origins of Mexican National Politics, 1808–1847*. Wilmington, Del.: SR Books, 1997.

—————————. *Political Culture in Spanish America, 1500-1830*. Lincoln: University of Nebraska Press, 2017.

Santos, Richard G. *Santa Anna's Campaign Against Texas, 1835–1836*. Waco: Texian Press, 1966.

Stagg, J. C. A. *Borderlines in Borderlands: James Madison and the Spanish-American Frontier, 1776–1821*. New Haven, Conn.: Yale University Press, 2009.

Stuntz, Jean A. *Hers, His, and Theirs: Community Property Law in Spain and Early Texas*. Lubbock: Texas Tech University Press, 2005.

Schwarz, Ted. *Forgotten Battlefield of the First Texas Revolution: The Battle of the Medina, August 18, 1813*. Austin: Eakin Press, 1986.

Siegel, Stanley. *A Political History of the Texas Republic, 1836–1845*. Austin: University of Texas Press, 1956.

Smith, F. Todd. *The Wichita Indians: Traders of Texas and the Southern Plains, 1540–1845,* College Station: Texas A&M University Press, 2000.

_____. *From Dominance to Disappearance: The Indians of Texas and the Near Southwest, 1786–1859.* Lincoln: University of Nebraska Press, 2005.

_____. *Louisiana and the Gulf South Frontier, 1500–1821.* Baton Rouge: Louisiana State University Press, 2014.

Spaw, Patsy McDonald, editor. *The Texas Senate, Volume 1: Republic to Civil War, 1836–1861.* College Station: Texas A&M University Press, 1990.

Struck, Walter G. *José Francisco Ruiz, Texas Patriot.* San Antonio: Witte Memorial Museum, 1943.

Sullivan, Roy F. *The Texas Revolution: Tejano Heroes.* Bloomington, Ind.: AuthorHouse, 2011.

Taylor, Quintard. *In Search of the Racial Frontier: African-Americans in the American West, 1528–1890.* New York: W. W. Norton & Company, 1998.

Thonhoff, Robert H. *The Texas Connection with the American Revolution.* Austin: Eakin Publications, 2000.

Tijerina, Andrés. *Tejanos & Texas Under the Mexican Flag, 1821–1836.* College Station: Texas A&M University Press, 1994.

Uecker, Herbert G., Frances K. Meskill, and I. Wayne Cox. *Archaeological Investigations at The Ruiz Family Property (41 BX 795), San Antonio, Texas.* San Antonio: Center for Archaeological Research, University of Texas at San Antonio, 1991.

Ulrich, Kristi M., Jennifer L. Thompson, Kay Hindes, Bruce K. Moses, Jon J. Dowling, Lynn K. Wack, and Barbara A. Meissner. *Testing and Data Recovery at the Pérez Ranch (41BX274).* San Antonio: Center for Archaeological Research, University of Texas at San Antonio, 2010.

Valdés, Pablo M. Cuellar. *Historia de la Ciudad de Saltillo.* Saltillo, Coahuila: Biblioteca de la Universidad de Coahuila, 1982.

Villegas, Daniel Cosío, editor. *Historia General de México.* Mexico City: El Colegio de México, 2000.

Weber, David J. *The Mexican Frontier, 1821–1846: The American Southwest Under Mexico.* Albuquerque: University of New Mexico Press, 1982.

Weddle, Robert S. *San Juan Bautista: Gateway to Spanish Texas.* Austin: University of Texas Press, 1968.

_____, and Robert H. Thonhoff. *Drama & Conflict: The Texas Saga of 1776.* Austin: Madrona Press, 1976.

Winders, Richard Bruce. *Sacrificed at the Alamo: Tragedy and Triumph in the Texas Revolution.* Abilene, Tex.: State House Press, 2004.

Dissertations and Theses

Cantú Rios, Nora Elia. "José Francisco Ruiz, Signer of the Texas Declaration

of Independence." M.A. Thesis, Texas Tech University, 1970.
Milligan, James Clark. "José Bernardo Gutiérrez de Lara: Mexican Frontiersman 1811–1841." Ph.D. Dissertation, Texas Tech University, 1975.

Websites
Friends of Casa Navarro, http://casanavarro.org/casa-navarro-history/José-
antonio-navarro.
The Handbook of Texas Online, https://tshaonline.org/handbook/online.
Justia: United States Supreme Court, https://supreme.justia.com/
San Antonio Express-News, http://www.mysa.com.
Sons of the DeWitt Colony of Texas, http://www.sonsofdewittcolony.org/
Texas Constitutions, 1824–1876, https://tarltonapps.law.utexas.edu/constitutions.

Index